The Negro in Illinois

THE NEW BLACK STUDIES SERIES

Edited by Darlene Clark Hine
and Dwight A. McBride

*A list of books in the series
appears at the end of this book.*

The Negro in Illinois

The WPA Papers

Edited by
BRIAN DOLINAR

UNIVERSITY OF ILLINOIS PRESS
Urbana, Chicago, and Springfield

Library of Congress Cataloging-in-Publication Data
The Negro in Illinois : the WPA papers /
edited by Brian Dolinar.
pages cm. — (New Black studies series)
Includes bibliographical references and index.
ISBN 978-0-252-03769-6 (hardcover : alk. paper)
1. African Americans—Illinois—History.
2. African Americans—Illinois—Social conditions.
3. Illinois—History. 4. Illinois—Social conditions.
5. African Americans—Illinois—Chicago—History.
6. African Americans—Illinois—Chicago—Social conditions.
7. Chicago (Ill.)—History. 8. Chicago (Ill.)—Social conditions.
I. Dolinar, Brian. II. Writers' Program of the Work Projects
Administration in the State of Illinois.
E185.93.I2N44   2013
305.896'073077311—dc23   2012044794

Contents

Acknowledgments

This book is dedicated to those who, over the years, have been the caretakers of the Illinois Writers' Project papers. Foremost is the role played by librarian Vivian G. Harsh, who in 1943 first agreed to house the IWP papers in her Special Negro Collection at the Hall Branch Library. In 2007, what is now named the Harsh Research Collection celebrated its seventy-fifth anniversary as the "Black Jewel of the Midwest." Today, due largely to the vision of its founder, it is the largest repository of African American literature and history in the Midwest.

Current curator Robert Miller has built up a staff that keeps a watchful eye over the collection. Archivist Michael Flug, who first organized and produced a finding aid for the IWP papers, has been the most knowledgeable and gracious collaborator a researcher could ask for. Additionally, assistant curator Beverly Cook, librarian/preservationist Denise English, librarian Cynthia Fife-Townsel, and archive clerk Lucinda Samuel were extremely kind to me during my visits and patient in accepting my many requests for boxes of IWP materials. I benefited tremendously from a Timuel D. Black, Jr. fellowship awarded by the Vivian G. Harsh Society, which allowed me to spend the summer of 2010 at the Harsh collection to complete the research for this project.

The other library institutions that have materials from the IWP papers within their collections should also be acknowledged. I am grateful for a fellowship I received in 2009 to examine the papers of Jack Conroy at the Newberry Library, where there is a significant holding of IWP documents. I am also thankful to historian James Grossman, then at Newberry, for talking with me at length about the historical significance of *The Negro in Illinois*. At Syracuse University's Special Collections Research Center, Kathleen Manwaring was enthusiastic and helpful in guiding me through the Arna Bontemps papers. The late Beth Howse at Fisk University Special Collections and Archives was always kindly willing to assist in tracking down a document or photograph.

I also utilized the collections at several other institutions. I am indebted to librarians at the Library of Congress, National Archives, Abraham Lincoln Presidential Library, Iowa University Special Collections, Beineke Rare Book and Manuscript Library at Yale University, Chicago History Museum Research Center, and University of Chicago Special Collections Research Center.

There were also many conversations with those who graciously shared their insights and provided me with context for *The Negro in Illinois*, including Timuel D. Black, Jr., Darlene Clark Hine, Douglas Wixson, Bill Mullen, Anne Meis Knupfer, Sonja Williams, Richard Courage, Ayesha Hardison, Michelle Y. Gordon, June O. Patton, Maryemma Graham, John Edgar Tidwell, Richard Yarborough, Christopher Reed, Chris Benson, Sundiata Cha-Jua, Abdul Alkalimat, Mary Helen Washington, and the late Susan Cayton Woodson. I am also grateful to my editor Larin McLaughlin for her patience and persistence in helping to bring this manuscript to print.

I am deeply indebted to the Scott family for introducing me to Chicago's South and West Sides. Gregory Koger and Eric Myers kindly provided me a place to stay in the city while I was doing research.

Finally, I would like to recognize all of the unknown writers who worked on the Illinois Writers' Project, who struggled and survived during the hard times of the Depression to leave us this manuscript.

Editor's Introduction

BRIAN DOLINAR

When the first editions of the American Guide Series were published by the Federal Writers' Project, one of President Roosevelt's innovative New Deal programs, they depicted a lily-white image of America. In the 1930s, blacks still remained largely invisible in the textbook accounts of American history. There was a great unwillingness to recognize the racially mixed American past. The Harlem Renaissance of the previous decade was a relatively obscure movement led by a small group of artists and intellectuals. With the establishment of the Federal Writers' Project, black leaders saw an opportunity to include African Americans in the image of the nation being presented by the guidebooks. By pressuring the Roosevelt administration for more black representation, they were engaging in a struggle for recognition.

A campaign was mounted in Washington, D.C., and the accomplished black poet and professor Sterling Brown was chosen as Editor of Negro Affairs. At his post, Brown planned a series of seventeen projects collecting African American history, folklore, and culture. The one best known today is the collection of interviews with hundreds of ex-slaves. Another was *The Negro in Illinois*, a study conducted by the Illinois Writers' Project (IWP). It was the first-ever attempt to present a comprehensive social history of African Americans in Illinois. The study was supervised by New Negro poet and novelist Arna Bontemps and Jack Conroy, a white proletarian writer. The twenty-nine-chapter outline for the book included chapters on housing, health, religion, literature, music, and culture. A manuscript was completed, but due to the nation's entrance into World War II, funding for the project was diverted to the military, and a book was never produced.

After the project was shut down, Conroy and Bontemps continued to rework the manuscript. In the following years, it was significantly rewritten to address the black migration more generally and then released as *They Seek a City*, a book that was well received when it was published in 1945. While approximately one-quarter of the chapters resembled ones from the earlier manuscript, the book lost its Illinois focus and did not include much of the valuable material collected by IWP workers. The original manuscript for *The Negro in Illinois* contains many folksy tidbits, fascinating anecdotes, and lost jewels of African American history. Most important, it contains much raw data on blacks in Illinois never before made available to the public. While Harlem is still considered by scholars to be the "black mecca," the publication of *The Negro in Illinois* shows the significant contribution of Chicago's South Side to the African American experience.

True Guides of American Life

During the Depression, Chicago was a rapidly growing city with thousands of black migrants from the South. For sociologists at the University of Chicago, the city embodied all the problems of modern urbanization. Horace Cayton and St. Clair Drake were graduate students at the school when they conducted a massive investigation of the South Side under the auspices of the Works Progress Administration (WPA), which funded their work. They eventually used this research in the writing of their landmark study, *Black Metropolis: A Study of Negro Life in a Northern City* (1945).[1] Roosevelt had allocated millions of dollars in government aid to help pull the country out of the economic crisis. Chicago's South Side, as Cayton later wrote in his autobiography, was a "solid New Deal town" (183). Among the workers on relief were black writers who had been shut out of the white publishing industry and the mainstream press. The 1930s saw a new spirit of militancy among these writers, some of whom had participated in the "New Negro" movement of the previous decade, others of them coming of age during the hard times of the Depression.

In these years, there occurred what literary scholar Robert Bone first called the "Chicago Renaissance," a more socially and politically informed movement than its predecessor in Harlem.[2] According to Bone, the University of Chicago was largely responsible for the sociological interest of many of these writers, most notably Richard Wright. More recent scholars have suggested that the Black Chicago Renaissance sprang from the Communist Party's Popular Front strategy, the emergence of a black consumer culture, black civic leadership, or women's activism.[3] Institutions such as the South Side Community Art Center, Wabash YMCA, Chicago Urban League, and Hall Branch Library were all influential. *The Negro in Illinois* has been one of the most frequently cited but widely unknown documents of the Black Chicago Renaissance. It was collectively produced by a group of black writers in Chicago responsible for a remarkable amount of literary and artistic output from Richard Wright, Margaret Walker, Katherine Dunham, Arna Bontemps, Fenton Johnson, Frank Yerby, Onah Spencer, Kitty Chapelle, Robert Lucas, Robert Davis, George Coleman Moore, and Richard Durham, among others.[4] Their time on the Illinois Writers' Project is a reminder that the Black Chicago Renaissance benefited greatly from the federal funding of the arts.

The idea of creating a taxpayer-funded project to put unemployed writers back to work might seem like a far-fetched idea today, as politicians call for reducing the size of "big government." Even in the depths of the Depression, WPA programs were referred to as wasteful and those who received relief ridiculed as being lazy. The boldness of the undertaking known as Federal One—establishing the Federal Art Project, Federal Music Project, Federal Theatre Project, and Federal Writers' Project—cannot be underestimated. It employed some twenty-five thousand workers at its height, approximately one-quarter of whom were on the Federal Writers' Project. The initial idea came out of an early stimulus package of sorts wherein the Treasury Department, with funding from the Civil Works Administration, oversaw a series of construction projects building federal facilities throughout the country. One percent of the budget went to the Public Works of Art Project (PWAP), which oversaw the installation of murals in post offices, courthouses, and most famously in San Francisco's Coit Tower, where controversy erupted after one artist incorporated a hammer and sickle into one of the murals. The PWAP was the first time the government had sponsored a national arts program and paved the way for Federal One. It was largely the brainchild of George Biddle, who betrayed his family's plans for him as a powerful attorney and instead became a painter. A former classmate of Roosevelt, Biddle lobbied the president for a government-subsidized arts project.

Several leftist groups such as the John Reed Clubs and Writers' Union were also agitating for public sponsorship of the arts, inspired by similar efforts in the Soviet Union and France. Heywood Broun's Newspaper Guild, which was working to unionize journalists, joined the chorus of voices lobbying for a federal arts project. They argued that in addition to artists, writers too deserved relief. Indeed, in his history of the Federal Writers' Project, *The Dream and the Deal* (1972), former project editor Jerre Mangione writes, "without the prolonged insistence of professional artists' and writers' organizations and leftwing activity, Federal One, as it was finally conceived, might never have come into being" (34).

In August 1935, the launching of Federal One was officially announced, with Henry G. Alsberg appointed head of the Federal Writers' Project. Alsberg had previously worked at the Federal Emergency Relief Administration (FERA), editing two government magazines, and had close contacts in the Roosevelt administration. Earlier in his life he was an anarchist and friend of anarchist Emma Goldman. He visited the Soviet Union shortly after the revolution but had become disillusioned by the Communist project. Now in his late fifties, he was a New Deal liberal who had left his radicalism behind and knew many people in the New York literary scene. Alsberg oversaw the writing of the American Guide Series, modeled after the Baedeker travel books in Europe, which began with history and general information about each state and followed with several tours of important landmarks, accompanied by maps and photos. Together, they would document the American character and had the stated intent of promoting a national culture.[5]

Yet when the first state guidebooks came out, African Americans were glaringly absent from their pages. This was due in part to the dismally low numbers of black writers on the project. Members of Roosevelt's unofficial "Black Cabinet" pressured the administration to hire more black writers. A delegation made up of John P. Davis, New Deal critic and executive director of the National Negro Congress; Ralph Bunche, political science professor at Howard University; and Alfred E. Smith, chief assistant on black affairs for New Deal architect Harry Hopkins, went to the home of Sterling Brown, a professor of literature, also at Howard.[6] They convinced him to accept a position as Editor of Negro Affairs on the Federal Writers' Project.[7] Remarkably, Brown still held his position at Howard while working part time for the WPA. He set up an office with two assistants, Eugene Holmes, professor of philosophy at Howard, and Ulysses Lee, who was later co-editor with Brown on *The Negro Caravan* (1941). As Brown later recalled, "We had quite a staff" (Rowell 302).

When Brown got started in April 1936, his first task was to take stock of what research had already been collected on African Americans and get a count of black writers on the different state projects. These numbers fluctuated significantly from month to month. In a memo dated August 11, 1936, reporting the numbers of African Americans working on the state guidebooks—skilled, unskilled, and professional—Illinois ranked among the highest with eleven workers.[8] Later that year, Illinois acting state director George A. Rollins wrote in a letter to Henry Alsberg and marked for the attention of Sterling Brown that just before a round of staff reductions were to begin, there were eight African Americans employed.[9] In 1937, Brown sent a letter to the newly appointed state director John T. Frederick, providing him with the names of six black writers in Chicago whom he might consider to work on the project: Barefield Gordon, poet and book reviewer for the *Chicago Defender*; William Attaway, future novelist; Garfield Smith, an editor for the *Chicago World*; Marita Bonner Occomy, the only one Brown knew personally, a black woman writer who had produced some "rather interesting stories" during the Harlem Renaissance; Isaac Clark, recently returned to Chicago to get a teacher's certificate at the Chicago Normal School; and Hugh Gardner, former city editor for the *Chicago Whip* and at the time a writer for the *Chicago World*.[10] Of these, only Barefield Gordon eventually worked on the Illinois Writers' Project.[11] Many were restricted from working on the project because they were not unemployed and therefore ineligible for relief. Frederick replied to Brown, thanking him for the suggestions but remarking, "I have encountered some difficulty in making additions to our staff because of the restrictive policy, particularly in reference to non-relief workers." The two men appear to have shared a good rapport. Frederick ended his letter by telling Brown that he enjoyed his recent trip to Washington, D.C., "especially [the] visit which was spent in your office."[12]

A list of essays about African Americans in Illinois and their authors was prepared and sent to the Washington, D.C., office for review. They were returned to Illinois state director George A. Rollins with a letter from George W. Cronyn, associate director of the Federal Writers' Project, who said they were of "practically no use." A comment was attached from Alfred E. Smith, who remarked harshly, "[T]hese thirteen articles have been floating around for a good while. They should have kept on floating, right down the Potomac."[13] Although the specific list of thirteen articles does not exist, a list of almost one hundred different articles sent to Washington in March 1937 does remain.[14] The following month, a report was sent back to the Illinois office by Sterling Brown. Some of the articles were "well handled," in Brown's view, although many of them did not focus on Illinois, but rather on the country in general. "Almost all of the material," he wrote, "on Industry, Ethnography, History and Amusements is valuable." He wrote brief reviews for forty-two of the more relevant articles. There were already ones by writers who would make valuable contributions to the project, including Richard Wright, Fenton Johnson, Lillian Harper, William Page, and Orange Winkfield.[15]

In reviewing reports from the state projects, Brown was disappointed by the lack of information on African Americans. He complained to Henry Alsberg, "In reading State Copy I have been struck by the fact that in many cities where the Negro population is large the Negro is barely mentioned, if at all. This New South (or New Midwest or New North) from which the Negro is an exile, not self-imposed in this case, is hardly recognizable." Brown acknowledged that the guidebooks were to present a positive image to potential tourists. As he continued, "I appreciate the fact that frequently in these cities the Negro belongs to the backyard problems. These cities will hardly wish tours to call attention to the slums where the Negro is usually forced to live." As of yet, there was too little information available to include in any of the guidebooks soon to be published. But if they were to be "true guides of American life," Brown concluded, "the Negro cannot be so completely relegated to the background."[16]

Brown initiated a plan to create a portrait of Negro America as it had never before been presented. As historian Jerrold Hirsch has argued, Brown wanted to concentrate not just on the contributions of African Americans, but their participation in making up the very fabric of American culture.[17] His was ultimately an integrationist approach, as he intended to develop a book-length study, which would be his summary statement while on the project, "The Portrait of the Negro as American." As Brown explained in early 1940, "The Negro in America has been greatly written about, but most frequently as a separate entity, as a problem, not as a participant." African American historians had often tried to correct this neglect, but the result was overemphasis. "Where white historians find few or no Negroes and too little important participation, Negro historians find too many and too much."[18] Such racial biases had clouded the interpretation of history. There was a need, Brown believed, for an "adequate" and "accurate" depiction of African Americans. This was the mantra he repeatedly stressed as editor. He eventually outlined a list of seventeen book projects that would be undertaken under his watch:

1. A History of Negroes in Virginia
2. Drums and Shadows
3. The Survey of Negroes in Little Rock and North Little Rock, Arkansas
4. The Negro in Pittsburgh
5. The Negro in Philadelphia
6. Negroes in New York
7. The Florida Negro
8. History of Negroes in Louisiana
9. Book of Negro Folklore
10. Narratives of Ex-Slaves
11. Underground Railroad Book
12. Portrait of the Negro as American
13. History of the Negro
14. The Negro in Boston
15. The Negro in Chicago
16. Negroes in Oklahoma
17. Selected Bibliography[19]

In memos sent to Henry Alsberg for approval, Brown gave details of what a more "adequate" depiction of the sizable black populations in northern cities would look like. These instructions were then passed on to state projects. He wanted field workers to investigate prominent figures in the early history of a given place and the "nativity" of local black populations. He wanted to know where early founders had migrated from and when. Nineteenth-century history of fugitive slaves and the Underground Railroad was to be dug up. They should tell the story of the black migration in the early twentieth century. The work of black laborers, skilled and unskilled, was to be recorded. Instances of black workers being used as strikebreakers were to be explained, as well as efforts toward unionization. Workers should research issues such as housing, health, education, recreation, business, and politics. Church life was to be covered, both traditional churches, and nontraditional "storefront" churches, such as those of Daddy Grace and Father Divine. Information on cultural activities was to be gathered, such as drama, choral and music groups, theaters and libraries, writers and artists. The current conditions of the Depression were also of interest, the number of blacks unemployed, and an enumeration of those who relied upon WPA and other relief programs.[20] While Brown had a heavy hand in the publication of *The Negro in Virginia* and collection of the slave narratives, there is little evidence that he had any sway over the Illinois Writers' Project. In 1940, when he resigned from his post, *The Negro in Illinois* was just beginning.

Of the seventeen projects planned, only two—*The Negro in Virginia* (1940), edited by Roscoe E. Lewis, and *Drums and Shadows* (1940), conducted by the Georgia Writers' Project—were published before the Federal Writers' Project was closed down. Additionally, a short booklet titled *The Negroes of Nebraska*, co-sponsored by the Omaha Urban League, was published in 1940. Roi Ottley, the supervisor of the New York project, was in the process of rewriting *The Negro in New York* but passed away before it was completed. The book was published in 1967 by William Weatherby, whose editorial approach was to do "as little as possible to the narrative" (xiii). *The Florida Negro*, which Zora Neale Hurston worked on extensively, had not neared completion but was significantly rewritten from draft fragments by editor Gary McDonogh and published in 1993. In 2004, *The WPA History of the Negro in Pittsburgh* was published by editor Laurence Glasco from an unfinished manuscript with a layer of footnotes explaining his process of reconstructing the work. What was at first "The Negro in Chicago" became a statewide study called *The Negro in Illinois*. The manuscript was finished, although it never reached publication. Next to New York, it attracted a greater number of talented writers than any other of Brown's projected studies.

Almost as soon as the Illinois Writers' Project began, black writers applied for employment on its staff. Richard Wright was among the first to be hired. Although he may have started earlier, the first document bearing Wright's name is "Ethnographical Aspects of Chicago's Black Belt," dated December 11, 1935. The title suggests that the anthropological and sociological methods being practiced at the University of Chicago had already made an impact on the aspiring author. According to Wright, he first encountered these ideas after meeting his relief worker's husband, Louis Wirth, a sociology professor at the University of Chicago. Horace Cayton recalled he was in Wirth's office one day when Wright knocked on the door and introduced himself, "My name is Richard Wright. Mrs. Wirth said that her husband might help me. I want to be a writer" (Hill et. al, 196–97). Wirth supplied him with several readings, and he became an informal student at the "Chicago school" of sociology. Cayton would also provide Wright access to the maps, tables, and graphs he had collected. These perspectives deeply influenced Wright and would leave an imprint on his fiction.

Other writings Wright completed while on the project were routine assignments that workers performed in preparation for the guidebooks. He took an account of the material held in the files of the Chicago Urban League for future researchers. He created a bibliography of works on African Americans in Chicago. He reported on tourist destinations throughout the South Side such as Washington Park, Bronzeville's free speech park. He wrote about the "White City" amusement park, modeled after the original 1893 World's Columbian Exposition, which was located on the South Side but excluded blacks from

Horace Cayton and Richard Wright examine a map of the South Side.
(Vivian G. Harsh Research Collection of Afro-American History and
Literature, Chicago Public Library, Horace Cayton Papers 015)

entry. Any social or political commentary was eliminated from these writings, as they were to present a positive image for potential tourists. Wright's address at 3743 Indiana Avenue is listed on the front page of these essays, suggesting he was allowed to work at home rather than at the downtown office on 433 E. Erie Street, a privilege given to few writers.[21] He was also paid to work on his fiction and wrote a draft of "Big Boy Leaves Home" while at the Illinois Writers' Project.[22]

For a brief period in early 1936, Wright was transferred to the Federal Theatre Project.[23] According to his account in "I Tried to Be a Communist," he already had considerable pull among WPA administrators, enough to have the current director of the Negro Federal Theatre in Chicago replaced by Charles DeSheim, who had recently directed a local production of Clifford Odet's *Waiting for Lefty*. With hopes of creating a "genuine Negro theater," Wright had proposed a local production of Paul Green's *Hymn to the Rising Sun*, a one-act play about a southern chain gang. The play was to be staged in October 1937 but was shut down after being deemed "immoral" by the state head of the WPA.[24] Wright's gives a much different account, claiming that it was shut down by the actors themselves who refused to perform in the play. He tells the sensational story of an angry group of actors who threatened him with pocketknives. After this incident, he says he demanded to be taken off the project immediately. He was placed back on the Illinois Writers' Project, but the exact date he returned is uncertain.

A young Margaret Walker lied about her age on her application, and on March 13, 1936, she arrived for her first day at work on the Illinois Writers' Project. She recalled seeing Wright, who was then on the Theatre Project. At this time, the Theatre Project and the Writers' Project shared the same offices on Erie Street. Wright and Walker soon became friends and began sharing their writings. According to Walker, she wrote a story titled "Goose Island" that Wright "took from me" as inspiration for *Native Son* (Tate 34). Years later Walker would publish the biography *Richard Wright: Daemonic Genius* (1988), wherein she recounts these years when she knew him best. "The explosion of his creative genius," she wrote, "coincided with this cultural explosion of the WPA" (81).

On June 24, 1936, Claude Barnett, founder of the Associated Negro Press (ANP) and an early supporter of Wright's career, wrote a letter to George Davis, the state supervisor of the Federal Theatre Project, regarding a "young man on your staff who has newspaper talent" named Richard Wright.[25] He requested that Wright be assigned to work on publicity for the Associated Negro Press and spend his days at their office. This was quite an unusual request, for Barnett could obviously hire Wright if he wanted to employ him. By August 1936, Wright had been reassigned to the Illinois Writers' Project, but not due to Barnett's intervention. George A. Rollins, Illinois state director of the Writers' Project, wrote back to Barnett saying that he appreciated his suggestion but Wright was "a valued member of our staff and is now doing important rewrite work which, of course, must be done in this office." If Barnett had private employment for Wright, Rollins said he could give him a high recommendation.[26]

However Wright ended up back on the Writers' Project, he was promoted to a supervisor position when he returned, another sign that he was appreciated by WPA administrators. In March 1937, Wright outlined a plan for a book to be called "20 Years of Negro History through Negro Eyes." It would be conducted under the auspices of the Federal Writers' Project and utilize the files of the Associated Negro Press. The idea had come out of a series of conversations with Claude Barnett about a book on recent black history. The book would be a creative arrangement of interesting newspaper items, Wright suggested, employing the "camera eye" technique John Dos Passos had used in his novels.[27] It had the blessing of Barnett, who wrote a cover letter for the proposal that was sent to Sterling Brown.[28] Brown responded to Barnett a week later, explaining that while the plan was well thought out, it ran parallel to the project already approved by national director

Henry Alsberg and underway, what was presumably "The Negro in Chicago." The book, Brown wrote, would be "neither sociological nor historical" and cover a wider period than twenty years.[29] Brown still hoped that Wright could serve in an editorial capacity, but he would move to New York in May 1937 before he could contribute any further to the study of African Americans in Illinois.[30]

The Writers' Project was not the only WPA office interested in documenting black life on the South Side. There was also an in-depth sociological study headed by Horace Cayton. Cayton had come to Chicago in 1931 to attend the University of Chicago as a graduate student in the Sociology Department. He would study under Professors Robert Park, Louis Wirth, Ernest Burgess, and W. Lloyd Warner. In November 1936, Cayton began as supervisor of a WPA-sponsored study of the South Side under the guidance of Warner, a professor in anthropology and sociology. The data they compiled, known as the "Cayton-Warner papers," became the basis for several later works. Those who worked on *The Negro in Illinois* also drew from these materials. Yet again, this WPA project did not come without a challenge.

A New Deal Town

When Cayton first found out that the University of Chicago was to be sponsoring a government study of conditions among African Americans on the South Side, he penned a scathing letter to WPA administrators denouncing the institution that was, he said, largely responsible for racial segregation and overcrowded housing. The Institute for Juvenile Research at the University of Chicago was embarking on a survey of delinquency among black children in Chicago. Cayton registered his "most emphatic protest," he wrote in the letter, not to the idea itself but to its sponsorship. The University of Chicago, he said, had exhibited a "hostile, unfriendly, and basically unjust attitude" toward their neighbors in nearby Bronzeville, the black community adjacent to Hyde Park where the university was located. As evidence, he pointed to the University of Chicago's medical school, which refused to allow its students of color to intern at its own hospital in fear of protests from white patients who did not want to be treated by blacks. Instead, they gave funding to the newly built Provident Hospital, where black medical students were sent to treat the African American population it served. The University of Chicago also gave large contributions to a white neighborhood association that enforced restrictive covenants in the Woodlawn neighborhood, maintaining a buffer zone between the campus and the black community. Therefore, he wrote, this institution from which "oozes a constant secretion of racial prejudice and intolerance" should not be permitted to prey upon residents of the South Side. Any study conducted by the University of Chicago was incapable of producing an honest account of juvenile delinquency among black youth or assigning blame where it rightly belonged.[31]

Ironically, Cayton was appointed to supervise just such a study, a daunting task for this young scholar and a job he would approach with much enthusiasm. Contrary to what might be expected, there was not a great deal of bureaucratic red tape constraining what could be done. If a compelling proposal were submitted to put Americans back to work, there was WPA money available. As Cayton recalled, "It was not too difficult to secure such funds at this time, since millions were being spent to provide jobs for the unemployed.

The procedure was for some responsible organization or institution to suggest a project; workers and limited supplies were then furnished by the government" (236). With the backing of the Institute for Juvenile Research and W. Lloyd Warner, Cayton launched his study. He began by gathering the original field materials from previous studies done by E. Franklin Frazier, Howard Gosnell, Earl Johnson, Ernest Burgess, and Philip Hauser.[32] This was eventually published in 1972 as *Chicago Afro-American Union Analytic Catalog*, a bibliography of some seventy-five thousand entries. Over a period of three and a half years, Cayton oversaw more than twenty different WPA projects with a staff of some two hundred people, recruiting graduate students from the University of Chicago to lead projects. Approximately 90 percent of the workers were African American. They collected data on housing, population growth, migration, occupations, business, politics, education, family, voluntary associations, churches, social stratification, social agencies, newspapers, and juvenile delinquency.[33]

Headquarters for the study were located in the basement of the Church of the Good Shepherd at 5700 Prairie Avenue, which rented the space for a nominal fee. Other projects were based at the University of Chicago and Hall Branch Library. In early 1939, they held an exhibit on the South Side attended by some five hundred people, where they presented maps, charts, graphs, and tables that had been created.[34] Out of this research came three books published in December 1939: *The Chicago Negro Community: A Statistical Description*, by Mary Elaine Ogden; *Occupational Changes among Negroes in Chicago*, by Estelle Hill; and *Churches and Voluntary Associations in the Chicago Negro Community*, by St. Clair Drake. The Cayton-Warner papers were offered to Gunnar Myrdal for his Carnegie-funded study, *American Dilemma*. But when Myrdal would not offer compensation, Cayton refused to hand over his years of work.[35] Instead, the papers provided the bulk of the material for *Black Metropolis*, the book he wrote with St. Clair Drake, whom he had hired to work on the WPA.[36] A proposal for an institute to house the Cayton-Warner papers never came to fruition, and the collection has since disappeared.[37] Yet the papers represent, according to Margaret Walker, the "sociological backbone of the Chicago School of Social Protest of the 1930s."[38]

There was significant overlap between the twenty-plus WPA programs run by Cayton and the Illinois Writers' Project. Several of the studies conducted under Cayton's leadership were carried out by those on the Illinois Writers' Project and folded into *The Negro in Illinois*. Among them was a survey of black newspapers titled "The Negro Press in Chicago," which was to eventually become a book. A plan for the study was outlined by Cayton in November 1938 and a manual was prepared for field workers.[39] It included a comprehensive list of black periodicals to be researched. A questionnaire was developed and administered by Henry N. Bacon, who was former managing editor of black literary magazine *The Bronzeman* and had many contacts among the local black press. The questionnaire was then filled out by field workers who interviewed several founders of black periodicals, names provided to them by Bacon. One of those to conduct interviews was Richard Durham, who filled out questionnaires on the *Chicago Bee*, *Flash*, *Bronzeman*, *Reflexus*, *Chicago World*, *Original Illinois Housewives Association*, *Chicago Leader*, *The South Side Business and Professional Men's Review*, and *Chicago Conservator*.[40] While writing radio scripts for the Illinois Writers' Project, Durham found his true passion and later created *Destination Freedom*, a radio program broadcast on WMAQ in Chicago from 1948 to 1950.

Margaret Walker, 1942. (Vivian G. Harsh Research Collection of
Afro-American History and Literature, Chicago Public Library,
George Cleveland Hall Branch Archives 050)

Also working on the survey was Margaret Walker, who would become known for her
poetry and fiction. Two questionnaires she filled out remain in archives, one for the *Royal
Messenger* and the other for *Woman's National Magazine*. She copied several editorials on
matters of race from the *Metropolitan Post*. She also performed several other routine assignments during her three years on the project. [41] She was finally laid off in 1939 after
Congress passed a law limiting the time to eighteen months that someone could work
on WPA. [42]

Once material was collected, there were plans for a book project on the history of the
African American press in Chicago. There was an outline for ten chapters, several of which
were completed. [43] Four chapters were authored by Henry N. Bacon: "To Arms for Liberty,"

written in April 1939; "The Political Pot Boils," and "News That is News," both written in June 1939; and the undated "Am I My Brother's Keeper?" Margaret Walker wrote a twenty-two-page essay titled "The Bronzeville Press—Its Cultural Impress."[44] For other chapters the authors remain unknown. "Bronzeville Finds Its Voice" is a history of black newspapers from the *Conservator* to the *Defender*. "A Good Neighbor Speaks" includes full quotes out of Anthony Overton's *Chicago Bee* from the 1930s, many copies of which today are nonexistent. Perhaps the most powerful is the concluding chapter, "Don't Spend Your Money Where You Can't Work," by Richard Durham, about advocacy in the black press for jobs and the fight against what he calls "economic discrimination." Durham discusses African American interest in Communism, their growing involvement in labor unions, and support for New Deal programs. This chapter describes the radicalization of black residents in Bronzeville and also reflects the impact it had on writers like Durham. It was during these years that Durham briefly joined the Communist Party and also met his wife Clarice Davis (the sister of Robert Davis) at the local branch office of the National Negro Congress at 47th and South Parkway.[45] Addressing the growing war in Europe in the essay, he noted that African Americans were not unfamiliar with fascism—"it is already here."[46]

Several talented black writers who could not find work during the Depression were sustained by the WPA. One of the most established black writers forced to go on relief was poet Fenton Johnson. Born in Chicago in 1888, Johnson had self-published three books of poetry in the 1910s, written short stories and plays, founded two literary magazines, and worked as a journalist, but he still struggled to find employment. When Johnson was hired on the Illinois Writers' Project, he was given free rein to write on a variety of topics. For example, he wrote fascinating personal reminiscences of famous African Americans he had met: John R. Marshall, colonel of the all-black Fighting Eighth; Bishop Reverdy C. Ransom of the A.M.E. Church; and composer Will Marion Cook. He wrote several notable essays such as "Racial Friction in Chicago," about incidents leading up to and following the 1919 race riots. Another essay, "Americanization," was a history of blacks in education. In an essay called "Negro Aristocrats," he wrote about the African American upper class. Writings documenting Johnson's time on the project are dated as early as April 1937, although he probably did not work there consistently. He would write chapters on literature and theater for the *Cavalcade of the American Negro*, a booklet produced for the 1940 American Negro Exposition. He also wrote early drafts for the first chapters of *The Negro in Illinois*. The project benefited from Johnson's extensive knowledge of Chicago's early black history. In turn, his time on the project helped Johnson to stay afloat during years that were for him troubling both financially and emotionally. As Jack Conroy recalled, Johnson was "always morose and taciturn" when he checked in at the office ("Memories of Arna Bontemps" 605). Yet Johnson produced an impressive collection of "WPA Poems" that he wrote while on the project and gave them to Conroy. Conroy showed the poems to Bontemps, who tried to find a publisher, although they never reached print. In the years afterward, Bontemps remained the greatest champion of Johnson's work.

Another writer who collected a government paycheck while writing freely on special topics was Katherine "Kitty" de la Chapelle, about whom little is known. Originally from Louisiana, Chapelle spoke with a Creole-French accent. She was hired by Horace Cayton and worked on the Illinois Writers' Project for a little more than a year, with documents dating from May 1937 through June 1938. She wrote at length about various forms of

African American cultural production. One essay titled "Development of Negro Culture in Chicago" began with a discussion of Chicago's black founder Jean Baptiste Point Du Sable and the small collection of pictures attributed to him in historical records, which, she says, reflects his appreciation for art and culture. She wrote nearly seven hundred pages in a series of writings titled "Colored Culture in Chicago."[47] It is a lengthy stream-of-consciousness narrative that addresses art, music, theater, and literature in a way that recognizes the interrelatedness of these forms. She frequently speaks of an artistic movement underway, what scholars today refer to as the Black Chicago Renaissance. It had its earlier roots such as the 1927 publication of *Letters* magazine. "With such a distinguished line of forebears," she wrote in one inspired passage, "we can but urge the rising Negro poets keep their eyes fixed fast upon that brilliant heraldry of 'Letters' and follow on. But in following on we admonish them, for their own greater glory, to forgive and forget, blotting out from memory entirely those baneful years of slavery, with the temporary arrestment of development. They have a glorious past!" More than just describing this movement, Chapelle was ushering it in. She continued, "Though the more recent years have produced such poets as Dunbar and Phillis Wheatley, we look to the new rising generation for a happier spirit, a surging forward into new life, rather than a looking backwards at the smoking embers of a yesterday." She cited as an example the poetry of Frank Marshall Davis, which captured the "dauntlessness" of this new generation.[48]

When John T. Frederick became state director of the Illinois Writers' Project, he took seriously the mandate from Sterling Brown to hire more black writers and cover more black history. The author of two novels, founder of *Midland* magazine, and professor at Northwestern University, Frederick was a well-respected writer and scholar. He was hired as state director in August 1937, and the following year he was promoted to regional director also overseeing projects in Indiana, Michigan, Missouri, and Ohio. When national director Henry Alsberg was forced to resign in 1939, Frederick was asked to take his place, but he gracefully declined. In January 1940, Frederick resigned from the Writers' Project, citing health reasons. While no radical, Frederick had a liberal view of race. He included African American authors in his edited anthologies and invited them on his popular radio show, "Of Men and Books."[49]

In his position, Frederick hired several black writers to focus on specialized assignments. Among them was educator Alonzo Bowling, who conducted the study "A History of Negro Education in Illinois" under Frederick's direction. Born in Lincoln, Illinois, in 1881, Bowling was, like Fenton Johnson, of an older generation. He had more than twenty-five years' experience in the field of education. He had been an editor of the *Conservator* and frequent contributor to the *Broad Ax* and *Chicago World*. He had begun to research the educational system in Illinois while in the office of the superintendent of the Department of Public Instruction in Springfield, a study he continued for a year and a half while working on the Illinois Writers' Project. Documents date his time on the project from May 1938 to January 1939.[50] The central problem guiding his investigation was that although there was no state law in Illinois for the separation of black and white students, it was a standard practice in many communities.

A study of black religious groups, what were called "cults" and "storefront churches," was also initiated under Frederick's leadership. The term "cults" was commonly used in the day, even though it was viewed by some as offensive, and has since continued to frame the discussions on fringe black religious groups, in particular black Muslims. In *Churches and Voluntary Associations in the Chicago Negro Community*, St. Clair Drake intentionally refrained from using such dismissive language. In 1944, Arthur Huff Fauset was rebuked for his use of the term "cults" in his book *Black Gods of the Metropolis*. The 1972 publication *Black Sects and Cults* by Joseph Washington reflects this same bias. Even more recently, Manning Marable, author of the 2011 biography *Malcolm X: A Life of Reinvention*, has been criticized for his reference to the Nation of Islam under Elijah Muhammad's leadership as a "cult" and a "sect."[51] Although workers on the Illinois Writers' Project referred to these groups as "cults," they conducted a unique study into the religious folk practices on the South Side and were among the first to document the appearance of the Nation of Islam, today one of the most influential black religious groups in the United States.

The study began as early as September 1938 under the supervision of dancer Katherine Dunham. Previously, Dunham had worked as director of the Chicago branch of the Federal Theatre Project, where she staged "L'Ag'Ya," a ballet incorporating Caribbean dance.[52] While she was a graduate student in anthropology at the University of Chicago, one of her professors, Robert Redfield, had suggested she show her work to John T. Frederick of the Writers' Project. Impressed by her manuscript for *Journey to Accompong*, Frederick appointed her as supervisor to a study of black cults and storefront churches in Chicago.[53] According to an internal memo from Frederick, the study was especially focused on the "survivals of primitive religious practices."[54] This was a task well suited for Dunham, who had studied the survival of African religious beliefs in the voodoo practices of Haiti. In an unpublished autobiography to be called "Minefields," Dunham recalled that the planned title for the study was "The Occurrence of Cults among Deprived Peoples," although she says it changed a few times. She remembered selecting a team of researchers that included Mary Fujii, one of the few women in the anthropology department, Barefield Gordon, who was a friend, and his cousin, Frank Yerby. An outline for the project, dated April 24, 1939, indicates the study was at this time titled "Revolt in Green Pastures" (a twist on the title of the play by Marc Connolly) and included six chapters: "Exodus," covering the period from the African slave trade to World War I; "Prophet from the Islands," about Marcus Garvey; "King Sheba" about the Abyssinians; "I, Your Prophet," about Noble Drew Ali and the Moorish American Science Temple; "The White Devil," a chapter just being started about what was then referred to as the Temple of Islam; and a conclusion not yet completed.[55] Dunham recalled visiting the Nation of Islam's Temple Number Two. There she met Elijah Muhammad and was "impressed by his sincerity" (*Kaiso* 89). Dunham also sent other IWP field workers to conduct participant observation among black religious groups of the South Side.

Field workers initially faced obstacles from groups that were suspicious of outsiders. Black Muslims were openly hostile to whites, whom they referred to as "Caucasian devils." Likewise, women could not gain full access due to a strict separation of the sexes. Jack Conroy, who took over the study when Dunham quit to pursue her dancing career, recalled the difficulties workers faced, but eventually one of them was successful: "One of our alert Negro field-workers managed not only to obtain the cult's secret rituals but also to be accepted as a member and to take part in some of the meetings. He was told that Allah had had about enough of the 'spook' civilizations of the white 'caveman' and would soon bring it to a halt and would replace it with a Muslim order of things. This would bring opportunities for black men as government officials, diplomats, etc., and our representative was assured that his temple membership and his educated bearing would assure him of a desirable post" ("Memories of Arna Bontemps" 603).

One of the black workers who gained access to these groups was Frank Yerby, whose name is on more than a dozen essays dated between September 1938 and February 1939. Yerby wrote fascinating, firsthand accounts from his observations of the Spiritualists, the First Church of Deliverance, the Moorish American Science Temple, and Bishop Daddy Grace.[56] He described the halls they worshiped in, the colorful costumes they wore, and the hymns they sang. After attending services, he wrote down his observations of the charismatic figures who headed these congregations, such as "Mother" Mattie Thornton, assistant pastor of the First Church of the Deliverance, who handed out, for a quarter a piece, sacred flowers that were believed to cure illnesses. Yerby was also present in 1939 at the Moorish American Science Temple for the birthday of Noble Drew Ali, the group's prophet. Although Ali had since died, every January 8 there was a celebration that, Yerby remarked, was regarded as the group's Christmas. Yerby later became successful writing bestselling novels, but he got an early start on the Writers' Project. By the time Arna Bontemps arrived on the project, Yerby had already left, although the two men corresponded in later years. Bontemps characterized Yerby as a "wraith-like" figure whose presence on the project was remembered "dimly" by those who worked alongside him ("Famous WPA Authors" 45).

The study of black cults and storefront churches originally focused on four general groups: the Moorish American Science Temple, the Nation of Islam, Sanctified Churches, and Spiritualist Churches. Each group had its own origins and specific practices, which were described in detail by field workers. The Moorish-American Science Temple and Nation of Islam were both followers of Allah, although each had their own interpretations of the Koran. The Spiritualist and Sanctified churches were of Christian faith but believed in divine healing and direct communication with the heavenly world. Others who collected research include Alvin N. Cannon, Ann Williams, William Page, Robert Davis, William Henry Huff, and Robert Lucas.[57] A three-page essay was prepared by Robert Lucas describing his visit to the "King Solomon's Temple of Religious Science," which was located in the basement of the Oriental Incense Company. "The sweet smell of incense and perfume," he reported, "which pervaded the low-ceilinged worship space was blown about in nauseating waves by the breeze from an open window."[58] When it appeared in *The Negro in Illinois*, this material was split up into two different chapters. What was collected on storefront churches and cults was used in the chapter "And Churches," and research on the Moorish American Science Temple and Nation of Islam was used in the chapter "What is Africa to Me?" as the two groups were seen as expressions of black nationalism.

Arna Bontemps, who would later become supervisor of *The Negro in Illinois*, was also hired by Frederick to work on the project. His first assignment was to supervise a study of black music in Chicago. In their book *The Muse in Bronzeville*, authors Robert Bone and Richard Courage place Bontemps, born in 1902, among older members of the Chicago Renaissance. Working in conjunction with younger artists, they "formed the very center of Bronzeville's cultural ferment" (6). Bontemps had made a name for himself during the Harlem Renaissance by writing such poems as "Nocturne at Bethesda" which won the

King Solomon's Temple, one of the storefront churches studied by members of the
Illinois Writers' Project. (Abraham Lincoln Presidential Library & Museum,
Illinois Writers' Project Papers)

top prize in the first-ever poetry contest held by *Crisis* magazine in 1927. It was in these youthful years that he was introduced to Langston Hughes, who became his best friend and collaborator. In 1935, Bontemps moved to Chicago to begin a master's degree in English at the University of Chicago. He quickly met other Chicago writers and was a founding member of the South Side Writers' Group. In 1936, he published the acclaimed novel *Black Thunder* about Gabriel Prosser's slave revolt in Virginia. John T. Frederick read the book and offered Bontemps a position as supervisor on the Illinois Writers' Project, which he began in late 1939.[59] Bontemps had a lasting interest in jazz and the blues. In 1941, while working on the project, he assisted W. C. Handy in writing his autobiography, *Father of the Blues*. An outline Bontemps had written for a book-length study to be called "History of Negro Music and Musicians in Chicago" includes chapters with titles such as "The Heritage," "Darktown Strutters," "State Street Blues," "Spirituals of Today," "Concert and Parlor Music," "The Heavy Load," and "Boogie Woogie."[60] One of the workers most involved with this study was George D. Lewis, who performed numerous interviews with local musicians and conducted extensive research. Some of the material was collected by

Arna Bontemps, 1939. (Library of Congress,
Carl Van Vechten Collection)

Onah Spencer, African American folklorist and music historian. Eventually, this study was utilized for the chapter "Music," written by Robert Lucas.

In 1940, those in Chicago who were planning the American Negro Exposition, the first black-organized World's Fair, called on Arna Bontemps and his staff at the Illinois Writers' Project to write the official booklet for the event. Called the "Diamond Jubilee," celebrating seventy-five years since emancipation, the exhibit was to feature a number of displays highlighting African American achievements in health, industry, education, sports, art, music, and literature. That the exposition was held in Chicago rather than New York signaled, Adam Green writes, "a shift in the balance of cultural power in black America" (24). Chosen as executive director was Truman Gibson Jr., a local attorney who had many contacts among the black intelligentsia and business class. Claude Barnett threw his support behind the exposition and assigned ANP journalist Frank Marshall Davis as publicity director. Horace Cayton, now head of the Good Shepherd Community Center, was the assistant to Gibson. Vivian Harsh of the Hall Branch Library offered her expertise. Curtis D. MacDougall, hired to replace John T. Frederick as state supervisor of the Illinois Writers' Project, served on the board of the Exposition Authority, giving it the blessing of his office.

The American Negro Exposition was financially supported by a $75,000 grant from the Illinois state legislature that was matched by another $75,000 from the federal government. It was befitting that the Illinois Writers' Project, a government-sponsored program, would produce the publication promoting the fair. The *Cavalcade of the American Negro* was edited by Arna Bontemps with the help of Henry N. Bacon, Alvin Cannon, Herman Clayton, Fenton Johnson, Edward Joseph, and George D. Lewis. The *Cavalcade* was largely national in scope and included little Illinois history. There were fifty thousand copies printed, reflecting the high hopes of the organizers. It was forecast that two million people would attend the exposition. Yet the initial letters of support were sent in March 1940, leaving little time for preparations before the July 4th opening. As a result, the manuscript for the *Cavalcade* was not vetted by the Washington office, leaving Sterling Brown disappointed with the final product. Brown gave his opinion in an internal memo dated July 23, 1940. The story was presented "simply as smoothly," he said, but it largely relied on secondary sources. The book's "fluency" was attributable to the fine editorship of Arna Bontemps. He characterized the book as "cautious" and found it contained "nothing to disturb either Negro or white reading publics." Reiterating his theme of accuracy, Brown noted there was more racial praise than interpretation, "but this befits an exposition." The *Cavalcade* left much room for improvement. Its publication without any editorial advice was "unfortunate and a bad precedent."[61] Bontemps was also disappointed in the exposition, which was, as he wrote in a letter to Harold Jackman, "too many shooting galleries and cheap amusements, too much attempt to mix culture with hot dogs, too much tawdry advertising, too much confusion and noise, too little imagination."[62]

For a brief time, IWP workers were considered to assist W. E. B. Du Bois with his *Encyclopedia of the Negro*, the uncompleted project that preceded the *Encyclopedia Africana*. Since 1909, Du Bois had tried to produce a comprehensive encyclopedia written by and about African Americans. Du Bois had resurrected the project in the mid-1930s, but it was waylaid by a lack of funding. In early 1941, Bontemps wrote to Du Bois, whom he had spoken with a month earlier about the status of the encyclopedia.[63] In the letter, Bontemps proposed that IWP workers be used to conduct the project. Bontemps arranged for state supervisor Curtis MacDougall to go to Washington, D.C., to promote the idea but he got nowhere. WPA officials were in a state of "despair," fearing that the Writers' Project would soon be shut down, but Bontemps was persistent. A trip to Washington made by Du Bois himself, he suggested, would be the "most helpful move." There was hope that various state projects would work on the encyclopedia, but at a minimum the Illinois Writers' Project could "participate on its own authority as things stand now and could contribute substantially." Bontemps said he had "very great interest" in the encyclopedia and thought that much of the "spade work" could be done by project writers. Perhaps Du Bois had other plans, but Bontemps believed that "there are possibilities." Whatever came of these conversations is unknown, but it appears Du Bois never took him up on the offer.

African Americans in the Land of Lincoln

When it was officially launched in October 1940, *The Negro in Illinois* would draw upon the previous five years of work and be drafted by the collective effort of many different writers and field workers.[64] Earlier that year, *The Negro in Virginia* had been published by the all-black unit of the Virginia Writers' Project. Headed by Roscoe E. Lewis, it was the first book published of Sterling Brown's seventeen planned projects. When Arna Bontemps read it, he was "struck by the idea that a similar book about Illinois Negroes should be even more interesting."[65] With the help of IWP editor Parker Van de Mark, Bontemps put forward a proposal to the Rosenwald Fund, a Chicago-based philanthropic organization that donated millions to establish schools for black children throughout the South and also awarded grants to black artists and writers. On October 9, the fund's Board of Trustees voted to sponsor the book. (It was standard practice for guidebooks to find a private backer, so as not to interfere with the free market.) The project was housed in the Rosenwald mansion at 4901 S. Ellis Avenue, where the Rosenwald Fund was headquartered. Arna Bontemps and Jack Conroy were appointed co-supervisors of a staff that included six writers and seventeen reporters.[66] The book was projected to take nine months to complete. It originally consisted of twenty-two chapters, although it was later expanded to twenty-nine chapters. What was at first a study of "The Negro in Chicago" gained a statewide focus with assistance from those such as Eugene Covington, based in Peoria, as well as individuals from other IWP offices across the state.

Perhaps one of the most surprising aspects of *The Negro in Illinois* was the involvement of white fiction writer Jack Conroy. While on the Illinois Writers' Project, Bontemps and Conroy formed a close friendship that lasted for many years and would lead to their collaboration on five books.[67] As editor of a succession of little magazines—*Rebel Poet*, *Anvil*, and *New Anvil*—Conroy helped to promote a period of midwestern literary radicalism in the 1930s. When he published his novel *The Disinherited* in 1933, it was hailed as a classic of proletarian literature. Although Conroy was close to the Communist Party and participated in the John Reed Clubs, he carried out his own cultural program of publishing working-class writers. He spent two years on the Missouri Writers' Project but was forced to resign for his union activity.[68] In March 1938, he moved to Chicago, enticed by the opportunity to revive his magazine as the *New Anvil* with his friend and fellow writer Nelson Algren. Algren, who was already working on the Illinois Writers' Project, introduced him to John T. Frederick. Conroy was hired by Frederick to collect industrial folklore—the tall tales that factory workers would tell to one another. It was a project he had started earlier with the assistance of a Guggenheim fellowship, and from it he planned to write a book about black migrants to be called "Anyplace But Here." Conroy began working on the IWP as early as July 1938 and by September he had completed a manuscript of stories.[69] When Frederick resigned in January 1940, he was replaced by Northwestern University professor Curtis D. MacDougall. Frederick had refused to promote Conroy because of his radical politics. The more progressive MacDougall implemented an exam process by which Conroy, after scoring highly, was made into a supervisor.[70]

It may seem unlikely that Conroy and Bontemps would become such close friends. Bontemps was mild-mannered and scholarly, a middle-class family man who steered away from politics and controversy. Conroy was proudly working class, the son of an Irish

Jack Conroy, photo taken while on the St. Louis Writers' Project, 1936.
(Photo courtesy of the Newberry Library, Chicago.
Call # MMS Jack Conroy Papers, box 92, folder 2972)

coal miner, who had a gregarious personality and openly associated with the Communist Left. Their relationship was a unique interracial collaboration that defied social norms of the period. The two men shared a common interest in depicting folk language and lore in literature. They first met in the Erie Street offices of the Illinois Writers' Project, although they were assigned to separate studies. Langston Hughes was a mutual friend who insisted they meet one another. Bontemps and Conroy struck up a friendship that grew as they worked side-by-side at the Rosenwald mansion. A publisher had suggested to Conroy that he consider writing a juvenile novel from one of his industrial tales, "The Boomer Fireman's Fast Sooner," the story of a dog who was as fast as a locomotive train. Conroy had never written for children. He showed the story to Bontemps, who had co-authored the juvenile *Popo and Fifina* with Hughes. "Why not tackle it together," Bontemps offered. The book they co-wrote, *The Fast Sooner Hound*, sold over a half million copies. Thus began a long and fruitful literary collaboration that, Conroy said, "aroused me from a rather dormant period insofar as creative work was concerned" ("Memories of Arna Bontemps" 604).

Together, Bontemps and Conroy made a skillful set of editors. The writers on the project had a range of experience, and managing them was a delicate task. Bontemps most likely chose Conroy as co-supervisor because of his research on the black migration. But Conroy also had a reputation for encouraging African American authors in Chicago. As editor of the *Anvil*, he had published some of Richard Wright's earliest poems. The *New Anvil* included among its associate editors Frank Marshall Davis and published short stories by Margaret Walker and Frank Yerby, both of whom Conroy had met on the project. As correspondence letters in his papers reveal, Conroy offered words of encouragement to numerous young black writers and was well-liked by those such as Margaret Burroughs, Gwendolyn Brooks, Alice Browning, Onah Spencer, Willard Motley, and Frank Marshall Davis. Richard Wright affectionately referred to Conroy as "the old daddy of rebel writing in the United States."[71] Bontemps also had a gentle hand as an editor and was committed to assisting other black writers. In his 1941 collection *Golden Slippers*, he included poems by Fenton Johnson, Richard Durham, and Josephine Copeland, all of whom worked on the IWP. As mentioned previously, Bontemps had pursued getting Fenton Johnson's "WPA Poems" published. After Bontemps died, Conroy penned the tribute "Memories of Arna Bontemps, Friend and Collaborator" in which he recalled how Bontemps had "tried persistently to find publication for the works of writers he considered unjustly neglected" (606).

It is significant that the editors of *The Negro in Illinois* began with the story of Jean Baptiste Point Du Sable for the opening chapter, "First, the French." The decision was part of a local campaign to raise awareness of Chicago's first settler, who was a black man. In 1928, the National Du Sable Memorial Society was formed by Annie Oliver and other prominent black Chicagoans who joined in a concerted effort to claim the city as their own. Immediately, the group set its sights on the coming 1933 World's Fair, dubbed "A Century of Progress" (Chicago was incorporated in 1833). For the next five years, they fought to convince city leaders to acknowledge Chicago's black founder. Eventually, the city agreed to include a replica of the cabin inhabited by Du Sable at the fair. After this initial victory, the Du Sable Society continued to educate the public. This time they led a campaign to have Wendell Phillips High School, which had been rebuilt after burning to the ground in 1935, renamed the Du Sable High School. The high school had gone from white to black, as had the rest of the South Side. After a campaign was mobilized, the board of education agreed to change the name to the DeSaible High School, the spelling of the settler's name the society had agreed to up to that point. Yet this caused confusion when some white children mispronounced the name and began referring to the black school as "the disabled school." The society decided they should change the name to Du Sable, the spelling now used today. On June 9, 1936, a formal ceremony was held renaming the new building at 49th and Wabash Avenue the Du Sable High School.[72]

In writing other chapters on the early history of African Americans in Illinois, authors relied on newspaper clippings collected by IWP workers, historical documents, and secondary sources, among them an unpublished manuscript by African American historian Lawrence Dunbar (L. D.) Reddick. The 137-page essay, "A Sociological History of the Negro in Chicago," was prepared as a WPA-sponsored study directed by Horace Cayton and Lloyd Warner.[73] Although Reddick did not work on the Illinois Writers' Project, his was another WPA study that was used by those writing *The Negro in Illinois*. As a student at Fisk University in the late 1920s, Reddick had interviewed ex-slaves for Charles S. Johnson's Social Science Institute under the direction of Ophelia Settle Egypt. It was Reddick who initiated an early FERA project in 1934, collecting some 250 slave narratives.[74] Although the study was cancelled, the collection was picked back up by the Federal Writers' Project.

Members of the National Du Sable Memorial Society stand outside the replica of
the cabin inhabited by Chicago's first permanent resident, then spelled DeSaible,
at the 1933 World's Fair. Founder Annie Oliver sits out in front of the first row.
(Vivian G. Harsh Research Collection of Afro-American History and Literature,
Chicago Public Library, Esther Parada Papers 001)

While a professor of history at Dillard University in New Orleans, Reddick worked on
the Louisiana Writers' Project as supervisor of "The History of the Negro in Louisiana,"
another one of Brown's projects. Reddick took a leave of absence from Dillard to study at
the University of Chicago for the academic year 1936–37.[75] It was during this time that he
wrote "A Sociological History of the Negro in Chicago." That year he was also a featured
speaker at the national conference of the Association for the Study of Negro Life and
History in Virginia where he delivered the influential address, "A New Interpretation for
Negro History."[76] When Arthur Schomburg died in 1938, Reddick was named as curator
of the African American collection at the Harlem branch of the New York Public Library.
For the short time he lived in Chicago, Reddick produced an important manuscript that
was heavily drawn upon for the chapters "First, the French," "Abolition," and "The Underground Railroad."

There are many compelling stories of both familiar and little-known aspects of black
history contained in the pages of *The Negro in Illinois*. Although slavery was officially outlawed by the Illinois state constitution, the Black Laws significantly curtailed the rights
of African Americans. Of course, Illinois is commonly referred to as the "Land of Lincoln," but few know about William de Fleurville, Lincoln's black barber who influenced
his views on race. The abolitionist movement was strong in Illinois and had as its first
martyr Elijah Lovejoy, publisher of the *Alton Observer* who was murdered for his anti-

slavery editorials. The Underground Railroad passed through Illinois, with Chicago as a destination for many seeking refuge.[77] The editorial hand of Arna Bontemps, who had written two novels of black slave rebellions, is evident in these chapters on early Illinois history. "The Negro himself," he writes, "never a docile slave, struck out boldly for his freedom." It was during these years that Chicago gained the reputation as a "sink hole of abolitionism." Among the abolitionists of color was John Jones, a former slave who had bought his freedom, was trained as a tailor, and became one of the most successful black businessmen in Chicago. During the Civil War, some eleven hundred African Americans from Illinois fought in the Union Army. The first black military regiment, known as the "Fighting Eighth," was later founded in Illinois.[78]

African Americans migrated north in the postbellum period, searching for well-paying jobs, a better future for their children, and an escape from the brutal conditions of the South.[79] Those working on *The Negro in Illinois* collected census records showing how the black population rapidly multiplied in cities across Illinois. As the newly arrived migrants set down roots, they formed their own businesses, restaurants, churches, and newspapers. A chapter titled "Rising" covers the history of black achievement in education, building on the early IWP study by Alonzo Bowling. The chapter "Exodus Train" cites the advertisements in the *Chicago Defender* that announced the many employment opportunities in the North for those willing to make the journey. As laborers were needed in plants gearing up for World War I, black migrants competed with whites for jobs and were often used as strikebreakers. In 1917, a race riot took place in East St. Louis, where whites set fire to black homes and shot those who tried to escape. Two years later, in 1919, riots occurred in Chicago after a black youth swimming in Lake Michigan was drowned by whites throwing rocks at him because he had crossed over into an assumed whites-only section of the beach. The incident quickly escalated and led to five days of rioting, with white gangs roaming through the South Side randomly attacking blacks.

As it grew in numbers, the South Side of Chicago became the modern day "Black Metropolis" where African Americans established their own independent institutions to cope with de facto segregation. Other chapters in *The Negro in Illinois* tell about these institutions and the men and women who built them. There was Jesse Binga, who in 1908 opened the Binga State Bank. There was also Annie Malone, who sold black beauty products and founded her own beauty school, Poro College. Ernie Henderson, believing that many preferred fried chicken over barbeque, opened his famous chicken shack, said to be the setting for a scene in Richard Wright's *Native Son*. Refused service by white taxi drivers, blacks rode in "jitneys" that operated on the South Side. African Americans had their own public library, the George Cleveland Hall Branch, which was run by librarians Vivian Harsh and Charlamae Rollins. They had their own YMCA and YWCA facilities. Kept from participating in "America's greatest pastime," African Americans created their own baseball league. There were stars such as Rube Foster from Chicago who played for the Leland Giants and was a founding member of the National Negro Baseball League. Other famous black athletes who had connections to Chicago included Olympian track runner Ralph Metcalfe and heavyweight boxing champion Joe Louis.

The chapter "Health" documents the high rates of tuberculosis among blacks on the South Side. It also gives the history of Provident Hospital, which had been started by black doctors in the late nineteenth century to address the poor health conditions among African

Americans in Chicago. In 1933, Provident was moved into a seven-story building on 51st Street next to Washington Park, viewed by many as a great benefit to the community. Yet to others Provident was seen as a Jim Crow facility. This controversy was not mentioned by the editors of *The Negro in Illinois*—perhaps for fear of drawing attention to the already politicized, government-sponsored project.

As they moved to urban areas, black migrants brought with them their own religious practices and adapted them to a new setting. The chapter "Churches" discusses several prominent black religious institutions, most notably Quinn Chapel, which still stands today at 24th and Wabash Avenue in Chicago. They were to be distinguished from the storefront churches written about in the chapter "And Churches," which retained many of the folk methods of worship imported from the South. There existed what was called an "undeclared religious war" between the two, with some finding the storefront churches "homier" and others believing they promulgated "superstition." Much of this material comes from the earlier study initiated by Katherine Dunham. Also noted among black churches was a "modern independent trend" born out of the conditions of the Depression and best expressed by Reverend Kingsley of the Good Shepherd Church, who preached about the problems of "slums and dives."

The Negro in Illinois is most unique as a document of the Depression, the turbulent years of the last decade still fresh in the minds of its authors. In the chapter "Houses" they told about the rent strikes organized by the unemployed councils in the early years of the economic crisis. These groups appeared as African Americans were being evicted from their homes on the South Side and moved them back in, occasionally clashing with police. Recollection of these actions was provided by a young black radical who wished to remain anonymous and appears only as "Mr. X." In an interview with a WPA worker, he recalled how resistance to evictions began on the South Side and eventually spread to white neighborhoods. Both blacks and whites joined in the efforts to return furniture and belongings to apartments that had been emptied out. A battle between police and protesters on August 3, 1931, left three African American activists dead and prompted the mayor to halt all evictions.[80] Rent for apartments on the South Side still remained high, and the properties were often run down. Those who could afford to buy homes were confined to the South Side by restrictive covenants forbidding the sale of homes to African Americans in white neighborhoods. In downstate Illinois, where prejudice was much greater, blacks lived in segregated communities such as those in Quincy, Cairo, Mound City, Champaign, and East St. Louis.

A group of black women standing on the corner in the downtown Chicago Loop was a common sight during the Depression. These women were waiting for day jobs doing domestic work in the homes of white women. A chapter called "Slave Market" begins with this image as a starting point for discussing the poor working conditions for African Americans and those within the labor movement trying to improve them.[81] As black migrants came from the South, they were often excluded from unions. Some in the meatpacking and garment industries allowed African Americans into their unions after seeing them used as strikebreakers. In 1925, the Brotherhood of Sleeping Car Porters, made up entirely of black porters, was launched in Chicago and eventually admitted into the American Federation of Labor. The most important development for blacks in labor was the formation of the Congress of Industrial Organizations (CIO), which organized workers industry-wide and openly recruited African Americans. The Fair Employment Practices Commission (FEPC) was established after A. Philip Randolph threatened to hold a march on Washington. An FEPC hearing held January 1942 in Chicago received mention in *The Negro in Illinois* as the latest sign of advancements in labor.

There was a rising tide of racial consciousness in Chicago, as there was in Harlem and throughout the Black Diaspora. This is the subject of one of the most interesting chapters, "What is Africa to Me?" It begins with early efforts by African Americans to return to their ancestral homeland. More recently, Marcus Garvey had attracted a large following in Illinois. In 1930, Garvey had some seventy-five hundred supporters in Chicago and other active branches throughout Illinois. The chapter tells of the bitter feud between Garvey and the *Defender*'s Robert S. Abbott, as well as Garvey's one and only visit to the South Side in 1920, where he held a rally at the Eighth Armory. After Garvey was sent to prison for mail fraud, the movement in Chicago was beset by internal schisms. Also discussed in this chapter are two organizations—the Moorish American Science Temple and the Nation of Islam—that fostered "racial pride" among their congregations. Noble Drew Ali spoke of Garvey as his spiritual forefather. While his descendants are regarded as religious fakers, Garvey's influence is described as "immeasurable."[82]

The final four chapters of *The Negro in Illinois* look at African American cultural production in the fields of literature, theater, music, jazz, and the blues.[83] These chapters delineate the artistic roots of the Black Chicago Renaissance. They build on the cultural writings of Kitty Chapelle and the interviews with local musicians conducted by George D. Lewis. The literature chapter was written by Jack Conroy, which may be somewhat unexpected for a white writer, but he had gained a deep understanding of African American literature in the Midwest as the editor of several journals. It begins with the literary societies, orators, and slave narratives of the nineteenth century. A more literary turn was marked by the dialect poetry of Paul Lawrence Dunbar, James Edwin Campbell, and James David Corrothers, all of whom passed through Chicago. Fenton Johnson is credited with being the first modern black poet to experiment in free verse. The most "assertive" poet of the recent renaissance was Frank Marshall Davis, today referred to by some as President Obama's "Communist mentor."[84] William Attaway, Waters Edward Turpin, and Arna Bontemps were notable contemporary black writers who had lived in Chicago. Of course, Richard Wright had attained "major stature" by this time for his novel *Native Son*. As well, Conroy includes a number of white scholars, poets, and novelists from Illinois who had written sympathetically about African Americans.

Just about every major black musician had passed through Illinois, often en route to Chicago. As early as 1870, piano prodigy "Blind Tom" Wiggins visited Chicago. The Hampton Singers came through Illinois on their fundraising tour for Hampton Institute. The Fisk Jubilee Singers appeared in Springfield in 1880 and Chicago in 1886. Those in Illinois who were inspired by their example founded their own choral groups. The Chicago Choral Study Club was among the first to perform the works of black composer Samuel Coleridge-Taylor. These groups were best known for singing spirituals. As author of the "Music" chapter Robert Lucas wrote, the "strange, haunting quality" of the spirituals stood in sharp contrast to the minstrel songs popular in the late nineteenth century. Chicago also had its share of minstrel shows, the comedic routines performed by actors in blackface. The famous team of Bert Williams and George Walker frequently visited Chicago, making their first appearance there in 1902. When the Pekin Theater was opened by Robert Motts in 1905 at 27th and State Streets, it ushered in a new era of music and culture in Chicago. The first black-owned theater of its kind featuring black musicians and stage shows, the Pekin was opened ten years before a similar venue in New York. Charles Gilpin, Bill "Bojangles" Robinson, and Abbie Mitchell all got their start at the Pekin. In the following years, State Street became known as "the Stroll" with other clubs opening up and musicians including it on their tours. During these years, Chicago provided fertile ground for innovations in ragtime, blues, boogie woogie, jazz, and gospel. It was King Oliver who first brought jazz to Chicago. Louis Armstrong and Cab Calloway followed in his footsteps. They all made a name for themselves in Chicago before moving to New York and becoming famous. As Calloway later recalled, when the Duke Ellington Orchestra came to the Cotton Club in late 1927, they replaced King Oliver's band from Chicago. "In fact, the entire original Cotton Club staff, including the band, was imported from Chicago" (Travis 232). In some aspects, the New Negro Renaissance in Chicago predated the one commonly associated with Harlem. As the South Side expanded, the black business and entertainment district shifted from State Street to 47th and South Parkway, what is today recognized as the historic center of the Bronzeville community.

Golden Apples

Not long after the United States entered World War II, funding for New Deal projects was quickly diverted to the war, and the Federal Writers' Project came to an end. Arna Bontemps resigned on May 29, 1942, to pursue a master's degree in library science at the University of Chicago. If he finished his degree, he was promised a job as head librarian at Fisk University. In his resignation letter to Jacob Scher, he wrote a personal note: "I have thoroughly enjoyed my work, and all personal contacts have been consistently harmonious. My interest in the unfinished book [*Negro in Illinois*] will continue. In fact, I plan to spend the 18th and 19th of June checking up on the outstanding chapters" (Jones 27). In June, Curtis MacDougall resigned to take a job with the *Chicago Sun* and shortly after the Illinois Writers' Project folded.[85]

In September 1942, Edwin Embree, president of the Rosenwald Fund, wrote to Merle Colby of the War Services Projects in Washington, D.C., inquiring about the status of *The Negro in Illinois*. In this letter, Embree mentioned that it had been "some time since the completion of the manuscript" and wondered whether a publisher for the book had been found. "I believe so much in the importance of the material," he wrote, "that I should like to see it placed before the public with as little delay as possible." He questioned who had legal ownership of the project, as the Rosenwald Fund had sponsored it, and whether Bontemps and Conroy could recast it in "popular fashion."[86] Because they were produced by the federal government with taxpayer money, the materials could not be copyrighted. There was no objection to Bontemps and Conroy moving forward with their idea.

After the astronomical success of Richard Wright's *Native Son* in 1940, there was a growing commercial market for books on African Americans. Jack Conroy wrote to his literary agent Maxim Lieber with hopes that a book he and Arna Bontemps (who was also one of Lieber's clients) had "finished" would be of unique interest to the public.[87] They had written what Conroy believed was the first exhaustive study of urban blacks, "irrefutably documented, sound sociologically, but spirited in pace." It emphasized the centrality of Chicago in the modern African American experience. "Just as New York is not America," Conroy wrote, "neither is Harlem Black America. Our book will show that historically and currently Chicago's South Side black belt yields more of social significance and reading interest." Roi Ottley had recently signed a contract with Houghton-Mifflin to publish a book (which would become *New World A-Coming*) utilizing much of the material gathered by the New York Writers' Project. Bontemps and Conroy would do the same with their proposed book. Conroy pitched his idea to Lieber and asked, "What enterprising publisher will be the first to seize this golden opportunity?" Lieber wrote back on January 6, 1943, saying that he did not think the manuscript was ready for publication.[88]

A year later, Doubleday editor Bucklin Moon asked Lieber about the manuscript by Bontemps and Conroy. If the authors would cover the African American migration to cities across the country, Moon wrote, "I'm sure we would have a great book."[89] Lieber wrote to Bontemps and Conroy with the news that he had been contacted by Doubleday. There was now, he said, "increasing interest in books on the Negro in America."[90] Ottley's *New World A-Coming* had since been released with much success. Horace Cayton and St. Clair Drake were also planning to publish their book *Black Metropolis*. For the first time, Doubleday was offering the George Washington Carver Award, which, Lieber said, they had a "likelihood" of winning. Excited by the idea, Bontemps and Conroy got started rewriting the manuscript.

In the summer of 1943, Bontemps finished his master's thesis and moved to Nashville to begin his position at Fisk University, where he would serve as librarian for twenty-two years. Before he left Chicago, he and Julia Waxman of the Rosenwald Fund arranged to have the IWP papers handed over to Vivian Harsh, who had established a "Special Negro Collection" at the Hall branch library. Harsh agreed to organize the papers and make them available to the public.[91] The Chicago Public Library's first African American librarian, Harsh had been named head of the George Cleveland Hall branch of the Chicago Public Library when it was opened in 1932 at 48th and Michigan. After visiting Arthur Schomburg's collection at the New York Public Library, she established a similar archive based in Chicago. Harsh was an active member of the local branch of the Association for the Study of Negro Life and History, founded by Carter G. Woodson in Chicago, and the collection was an extension of her work promoting black culture. Beginning with three hundred books, she built the Special Negro Collection at the Hall branch library. During the time of the Illinois Writers' Project, the Hall branch had served as the unofficial office for workers who were assisted by Harsh and relied heavily upon the collection she had compiled.

Bontemps and Conroy had other ideas of what to do with the materials they had collected, some of which they copied and kept for themselves. They contemplated writing a play or an entire book on black cults, or a producing history of the *Chicago Defender*.[92] When they set out to write *They Seek a City*, they split up the chapters between themselves. As Conroy said, "Our style was or had become so similar that most readers have been unable to determine which is a Bontemps and which is a Conroy chapter" ("Memories of Arna Bontemps" 604). Still living in Chicago, Conroy periodically borrowed IWP documents from Vivian Harsh to write the chapters he was assigned. In letter correspondence, Bontemps also asked Conroy to send him IWP materials in Nashville. The IWP papers thus became separated, with some eventually ending up in Bontemps' papers at Syracuse University, others in Conroy's papers at the Newberry Library in Chicago, and the rest of the collection remaining at the Chicago Public Library.

When it came out, *They Seek a City* was a much different book than what had been produced by the Illinois Writers' Project. It was broader in scope, telling the larger story of the Great Migration and covering other cities that were heavily impacted, such as Cleveland, Cincinnati, Detroit, Philadelphia, New York, Los Angeles, and San Francisco. Only about one-quarter of the chapters in the new book were based on earlier ones, with some of the passages taken word for word.[93] *They Seek a City* tells the story of the many "Mudtowns" across the country where African Americans were still segregated but had created their own vibrant communities. In his review for the *Chicago Sun*, Horace Cayton called the book an "eloquent explanation" of the black migration. In the *New Masses*, Alain Locke said the book was "scrupulously documented" and presented a panorama of black life as good as any other to date. Writing for *PM*, black playwright Owen Dodson said, "There are a hundred novels, and just as many plays, lying fallow in these pages."[94] Bontemps told Conroy that when Sterling Brown passed through Nashville he was praising the book "highly."[95]

The authors had high expectations for *They Seek a City* when it was released in May 1945. Doubleday editors told them they thought it would be more successful than the Ottley book and predicted sales would reach thirty thousand copies. The authors believed the Carver award had been "practically promised" to them.[96] They were therefore disappointed when the prize went to a white woman, Fannie Cook, for her novel *Mrs. Palmer's Honey*. In the end their book sold approximately seven thousand copies. This was comparable to similar titles, but still far from Richard Wright's bestselling novels. The authors directed their anger at Doubleday. As Conroy told Bontemps, they "threw us to the wolves."[97] Bontemps agreed, feeling that the publisher had "treated us like stepchildren." He was giving his next book to Houghton Mifflin.[98]

Those who worked on the Illinois Writers' Project would go their separate ways, but many of them would stay in contact and share memories of their days on the WPA. In the future, Bontemps and Conroy would collaborate on several different projects, including children's books, anthologies, and a new edition of their Great Migration book, renamed *Anyplace But Here*, published in 1966, which was significantly rewritten to address the contemporary civil rights movement. They maintained correspondence in letters until Bontemps died of a heart attack in 1973. After the project shut down, Conroy went on to write encyclopedias. He taught night classes in creative writing at the Abraham Lincoln School, a workers' school on State Street in the downtown Loop. Bontemps gave a talk in Conroy's class before he left for Nashville (Bontemps and Hughes 134). At Fisk, Bontemps found his role as a librarian exciting. He appreciated the "sober, intelligent, civilized group" and also fit in well with the "social corps."[99]

After the project days, some went on to play a role in the war effort. Among them was black poet and actor Robert Davis. Born in Mobile, Alabama, Davis had come to Chicago at age fourteen after his parents passed away. At Wendell Phillips High School, he wrote his first poetry and participated in amateur theater. The first meeting of the South Side Writers' Group was hosted by Davis at his home on South Parkway (Walker, *Richard Wright* 71). Like several others in the group, Davis was briefly a member of the Communist Party.[100] The single issue of *New Challenge*, which included a contingent of Chicago writers, ran a poem by Davis, "South Chicago, May 30, 1937," about the massacre of ten striking workers at Republic Steel Company. Davis researched organized labor for the Illinois Writers' Project as early as August 1937 and worked on the black cults study, but he was laid off after spending his eighteen months on the project.[101] For a short period, he worked with the WPA for Horace Cayton gathering magazine clippings, excerpting quotes from books, producing statistical tables, proofreading, and editing manuscripts.[102] In September 1943, Davis was commissioned into the Army and sent to Fort Huachuca in Arizona, where he was placed in an administrative and housekeeping unit.[103] In letters to friends he complained about his experience. He wrote to Langston Hughes bemoaning his three years in "this man's army" and said that if things did not change soon, "I'll have to blow my top."[104] He returned to Chicago briefly after the war, where Jack Conroy saw him at a fiction workshop he was teaching at the Parkway Center. According to Conroy, Davis was "very bitter about his experience."[105] In September 1946, Davis moved to Hollywood to pursue an acting career in television and film. He played "Sunshine" in the movie version of *Knock on Any Door*, based on the novel by Chicago writer Willard Motley. He began using the name Davis Roberts after finding out there was another actor with the same name in the Actors Equity union. During the 1960s, Davis was president of the local NAACP. In 1979, he advocated to get Paul Robeson a star on the Hollywood Walk of Fame. When he died in 1993, he had appeared in nearly forty movies and approximately two hundred television shows. His favorite role was when he played a prosecutor in the 1972 movie *The Catonsville Nine*, about the nine Catholic protesters who burned draft files in opposition to the Vietnam War.[106]

George Coleman Moore, who worked on the Illinois Writers' Project in late 1940 and 1941, went on to become a war correspondent. Moore was born in Uniontown, Alabama, in 1915, moved to Chicago with his family when he was two years old, and graduated from Du Sable High School. Moore had early success as a writer when he won first prize in an essay competition held by the *Chicago Defender* for his story "Women Make Good Soldiers."[107] As was the case for many aspiring writers, Moore found employment with the black press. He became theatrical editor for the *Chicago Bee*. For a short time he worked at the *Defender* before being fired for union activity.[108] In early 1943, Moore got a job at the Associated Negro Press. In May, he was chosen to be among sixteen war correspondents as a representative of the ANP and flew to Louisiana to observe training exercises. He traveled as a correspondent to France and Italy, sending back stories that were syndicated throughout the black press by the ANP. Moore also sent letters to Arna Bontemps while he was overseas. He was nostalgic about his days on the project. In a wartime "V-Mail" letter he wrote, "It has been a long time since we had the extreme pleasure of working with you on 'The Negro in Illinois.'"[109] Upon finding out that Bontemps was working on *They Seek a City*, he wrote back, pleased: "Since so much very wonderful material was included in many of the study reports on Negroes, it is gratifying to learn you and Jack Conroy plan to make use of it. We'll be interested to learn of the book's publication."[110]

During the war, Robert Lucas wrote several weekly radio scripts for the Women's Army Corps (WAC) recruiting office on the South Side that were broadcast by a small station in Chicago. Lucas said he first learned scriptwriting while on the Illinois Writers' Project. He was initially involved in the study of black cults with Katherine Dunham. He won a

Robert Lucas, 1945. (Fisk University Franklin Library
Special Collections, Julius Rosenwald Papers)

short story contest held for writers on the project. He had a hand in writing drafts for the chapters "Lincoln and the Negro," "Recreation and Sports," "Music," "The Theatre," as well as an "Art" chapter that was not included in the final book outline. After the project, he went to work as a journalist for the *Chicago Defender*. Former *Defender* editor Ben Burns remembered, "A sterling backstop staff member was bright-eyed gnome Robert Lucas, a slow talker and fast writer who was also a would-be radio scriptwriter" (20). While writing scripts for the WAC broadcasts, Lucas gained experience in what he called "the technique of radio."[111] Lucas collaborated with Richard Durham on radio scripts for *Democracy U.S.A.*, the predecessor to *Destination Freedom*. While working together on the Illinois Writers' Project and the *Chicago Defender*, Lucas and Durham developed a close friendship and were allies in the radio profession. Lucas was another ambitious young writer mentored by Bontemps. In 1948, with Bontemps serving on the review committee, Lucas won a grant from the Rosenwald Fund.[112] In gratitude, Lucas wrote to Bontemps after getting the news, "All I can say is thanks for the interest you've shown in me back in WPA days and through the years. It meant a great deal because there have been many times I was convinced I'd never be a writer. Now I think maybe there's some hope for me."[113] A year later, he reported on the progress he had made while on fellowship. He wrote excitedly to

Bontemps, "I'm really working. I'm writing. I can sit down at the typewriter (every day) and work on something profitable with no doubts or hesitancy. . . . I remember your very excellent advice when I first went to the Writers' Project—that it takes about 10 years for a writer to hit his stride."[114] Lucas was one of many black writers from this period who did not become a bestselling novelist, yet he still broke down many barriers in the culture industry and was able to make a living by his pen. In the 1960s, he was a columnist for the *Los Angeles Sentinel* and in 1980 he became associate editor for *Jet* magazine.

Another talented writer on the project was Onah Spencer, who collected a large portion of the material on music. Spencer was a staff writer for *Down Beat*, the jazz magazine founded in Chicago. He was the author of the 1934 pageant "O, Sing a New Song." Attended by a crowd of sixty thousand at Soldier Field, it featured Noble Sissle, Abbie Mitchell, and a young Katherine Dunham. Spencer had an extensive knowledge of blues and jazz. He was an authority on Louis Armstrong. He composed and recorded his own songs. He also published early versions of the blues songs "Stackolee" and "John Henry."[115] He was a frequent face in the local nightclubs on the South Side and gave Alan Lomax a tour of them when he visited Chicago. An outgoing (if, at times, demanding) personality, Spencer endeared himself to his supervisors on the Illinois Writers' Project. Conroy regularly kept in contact with Spencer. Yet in his correspondence with Bontemps, Conroy complained that he received hour-long phone calls from Spencer, sometimes late at night. When Bontemps was gathering writings for *The Book of Negro Folklore*, an anthology he co-edited with Langston Hughes in 1958, he asked Conroy to contact Spencer for permission to publish his "Stackolee." Conroy warned that Spencer would later make accusations they had "waxed rich off the sweat of his brain." He jokingly recommended that Bontemps disconnect his phone line. Still, Conroy wanted to lend Spencer his assistance. "I hope I didn't sound mean about Onah, as I'm really fond of him and think he has considerable, but wild, talent and wish I could do something for him."[116] Spencer granted Bontemps permission to publish the song, but he wanted to be acknowledged in the book as "one of the world's leading folklorists."[117] Over the years, Conroy remained friends with Spencer, even after he moved back to his hometown of Cincinnati. In letters written during the 1960s, Spencer referred to Conroy as his "old pal."[118] In one, Spencer told Conroy, "except my mother I have always loved you and your family more than anyone else on this planet."[119]

Among the more than one hundred workers who contributed to *The Negro in Illinois*, for the wide majority there is little or nothing known about them. Many were among the vast unemployed simply looking for a way to support themselves and their families during the Depression. Yet some of them had considerable talent and left their mark on *The Negro in Illinois*. Nothing is known, for example, about E. Diehl, not even his first name, although he wrote drafts for the chapters "Churches," "The Great Migration," "Slave Market," and "Recreation and Sports." Joseph Bougere, who worked on drafts for the chapters "Abolition," "Exodus Train," "Houses," "The Theatre," and "Rhythm," was also a Spanish translator and spent some time in Cuba during the late 1940s.[120] Andrew G. Paschal was on the Illinois Project for a short time in late 1940. The previous year he appeared as a reviewer along with Arna Bontemps for the Book Review and Lecture Forum at the Hall branch library. In 1971, when Paschal edited *W. E. B. Du Bois: A Reader*, Bontemps wrote the introduction. At this time, Paschal was listed as a writer, teacher, and lecturer in Chicago, but what he did in the decades between remains a mystery.

Barefield Gordon, who was employed by the project from early 1939 to mid-1940, was a conscientious objector in 1941 and worked for a time at a USO in Petersburg, but few other biographical details remain. Josephine Copeland, another IWP worker who prepared a substantial amount of source material, published her poem "The Zulu King: New Orleans," in *Golden Slippers*, the 1941 anthology of poetry for black children compiled by Arna Bontemps. A biography of Copeland is included in the book, indicating that she was born in Covington, Louisiana, went to high school in New Orleans, attended a two-year teacher's training at Dillard University, and moved to Chicago. She published numerous poems in the *Chicago Defender* and was part of a group of poets who called themselves "The Visionaries."[121] What became of Copeland after the project closed is unknown.

Other project supervisors returned to their careers, yet they still maintained contact with those they worked with on the project. John T. Frederick went back to his position as professor of modern literature at Northwestern University. He invited Bontemps to appear on his radio program "Of Men and Books" several times and chose him as one of his last guests before the show ended in 1944. Bontemps wrote to Frederick in 1946 saying that he was recently in Chicago and "saw several Alumni of the Writer's [*sic*] Project, all apparently making headway as writers."[122] Poet and attorney William Henry Huff, who worked on the study of black cults, wrote to Frederick in 1944. He commented on the recent success of Margaret Walker and Katherine Dunham. "It will ever be one of my cherished memories," he said, "that I worked with you and Miss Dunham on the good old Writers' Project."[123]

Curtis D. MacDougall became a journalism professor at Northwestern University and an outspoken voice of the American Left. In 1948, he ran for U.S. Senate as a Progressive Party candidate and campaigned for Henry Wallace in his challenge to Truman's Cold War agenda. Although MacDougall was "thoroughly disillusioned" with the direction of the U.S. economy in the postwar period, he said he never joined the Communist Party and had always been "fiercely independent."[124] He stirred up a brief controversy in the *Chicago Tribune* when he published a negative review of Jerre Mangione's history of the Federal Writers' Project, *The Dream and the Deal*. Although the book acknowledged the damage done to the project by Representative Martin Dies and the House Committee on Un-American Activities, he pointed out that the author gave little space to projects outside New York. The oversight reflected, MacDougall charged, Mangione's perspective as an "eastern burocrat [*sic*]." He had also failed to address the political differences on the project. He gave as an example the shift in policy when he took over as supervisor in Illinois. While John T. Frederick had held back several whom he suspected to be Communists, under his supervision they proved to be some of the project's most impressive writers. "The Reds were not the problem," MacDougall wrote. "The burocrats [*sic*] in Washington and Chicago were."[125] Mangione wrote a letter to the editor, which MacDougall then responded to with his own rebuttal, both of which were reprinted in the *Tribune*. A decade later, MacDougall said that most still neglected to recognize the "great contribution" of the WPA. "America is richer today," he wrote," because of WPA, which was one of the most successful projects in the history of the country."[126]

Bontemps and Conroy continued to work steadily, collaborating on other books and pursuing their own individual projects, yet neither of them would become widely celebrated writers. They attended to their day jobs—one churning out encyclopedias, the other working as a librarian—with the modest goal of simply providing for their families. They watched as former IWP writer Nelson Algren published his novel *The Man With the Golden Arm* to much acclaim and became something of a celebrity. In a letter to Conroy, Bontemps remarked about Algren's recent success and reminisced about their days together on the project: "It all goes to show that the old Erie street project group was really God's elect and that there are golden apples in store for even you and me."[127] Neither Bontemps nor Conroy would ever get to enjoy their "golden apples." Nevertheless, Bontemps was correct in his observation that many of those who passed through the Illinois Writers' Project were destined for greater things.

The Illinois Writers' Project was an incubator for several budding black writers to develop their skills. This innovative, government-sponsored program took the place of previous sources of white philanthropy that had dried up during the Depression and often came with strings attached. In June 1950, Bontemps reflected on the significance of the project in the article "Famous WPA Authors" for *Negro Digest*. This was a different group of writers, he said, than had been associated with the Harlem Renaissance. The writers who once wore "frayed overcoats" and inhabited the public libraries had since established "solid literary reputations" (44). There was not another writers' project in the country, Bontemps argued, that had launched the careers of so many black writers as the one in Illinois. Those worth mentioning included Richard Wright, Margaret Walker, Katherine Dunham, Frank Yerby, Robert Lucas, and Richard Durham. "Chicago was definitely the center of the second phase of Negro literary awakening," he wrote (46). The New York Writers' Project employed many black authors who had already established themselves, but only created one new writer, Roi Ottley, whose career later took off. If Harlem had its renaissance in the 1920s, Chicago experienced one a decade after with the help of the WPA. This literary movement took place, as Bontemps put it, "without fingerbowls but with increased power" (47).

Margaret Walker was one of those Bontemps spoke about who went on to achieve acclaim. After leaving the project in 1939, she entered graduate school at the University of Iowa. In 1942, the collection of poems produced for her master's degree, titled *For My People*, won the Yale Series of Younger Poets Award, the first time a black writer had been so honored. When she published her novel *Jubilee* in 1966, it became a bestseller and inspired a new generation of African American women writers. Walker looked back fondly on her time at the Illinois Writers' Project. She said the WPA did two things for black writers: it paid them to produce their art; and it created an environment where writers, especially poets, were "no longer entirely isolated from other writers" ("New Poets" 346). In the Writers' Projects of the North (distinct from those in the South), black writers worked side by side with white writers. Walker recalled working with Studs Terkel, Nelson Algren, Jack Conroy, John T. Frederick, Saul Bellow, and Meridel LeSueur while on the Illinois Writers' Project. It was the 1930s, according to Walker, when the New Negro "came of age" (349). The black writer was no longer just an "exotic" figure, but during these times of social upheaval the poet took up the cry of "social protest" (349–50). For at least a decade longer, Walker said, African American poetry reflected "the mood of the Thirties" (348).

Restoring the IWP Papers

While today the papers of the Illinois Writers' Project are heavily used by scholars researching the history of African Americans in Chicago and Illinois, for several decades the volume of work sat largely disorganized. After a bout with illness, Vivian Harsh retired on November 10, 1958, and Ollye Marr Coffin was hired to take her place as head librarian at the Hall branch. Although she had initially expressed support for the Special Negro Collection, Coffin closed it to the public and moved it to the basement. This was a great affront to Harsh, who had dedicated her life to building up the collection. Harsh died on August 17, 1960, less than two years after she retired.

When Coffin left the Hall branch to pursue her career as a concert singer, she was replaced by Donald Franklin Joyce, who is responsible for the resurrection of the Special Negro Collection. In 1970, Joyce was named curator of the collection. One of his first initiatives was to change its name to the Vivian G. Harsh Research Collection of Afro-American Literature and History. In early 1970, Joyce secured an $89,000 grant to update the collection. At that time the IWP papers sat in two file cabinets. In June, the Center for Inner City Studies at Northeastern Illinois State College, headed by Director of Research Carol Adams and librarian Dorothy Robinson, completed the project of microfilming the IWP papers. Although they were divided into folders, the papers were not organized in any order.

Seeing the need for a more modern facility to house the growing collection, Joyce advocated for a new branch library on the South Side. The board of directors for the Chicago Public Library, which included John Hope Franklin and Lerone Bennett Jr., voted to move the Harsh Research Collection to the newly constructed Carter G. Woodson Library, located at 95th and Halsted, which opened its doors to the public in 1975. After Joyce resigned in 1981, poet Alfred L. Woods and Sharon Scott served for short periods as acting curators. Steven Newsome was hired in 1983 as permanent curator.

In 1986, Robert Miller became curator. According to Miller, when he arrived at the library the IWP papers were in "disarray." There was no protocol to collect identification and keep a log of guests who visited the papers. University professors, library patrons, and local historians routinely absconded with materials from the collection. Miller would receive donations from individuals, only to find they contained IWP documents that had been stolen from the library. When he took over, he immediately closed the papers to the public. The IWP papers then became the impetus for his future expansion of the Harsh Research Collection. Miller applied for and received a $70,000 grant from the Secretary of State's office for encapsulation and de-acidification of the IWP papers. Miller tells the story of the day when then Secretary of State Jim Edgar (later elected Illinois governor) came down to the Woodson library for a photo opportunity with him and the IWP papers.

Miller began to assemble a staff to support the Harsh Research Collection. Michael Flug started in 1989 as a librarian at the Woodson branch and two years later was promoted to archivist of the Harsh Research Collection. In 1992, Flug tackled the long-overdue task of organizing the IWP papers. He arranged them according to the outline for the original twenty-nine chapters. A year later, a finding aid in typewritten form was available for use by researchers at Harsh, and today it can be accessed online.

When I first looked through the IWP papers in 2004, I was immediately struck by what was a veritable treasure trove of materials produced by an impressive group of writers. Michael Flug told me this was the most frequently visited collection at the library. He had previously tried to convince at least half a dozen scholars to publish a book from the papers, but all of them had declined. He warned me it would be a formidable task. Only about two-thirds of the chapters were at the Harsh, and the location of others was uncertain.

After the Illinois Writers' Project was shut down, the papers were scattered to the four winds. Bontemps and Conroy had taken some of the materials to write *They Seek a City*. Other papers have since disappeared. Some of the IWP files resurfaced when the Newberry Library acquired Jack Conroy's papers. Undaunted, I embarked on a journey to retrieve the lost chapters and restore *The Negro in Illinois* manuscript to its original form. Some of the chapters turned up at Newberry, but three were still unaccounted for—"John Brown's Friend," "What is Africa to Me?" and "Music"—leaving gaping holes in the narrative. Next, I traveled to Springfield, the state capital, and Washington, D.C., where IWP workers routinely sent copies of what they produced, but I found no more chapters. Finally, while visiting the Arna Bontemps papers at Syracuse University, I discovered the three missing chapters in a file labeled "God's Country: The Negro Comes to Illinois" (an alternate title). I excitedly telephoned Flug from the library lobby to tell him that all of the chapters had been found.

For the first time since the project doors were closed, the twenty-nine chapters of *The Negro in Illinois* have been reunited. With this publication, scholars and the public now have access to one of the primary source documents of the Black Chicago Renaissance.[128] The Illinois Writers' Project was an important institution that gave many talented writers the confidence and skills to make a living at their chosen craft. They left behind a document that, in telling the history of African Americans who came to Illinois, gives us a unique story of the richness and diversity of American life.

Editor's Note

Although *The Negro in Illinois* reached completion, it did not reach publication in its day, and the final manuscript has not been discovered. According to correspondence, Jack Conroy finished the manuscript some time during the second half of 1942. In the version presented in this volume, I have attempted to adhere as closely as possible to what we today can only imagine was the final version.

To assemble this work I have culled chapters from collections at three different libraries—the Illinois Writers' Project/"The Negro in Illinois" Papers at the Vivian G. Harsh Research Collection of Afro-American History and Literature, Chicago Public Library (hereinafter referred to as the IWP papers); the Jack Conroy Papers at Newberry Library; and the Arna Bontemps Papers at Syracuse University Library. The chapter order was based on a copy of the table of contents located in the IWP papers at the Harsh Research Collection. Titles of chapters were commonly written in Arna Bontemps's handwriting on the upper left corner of the front page of source materials corresponding with the chapters in the outline.

There is repetitious material in some chapters and incorrect information in others that may have been corrected in a final manuscript. The reader will notice the absence of an introduction or conclusion by the editors. I have preferred to preserve the surviving manuscripts rather than intervene in the narrative myself.

I have provided headers for each chapter telling which library it came from and who was its author. In the headers I also explain the editorial process of selecting which draft is the most recent for each chapter. I did this by examining the editorial comments in the handwriting of Bontemps and Conroy, or by reading correspondence letters and internal memos. In some cases chapter drafts were dated; in others, dates in the narrative help to identify when the essay was written. The editors typically preferred short chapters to long ones. One example is the chapter on the black press. This is also the only case wherein I departed from the chapter outline. A forty-eight-page draft of chapter 22, "Newspapers," written in 1941, covered black newspapers throughout the state. I replaced it with a fourteen-page essay, "Defender," dated May 1942 (just before Bontemps left the project), which focuses on the history of the *Chicago Defender*.

The Negro in Illinois, like other works of the Federal Writers' Project, is unique in American letters, as it was collectively written by a large staff of writers, some of them already well established and others who remain unknown. It was standard practice to acknowledge the supervisors of the state projects, but the names of the thousands of federal workers who contributed as writers and researchers were omitted. It is unfair to say that a work like *The Negro in Illinois* was written only by Arna Bontemps and Jack Conroy. There were more than one hundred men and women who worked on the study. Some of the early chapter drafts have names on them. On others the name has been crossed out by the editor. Yet most of the final drafts have no name on them. From letters, internal memos, and early drafts, I attempted to best identify the author of each chapter. The reader will notice that chapters by Bontemps often end with a witty commentary.

In reconstructing the manuscript, I have tried to alter it as little as possible. If handwritten corrections were not yet incorporated, I made the changes myself. It was the policy of the Federal Writers' Project not to include footnotes to make their publications more accessible to the general public. I have eliminated all of the original footnotes, if they had not already been removed by Bontemps and Conroy—yet I have added some notes to convey the breadth of the project and show how many people worked on it. While drafts for the twenty-nine chapters were all found either at the Harsh Research Collection, Newberry Library, or Syracuse University Library, there are many important materials at the Abraham Lincoln Library in Springfield, Illinois, and at the Library of Congress and National Archives in Washington, D.C., where copies of documents were often sent. There was also useful information in the John T. Frederick Papers at the Iowa University Special Collections, Louis Wirth Papers at the University of Chicago Special Collections Research Center, and Claude Barnett Papers at the Chicago History Museum. I have indicated in the notes the libraries where scholars can find such further information.

Title of Article_____Author's name if any_____

terest in art. He possessed twenty three paintings, among them

portraits of Lady Strafford and Lady Fortescue. It is also sur-

mized that Du Sable was a distiller, probably for the purpose of

trading with the Indians.

That he was influential throughout this part of the North-

west is evident in more respects than one. In 1796 he led a

group of Indians in birch bark canoes; and was surprised when

he reached Mackinac to receive from the British a salute of

cannons. He, also, was personal friend of the political figures

of the Northwest, including Clamorgan of St. Louis.

In 1788 Du Sable and his Indian wife, Catherine, underwent

the marriage ceremony of the Roman Catholic Church, thus legaliz-

ing their union. We have no description of Catherine; but her

husband was a man about six feet tall, quite gray,and as he ad-

vanced in age venerable in appearance.

There, in the Chicago wilderness, Du Sable was an af-

fable host to any who might in journeying up the Chicago river

stop at his establishment. He was a gay conversationalist and

always had a glass or two of liquor ready for his guest. Often

he would take his guest for a stroll, revealing to him the beauty

of the Chicago wilderness — the great oaks, the slender willows,

Worker's Item No._____Worker's Name_____
WORK PROJECTS ADMINISTRATION (Illinois)
Illinois Writers' Project, 4901 Ellis Avenue
% Julius Rosenwald Fund
Chicago, Illinois

Draft manuscript page from the opening chapter on Jean Baptiste Point Du Sable.
(Vivian G. Harsh Research Collection of Afro-American History and Literature,
Chicago Public Library, Illinois Writers' Project/"Negro in Illinois" Papers)

1. First, the French.

There are three drafts of this chapter. Two early versions are located in the Illinois Writers' Project papers housed at the Harsh Research Collection. The earliest version was written by Robert Lucas. A third draft, the one used here, was written by Arna Bontemps and found in the Bontemps papers at Syracuse University with minor editorial changes in Bontemps's handwriting, which have been incorporated by the editor. Background for this and the subsequent chapters on early Illinois history came from two notable essays. One is "A Sociological History of the Negro in Chicago," a 137-page unpublished thesis by L. D. Reddick, produced as one of the WPA studies supervised under Horace Cayton and Lloyd Warner. The other is an essay written by Fenton Johnson and dated January 1, 1941, which begins with the early French in Illinois, mentions its first black settler Du Sable, discusses slavery before and after emancipation, and ends with Johnson's reflecting on the modern presence of the Ku Klux Klan, which he predicted would "melt as the snow flakes before the scorching sun."

In the spring of 1719 Phillip Francois Renault, a banker of Paris, set out on the adventure of his life. Versed in mining, he assembled complete tools, equipment, ships and men to develop mining interests for the company of St. Phillipe, a subsidiary of the Western Company. Of course, mineral treasures had not yet been found in Upper Louisiana, the area in which this group had rights, but one gathers that Renault had seen visions of a vast wealth buried in the American wilderness.

Forty-five days later, his ships entered the palm-fringed harbor of Cap Haitien, and Renault undoubtedly had occasion to compliment himself on getting "away from it all." But business was business, and the erstwhile banker was not in Haiti to sniff the fragrance of the tropics. He had stopped to purchase slaves. This he did forthwith, 500 of them to supplement the 250 miners and workers he had brought out from Paris. From the Haitian capital Renault sailed to New Orleans and continued up the river. Arriving in the vicinity of St. Philippe (Illinois), he and his party found a few forts erected by the French following the explorations of La Salle and Marquette. Prairie du Rocher, Cahokia, and Kaskasia were the most prominent of these settlements.

Renault's men prospected in the region of St. Philippe until 1744, but little came of their efforts. Then, perhaps discouraged, perhaps hungering for the glitter of his native Paris, Renault suddenly decided to pull out. He disposed of his slaves to the inhabitants of the district and returned home. Renault's unsuccessful mining venture succeeded in establishing slavery in Illinois.

The small farmers who purchased his slaves used them for domestic and farm labor. These Negroes "were treated everywhere with much leniency and kindness . . . and their children were taught the catechism." By 1778 half of Kaskasia's population of one thousand were Negro slaves. They were not at that time subject to the rigid enforcement of the Black Code as were the slaves in the southern districts of Louisiana. Hence in this country, where women were scarce, there was considerable intermarriage, the unions being sanctioned and solemnized by the Roman Catholic clergy of the community.

The scanty documentary records of colonial Illinois include the report of a crude census conducted in 1732. Negroes at that time numbered 69 men, 33 women, and 64 children, as compared with 159 white men, 39 women, and an uncertain number of children.

In 1750 a certain Monsieur Vivier, missionary to the Illinois Indians, described the region around Kaskasia in the following passage:

> We have here whites, negroes, and Indians, to say nothing of the cross breeds. . . . There are five French villages and three villages of the natives within a space of twenty one leagues. . . . In the five French villages there are perhaps 1,100 whites, 300 blacks and some sixty red slaves or savages. The three Illinois towns do not contain more than 800 souls (native) all told.

There is a certain vagueness in these categories, for the French did not usually hold mulattoes in strict bondage, and they were often numbered with the white population. On the other hand, no distinction was made between Indian-white mixed bloods and Negro-white mulattoes.

Another census was taken in 1752. This one revealed the presence of 187 Negro men, 113 women, 83 boys, and 62 girls. The white population was estimated at 134 men and 112 women.

Thus the Negro population, as officially recognized in colonial Illinois, increased from 166 to 445 within two decades.

Le Code Noir of 1724, by which Negroes were governed in French territory, provided for the "administration of justice, police, discipline, and traffic in Negro slaves in the Province of Louisiana." These rules appear mild when compared with the black codes of some Southern slave states. The slave had certain "rights" as well as "duties." While it defined bondsmen as real property, the code insisted that they be baptized, that they be given religious instruction, and that they be allowed certain primary liberties on Sunday and feast days. Under its provision a slave might purchase his freedom as many did.

In 1763 the Mississippi River Valley, with a population of about 3,000 (900 of them Negroes), was taken over by the English. Many of the inhabitants, not wishing to become British subjects, left the Illinois Country, either selling their slaves or taking them along. Of the 1,600 people remaining, 600 were Negroes.

In those times the Indians used to say that the first "white" settler in Chicago was a Negro. They had in mind, of course, Jean Baptiste Point Du Sable, the man who built his home at the mouth of the Chicago River in 1779 and lived there for more than sixteen years. Du Sable, also known as Au Sable, Du Saible, De Sable, Sabre, and Le Grand Sabre, was born about 1750. No one knows just where. The tradition is that Du Sable was a Haitian Negro who visited New Orleans prior to his coming to Chicago, his intention being to establish a colony of free Negroes in the lake Region. It is possible that he had been educated in France. But another story is told by Milo M. Quaife in his book *Checagou*. He says,

> The history of the Du Sable family can be traced to France in the early seventeenth century when the ancestral name was Dandonneau. After the migration of the Dandonneau family to Canada, the son of the emigrant was known as Dandonneau's Sieur du Sable. This was in keeping with the custom of the times of adding a second name to the ancestral name." (La Salle, the explorer, whose real name was Robert Cheveler, is a familiar example of this custom.)
>
> Succeeding generations of the family were known as Dandonneau and Du Sable, which names became prominent in the aristocracy of New France. Following the settling of Detroit, and subsequent migrations of the family to that city, the family name can be traced through the custom of the times, of the wife signing her name beside that of her husband on the church baptismal records. This custom left it possible for the children to be known by the name employed by the mother Dandonneau and Du Sable.
>
> For many generations the name of Du Sable was prominently associated throughout the Northwest Territory with Indian Traders.[1]

Thus several factors serve as connecting links between Jean Baptiste De Saible and the ancient Du Sable family of French ancestry: the similarity of the name, his occupation, and his location in the Northwest Territory. His patronage may be accounted for by a custom of the times: Negro and Indian slavery. "At Mackinac, as at Detroit, the baptismal register contains frequent records of both Indian and Negro slaves, and there is no lack of evidence that white men frequently cohabited with them. . . ." This account is substantiated by an existing document in which Point Du Sable referred to himself as a "free Negro."[2]

The first reliable record of Du Sable at Chicago is dated 1779. At that time the English had taken over the great Northwest from the French, and the American Revolutionary War was being waged. In the no man's land of the Northwest the loyalty of almost everyone was under suspicion. In his official report of July 4, 1779, Colonel Arent de Peyster, British commandant at Michilimackinac, wrote: "Baptist Point de Saible, a handsome Negro, well educated and settled at Eschikagou but was much in the interest of the French." Remembering Du Sable's name and connections, his sympathy for the French is not inconceivable. De Peyster ordered Du Sable detained because of suspicion of "treasonable intercourse with the enemy," but he left the vicinity and was later apprehended near what is now Michigan City. The report of the arresting officer, Lieutenant Thomas Bennet, throws some light on Du Sable's personality and position in the community.

> I had the Negro Baptiste Point de Saible brought prisoner from the River Du Chemin. Corporal Tascon who commanded the party very prudently prevented the Indians (English allies) from burning his home and doing him any injury. He secured his packs etc., which he had taken with him to Mackinac. The Negro, since his imprisonment, has in every way behaved in a manner becoming to a man of his station, and has many friends who give him a good character.

The charges of espionage against Du Sable were dropped and he was released. In fact, the British governor Patrick Sinclair, a man who was usually hard to please, was so impressed with Du Sable that he hired the former captive's services for the next three or four years. In the summer of 1780 the vicinity of the "Pinery," an establishment which Sinclair had developed on the St. Clair River just south of modern Port Huron, sent a delegation to Mackinac to complain of the manager. Sinclair complied with their request that Du Sable replace the incumbent, a Detroit Frenchman. Although Du Sable was in this location until 1784, his accounts with Detroit merchants, which have been preserved, show that he used Chicago as his "permanent" address. During the time he was not too busy to conduct his business and increase his land holdings. As early as 1780 he began developing a plot of eight hundred acres at Peoria, and in 1783 he satisfactorily proved his ownership to a federal agency.

In 1784 Du Sable returned to Chicago, and during the sixteen years he lived there his profits and influence increased. Hugh Howard, the agent of a Detroit merchant, journeyed to Chicago with several Canadian boatmen in the spring of 1790. The party stopped at Du Sable's place and on May 10 exchanged their canoe for a "pirogue." They also obtained 41 pounds of flour, 29 pounds of pork, and a supply of baked bread for which they traded 13 yards of valuable cotton cloth. Evidently Du Sable's establishment was of such size that it could supply these unexpected demands for goods.

In 1800 Du Sable's trading post consisted of a house forty feet by twenty two feet, a bake house, dairy, smoke house, poultry house, work shop, stable, barn, and horse mill. The presence of the mill indicates that he raised his own wheat, and the large number of tools suggests that he produced his own lumber. To care for his stock and help him in his business of trading, Du Sable must have had a large number of employees. He carried on a lively trade and the popular conception that his home was just a "cabin" is not borne out by the records.

Du Sable's wife was a Pottawatomie Indian named Catherine, and on October 27, 1788, their union, consummated years before, was legalized at Cahokia by a Catholic priest stationed there. Two years after her parents' formal marriage, their daughter Suzanne was married to Jean Baptiste Pelletier. They had a daughter, Eulalie, who was born at Chicago on October 8, 1796. Du Sable also had a son, Jean Baptiste Point, Jr.

Du Sable was a typical pioneer; he was a trader, cooper, husbandman, and miller not to mention a good many other occupations which the wilderness required. He is described as being "about six feet tall," of commanding appearance, "handsome," "venerable" in his old age, and "of very pleasant countenance." Some accounts say that he was "well educated," others that he could only "make his mark." The British greeted his arrival with a salute of cannons when he came to Mackinac in 1796, as the leader of a band of Indians in birch canoes. Jacques Clamorgan, an influential Spaniard of St. Louis, was his friend.

Du Sable was also a lover of art. In the inventory of 1800 two pictures were listed. Years earlier a list of the personal effects of Du Sable which appeared in the *Day Book of James May* of Detroit included twenty-three pictures. Some of the titles give an indication of his taste: *Lady Strafford, Lady Fortesque, The King and the Rain, The Magician, Love and Desire* (of *The Struggle*). This collection, modest though it may seem by modern museum standards, was unusual indeed in the primitive and almost isolated country in which Du Sable lived.[3]

In May of 1800 Du Sable sold out to Jean La Lime of St. Joseph. John Kinzie and William

CHAPTER ONE

Burnett witnessed the transaction, "and the bill of sale, written in French, was recorded in the Wayne County Building in Detroit." La Lime paid 6,000 livres, about $1,200 for the property. Why Du Sable sold his flourishing business and left Chicago is a mystery. Perhaps the region was becoming too "crowded"; perhaps he was seized with wanderlust. Perhaps disappointment was the cause, for Du Sable had recently failed to win election as chief of the surrounding Indian Tribes. Whatever the reason, Du Sable left his trading post on the shores of Lake Michigan, never to return.

Little is known of him after his departure.

In December 1800, Point Du Sable was a plaintiff in a case concerning some horses stolen by Indians and seen by him in the vicinity of Peoria. The case was brought to court in St. Clair County, Illinois, and the following March was transferred to the Indiana Supreme Court.

The years from 1805 to 1814 he spent in and about St. Charles, Missouri, where his son lived. Records of real estate negotiations document this fact. In June 1813, in return for her promise to care for him and to bury him in the Catholic Cemetery at St. Charles, Point Du Sable transferred a house, lot and other property in St. Charles to Eulalie Barode, his grand-daughter, wife of Michael Derais. These requests were probably not carried out. It is uncertain whether filial neglect or unavoidable circumstances is the explanation. At any rate, Du Sable "applied for the benefit of the law relative to insolvents" on October 10, 1814. He died soon thereafter.

2. Slavery

Three drafts of this chapter, as well as chapter fragments, are located at the Harsh Research Collection. The more recent version that appears below was written by Arna Bontemps and found at Syracuse University. The editor has incorporated minor corrections made in Bontemps's handwriting.

Early Illinois was anything but an asylum of liberty. In 1734 the laws of Louis XIV were enacted, regulating the traffic in slaves in the province of Louisiana—which included Illinois. A section in these regulations provided that if one parent was free, the child would follow the condition of servitude of the mother. It prohibited the sale of any slave where such sale would break up a family group. Slavery was legalized under English rule when General Gage took possession of the territory and allowed the French inhabitants the privilege of becoming English subjects. They were allowed to retain all the rights, including the holding of slaves, which they had held under their French king.

When George Rogers Clark came into the Northwest, the Virginia House of Burgesses charted the whole territory and enacted a law in October 1778, making it the county of Illinois. The residents were again allowed to keep their chattel, and slavery continued. Although the Ordinance of 1787 declared that "There shall be no slavery or involuntary servitude in such territory otherwise than in punishment of crimes whereof the party shall have been duly convicted," slavery in the Northwest persisted.

The perpetuation of slavery in the Illinois County was again assured in 1784 when Virginia, ceding the territory to the United States, stipulated that all the inhabitants who had embraced her citizenship should retain all their rights. Slavery hung on.

Soon, however, there came to the frontier a man whose destiny it was to consolidate the opposition to slavery and to lead this opposition effectively. His name was James Lemen, and he was born November 20, 1760 near Harper's Ferry, Virginia. It is a strange coincidence that the vicinity that saw the birth of James Lemen should one hundred years later be the scene of John Brown's historic adventure. From childhood Lemen had been a friend and protégé of Thomas Jefferson, who according to Willard C. MacNaul's *The Relations of Thomas Jefferson and James Lemen in the Exclusion of Slavery from Illinois and the Northwest Territory with Related Documents*, "consulted him not only on small matters but vital matters of state."[1] The same source reveals that by his "eloquence, tact and logic," Lemen influenced many of his friends to free their slaves. So impressed was Jefferson by Lemen's attitude and capabilities that he persuaded the latter to act as his secret agent in Illinois. Lemen's task was to help in the fight to exclude slavery from the entire Northwest Territory. Lemen's diary records the details of this unusual commission.

> Thomas Jefferson had me to visit him . . . as he wanted me to go to the Illinois country . . . to try to lead and direct the new settlers in the best way and also to oppose the introduction of slavery in that country at a later day, as I am known as an opponent of that evil, and he says he will give me some help. It is all because of his great kindness. . . . [I] have agreed to consider the case.

On May 2, 1784, Lemen wrote: "I saw Jefferson . . . today . . . I have consented to go to Illinois. . . . We had a full agreement . . . [which] is strictly private between us. . . ."

Jefferson's agent gave Lemen one hundred dollars to use as he saw fit. The entry for September 4, 1786, reads: "In the past summer, with my wife and children I arrived at Kaskasia, Illinois. . . ."

Lemen established the settlement of New Design, near the present town of Waterloo. The colony's quaint name was taken from Lemen's casual remark that he "had a new design to locate a settlement south of Bellefontaine."

Lemen's task was not an easy one. He relates,

> As Thomas Jefferson predicted they would do, the extreme southern slave advocates are making their influence felt in the new territory for the introduction of slavery and they are pressing Gov. William Henry Harrison to use his power and influence for that end. Steps must soon be taken to prevent that curse from being fastened on our people. (May 3, 1803)

Pressure from high officials did not deter Lemen from doing what he considered his duty.

> At our last meeting, as I expected he would do, Gov. Harrison asked and insisted that I should cast my influence for the introduction of slavery here, but I not only denied the request, but I informed him that the evil attempt would encounter my most active opposition in every possible and honorable manner that my mind could suggest or my means accomplish. (May 4, 1805)

Lemen continued his work, and on January 20, 1806, wrote,

> As Gov. William Henry Harrison and his legislative council have had their petitions before Congress at several sessions asking for slavery here, I sent a messenger to Indiana to ask the churches and people there to get up and sign a counter petition to Congress to uphold freedom in the territory and I have circulated on here and we will send it on to that body at next session or as soon as the work is done.

In 1809, when Illinois along with Michigan was organized as a Territory separate from Indiana (the name that had been given the Northwest after Ohio had been made a Territory), Lemen took definite steps to prevent the pro-slavery faction from introducing slavery if and when Illinois should become a state. The battle that followed resolved itself into a conflict between free-state and slave-state forces. When the division occurred, the

Black Laws that had existed in Indiana were not repealed in the newly created Territory of Illinois. In his fight for a free state, James Lemen organized an Anti-Slavery Church. On January 10, 1809 (1810), he wrote,

> I received Jefferson's confidential message on Oct. 10, 1808, suggesting a division of the churches on the question of slavery and the organization of a church on a strictly anti-slavery basis, for the purpose of heading a movement to finally make Illinois a free state, and after first trying in vain for some months to bring all the churches over to such a basis, I acted on Jefferson's plan and Dec. 10, 1809, the anti-slavery element formed a Baptist Church at Cantine [Quentin] creek. . . .

Jefferson sent a contribution of twenty dollars. This church, known later as "Bethel Meeting House," and still later as "Bethel Baptist Church," was originally named, "The Baptized Church of Christ, Friends to Humanity on Cantine Creek." Although this church was non-political, as it grew in strength, the members formed the Illinois Anti-Slavery League.

The proposed northern boundary of Illinois was drawn along the southern border of Lake Michigan. James Lemen had a surveyor draw a map with a new northern boundary which included sixty miles of frontage on Lake Michigan. This move, aimed "to counter balance the southern slave states," was introduced into the legislature by Nathaniel Pope. It gave Chicago and fourteen additional counties to Illinois.

James Lemen and his six sons (five of whom became preachers) dominated the early abolitionist movement in Illinois. According to his arch-opponent, William Henry Harrison, secretary of the Northwest Territory and alter governor of Indiana, Lemen had "set his iron will against slavery and indirectly made his influence felt so strongly at Washington and before Congress that all efforts to suspend the Anti-Slavery clause in the Ordinance of 1787 failed." MacNaul suggests that Jefferson refrained from revealing his role in the affair out of deference to the sensibilities of his slave-owning friends. James Lemen died on January 8, 1823, near Waterloo, Monroe County. Lemen is not only remembered for his activities—

> as a revolutionary soldier, territorial leader, Indian fighter and founder of the Baptist cause in Illinois, but . . . also [because] he was the companion and co-worker with Thomas Jefferson in setting in motion the forces which finally recorded the Anti-Slavery clause in the Ordinance of 1787, which dedicated the great Northwest Territory to freedom and later gave Illinois a free state constitution.

The ordinance of 1787, which had the effect of a constitutional amendment, signified to many that slavery had been officially condemned, and that it should not be extended, even though it continued to exist where it was already established. One of the most important provisions of this document was Article VI, which stated,

> There shall be neither slavery nor involuntary servitude in the said territory, otherwise than in the punishment of crime, whereof the party shall have been duly convicted; provided always, that any persons escaping into the same, from whom labor or service is lawfully claimed in any of the original States, such fugitive may be lawfully reclaimed and conveyed to the person claiming his or her labor or service as aforesaid.

Slave holders in the territory, worried by this Article, challenged its validity and threatened to move rather than relinquish their property. Governor Arthur St. Clair, a Revolutionary general appointed governor of the Territory in 1788, gave a new interpretation of the clause and thus appeased the owners. He decided that the clause prevented the introduction of new slaves but did not affect previously acquired slave property. Encouraged by this concession, the pro-slavery forces doubled their efforts to have the article repealed. Petitions were presented to Congress seeking permission to introduce slaves from other states, and the anti-slavery group, again led by Lemen, countered with petitions denying that the pro-slavery spokesmen voiced the sentiments of the majority. The Senate committee reported that legislation would be inexpedient, and action was suspended until after Illinois should become a state.

Under the Black Laws of the Territory of Illinois Negroes and mulattoes were considered taxable property and were denied citizenship. To satisfy judgments against himself, a master could sell his bonded servants; he could also sell the unexpired time of indentured Negroes. No Negroes could be a witness against a white man. There were laws which provided for the lashing of lazy, misbehaving and disorderly servants, but Negroes could not take advantage of the courts in registering complaints against mistreatment by their masters, as could white servants.

These regulations were modeled after *Le Code Noir* of the French and formed the basis for the Black Laws which were to come later.

Negroes were further differentiated under the law. It held that "In all cases of penal laws, where free persons are punishable by fine, servants shall be punished by whipping, after the rate of twenty lashes for every eight dollars. . . ."

A master and his servant could not enter into a contract—

and if any person shall presume to deal with any servant without . . . consent [of the owner,] he . . . shall . . . pay to the master . . . four times the value of the thing bought, sold or received . . . and shall also forfeit . . . twenty dollars . . . or receive . . . on his bare back, thirty nine lashes, well laid on, at the public whipping post. . . .

Tavern keepers were not allowed to sell beer or liquor to slaves or bonded servants. Another section provided that—

No Negro [or] mulatto . . . shall at any time purchase any servant, other than of their own complexion; and if any of the persons aforesaid, shall nevertheless presume to purchase a white servant, such servant shall immediately become free, and shall be so held, deemed and taken.

Yet in Chicago in 1833 there occurred an incident which raises the question of how effective this law operated. A white man named Harper, the first person to be confined in Chicago's first jail, was put on the auction block under the Illinois vagrancy law. A large and curious crowd attended the sale, but the only bid was that of the town crier, George White, a Negro. Harper was sold to White for a quarter. What became of Harper after the transaction is not recorded.[2]

If an owner brought his slaves or indentured servants into the territory, he was required to register them within thirty days and at that time agree upon and record with the county clerk the length of service. If a servant refused to serve, he might be removed from the territory within sixty days. The servant was declared free if the master failed to comply with the requirements. Any one who helped a slave escape from the territory was liable to a fine of one thousand dollars and if caught harboring a runaway was forced to pay a dollar a day to the master.[3]

The regulations governing the behavior of slaves and servants were particularly strict:

> . . . if any slave or servant shall be found at the distance of ten miles from the tenement of his or her master . . . without a pass . . . it shall . . . be lawful for any person to apprehend and carry him . . . before any Justice of the Peace, to be . . . punished with stripes. . . .
>
> If any slave or servant shall presume to come . . . upon the plantation . . . of any person . . . without leave from his . . . owner . . . it shall be lawful for the owner of such plantation . . . to give, or order such slave or servant; ten lashes on his . . . bare back.
>
> Riots, routs, unlawful assemblies, trespasses and sedition speeches by any slave . . . or . . . servant . . . shall be punished with stripes . . . not exceeding thirty-nine.
>
> . . . if any person . . . shall permit . . . any . . . slave . . . or servant of colour, to the number of three, or more, to assemble in his . . . house, out house, yard, or shed, for the purpose of dancing or reveling, either by night, or by day, the person . . . so offending shall forfeit . . . the sum of twenty dollars . . . to any person . . . who shall sue for . . . the same.

The indenture system, with its restrictions on servants, amounted to virtual slavery, so it made little difference if a Negro or mulatto was called a slave or an indentured servant.

In evaluating these slave laws it is necessary to keep in mind the character of social legislation at that time. In 1788 a thief who was unable to restore the value of stolen goods and pay the fine assessed could be lashed and sold to labor. A debtor with no estate had to satisfy his debt by "personal and reasonable servitude." In the early part of the nineteenth century vagrants and the poor were also hired out. "The jail, the lash, and compulsory labor, far from being confined to the criminal law, were part and parcel of family government, of township government, and even the law's charity for the weak and poor." Even considering all this, the Black Laws were far from human, just or civilized.

When Illinois became a state in 1818, the constitution included the anti-slavery provision of the Ordinance of 1787, but not without compromising clauses. The delegates who voted for these compromises were backed by wealthy slave-owners, many of whom were officials at the constitutional convention. Article VI, Section 1 read:

> Neither slavery nor involuntary servitude shall hereafter be introduced into this State otherwise than for the punishment of crimes, whereof, the party shall have been duly convicted. . . . Nor shall any indenture of any Negro or mulatto, hereafter made and executed out of this State, or if made in this State, where the term of service exceeds one year, be of the least validity except those given in cases of apprenticeship.

Section 2:

> No person bound to labor in any other State shall be hired to labor in this State, except within the tract reserved for the salt works near Shawneetown; nor even at that place for a longer period than one year at any time; nor shall it be allowed there after the year 1825. . . .

Section 3:

> Each and every person who has been bound to service be it contract or indenture in virtue of the laws of Illinois territory heretofore existing, and in conformity to the provisions of the same, without fraud or collusion, shall be held to a specific performance of their contracts or indentures; and such Negroes and mulattoes as have been registered in conformity with the aforesaid laws, shall serve out the time appointed by such laws; provided, however, that the children hereafter born of such person, Negro or mulatto, shall become free, the males at the age of 21 years, the females at the age of 18 years. Each and every child born of indentured parents shall be entered with the clerk of the county in which they reside, by their owners, within six months after the birth of said child.

The Illinois Bill of Rights avowed, "That all men are born equally free and independent, and have certain inherent indefeasible rights, among which are those of enjoying and defending life, liberty, and of . . . pursuing their own happiness." Yet the Negro was denied the right to vote and many other privileges which citizens enjoyed. Probably only the fear that such action would have prevented admission of Illinois to the Union kept the framers of the constitution from officially recognizing slavery. Once statehood had been attained, the pro-slavery forces began agitation for legislation to make Illinois a slave state. In the struggle to prevent this move Edward Coles, second governor of Illinois, played the leading role.[4]

Coles's background was that of a southern aristocrat. He was born in Albermarle County, Virginia, on December 15, 1786, the son of a wealthy plantation owner. His family often entertained such distinguished visitors as James Madison, James Monroe, Patrick Henry, and Thomas Jefferson. When he was twenty-two, young Coles fell heir to his father's estate, but he had no wish to be a slave holder. During his college days he had become convinced of the fundamental equality of man. He left his estate and became President James Madison's private secretary. In 1816 he was sent by the president to Russia on an important diplomatic mission. Coles traveled extensively and made two trips to Illinois. He decided to take his slaves and settle there.

Under the leadership of a mulatto named Ralph Crawford, who had previously accompanied Coles to Illinois, the wagon train began the long haul over the Allegheny Mountains. Coles joined his slaves at Brownsville where the entire party embarked on flat-bottom boats and continued the journey. The pilot whom Coles had engaged to guide them on the six hundred mile journey was discharged at Pittsburgh because of drunkenness, and Coles himself piloted the lead boat to New Albany, just below Louisville. There he sold the boats, and the party, again under the leadership of Crawford, continued to Edwardsville, Illinois.

When they left Pittsburgh, Coles assembled his slaves and made an astonishing announcement. He declared all his slaves unconditionally free and let each decide whether he would go ashore or proceed to Illinois. They all chose to accompany their former master to Edwardsville. Before their arrival there, Coles gave certificates of freedom to the liberated slaves. He prefaced these documents with these words:

> Not believing that man can have of right a property in his fellow man, but on the contrary, that all mankind were endowed by nature with equal rights, I do therefore, by these present restore to (naming the party) that inalienable liberty of which he has been deprived.

He also deeded to the head of each family one hundred sixty acres of land and obtained work for all others. Coles was appointed Registrar of the land office at Edwardsville by President Monroe, March 5, 1819. He made many friends and contacts which later proved valuable to him politically. Coles ran for office in the gubernatorial election of 1822 and was elected by a plurality of fifty votes. The lieutenant-governor was a pro-slavery man who offered the new governor strong and consistent opposition throughout his term. In his inaugural address Coles denounced slavery bitterly and urged the adoption of measures which would abolish the slavery which still existed in Illinois despite the declaration against it in the Bill of Rights. The pro-slavery faction took up the challenge and passed a resolution calling for a referendum and a convention to amend the constitution. Opposing this move to write slavery into the letter of the law, the anti-slavery forces issued an appeal which ended with these words:

> In the name of unborn millions who will rise up after us, and call us blessed or accursed, according to our deeds—in the name of the injured sons of Africa, whose claims to equal rights with their fellow men will plead their own cause against their usurpers before the tribunal of eternal justice, we conjure you, fellow citizens, TO PONDER UPON THESE THINGS.

During the period of eighteen months between the passage of the resolution and the actual vote, both sides sought to strengthen their forces. The Friends of a Convention, the pro-slavery advocates, sought to discredit their opponents by attacking their leader Coles. His farm buildings were destroyed; he was denounced, threatened and burned in effigy. A suit was filed against him for the recovery of two hundred dollars for each slave he had brought to Illinois and emancipated. The law under which the suit was filed was passed on March 30, 1819, but was not published until the following October. His enemies sought to convict him on a legal technicality, for Coles had come to Illinois in May of that year. In September 1824, the jury decided against Coles and he was assessed two thousand dollars plus costs. The case was carried to the Supreme Court, and Coles was finally vindicated. This attempt to destroy the effectiveness of the anti-convention campaign failed, for the Friends of a Convention lost by more than 1,800 votes. The question was settled: Illinois was to practice a system of servitude, but slavery was not to exist—legally.

Later, Edward Coles took up the fight against the Black Laws and was induced to run for Congress. He lost the election and finally left Illinois and moved to Philadelphia where he died July 7, 1868. Coles County, named in honor of this champion of freedom, is a memorial which keeps alive his name in Illinois.

Three years after the enactment of the federal Fugitive Slave Law in 1850, Illinois passed a supplement to it which provided that—

> If any Negro or mulatto, bound or free, shall hereafter come into the State and remain ten days with the intention of residing in the same, every such Negro or mulatto shall be deemed guilty of a high misdemeanor and for the first offense shall be fined the sum of $50 to be recovered before any Justice of the Peace in the county where said Negro or mulatto may be found. . . .

In an attempt to compensate for the admission of California to the Union as a free state, the pro-slavery group secured the passage of the Kansas-Nebraska Act in 1854. This bill provided that when the territory should apply for admission as a state, the request would

CHAPTER TWO

be granted regardless of whether its constitution permitted or prohibited slavery. The territory was divided into two parts, Kansas and Nebraska, because it was feared that the northerners would take the initiative in settling the northern section. Because Stephen Douglas introduced this provision, he lost much of his popularity and prestige in Illinois.

In 1834 an army officer named John Emerson, traveling—as was his custom—with his personal slave, came to Rock Island, Illinois. Two years later the officer was on the move again, this time into the Minnesota country. Again John Emerson took his slave along. Eventually the army officer returned to his home in St. Louis and settled down with his family and his slave. In 1844 he died.

Meanwhile, the slave—whose name was Dred Scott—married a young girl who was also owned by John Emerson. When the master died, title to the two slaves passed to his wife. One may be excused for imagining that she was the scolding type, for the death of John Emerson proved to be the signal for the slave couple to assert themselves. In 1846 Dred Scott sued for his freedom on the grounds that he had lived in Illinois and Minnesota, both north of the 36" 30' line designated by the Missouri Compromise, and hence could not be held. He won the decision of the lower court, but the case was appealed and the judgment reversed on plea that Scott had reverted to his former status of a slave by returning to Missouri.

In 1850 Mrs. Emerson married an abolitionist congressman from Massachusetts and transferred the ownership of her slaves to her brother, John Sanford of New York. The Dred Scott case went on. Finally it reached the Supreme Court of the United States, where the court held that under the "due process" clause of the Constitution, Congress could not destroy the right of an owner to his slaves simply because he took them into a Territory. The Missouri Compromise was therefore invalid. Two justices dissented but Scott's suit was dismissed and he remained a slave.

The North protested. The Court had said in effect that slavery could not be limited anywhere in any state or territory. In Lincoln's words, slavery could now "follow the flag."

The *Illinois State Journal* asked indignantly, "Where will the aggressions of Slavery cease?" The *Aurora Beacon* declared,

> The infamous decision of the Dred Scott case has aroused the whole North to a realization of the danger which our free institutions are subject to at the hands of the slave power and their adherents in the Supreme Court.

The struggle was on.

3. Abolition

There are three drafts of this chapter at the Harsh Research Collection, all written by Joseph Bougere. Editorial comments made in Bontemps's handwriting, including the omission of two paragraphs, from a draft found at Syracuse University were incorporated by the editor in the version that appears below.

Many of the settlers of southern Illinois had come from the slave belt. These men brought with them their outlooks and habits of life, and southern Illinois, later known as "Egypt," became a stronghold of pro-slavery sentiment. With the opening of the Erie Canal, New Englanders, New Yorkers, and immigrants direct from Europe settled in Ohio, Michigan, Illinois, and Wisconsin. These pioneers, too, "packed their beliefs in their traveling bags." It has been contended by some that the construction of the Erie Canal was more influential in freeing the Southern slaves than were such abolitionists as William Lloyd Garrison. For the Canal brought in the men who gave Abraham Lincoln an edge in the Northwest when he stood for election in 1860.

The newcomers from New England and the North Atlantic States came from a region which had abolished slavery as far back as the era of the American Revolution. In this section of the country slavery had been tried and rejected. Then, too, anti-slavery societies in the South as well as in the North were stirring up a growing sentiment against the institution. Soon the emancipation societies in the South died out because the changing economic structure made slavery a sectional institution, yielding vast profits. The South decided to retain, defend, and increase her supply of slave labor. At the same time abolition societies in the North flourished. From the 1830s onward they dropped their emphasis from persuasion, gradual emancipation, and colonization and struck out boldly for abolition. They were dedicated to the destruction of the "evil" institution. Such sentiments were more and more frequently expressed above the Mason-Dixon Line. Below that line were Fitzhugh, Dew, Harper and others who spread the illusion that slavery constituted a positive good for all concerned. This propaganda held that the African was never luckier than on the day the slavers caught him, for slavery was his redemption from the savagery of the jungle. Slavery blessed the poor white, on the other hand, by giving him color prestige. Society was thus stabilized. Knighthood flowered again. Fairy-like women came out of the great houses and languished under magnolia trees. Fortunately not everyone in the South succumbed to what they saw of the "dream." There were those who observed that less than one tenth of the total population enjoyed the fruits of this system.

The North, on the other hand, failed to present a united front against the evil of slavery. The abolitionists constituted a minority, which, though small, made their presence felt. Until the bitter end most Northerners regarded abolitionist speakers as interlopers and mobbed, tarred, and feathered them and rode them out of town on rails.

Emigrants from Europe usually cast their lot with the abolitionists. A definite stand against slavery was taken by the English settlers who had established a colony at Edwardsville, Illinois. Because they felt that slave labor would be required on the large grain plantations they planned, these Englishmen turned to raising cattle instead. They boasted that "there never was a slave taken in our neighborhood." They also assisted Negro emigrants from Illinois at the time when colonization of Negroes in Liberia and Haiti was proposed.

The German settlement at New Harmony was a community similar to that at Edwardsville. The attitude of the people in these two towns did much to neutralize some of the anti-Negro sentiment current at that time.

While Harriet Tubman was carrying on her work of personally liberating all the slaves she possibly could, and Garrison, Sojourner Truth, Fred Douglass, and others were campaigning through other parts of the country, the men of Illinois were not idle. By defending Negroes in the courts, often without remuneration, by lecturing and recruiting members to the abolition societies, and by publishing anti-slavery newspapers, they did their part; often they forfeited reputation, property and life, for the stand they took. Heading this list is Elijah Parrish Lovejoy, minister of the gospel, journalist, and martyr.

"That an American citizen is in a state whose Constitution repudiates all slavery, should die as a martyr in defense of the freedom of the press, is a phenomenon in the history of this union. . . . Here is the most effective portraiture of the first American martyr to the freedom of the press and freedom of the slave." These lines were written about Lovejoy by ex-president John Quincy Adams in 1837.[1]

Elijah Lovejoy was a pensive young Presbyterian minister who came to Alton in 1836 with his printing press. The anti-slavery sentiment and the pro-slavery point of view which was co-existent in Illinois became concentrated in a small area in Alton, which was just across the river from a slave state. Lovejoy and his printing press provided the local issue which threw these elements of conflict into open opposition.

Lovejoy, the son of a Presbyterian minister, was born at Albion, Maine, November 9, 1802. He became assistant editor of the *St. Louis Times* shortly after he arrived there in 1827. In 1832 he became converted to Presbyterianism at a revival, entered the Princeton Theological Seminary in New Jersey, and was ordained. He then returned to St. Louis and became editor of the *St. Louis Observer*, a religious organ of the Presbyterians of Missouri and Illinois. Soon his opinions on the slave question were being criticized by the local supporters of slavery. He publicly asserted he was not an abolitionist, for he advocated colonization of the Negro, a reform that had supporters even in the South. But when he denounced the public whipping of men who aided fugitives, the pro-slavery press cried "Abolitionist," and the name stuck. The owners of the paper became fearful of possible violence in the conflict that ensued, and since the profits from the *Observer* were small, they decided to retain Lovejoy providing the paper was moved to Alton. Before the move could be made, an incident occurred which enabled Lovejoy to take a parting shot at his opponents. A Negro deck-hand named Francois McIntosh stabbed and killed a deputy sheriff in a waterfront brawl, and before he could be brought to trial, a mob snatched him from the jail and burned him to death. When the grand jury convened on the case, the judge (who was named Lawless!) instructed the jury that a murder indictment was not possible because the lynching had been the action of a mob, and was beyond their legal jurisdiction. Lovejoy immediately denounced the judge's reasoning and his editorial incited further mob violence. The *Observer* was stormed, some type destroyed, and the office wrecked.[2]

The press of the *Observer*, which had escaped destruction, was landed safely on the Alton wharf on Sunday, July 21, 1836, but that night a mob, composed of men from Illinois as well as Missouri, seized it, smashed it beyond repair, and threw it in the river. The next day a meeting was held, and though there were some who argued that the issue did not concern a town of free men, a subscription was made to buy a new press. Because of this, Lovejoy felt obliged to state his position. He said,

> I do not know that I shall feel it my duty to discuss it [slavery] here as fully as I did in St. Louis. There where its enormities were constantly before, I felt bound to lift up my voice against it, as in the murder of McIntosh. This I claim as my constitutional right, a right I shall never relinquish to any man or body of men. But to discuss the subject of slavery is not the object of my paper, except as a great moral subject in connection with others. My object is to publish a religious journal which shall be instructive and profitable to my fellow-citizens. As to the subjects I shall discuss, and the manner of doing them, I shall ever claim the right of determining for myself, always accepting counsel from others with thankfulness.

There were some who interpreted this rather guarded statement as a "solemn pledge" not to discuss the slavery question in Alton, but such a promise would have run counter to all that Lovejoy lived by.

He became the first pastor of the Presbyterian church in Upper Alton, and the circulation of the *Observer* rose to several thousand under his editorship. For a year Lovejoy found peace, but on the Fourth of July 1837, he broke his silence on slavery with an impassioned plea to "unloose the heavy burdens, and let the oppressed go free." As an immediate step he proposed the formation of an Illinois State Anti-Slavery Society. A meeting was called of the pro-slavery element and a resolution was passed expressing—

> disapprobation of the course pursued by the Rev. E. P. Lovejoy, Editor of the *Alton Observer*, in publishing and promulgating the doctrine of Abolitionism, and that too in violation of a solemn pledge, voluntarily given by him at former meeting of the citizens of Alton . . . that he would not interfere with the question of Abolitionism, in any way whatever. . . .

Lovejoy said in reply:

> It is far from my intention to bring on an "unwise agitation" of the subject of slavery to this community. It is a subject that . . . must be discussed, must be agitated . . . I hope to discuss the overwhelmingly important subject of slavery with the freedom of a republican and the

meekness of a Christian. If I fail in either respect, I beg that you will attribute it, gentlemen, to that imperfection which attends us all in the performance of our best purposes.

The issue was now in the open and the *Observer* called upon its subscribers to petition the abolition of slavery in the District of Colombia. The Madison Anti-Slavery Society was organized in Upper Alton on August 6th, with the Reverend Loomis as president, Enoch Long and C. W. Hunter as vice presidents, and Lovejoy's brother, Owen, as secretary. The pro-slavery *Missouri Republican*, commenting on the new organization, said editorially:

> The good people of Illinois must either put a stop to the efforts of these fanatics or expel them from the community. . . . Everyone who desires the harmony of the country and the peace and prosperity of all, should unite to put them down.

Lovejoy's press was destroyed three times, and his life was threatened if he did not leave town. He had been driven almost frantic by fear for the safety of his wife and child, yet he answered defiantly:

"I have been beset night and day at Alton. And now if I go elsewhere violence may overtake me in my retreat. . . . I have concluded . . . to remain at Alton, and here to insist on protection to exercise my rights. If the civil authorities refuse to protect me, I must look to God." He concluded with this grimly prophetic pronouncement, "And if I die, I have determined to make my grave in Alton."[3]

The fourth press arrived on the night of November 6th. It was unloaded and stored in a warehouse adjoining the wharf, and an armed guard was posted. The next night the warehouse was attacked by a drunken mob and in the exchange of shots, Lovejoy was killed. The defenders of the warehouse, as well as the members of the mob, were brought to trial but all were acquitted.

By murdering Lovejoy, the pro-slavery faction placed a weapon in the facile hands of their opponents. The effects of Lovejoy's death were felt all over the country. The historian Harris says, "The anti-slavery movement in Illinois had its origin in the work and death of Elijah P. Lovejoy."[4]

Three positive results grew out of the incident at Alton. First, the Underground Railroad grew and was extended; second, a definite propaganda machine for Negro rights was formed; and third, anti-slavery societies were established throughout the state.

One positive result of the incident at Alton is seen in the growth and establishment of anti-slavery societies in the state. Eighteen such groups were organized between 1837 and 1839. In another year or two the Illinois State Anti-Slavery Society was contemplating political action. Rev. Chauncey Cook, one of its most active members, reported the following year's work: fifty-three lectures delivered in twenty-four towns, seven anti-slavery societies founded, two hundred and sixty-six new members recruited. Throughout these activities he was supported by voluntary contributions.

The first anti-slavery meeting in Chicago was held in the City Saloon Building. The group was headed by such prominent citizens as Dr. Charles V. Dyer, Robert Freeman, Philo Carpenter, and Calvin De Wolf of the Presbyterian church. A few Baptists and Methodists were included. Other groups joined and by 1844 there was a women's auxiliary added. The Chicago organization was quite influential in state conventions.

Owen Lovejoy, pupil of his martyred brother Elijah, was an untiring worker in the abolitionist cause. He, too, studied for the ministry and for seventeen years was the pastor of the Congregational Church at Princeton. In defiance of the state laws, he held open anti-slavery meetings and was subjected to persecution. Although his colleague, Ichabod Codding, was an able orator, Lovejoy did more to advance the cause of abolition in the state. He became influential in the Republican Party and was Lincoln's ardent supporter.

In 1843 Lovejoy was indicted on two counts. He was charged in one with harboring a Negro slave named Agnes, and in the other, with harboring a slave named Nancy. Because of the prominence of the defendant the trial created much interest throughout the state and nation as well. Lovejoy was acquitted, and because he and his counsel, James H. Collins, were both outstanding abolitionists, the outcome of the trial was a great triumph for their cause.[5]

To Owen Lovejoy fell the honor of proposing the bill which abolished slavery forever. He died the next year in 1864, after having seen the close of one phase of the anti-slavery struggle.

Ichabod Codding was a militant clergyman, who, while he was still a student at Middlebury, Vermont, began giving anti-slavery lectures. After leaving college he served five years as agent and lecturer for the Anti-Slavery Society. Like other abolitionists he was often exposed to mob violence. In 1842 he entered the Congregational ministry and held pastorates at Princeton, Lockport, Joliet, and other cities in Illinois. Codding was the colleague of Owen Lovejoy and was a power in the organization of the Republican Party. He was born at Bristol, New York, in 1811 and died at Baraboo, Wisconsin, June 17, 1866.

Edward Beecher, the brother of Henry Ward, and Harriet Beecher Stowe, author of *Uncle Tom's Cabin*, were other Illinois abolitionists. Beecher gave up the pastorate of a prominent church in Boston to become the president of Illinois College at Jacksonville. Some of his students were indicted for harboring fugitive slaves. He stood guard at the warehouse when Lovejoy was murdered and two years later wrote the *Narrative of the Alton Riots*.

Zebina Eastman was an anti-slavery journalist who was born at Amherst, Massachusetts, on September 8, 1815. He worked on various newspapers in the East and although at first he was not sympathetic toward the abolitionist movement, in 1839 he joined Benjamin Lundy at Lowell, La Salle County, in the latter's efforts to revive *The Genius of Universal Emancipation*. After Lundy's death, Eastman with Hooper Warren began the publication of *The Genius of Liberty* as successor to Lundy's *Genius*. The *Genius* (published in Chicago) became the *Western Citizen*, then *The Free West* and finally merged with the *Chicago Tribune*. In 1861 Eastman was appointed United States Consul at Bristol, England, by president Lincoln. He died at Maywood, Illinois, on June 4, 1883.

Hooper Warren was another abolitionist who was also a journalist. He was born at Walpole, New Hampshire, in 1790. In March 1819 at Edwardsville he established *The Spectator*, the third newspaper in Illinois. The contest over the effort to introduce a pro-slavery clause into the state constitution soon brought the paper into prominence. *The Spectator* made a fight against the scheme which ended in its rejection at the polls. Warren left Illinois for a brief period but returned to establish the *Sangamon Spectator*, the first paper to be published at the present state capital. In 1832 he removed to Hennepin where he held public office during the next five years. Later he was associated with Zebina Eastman in the publication of *The Genius of Liberty*, *The Western Citizen*, and *The Free West*. He died at Mendota in 1864.[6]

Benjamin Lundy, who in 1815 organized the first abolition society, was born in Hardwick, New Jersey, January 4, 1789. He published the first issue of *The Genius of Universal Emancipation* at Mt. Pleasant, Ohio, in 1821. In 1825, when his wife died, Lundy determined to devote the rest of his life to the cause of freedom. He journeyed through the middle and eastern states to arouse sentiment, organize societies, and get subscriptions for *The Genius*. He was the inspirer and teacher of William Lloyd Garrison, who joined him in Baltimore to help him edit *The Genius*, but on August 22, he died and was buried in Putnam County, Illinois.[7]

Lyman Trumbull was an old-time Democrat with no leanings toward abolition, but with an honest desire to see justice done the Negro in Illinois. He was one of the able lawyers who fought cases for the Negro in the courts with little or no pay.[8]

Not all the abolitionists stood by their principles. *The Quincy Whig* reported in November 1843:

A late number of the Quincy Whig contains . . . [a] letter from David D. Nelson of Adams County renouncing political Abolitionism, and assigning his reasons for the course thus adopted by him. Mr. Nelson has heretofore been one of the most prominent Abolitionists in the State, and we hope the example he has set will be speedily followed by others whose action . . . has done more to rivet the chains upon the slave, and entail permanently upon the slaveholding States, the curse of slavery, than all other causes combined.

The rest of the news item gives a point of view held by many of the people of Illinois.

But for Abolitionism, and its proscriptive, uncharitable course, we entertain not a reasonable doubt, but that are this, Kentucky, Virginia, and several other states, would have been in a progressive course of gradual emancipation and so soon as Abolitionists cease their abuse and proscription of the slave-holder then and not till then, can we with any degree of confidence expect to witness in the slave-holding states efficient measures taken for the gradual but permanent emancipation of the slave. Of this we have been long convinced, and feel gratified at the course taken, and the views expressed by Nelson in his communication.

However, the Abolitionists, impatient with talk of "gradual emancipation," continued the fight for freedom in their own way.

The newspapers by directing a steady stream of "tracts, pamphlets, sermons, lectures, slave narratives, Sunday-school lessons, catechisms, and picture books," aroused the public to "the influence of the slave power." The files of old newspapers furnish an excellent record of this gradual change in the attitude of the courts and the general public toward the Negro.

A notice which appeared in the *Illinois State Register and People's Advocate*, October 1838, reads:

Was committed to my custody . . . a runaway Negro . . . whom I have in jail in Carlyle, Clinton County, Ill.

N. B. He says . . . that he was hired out for 9 months to Hicks, Capt. Steamboat Tuckahoe, at Clarksville . . . unless the said Negro is claimed before six weeks I shall proceed to hire him out according to law.

Sheriff

Thirteen years later similar cases were reported in this manner:

Some weeks since a Negro was committed to jail in Gallatin County, charged with being a fugitive slave. On the 17th he obtained a write of habeas corpus, and was heard before Judge Denning at Elizabethtown, where his counsel contended that the imprisonment was illegal, for that the section of our statue under which the commitment was made, being intended to assist the Master to recapture his fugitive slave, was void, as Congress had the exclusive right of legislation over the subject. In support of this decision of the Supreme Court of this State in the case of Thornton was read, which case is precisely similar to this, also the case of *Prigg vs. Commonwealth of Pennsylvania* was referred to as sustaining the same position.

Judge Denning after due reflection, thought proper to discharge the fugitive. The Judge stated that he thought the decision of the Supreme Court of this State was wrong, and that it was the duty and right of the States individually to pass laws for the purpose of enabling the Master to recover his fugitive slave, but that he was constrained (against his feelings and private opinions) by the decision of the highest judicial tribunal of the State, to set the Negro at Liberty.

—Morgan Journal

March 30, 1855, *Chicago Daily Democrat*
Rosetta, a colored girl who was sometime since brought to this state from Kentucky by an agent of her master, and declared free by the state court of Columbus, was today arrested under the Fugitive Slave Act. The case came before Judge Parker, who decided that the girl was entitled to her freedom, having been brought into the state by her owner or his representative.

The reaction of Chicagoans to the Fugitive Slave Law and the militant action they took is shown in this news item from the *Quincy Whig*.

By *The Telegraph*, Chicago, Oct. 23, 1850.
The excitement here about the recapture of fugitive slaves under the late law is very great; the City Council, by an almost unanimous vote, required the city police and requested all citizens to give no aid to the recapture of slaves.

They also passed a series of resolutions in condemnation of the law, and censured those Senators from the Free States who voted for the bill or avoided the responsibility of voting.

Last night the opponents of the law held a meeting in the city hall—the hall was full, and the most violent speeches were made, which created great cheering, resolutions were offered, declaring the blacks to be justified in resisting all attempts to recapture them; even if they have to do so to death. The meeting adjourned to Friday evening to consider and act upon the resolutions.

In the East, New York, Boston, and other cities, similar protest meetings were held with Negroes and whites vowing to oppose "to the death" the Fugitive Slave Law.

Although opinion was divided as to whether or not the anti-slavery movement should be linked with politics, the Illinois abolitionists in the early 1840s diverted some of their energy to the building up of the Liberty Party. They campaigned during the presidential election of 1844 with much enthusiasm. William Jones, "a free colored man of Chicago," told how he had been robbed and kidnapped, and stories such as this helped them greatly.

However, the Liberty Party polled only 3,496 votes. Larger gains were made in the Gubernatorial elections of 1846, when Richard Eels, who had been persecuted for aiding fugitives, was nominated for Governor. Another abolition paper, the *Liberty Banner*, was started in Rock Island, and Eastman and Davidson began publishing a monthly periodical called the *Liberty Tree*. The Liberty vote for Governor was 5,147, an increase of more than 1,600 over the vote two years before. The Congressional vote totaled 6,220. This gain, though slight, stimulated that party to continue its efforts. In 1848 the Liberty Party recognized other political issues and joined with the Free Soil group. This campaign was noteworthy because the Whigs and the Democrats, sensing the growing anti-slavery sentiment, decided to incorporate in their platforms and stand against the extension of slavery. Fewer votes were polled this time than before, and for a time the abolitionists were disheartened because of the fall of the Liberty Party. However, a firm stand against the extension of slavery was almost universally adopted and the State Anti-Slavery Society reorganized into a more efficient organization.

Throughout the fight against slavery the abolitionists were invariably in the minority. At first their general plan was a scheme of gradual emancipation, recompensing slave owners for the loss of their chattel, and the colonization of the liberated slaves. The entrenchment of slavery as an institution of vast economic power made such plans futile indeed as the South sought, through the courts and in practice, to limit further the activities and rights of the Negro. Lovejoy's death at Alton gave impetus to the struggle, and the abolitionists in Illinois, as well as those throughout the country, worked to bring about complete emancipation, some of them realized that not "through the processes of discussion and balloting; rather through fire and blood were Southern slavery and Illinois's Black Code to be washed away."

The firing on Fort Sumter in April 1861 marked the beginning of the end of the struggle. Prophetic of the coming storm were Owen Lovejoy's words at Alton in 1860.

Twenty-three years ago the blood of my brother, slain in these streets, ran down and mingled with the waters of the mighty river which sweeps past your city to the sea:

'The Avon to the Severn runs,
The Severn to the sea—
And scattered wide as Wycliffe's name
Shall Wycliffe's ashes be.'

4. The Underground Railroad

There are two drafts of this chapter in the IWP papers at the Harsh Research Collection. The more recent one, printed here, was written by Arna Bontemps.

On July 13, 1844, the following advertisement appeared in the pages of the *Western Citizen*, a Chicago newspaper:

LIBERTY LINE
New Arrangement—Night and Day

The improved and splendid Locomotives, Clarkson with Lundy, with their trains fitted up in the best style of accommodations for passengers, will run their regular trips during the present season between the borders of the Patriarchal Dominion of Libertyville, Upper Canada. Gentlemen and Ladies who may wish to improve their health or circumstances, by a northern tour, are respectfully invited to give us their patronage.

SEATS FREE, *Irrespective of color.*
Necessary clothing furnished gratuitously to such as have *"fallen among thieves."*

"Hide the outcasts let the oppressed go free."
   —Bible

For seats apply at any of the trap doors, or to the conductor of the train.
   J. Cross, *Proprietor*

N.B. For the special benefit of Pro-Slavery Police Officers, an extra heavy wagon for Texas will be furnished, whenever it may be necessary, in which they will be forwarded as dead freight, to the "valley of Rascals," always at the risk of the owners.

Extra overcoats provided for such of them as are afflicted with the protracted *chilly-phobia*.[1]

Citizens of Bond County, Illinois, had been harboring runaway slaves as early as 1819. The first known case of dispatching a fugitive from Chicago to Canada occurred in 1839, and in 1844, the decade which saw the rise of the Underground Railroad generally, the Illinois System was bold enough and well enough organized to insert advertisements in local newspapers.

Lawrence D. Reddick states in a recently unpublished study that:

The chief stimulation to the Underground Railroad growth was the Fugitive Slave Law of 1850, a law which put teeth into the weak Act of 1793. The Southern slaveholders were determined to take advantage of these new provisions and sent their agents North to retrieve their lost property. Often these agents were rude, unkempt, and unrefined specimens of the slave traffic. The sight of a human being, often with chains clanking from his ankles, being led through the Northern towns by such "human bloodhounds" did more to convert the citizens to an anti-slavery position than did all the abolition literature combined. Furthermore, as ever, "racketeers" took advantage of the law. Organized bands roamed the State kidnapping free Negroes, selling them into bondage. Communities were shocked when the news would break that some well known Negro, who had been living and working there for years, had been seized by either a legitimate or illegitimate slave catcher. The cries of anguish and defiance coming from the captive as he was torn from his family brought forth a sympathetic echo.[2]

Much of the communication relating to fugitive slaves was carried on in a guarded language. Special signals, whispered conversations, passwords, and figuratively phrased messages were the usual methods of conveying information about underground passengers, or about parties in pursuit of fugitives. The abolitionists knew these as the "grape-vine telegraph." These signals employed were of various kinds and were local in usage. Fugitives crossing the Ohio River at one point were sometimes announced at stations near the river by their guides by a shrill tremolo-call like that of the owl. Different neighborhoods had their peculiar combinations of knocks or raps to be made on the door or windows of a station when fugitives were waiting admission.

There were many means of conveying fugitives from station to station. In the early days of the Underground Railroad the fugitives were generally men. Unless there was some special reason for doing so, guides were not sent with them. The "passengers" were given necessary directions and put on their own. As the number of refugees increased, women and children were more frequently seen on the road. Pursuit became more common and the practice of transporting runaways on horseback or by vehicle was introduced. The steam railroad was a new means furnished to abolitionists by the progress of the times and used by them with greater or less frequency as circumstances required and when safety of passengers would not be sacrificed.

It is certain that during the 1850s there was some cooperation between the various railroad systems of the state and the Underground Railroad organization, although there is disagreement among the historians as to the extent of the participation of the railroads prior to this time. One historian records that the Chicago and Rock Island, the Illinois Central, and the Burlington and Quincy roads were used in transporting fugitives.

The number of runaways that passed over the route has been estimated at various times. One announcement which ran in the *Western Citizen* read:

This road is doing better business this fall than usual. The Fugitive Slave Law has given it more vitality and more activity; more passengers and more opposition, which accelerates business. We can run a load of slaves through almost any part of the border states into Canada within forty-eight hours, and we defy the slaveholders to beat that if they can.

This same abolition newspaper in 1854 placed the number of fugitives "escorted" to freedom in Canada at one hundred and seventy-six during one three-month period. "The total number of fugitives escaping from slavery to the North elsewhere may be estimated roughly at between fifteen hundred and two thousand annually," states one researcher. It would be impossible to ascertain what percentage of this number passed through Illinois and Chicago.

Despite the friendly attitude of Chicago as a whole, an escaped Negro was as liable to seizure as elsewhere in the country. This was due to the provisions of the Compromise of 1850. The passage of this law caused great excitement among the Negroes of Chicago as well as other communities. Men who had escaped years before and had begun a new life were once again haunted by the thought of recapture and re-enslavement. Many determined to remain where they were and fight back, but some fled the country—headed for Canada. It is reported that approximately 60,000 Negroes went to Canada, 20,000 of these during the decade of the 1850s. The attitude of the Canadians in the border provinces was generally favorable to the fugitives, and in spite of attempts upon the part of the Southern interests to extradite the runaways, the people of Canada clearly stated that Canada was a free land and that there was to be no pursuit of slaves over her border.

The kidnapping and sale into slavery of both free Negroes and fugitives reached such proportions that a statute of "To More Effectively Prevent Kidnapping" was enacted in 1825. Severe penalties instrumented the act but it failed to halt the practice which grew into a large lucrative business. The law provided that citizens of Illinois would be guilty if they transported Negroes across the state line. This clause was evaded by simply taking them to a point near the state line and turning them over to non-resident slave agents.

A favorite method of the kidnappers was to transport their victims to the Ohio or Mississippi Rivers and smuggle them by boat to Memphis and New Orleans.

One writer has aptly said: "To ask for a map of the route of the railroad is to ask for a map of the route by which the wily fox evades the hounds. Circumstances and a close local knowledge determine them."[3]

Alton, Quincy, and Chester were the most common points of entry of slaves from the South. One route ran from Alton, northeast by Jacksonville to the Illinois River which was followed to La Salle and Ottawa. This route led into Chicago by way of Plainfield and Lyons. One road that,

> extended through McDonough County started at Quincy, which was station No. 1, receiving Negroes from across the Mississippi River in Missouri. Station No. 2 was down at Round Prairie in Hancock County, at the Pettyjohn or Burton home. Station No. 3 in McDonough County was generally at the home of Uncle Billy Allison, or one of his sons on Troublesome Creek. Part of them lived in Chambers and the others in Scotland Township. Station No. 4 was at the home of Henry Dobbins in Fulton County from whence cargoes of Negroes were dispatched to Galesburg, Princeton, and on to Canada, the terminus of all Underground Railroads. It is interesting to recall that the Princeton station was in the charge of the Lovejoy family, which played an important part in the early abolition movement.

Another well-traveled route led from Chester to Sparta, then to Centralia, through Will County to Chicago. Still another route passed through Quincy, Farmington, Galesburg, Princeton, La Salle, and to Chicago.

Among the conductors of the Eden-Nashville route were the Hoods, Moores, McClur-kins, and Milligans, all of whom played prominent roles in the operation of the road. Van Dorn, of Quincy, is said to have aided some two or three hundred fugitives during his twenty-five years of activity. In Chicago, Philo Carpenter gave assistance to two hundred or more Negroes embarking from that city, and Zebina Eastman and Dr. C. V. Dyer, friends of Carpenter, often secreted escaping slaves in their own homes.

H.B. Leeper, son of an early abolitionist says of his father,

John Leeper moved from Marshall County, Tennessee, to Bond County, Illinois, in 1816. Was a hater of slavery. . . . Remained in Bond County until 1833, then moved to Jacksonville, Morgan County, and in 1831 to Putnam County, and in 1833 to Bureau County, Illinois. . . . My father's house was always a hiding place from slavery.

D. N. Blazer in his "History of the Underground Railroad of McDonough County, Illinois" writes, " . . . Andrew and Harmon Allison like the Blazers, my father James and his brother John Blazer and their families were ardent abolitionists and a part of the Underground system."[4]

In every town through which the Underground Railroad passed there were men who risked their fortunes and often their lives for the principles upon which the system was based. "At Quincy Dr. Richard Eels was most active in receiving and forwarding fugitives. In retaliation, it was sought in 1843 to have him extradited to Missouri. One mob crossed the river to burn part of his Mission Institute.

The home of Thomas W. Melendy was one of the Underground depots in Jacksonville until, as was often the case, the place became too well known. Bob and Emily Logan, a Negro boy and girl from Kentucky, were brought to Jacksonville and set free. Bob was captured and shipped back South, but his sister Emily sued for her freedom. Elihu Wolcott, D. B. Ayers, and T. W. Melendy provided her bond and fought the case up to the Supreme Court where a decision in favor of the girl was handed down.

Isaac Shedecker who lived near Jacksonville was an active conductor for the Railroad. Benjamin Henderson, a Negro teamster, came to live in Jacksonville in 1841. His home was a regular stopping place for fugitives, and he often made two trips a week transporting runaways to Springfield, Farmington, and other places. He could always get supplies for the fugitives from Joseph and Horace Bancroft, J. W. Lathrop, T. D. Eames, Asa Alcott, Hoyt Burdette and others. Henry Irving and the Reverend Kirby could also be counted on to help wherever needed. In Springfield, Henderson turned his charges over to Daniel Callahan and William Butler who were the station keepers there. Other men who were active in the movement in Jacksonville were Joseph C. King, William Holland, William Carter, Julius Willard, Axel Pierson, William Strawn, Samuel Adams, J. B. Turner, Timothy Chamberlain, and William H. Williams.[5]

In Tazewell County there were four stations or "depots." Agents were Joseph Mathew at Tremont, Uriah Crosby of Morton, who built the first house in that town in 1833, a Mr. Kean at Washington, and Absalom Dillon of Dillon. In Peoria there was a Mose Pettingill who was an agent. A well-known station in the same city was located on the corner of Jefferson and Liberty Streets, where the Jefferson Hotel now stands, but who the agent was is not well known. The number of fugitive slaves that are said to have passed through these stations averaged 25 or 30 a year.

On September 5, 1842 the *Peoria Daily Transport* reported:

The law caught the agent of the Underground Railway in Peoria today as he was aiding three Negro slaves, two women and a child, to escape to Canada. A magistrate sent to arrest the agent was assaulted but he gained possession of the slaves and placed them in jail in Knoxville to await the arrival of their owner. A crowd of a dozen Abolitionists who gathered at the jail and demanded the release of the prisoners was ignored.

In compliance with the fugitive slave law Sheriff Peter Franz of Knoxville advertised in the newspaper several days later that he was holding five runaway slaves, a mother and her four children for their master Daniel Robinson, Esq.[6]

On the banks of the Ohio River at Cairo stands today the Halliday Hotel, one of the largest and most important Underground Railroad stations in Illinois. Slaves were brought across the river in boats to the Illinois shore and were led through tunnels to cells located beneath the street adjoining the hotel. There were sixteen of these windowless cells constructed with cement walls, and fugitives were hidden in them until it was safe for them to be moved further north. Food and water were passed through a hole in the street. Later, these same cells were used by General Grant for the internment of military prisoners during the Civil War.[7]

Beecher Chapel of Knox College at Galesburg was once the old brick church. The original building was destroyed by wrecking in 1894. This old building may be set down in history as the guardian and protector of the Underground Railway in Knox County. Many were the times when fugitives were sheltered beneath its roof and in its belfry. Its walls echoed to the condemnation of slavery, the fugitive slave laws, the Missouri Compromise, and everything and everyone that approved of slavery.

Stories of exciting escapes and harrowing incidents in the operation of the "Railroad of Freedom" are numerous in Illinois history.

Several escaped slaves were cooped in a small room at the home of one of the Blazers in McDonough County. Among them was a child with whooping cough. At times the youngster was half-smothered under pillows as its mother sought to muffle its retching and hacking. Beyond the thin concealing wall of the room, hour after hour, sat "John Potter, a spy." He was visiting and eating with the Blazer family, hopefully waiting to ferret out one of their periodic, punishable secrets, unaware that he was so close to success. Fearful, the keen-eared Blazers, on the first sound of stifled whooping, scraped feet and chairs, coughed, talked, and laughed loudly. Thus they frustrated their cordial, unfriendly caller who must have been either uncommonly obtuse or afraid to press an inquiry.

Dr. Richard Eels was caught violating the law against aiding fugitive slaves while operating out of his home in Quincy. His case is an example of the hardships many of the Underground Railroad agents endured because of their efforts to help the cause of freedom. One evening in the early fall of 1837 a tall, rather lean black man swam across the Mississippi River from the Missouri shore and landed in Illinois at Quincy. A Negro Underground agent notified Dr. Eels of the fugitive's arrival and preparations were made to help the runaway to Canada. Dr. Eels and the fugitive headed for the next station in a good buggy with a fast horse, but they were pursued by the master of the slave and a searching party. One group of the slave hunters was about to overtake the agent and his passenger, so Dr. Eels ran his buggy close to a fence to enable the fugitive to escape and

CHAPTER FOUR

hide. Later the slave was captured and the doctor was arrested and jailed. His case was fought through all of the lower courts up to the Supreme Court of the United States. The costly trial and the succession of suits and counter-suits impoverished the physician and he lost even his home in Quincy. In 1846 he went to Chicago and later became the Liberty Party candidate for governor. The great notoriety of the Eels case brought many new supporters from all parts of the country to the anti-slavery crusade.[8]

In July 1841 three other citizens of Illinois were indicted, tried, and sentenced to twelve years in the penitentiary for their work on the Underground Railroad.

By the 1850s Chicago had earned the reputation of being a "nigger-loving" city. The *Shawneetown Gazette* remarked, "We of the South do not regard Chicago as belonging to Illinois. It is as perfectly a sink hole of abolition as Boston or Cincinnati." The *Cairo Weekly Times* added, "The [Chicagoans] are undoubtedly the most riotous people in the state. Mention nigger and slave catcher in the same breath and they are up in arms."[9]

The Chicago Common Council took action against the Fugitive Slave Act of 1850 by resolution and by refusing the cooperation of the city in complying with the provision in that law requiring the return of fugitives. Memorials were submitted to the people of the city who, in a public meeting, endorsed the action of the Council. Lemuel C. P. Freer, Isaac Arnold, and George Manierre were among those who served on the Committee of Resolutions. Spokesmen of this enthusiastic meeting were J. H. Collins, an eminent lawyer, Dr. C. V. Dyer, and E. C. Larned. Collins began his speech with the words:

> Honor, eternal honor, to the Chicago Common Council, Damnation eternal to those who voted for or dodged vote on the infamous slave bill. The men who voted for it are bad. The men who sneaked away to avoid their responsibilities to their constituency are both bad and base.

His speech was received with much applause and cheering.

In addition to these men who took a positive stand against slavery was Dr. David Nelson, a Virginian and a former slaveholder. He was ousted from the presidency of Marion College in Missouri because of his anti-slavery views. Later he founded an institute in Quincy, Illinois, where each Sunday he and his students would patrol the river in rowboats and by softly tapping stones together signal to slaves hiding in the woods. They took the fugitives 16 miles inland to a red barn which served as a "waiting room." Later, a pro-slavery mob burned Dr. Nelson's Institute to the ground.

The abolitionists of Illinois did not become politically conscious until 1840. In that year they polled one hundred and sixty votes for James G. Birney, the presidential candidate of the Liberty Party. This was accomplished without organization or any of the other adjuncts of political effort such as campaign funds, literature distribution, county and district headquarters, or a sympathetic press.

In each of the following years, 1841 and 1842, the vote of the anti-slavery group doubled. This was the result of better state and district organization of the Illinois Anti-Slavery Society. They campaigned on a platform adopted by the hundred and six delegates who formed their state convention. This platform was a declaration of opposition to slavery and the political Illinois Black Laws. The increasing political strength of the abolitionists was due in large part to their anti-slavery publications.

In 1848 the Liberty Party (the name under which the abolitionists campaigned) decided, for the sake of political expediency, to merge their forces with the Free Soil Party which nominated Martin Van Buren for president. But the Free Soilers were much too moderate to suit the abolitionists, and they lacked the zeal of the old Liberty group. The result was a slowing down and a serious dampening of that spirit that kept the abolitionists always ready for work and sacrifice for the anti-slavery cause. The charge of apathy to the "cause" is substantiated by an analysis of the vote which showed that while the anti-slavery presidential vote in Illinois was four times as large as heretofore, the well-known anti-slavery candidates on the state ticket failed to show even their former strength. At the same time the Whig candidates, running on the Free Soil platform, made appreciable gains over the same period. The abolitionists, who had formed the left wing of the Free Soil Party, decided not to continue the coalescence and set about reforming their own independent party.

However, in 1854 a new national party was organized and the first convention held in Wisconsin. This new political group was incorporated as the Republican Party. Its anti-slavery platform was acceptable to Whigs, Free Democrats, Free Soilers, and Abolitionists, and on the 30th of August the first Republican district organization was formed in Illinois. The latter group adopted a platform calling for the repeal of the Fugitive Slave Laws, restricting slavery to those states where it was already established, and "the prohibition of slavery in the Territories and opposition to the creation of more slave states."

The preliminary meeting for the formation of a state organization was held in Decatur in February 1856. In this year Abraham Lincoln was nominated by the Republican Party to run for the senate in opposition to the incumbent Stephen A. Douglas, noted for his opposition to governmental action in the restriction of slavery. The famous Lincoln-Douglas debates highlighted this contest; and although Lincoln was defeated, his platform ability was responsible in large part for his later election to the presidency and the final triumph of the anti-slavery forces.

Throughout the struggle of the anti-slavery groups, whether they fought for total abolition or mitigation of the slave evil, the press, or lack of it, was an important factor.

Each progressive group strove to maintain an official organ, not to mention additional weekly and monthly publications. Among those newspapers that played leading roles in anti-slavery agitation were *The Genius of Liberty*, *The Liberty Banner*, the *Western Citizen*, *The Free West*, and the *Edwardsville Spectator*. Preceding all these (with the exception of *The Spectator*) and ranking higher in importance was the *Alton Observer*, edited by Elijah P. Lovejoy, Illinois's first prominent martyr to the cause of freedom. All of the foregoing papers were published within the state and were responsible for much of the anti-slavery propaganda. But credit must also be given to papers from outside the state for sowing "the seed of abolition." Of these *The Liberator*, *The Emancipator*, and *The Philanthropist* were of major importance. The *Edwardsville Spectator*, however, first issued in 1824, appears to have been the first Illinois paper to seriously concern itself with the evils of slavery.

Accounts of the hairbreadth escapes of many of the fugitives and the adventures of some of the men who aided them are given by the Rev. John A. Ryan in his book *A Sketch of the Sturdy Abolitionist John Hossack*.

September 14, 1859, three slaves escaped from the plantation of Richard Phillips, near New Madrid, Missouri, and one, Jim Gray, was captured in Union County and imprisoned under the State law. This being irregular, a man named Root interested himself in behalf of the Negro and swore out a writ of Habeas Corpus before Judge J. D. Caton of the Supreme Court of Ottawa. [In Ottawa] . . . lived Dr. Gooding, William Carter, James and Joe Stout, H. L. and John Hossack, the last named the most conspicuous in courageous fidelity to the inner light, even to bonds and imprisonment.

The first slave he helped to freedom was sent to him by Ichabod Codding in 1844; he was then living on a farm at Hossack's Grove, 22 miles from Chicago. He hitched his team to a wagon and started with these slave entrusted to his care. On the way they passed a group of workmen on the canal, who cried derisively "the niggers," and ran menacingly towards them, but a good team made their escape possible, even though a shower of stones, which fortunately, did little damage, and another attack was made further along the canal. As they neared Chicago, they waited till dark, and then drove in, delivering the slaves to that grand philanthropist Dr. C. V. Dyer.

Another time while "nigger Jim," an escaped slave, was en-route to Ottawa, Hossack received an unpretentious telegram, signed "Haugh." It ran, "Meet friends at the depot." Hossack obeyed and as the train stopped a colored man was taken off and with him Phillips, his son, Constable Albright, and three notorious kidnappers Jones, Curtley, and McKinney.

The slave had a trace chain fastened to his legs, his arms pinioned, and rope around his neck and down between his legs the end held by a white man, the Negro walking in front.

Hossack's intense nature, quickened by the antagonism of years of conflict, challenged the brutality and asked, "What crime has he committed? Has he done anything but want to be free?" And to an impertinent answer he responded that, "No man could be taken through the streets of Ottawa while John Hossack lived." It is needless to say that the exhibit was made less offensively—and the Negro was quietly encouraged to look up and expect friends.

Following this episode mass meetings were called by both the anti-slavery and pro-slavery factions. The pro-slavery attempted to turn public opinion against the slave while the anti-faction sought to arouse sympathy for him. The case was tried by Judge Caton, who had discharged Lovejoy on the charge of harboring a fugitive. John Caton prefaced his decision with

a conciliatory appeal to the common respect for the Constitution, the laws, and the good name of the town. He then discharged the Negro from the custody of the State, deciding his arrest to have been illegal, but held him under writ issued by the United States Commissioner under the United States "Fugitive Slave Law" remanding him to the custody of the United States Marshal to be taken before Commissioner Conreau.

The Judge's pathetic appeal had for a time paralyzed the "Tigers," as the Abolitionists were called, and some heroic move must be made to bring concert of movement in the courtroom rather than a battle in the streets. James Stout, whose wit saved him on other occasions, moved "that the meeting resolve itself into a committee of the whole to carry out the law," meaning the higher law. Hossack said, "If you want your liberty, come." Dr. Stout separated the Negro from the marshal, and Hossack threw himself in the way of the officer. A lane lined the Abolitionists, made a path for the Negro, which closed behind him, but his way was blocked at the door; Dr. Hopkins, an athlete, who had been standing outside, caught the Negro by the shoulder and lifted him free of the crowd.

Someone cried, "The carriage," and not seeing the gate the Negro leaped the fence at a bound and plunged head first in and through the carriage, both extremities sticking out. Campbell leaped into carriage in company with two others, Peter Myers made a dash at the prancing horses, but Hossack sent him to the dust of the street, and the wild black team sped away leaving only a cloud of dust, and a bewildered, baffled, angry crowd surging about the scene of the well-executed escape.

The fugitive, Jim, made his escape to Canada via Chicago.

For this violation of the law, John Hossack, Dr. Joseph, and James Stout, with ten or fifteen others, were indicted. The first three, being the offenders, were taken to Chicago and lodged in jail; most of the others were released upon recognizance.

John Hossack was defended by six able lawyers—Hon. Isaac N. Arnold, Joseph Knox, B. C. Cook, J. V. Eustace, E. Leland, and Hon. E. C. Larned, but the Fugitive Slave Law and the machinery of justice was against him and he was convicted.

When asked by the court why sentence should not be passed, Hossack replied in a speech of 15,000 words that has become memorable. Hossack's eloquent words were printed again and again as the press through the land championed his cause.

John Wentworth, mayor of Chicago at that time and owner of the *Daily Democrat*, wrote, following the conviction:

Last night Hossack and his two companions in their bondage stood at the grated windows of their calls and beheld the long lines of men dressed in uniforms, bearing torches, marching to the sounds of martial music, and filling the cars of the night with acclamations of honor to Stephen A. Douglas.

On one side of the gates were men who had done only what Christ and his apostles would have done—what every man with a heart true to humanity must have done. On the other side a man, who at best, cares not whether slavery is voted up or down—cares not whether the laborer shall own his own sinews and the fruits of his own toil, or whether they shall be the property of another.

The Rev. John A. Ryan gives a picture of the situation as it stood the next year.

This was October 1860. What momentous issues were running to their culmination? In five short months Stephen A. Douglas, defeated candidate for the presidency, James Buchanan, retiring president, of whom it is only respectful to speak in pity, and Chief Justice Taney of Dred Scott fame, stood on the inaugural platform with Abraham Lincoln. An old school of political thought was passing, a new series of events had been ordered, in which only one of that group could have a part. Abraham Lincoln stood in the full light of the new day that had broken upon the nation. But Benjamin Lundy, Eastman, Carpenter, Codding, and John Hossak, like mountain peaks, high-lifted above the mists of doubt and fear, caught the first rays of the coming day.

The Negro himself, never a docile slave, struck out boldly for his freedom. There is a story in the *American Guide Series* (Macomb County) about one fugitive

. . . white as any Caucasian, his back lacerated . . . by scourgings . . . [who] was armed with a revolver and a bowie knife. [He] expressed . . . determination never to be taken back [into slavery] alive. Traveling across country he was . . . advised to [lie] down in the wagon [but he refused]. Doubtless thinking, with pardonable venom, of furtive and irresponsible ancestry, he declared that he was "white as any man" [and] would "exercise a white man's privilege."[10]

Well remembered by McDonough Underground crew was, a youthful slave, "Young Tom" who,

hands tied for a flogging, fled from bondage when his master went for a withe. He eluded capture by calling to pursuing hounds, which he had trained to fear him, lashing them severely with a rope he had wriggled from his hands, and sending the dogs to his would-be captors yelping in such pain that they would not track him further.

Best-known underground passenger to travel to the McDonough County route was "Charlie," who became a regular commuter, making frequent round trips from the North after his initial escape, in effort to liberate his wife and children. Several unsuccessful attempts to free his family, his own capture and re-escape left him undaunted. Once, near Macomb, he slashed his way free of two would-be-retrievers, one of them, wounded, told how he had fallen against a plowshare, perhaps thinking "it would not be of any credit . . . to acknowledge that (one) Negro was too much for two" white men. Charlie's family joined him in Canada after Emancipation.

A mulatto slave girl, who had traveled in Europe and received a good education, charmed a hostile, pro-slave white into aiding her and another girl to escape. The two girls being aided by an agent of the Underground Railway whose horses had tired, and the pro-slavers in the community planned to search his house that night. When one of them came over to the house where the fugitives were hiding, the mulattress conceived a plan. She dressed herself in a fine dress and accessories and acted as hostess to the pro-slavery minded neighbor of the Underground Railroad agent and so impressed him that when she excused herself and returned in the rags of slavery and begged his aid in escaping, he gladly consented to help. He later became a fervent abolitionist.[11]

The *Quincy Whig* covered an attempted escape and quaintly reported:

There was a tolerably pretty race in some of our streets yesterday morning between two handcuffed Negroes and sundry other folks, the history of which we will relate.

Two Negro men belonging to the Hon. Mr. Colock of South Carolina, whom he had brought from his home to wait upon himself and family in this city, made their escape from him two or three months ago, and after diligent search, were found, a few weeks since. . . .

The fugitives had been aided by the servants of R. S. Cox. The owner and the jailer handcuffed the two Negroes together and hired two hacks in order to take the runaways to a southern mail boat at the dock. The white men rode in one hack and the Negroes in the other. Somewhere along the way the owner stopped at a store to buy another pair of handcuffs and the Negroes took advantage of the opportunity. The article continues:

. . . In a moment the alarm was given, but never did darkies scamper so swiftly. Two gentlemen pursued, the hue and cry was raised and everybody joined in the race, though few knew why. The handcuffs were not observed and it was wondered by many how close the contest was. At length the younger of the principal pursuers was gaining close upon the fugitives, when one of them lifted a stone or brick bat and would have leveled him to the earth had not some other person done the like for him at that moment. In an instant the brace of darkies were surrounded, and what appeared strange was the co-incidence of several slave dealers being amongst the crowd assembled. One of these with true business tact, made some remark about getting rid of trouble, but Mr. Colock replied emphatically that $5,000 would not buy either of them. They were . . . returned to jail . . . (and) . . . one of the officers spoke to them of the folly of their efforts, when the fellow who had attempted to throw the stone remarked, "I have but once to die, and I would sooner take a chance for it now, than to go home."

In a tone of bewilderment the article ends, "What is strange is that during all this fellow's life, prior to his present adventurous career, he was one of the most timid and bidable servants that ever lived."

The *Cairo City Times* in February 1855 printed an article entitled "Runaways."

Last week two runaway Negroes got on the train, we believe at section 16, and went as far up as Sandoval. There they were discovered and brought back to Cairo, it seems that a miserable dog of an abolitionist persuaded them to run away, got all the money and clothes they had and then left them to shift for themselves. This is what we term aboli-tion philanthropy.

We were glad that these Negroes were arrested and brought back, for the reason that the impression has gone abroad that there is to be an underground railroad from this place to Chicago, and that Negroes will be induced to run away from Missouri and Kentucky. We assure our friends abroad that such fears are entirely without foundation. It is to the interest of the citizens of Cairo, as well as to the interest of the railroad company to pre-vent such occurrences, and the utmost vigilance will be exercised by them in this respect. There are no abolitionists here. This is a free state—the climate doesn't agree with them.

John Jones, George D. Baptiste, and John Johnson were among the free men of color who received fugitives and concealed and fed them at their own expense. Mrs. Emma Jane Atkinson, who came to Chicago with her husband in 1847, prevented the capture of a woman whose master was in hot pursuit. The fugitive had red hair; Mrs. Atkinson disguised her by blackening her hair with soot. The ruse worked.

The Negro population of Chicago was reputed to be always ready to "relieve a slave owner of his property." S. J. Currey relates an instance in *Chicago: Its History and Builders*.

On one occasion, a certain Mr. Hinch came to Chicago searching for some lost slaves. He displayed his handbills describing the three persons and openly inquired as to their whereabouts. His assistant was a trusted slave. This Negro trusty seized the opportu-nity while near the lake front to board a steamer and sailed for Canada. A message was communicated to Mr. Hinch that a coat of tar feathers was being prepared for him. He appealed to a local justice for protection. He was advised that immediate flight would be his safest course.

Chicagoans used other devices in aiding Negroes in their flight to freedom. An officer named Moses Johnson received a bill describing several slaves he had in custody which stated that the runaways were copper-colored. Johnson compared the slaves with a piece of copper and some copper wire and deciding the description did not fit, allowed them to go on their way.

　　　　　　　　　　　　　CHAPTER FOUR

There is also the case of a Negro mechanic who fled to Illinois and successfully practiced his trade. Some white mechanics, regarding him as a competitor, accused him of being an escaped slave. He was arrested and finally put on the auction block for slave. A curious crowd gathered, but it was difficult to get anyone to bid. Finally a white man who knew the prisoner purchased him for "twenty five cents." He said to his "slave": "I have bought you and now I'm your master. Here's enough money to get you to Canada. Those are the only orders I have for you."

The *Chicago Daily Journal* reports that on April 4, 1861, some two hundred Negroes, armed with clubs, knives, pistols, and shotguns and "other utensils of war," were so irritated because several fugitives had been returned South that they threatened to take them away from the police and lynch a certain Hayes for having participated in the act of discovery and removal. The same newspaper on February 7, 1848, states that one hundred lashes laid on the bare back of a newly arrived Negro who was suspected of spying upon fugitives who had come into the city.

After the passage of the Fugitive Slave Law, the *Journal* reported that "a large and enthusiastic meeting of colored citizens of Chicago convened . . . in the African M.E. Church on Wells Street for the purpose of adopting a measure in relation to their action." The Rev. George W. Johnson called the meeting to order. Dr. D. C. Murray was temporary chairman and Richard L. Cooper, secretary. Alex Smith and John Johnson were appointed vice-presidents. The meeting resolved:

to form ourselves into a society to be called the Liberty Association . . . and we are loudly called upon, as colored men, to consider what position is best for us to assume in the present emergency and having assumed our position, pledge ourselves that we will stand by each other, in case any attacks are made upon our liberties, to reduce us to a state of servitude, and as we should not wish to offer violence to any person unless driven to the extreme, in which case we are determined to defend ourselves at all hazards, even should it be to the shedding of human blood, and that doing this, we will appeal to the Supreme Judge of the Social World to support us in the Justice of our cause, humbly invoking his guidance and protection in our behalf. We who have tasted freedom are ready to exclaim in the language of the brave Patrick Henry, "Give us liberty or give us death."

5. Lincoln and the Negro

There are five versions of the first draft of this chapter and one version of the second draft, both with Robert Lucas's name on them. What appears below is the second draft with significant corrections in Arna Bontemps's handwriting that have been incorporated by the editor. All copies are contained in the IWP papers at the Harsh Research Collection.

Among the people who abhorred slavery were some who objected to having large numbers of Negroes for neighbors. Two types of anti-slavery sentiment arose, one based upon moral principles and the other upon economic principles. There were those who advocated abolition to elevate the Negro to citizenship and contrasted to them were those who objected to slavery merely because it was an economic evil. But still the Negroes came North and where the Quakers and abolitionists were giving them industrial training intense struggles between white and black labor ensued. These conflicts spread to other sections of the population and became more and more overt. The result was an effort to keep Negroes out altogether.

In Illinois in 1853 a drastic law prohibiting immigration was passed. Any person bringing a Negro into the state was subject to prosecution. The Negro, if he remained for more than ten days, was liable to a fine of fifty dollars, and if he was unable to pay he could be sold to any person paying the cost of the trial. The anti-Negro sentiment in Illinois was led by the *Chicago Times*, copperhead daily, while its bitter opponent, the *Chicago Tribune*, championed the cause of Negro citizenship. These two widely circulated newspapers molded public sentiment to a great extent. The *Chicago Times* for October 14, 1862, printed an article entitled, "Shall Illinois be Africanized?"

> Alarmed at the influence upon the public mind of the Negro immigration which, should it continue for a few months to come as briskly as it has been carried on during the six weeks past, would Africanize Illinois, the abolition engineers announce that it has been stopped. If it be true that it has been stopped, the stoppage is only temporary, and it will be resumed after the election.
>
> Let nobody be lulled into the impression that the stoppage is otherwise than temporary. It is an expedient for the time being. It is a trick. It is designed to quiet an alarmed people

and to defraud them of their votes. When the election shall have passed, the floodgates will again be opened and the black stream will again flow in greater volume than before.

The unsympathetic attitude toward the immigrant which was then prevalent is further shown by another item in the *Times*.

Sometime ago we mentioned the case of a certain landlady in this city, who it was alleged had taken into her family of boarders an inspiring Negro. The affair brought about an indignation meeting which resulted in about one-half of her boarders leaving the house. Since then we have been called upon by an individual who represents himself to the cause of all the stir, and who feels very much aggrieved because he was called a Negro. He claims to be a Spaniard, in proof whereof he produced to us a Spanish document which he offered to translate. We shall certainly give him the benefit of a correction and we are pleased to know that there is one less Negro in Chicago than we had supposed.

Opposing this attitude were sentiments reported in the press as far back as the 1830s, which, though in the minority, made themselves heard. The *Chicago Daily Journal* advocated the extension of all rights and privileges to Negroes. It also condemned the Black Code of Illinois.

We do not advocate an interference with the constitutional rights of our sister States, but here in our own State, we can act. We can remove the disabilities of the colored free man and declare that so far as our efforts are concerned every man that wears the image and likeness of his Maker should be treated as a man.

The *Daily Democratic Press*, established in 1852, was almost as favorable to the Negro as was the *Journal*. The *Western Citizen*, a special publication, was for the rights of all men, Negroes included. The *Inter Ocean*, which appeared in 1873, was most objective of all in its treatment of news about the Negro.

An outgrowth of the divided opinion on the problem of the freed Negro was the African colonization plan. It appealed more generally to the people of both the North and South than any other proposal. Those who advocated the plan proceeded on the theory that the Negro had no chance for racial development in this country. The failure of the large numbers of immigrants to adjust themselves to their new environment was cited as proof of this contention. In December 1816, partly as a result of the "actual colonization feats" of Paul Cuffe, a Negro, the American Colonization Society was organized in Washington. Henry Clay was chairman, and Francis Scott Key, Bishop William Meade, and John Randolph were some of the members. The organization chose a site in Africa and named it "Monrovia" in honor of the President of the United States. Illinois, along with other states of the union, sent emigrants to Africa. The citizens of Edwardsville and New Harmony gave financial aid to Negroes in the community who wished to go.

In trying to rouse the masses of white people from their indifference to colonization and to gain their support, the American Colonization Society disseminated propaganda against the Negro which was quite as vicious as that spread by the forces that were openly anti-Negro. The prejudice stirred up made the situation more difficult.

Abraham Lincoln was sympathetic toward the plan to colonize freed Negroes.[1] But while the program of the American Colonization Society was in harmony with certain sections of public sentiment in both the North and the South, it never quite gained the confidence of any large numbers of Negroes. It did not agitate for abolition; it sought only to colonize legally liberated slaves. Yet it failed, and the free Negroes, the very element which the movement intended to send from the country, increased in number from 434,495 in 1850 to 488,070 in 1860. Africa was no longer their home.

The movement to gain the right of franchise for the Negro was another attempt to solve the problem of these strangers at the gate. While the majority opinion was against extending this privilege to include Negroes, there were a few influential proponents of universal manhood suffrage. General Rawlins of Galena in 1867 advocated universal manhood suffrage all over the country. General Ulysses S. Grant came out for Negro suffrage upon the Negroes of the District of Columbia by Congressmen who refused to grant it in their own states. The *Chicago Tribune* took a liberal point of view and declared that the Negro had never failed to make good, whether as a slave, freedman or citizen. It suggested that the opposition of the Democrats was due to the refusal of the Negroes to vote their ticket.

President Lincoln, an astute politician, steered a course midway between the two points of view, as a political expedient. In a letter to his friend Speed he wrote,

> I think I am a Whig; but others say there are no Whigs, and that I am Abolitionist. . . . I now do no more than oppose the extension of slavery. I am not a Know Nothing, that is certain. How could I be? How can anyone who abhors the oppression of Negroes be in favor of degrading classes of white people? Our progress in degeneracy appears to me pretty rapid. As a nation we began by declaring that "all men are created equal." We now practically read it, "all men are created equal, except Negroes." When the Know Nothings get control, it will read "all men are created equal, except Negroes and foreigners and Catholics."

Yet on another occasion he is quoted as saying, "I am not, and never have been in favor of making voters or generals of Negroes. . . ." In one of his debates with Stephen A. Douglas, Lincoln declared, "there is no reason in the world why the Negro is not entitled to all the natural rights enumerated in the Declaration of Independence, the right to life, liberty and the pursuit of happiness. I hold that he is as much entitled to these as the white man. . . ."

In his historic conference with Frederick Douglass in 1863, Lincoln, in answer to the Negro leader's questions, said,

> That the employment of colored troops at all was a great gain to the colored people; that the measure could not have been successfully adopted at the beginning of the war; that the wisdom of making colored men soldiers was still doubted by some; that their enlistment was a serious offense to popular prejudice; that they ought to be willing to enter the service upon any condition; that the fact that they were not to receive the same pay as white soldiers seemed a necessary concession to smooth the way to their employment at all as soldiers, but that ultimately they would receive the same.

These quotations suggest that perhaps Lincoln's private opinions were more liberal than some of his political utterances would suggest. He had to be "all things to all men." Yet, had he been an outspoken abolitionist he would probably have been less hated and less maligned by the slave-holding South. Lincoln was dreaded because he held the threat of being able to unify groups that were at odds and thus to command a majority. He was not a radical. He does not on the basis of his public utterance belong with the group which included Coles, Lemen, John Brown, and Lovejoy.

However, a more intimate and revealing portrait of Abraham Lincoln is seen through the eyes of the men and women who knew him and served him; ordinary people who loved him as their country lawyer friend and later revered his memory as their martyred liberator. Lincoln's faith in the ability of the Negro to respond to education and opportunity can be traced to his contact with the Negroes he had known in Illinois.

Most remarkable was his friendship with William de Fleurville, "Billy the Barber," of Springfield.[2] Fleurville was born at Cap Haitien, Haiti, about 1806, and was brought to this country during that country's revolution of 1821–22. He was placed in St. Mary's Convent in Baltimore by his godmother, his only living relative. When she died, the Orphan's Court bound him out as a barber's apprentice. He learned the trade, but when he grew older he longed for a warmer climate, a more familiar language. He found them in the old French town of New Orleans; he found the French language spoken there; he found a French atmosphere—he also found slaves (and free Negroes who could produce no "free papers" suffering the same treatment) being beaten and bartered on the block. Fleurville spent some time in St. Louis, but there too the traffic in human beings nauseated the freeborn Haitian, and because he was not in a position to prove he was a free man, he journeyed up the Mississippi into Illinois.

Late one evening in the fall of 1831, just outside the village of New Salem, Fleurville met a tall, red-shirted woodsman carrying an axe on his shoulder. The two men engaged in conversation and walked to a little grocery store. When the tall man learned that Fleurville was a barber, nearly out of money and heading for Springfield, he introduced the young Negro to the people in his boarding house, Rutledge Tavern, and obtained him for an evening's work. In this way a close friendship was born between the two men, and although Fleurville resumed his journey to Springfield the next morning, the friends were later reunited when the tall woodsman went to the Capitol and hung out his shingle—A. Lincoln, Lawyer.

In 1832, one year after he arrived in Springfield, Fleurville opened the first and only barber shop in the town.

William de Fleurville was a successful business man; soon he began to acquire property. At one time he owned almost an entire city block in Springfield, 8th Street to 9th Street on Washington. His adviser and attorney in all legal matters was Abraham Lincoln. Lincoln himself had little to invest in real estate but his astuteness in handling Fleurville's deals attests to his ability in civil as well as criminal matters.

Springfield,
Feb. 10, 1860

Mr. W. Packard, Esq.

Dear Sir:

William Fleurville, a colored barber here, owns four lots in Bloomington, on which I have been paying the taxes for him several years, but which I forgot to, through under promise, when I was at Bloomington last will you please collect the ten dollars fee we spoke of, add enough of your own money, pay all the taxes due, and send me the receipt or receipts? If you will I shall be greatly obliged; and besides, will return you the money you advanced by the first mail. William Thomas, Larrimore and others there knowabout these lots.

Yours truly,
A. Lincoln

Billy the Barber's shop was the meeting place of many important personages. Prickett, of the firm Allin, Gridly and Prickett, gave Fleurville two lots located in an addition these realtors had laid off in Bloomington "in consideration that he shave him during his lifetime."

Billy the Barber, who also owned Springfield's first clothes cleaning establishment, advertised his shop with unique newspaper ads, some of them in poetry.

WILLIAM FLEURVILLE

Hair Dresser & Barber Shop & etc.

They who could get the public favor
Must learn to utter some palaver;
Sound their own fame—or at least show
They'll hold the trump while *others* blow.

Know fashions votaries of either sex,
I am "Habile" in this art complex
For such as wish (if such there be so silly)
Mere red or white (buy why "paint the lilly")

Powders and puffs, cosmetics too I'll find—
All things, indeed, not needed to adorn the mind.
To such as care for curls, for top knots seek—
Heads I can dress as a la Kemble or as a la Grecque.

I've skill for those, whose hair to curl or cut,
Even those who dash with a bald occiput—
And I never force one unnatural grin
On those who yield to *me* their chin;

While waiting too for the art tonsorial
You may see my specimens of the art pictorial
Perhaps too it is well to hint, that
I'm at last becoming a democrat.

Fleurville's prices were $15 (75¢ a month) for shaving one year, 15¢ for cutting men's and boys' hair, and 20¢ for cutting girls' hair.

Fleurville was also a musician, and with his flute or violin often provided the music for evening entertainments. Many churches, especially the Catholic Church, received large donations from Fleurville, some as high as $700 at one time, and his contributions helped to establish the first Christian Church, now the largest Protestant church in Springfield.

In 1831 Fleurville married Phoebe Rountree of Glasgow, Kentucky. They had five children, Samuel, Alseen, Sineet, Varneel, and William, who he educated and provided for very well.

Lincoln spent much of his spare time at Fleurville's shop where there was always a crowd. Here he could relax and swap yarns with "the boys." Now and then he picked up a client there. Lincoln's actions as president, recognizing the independence of Haiti and his offer of free passage for any Negro who wished to go and live there, was no doubt due to the fact that his interest in the land and its people was aroused by Fleurville's stirring accounts. In spite of the objections of the State Department Lincoln received a Haitian Minister with all the honors accorded any other diplomat.

When Lincoln left Springfield, Fleurville felt he had seen his friend for the last time. He was never the same after the violent death of his friend, and although he was invited to join the funeral party with Lincoln's oldest and best friends, he elected to walk in the funeral procession with the Negroes of Springfield. On April 13, 1868, Billy the Barber died after a brief but severe illness and was buried by the same undertakers that buried Tad and Mrs. Lincoln. His wife, Phoebe, was executrix of his estate, and after her death the property was divided equally among his children and Samuel Henry Fleurville, his adopted son.

With his death there passed a man of whom the *Illinois State Journal* said in an editorial, "Only two men in Springfield understood Lincoln, his law partner William H. Herndon, and his barber, William de Fleurville." Springfield lost an honored citizen, a successful businessman and a colorful character who was indeed a friend of A. Lincoln, Lawyer.

Black Nance was another Illinois Negro who found in Lincoln a friend. She came to Pekin, Illinois, in 1829 as an indentured servant to Major Nathan Cromwell. Although she was a hard and faithful worker, in 1838 Major Cromwell agreed to sell her to David Bailey. Illinois laws prohibited slavery, but Cromwell accepted a note from Bailey for about $400 in payment for Nance. The note specified, however, that remittance would not be made until Bailey furnished documentary proof of the woman's slavery. Nance worked six months for her new master, and then, declaring her indentured period over, maintained she was free. Bailey had no legal power to hold her, and she soon obtained a job in Pekin. Meanwhile, Major Cromwell died without providing the promised evidence. Nevertheless, Cromwell's heirs demanded payment, but Bailey held that since the consideration remained unfulfilled he was not obligated to pay. The case was taken to the Circuit Court of Tazewell County in 1839 and Judge William Thomas ruled against Bailey.[3]

At this point Bailey turned the case over to Lincoln who appealed the decision to the Supreme Court of Illinois. Lincoln carefully avoided mentioning the legality of slavery in Illinois, since official leniency was then being granted to slave holders. Instead he based his case solely upon the stipulation in the note that the documentary proof of Nance's slavery was to be produced. In 1840 the Court reversed the lower court's verdict and Nance remained a free woman.

During his life William Donigan was also described as a friend of Lincoln. A resident of Springfield for fifty years, Donigan became a victim of a riot there in 1908. One of the eight Negroes who led the horses that drew President Lincoln's hearse was Martin Lewis. For ten years he worked as a messenger for the *Inter Ocean*; earlier he had worked for other Chicago newspapers. Joseph W. Moore was another of this group of eight who took part in Lincoln's funeral.

In addition to these individuals who were personal friends of Lincoln there were the many Negroes of Springfield who lined the streets and cheered, even though they felt a strange premonition, as their President rode by on his way to the station to board the train for Washington. When he returned they gathered tearfully to watch the funeral procession, all who could afford it wearing a little black band of crepe. Some of them even went to Chicago to attend the ceremonies.

The Committee of 100 which accompanied the body from Chicago was composed of the most prominent citizens of that city. Among them was a man who had years before enlisted in the fight for freedom, the cause for which Lincoln had died. Like Fleurville he was a free man of color and an outstanding businessman. His name was John Jones.

6. John Brown's Friend

This chapter was found at Syracuse University in the papers of Arna Bontemps, who is responsible for its authorship. It is the only draft of the chapter known to exist.

One night in March 1856, a band of men moved furtively through the unlighted streets of Chicago. They stopped before a darkened house. The leader went to the door and rapped sharply, while the others waited in the shadows. Presently the door was opened, and a shaft of yellow lamplight fell on the man outside. He was tall and gaunt, with piercing eyes and a heavy beard. The man inside extended his hand.

"Osawatomie!"

John Brown grasped the hand of Allen Pinkerton, famous detective and later Abraham Lincoln's bodyguard. Pinkerton, an active abolitionist, took some of the men into his house and found places for the others. They were all John Brown's men. All, that is, except eleven escaped slaves headed for Canada. Pinkerton then took Brown to the home of a mutual friend with whom Brown had stayed on other occasions—that of John Jones, free Negro and leader in the fight for equal rights, as well as prominent business man.

The following day the detective raised nearly six hundred dollars at a "lawyer's meeting" to assist the party on its way to Canada. He also obtained a car on the Michigan Central Railroad from Col. O. G. Hammond, general superintendent, "who personally saw to it that the car was stocked with provisions and water." Late in the afternoon the party left for Detroit. Brown himself had departed on an earlier train to make sure of meeting Frederick Douglass there. This was the last time the two old friends were to meet. John Brown went on to Harper's Ferry and his death. John Jones went on to become one of Illinois' most eminent citizens and a leader of his people.

To the activities of Jones and his friends may be credited Chicago's reputation in the South as a "sink hole of abolitionism." Among the early abolitionists, John Jones's most intimate friend was L. C. Paine Freer. Freer once chased a slave-catcher all the way across the state. For many years he was a master in chancery as well as an ardent and energetic foe of the slaver. He was among the first to sign the master roll of Chicago's famous regiment of homeguards in 1861. He served a number of years as president of the board of directors of Rush Medical College, the board holding its annual meetings at his office.

Another abolitionist friend of Jones was Dr. C. V. Dyer, a Vermonter who came to Chicago in 1835 at the age of 27. He has been numbered with the hardy pioneers who raised the city from its native swamps, and became a successful spectator and business man as well as physician. In those fierce days, when the cause of freedom seemed desperate, to be known as an abolitionist was to be pointed as a "nigger thief" and a harborer of fugitives from slave states. Dyer placidly ignored the name-calling of his enemies, and pursued his labors for abolition. Coming to Chicago to practice medicine, he soon amassed a large fortune and was elected a county commissioner. In 1837 he presided at an indignation meeting called to protest the slaying of Lovejoy, and in 1840 he and Calvin DeWolf voted for the Liberty Candidate for governor, James G. Birney. However, the official returns credited the party with only one vote in Cook County.

Dr. Dyer was a force in the Illinois Anti-Slavery Society and led his Democratic friends into that organization. He was responsible for the establishment of the *Western Citizen* in Chicago in 1842, and was chief manager of the Underground Railroad in Chicago about 1839, putting many fugitives on boats for Canada. Dyer's home was generally known as the central depot, where he kept "passengers" until they could be sent across the lakes. No charge could be made that he *secreted* runaways: he openly harbored and protected them! He claimed the right to "employ" around his house such persons as he chose, regardless of color. On one occasion a "servant" in Dyer's house was caught by his Kentucky master, who carried him away to the Tremont House. The doctor followed them to the hostelry, accosted the slave-catcher in the barroom and broke his elegant rosewood cane over his head, then retired in triumph with his "servant." A Virginian at the hotel presented Dr. Dyer with a stout hickory cudgel with his compliments, while the doctor's Negro friends had the shattered cane repaired and mounted with gold. He carried it with him on important occasions for the remainder of his life.

According to Zebina Eastman, an abolitionist editor and friend of Dr. Dyer, the good doctor once paid off an officious constable who had made him the particular object of his attention, frequently serving warrants on him for one offense or another. When asked to name the new-born child of a Negro woman with whom the constable had been overly intimate, the doctor bestowed upon him the name of the officer.

In 1846 at the great Northwestern Liberty Convention in Chicago, Dyer was appointed chairman of the committee to get out a national liberty paper in Washington. This newspaper, the *National Era*, first published Harriet Beecher Stowe's *Uncle Tom's Cabin*. In 1848, Dr. Dyer was the Liberty Party's candidate for governor of Illinois. It has been said that he always maintained that the only bill of sale for a human being which he would recognize as valid would be one from the Almighty.

Such were Jones's friends, the men who created the Chicago atmosphere so abhorrent to slave-owners and their sympathizers. John Jones was born on a plantation in Green County, North Carolina, late in the year 1816 or early in 1817. His mother was a free mulatto, his father a free German named Bromfield who had settled in the eastern part of the state, not far from the tidewater. As the child of a free woman, Jones himself was born free, but his mother, fearing that his father or his father's relatives might attempt to enslave him, apprenticed him at an early age to a man named Sheppard, who agreed that the boy should be taught a trade.

CHAPTER SIX

John Jones. (Vivian G. Harsh Research Collection of
Afro-American History and Literature, Chicago Public
Library, Grace Mason Papers, Atkinson 104)

Sheppard subsequently moved to Tennessee, and there bound the lad over to a tailor named Clere, who lived near Memphis. After working with Clere for a time, John was hired out by his employer to a Memphis tailor. It was in Memphis that the young man met and fell in love with Mary Richardson, daughter of a Negro blacksmith. Because they were dissatisfied with the lot of free Negroes in Tennessee, the Richardsons left the state and moved to Alton, Illinois, while John Jones stayed behind to finish his term of service.

Meanwhile, Jones was having troubles of his own. He learned that the heirs of Clere, whose death was expected momentarily, were planning to claim Jones as their property, and sell him. There were hints that he would be sent to Texas, then an independent republic, from which escape was almost impossible.

Jones immediately secured permission from his employer to return to North Carolina to obtain the evidence of his free state. It is said that he galloped his horse throughout the long, tedious journey, returning in a few days with the proof of his status.

In January 1838, Jones filed a petition addressed to Judge V. D. Barry, Judge of the Eleventh Judicial District, then holding court in Somerville. The petition set forth that John Jones, alias John Bromfield (for he was sometimes called by his father's name, sometimes by his mother's) was born free about the middle of November 1816; that he was brought from North Carolina to Tennessee by an individual to whom he was bound as an apprentice until he should be twenty-one; that by sale or otherwise he had passed among several bonds until by purchase he came to that of Richard Clere, a tailor, for the purpose of learning the trade; that Clere hired him out during the years of 1836 and 1837 and thereby forfeited all right to the custody of his person although he (Clere) had obtained articles of indentureship from the County Court of Rayette County until the petitioner was twenty-one years of age; that the petitioner was represented in the said articles as being, in 1831, nine years of age, which statement was false; that he was born free, was of lawful age, and that he was illegally, under said usage and false entry made in said County Court, held as a slave—hired out, offered for sale, or put to such kind of labor as might suit the convenience or pecuniary interest of said Clere. Therefore, he prayed for a writ of *habeas corpus* that he might be brought into court and discharged.

On January 16, 1938, the court, after considering Jones's petition, ordered his release from the service and custody of Clere, and he ruled that he be allowed to go at liberty. The discharge papers which Jones obtained that day are in the Chicago Public Library, presented by him.

The North Carolina background of John Jones has been credited with having much to do with the energetic action he took to secure his freedom. The state at that time was relatively liberal, and until 1835 free men of color were permitted to vote. Even after the Reconstruction period, a Negro or two sat at every session of the state House of Representatives for more than a score of years. The state paid homage to Frederick Douglass by adjourning its House of Representatives upon his death.

Jones remained in Memphis about three years, working and saving his money. Then he struck out for Alton, arriving there in 1841 with $100. He resumed his courting of Mary Richardson, and soon married her.[1] He was precipitated into the midst of seething events—the formation of anti-slavery societies, the organization of the Liberty Party, the spread of abolitionist sentiment, and increased activity of the Underground Railroad. Alton was the starting point of one branch of the road which ran northwest to Jacksonville, through LaSalle and Ottawa, and then to Chicago. Evidently the militantly anti-slavery atmosphere of Chicago, terminus of all the Illinois routes, attracted John Jones, for with his young wife and infant daughter, Lavinia, he headed northward. With his freedom papers in his pocket, he had little to fear from his suspicious fellow travelers during the seven-day journey by stage and canal.

The Jones family arrived in Chicago on March 11, 1845, and rented a one-room cottage at the northwest corner of Madison and Wells Streets. Jones also rented a small shop standing where the Clark Street entrance of the Sherman House is now situated. He set himself up as a tailor, and solicited the patronage of the townspeople. If, as reported, the abolitionists financed his business, he must have recommended himself to them before coming to Chicago. The Jones's capital of $3.50 was used to furnish the home, and, by pawning his watch, Jones procured two stoves, one for the home and one for the shop. From O. G. Hanson, a Negro grocer, the family secured credit to the amount of $2.00.

CHAPTER SIX

In the days that followed Jones was kept busy with work and study and unremitting activity on behalf of the less fortunate of his race. He learned to read and write, mainly by his own efforts. L. C. Paine Freer is supposed to have done all Jones's writing for him for a while after the tailor settled in Chicago. But when the kindly lawyer-businessman suggested that Jones acquire the art for himself, he studied and learned not only to write but to read with great proficiency. Through all the succeeding years, Jones and the courtly white abolitionist were associated in the most friendly intimacy, brought together constantly by their mutual interest in the defeat of slavery in all its forms. Freer survived John Jones by thirteen years, and lies buried in Graceland Cemetery, Chicago, a few yards from his old friend.

Jones was by far the most prominent man among Chicago's 958 Negroes in 1860. His business prospered from the first, his voice and pen were powerful in the struggle for emancipation, and his home was a popular rendezvous for abolitionists, black and white. It was also a station for the Underground Railroad through which many a fugitive passed on his way to Canada. As a moving spirit in the ranks of the progressives, he came to know all the outstanding anti-slavery men in the city. With George de Baptiste (also a free man of color and brother of the famous editor and churchman, Richard), Jones was foremost in the business of arranging safe "depots" in Negro homes and churches for slaves on their way to the border.

During the 1850s, Chicago Negro abolitionists participated in several of the state, regional and national anti-slavery conventions, invited in Negro lecturers (including Frederick Douglass), and raised funds to purchase freedom papers for runaways who could not be liberated otherwise. The Fugitive Slave Law, like previous oppressive measures and actions, only succeeded in arousing still greater determination among the freedom-loving citizens of the Northwest, and resulted in the Underground Railroad reaching its highest point of passenger service during the decade. By this time the Free Soil Party was the organization embracing the growing numbers opposed to slavery. The Chicago Free Soil League was formed August 21, 1848, and the following day a mass meeting of nearly 2,000 people was held in Public Square. A week later at Ottawa a "State Convention of Free Democracy" was held. The name "Liberty Party" was no longer heard; a Free Soil newspaper was started in Chicago, where large and enthusiastic meetings were held almost every night.

The new party, though it dissolved as soon as the unsuccessful contest of 1848 was over and left the anti-slavery movement without leadership, had aroused tremendous opposition in central and northern Illinois to the further extension of slavery, shared alike by Free Soilers, Whigs and northern Democrats. In fact, each party claimed the principle as its own, for in January 1849, all three parties joined in passing a resolution in the general assembly approving the Wilmot Proviso.

However, the work of Jones, de Baptiste, their people and the white friends of the Negroes was only beginning. In 1853 the state legislature passed a law prohibiting the immigration of free blacks to the state. The abolitionists sprang into arms, the Negroes themselves taking a prominent part in the campaign to nullify the measure, which had been maneuvered through in comparative quiet. John Jones was in the forefront of the fight, as were Freer and Dyer. Frederick Douglass was also active in Illinois, lecturing during October 1853 for the Free Democratic Party (the label of antislavery forces at that time.) The ex-slave orator and Jones worked closely together, and in subsequent years Douglass, when in Chicago, often stayed at Jones's home. Jones himself made speeches up and down the state, lobbied, and gave generously of his income, which had grown considerably since 1845. An incident which occurred during one trip to Wisconsin is told by Douglass in his autobiography:

> On an anti-slavery tour through the West, in company with H. Ford, Douglass . . . and my old friend John Jones . . . we stopped at a hotel in Janesville, and were seated by ourselves to take our meals. Thus seated I took occasion to say, loud and for the crowd to hear me, that I had just been out to the stable and had made a great discovery. Asked by Mr. Jones what my discovery was, I said that I saw there, black horses and white horses eating from the same trough in peace, from which I inferred that the horses of Janesville were more civilized than its people. The crowd saw the hit, and broke out into a good-natured laugh. We were afterwards entertained at the same table with other guests.

It is apparent that Negro leaders, determined to win their fight, had plenty of work to do in the decade preceding the conflict that was to settle finally the slavery questions. Yet John Jones, with all his activity, conducted his business so well that he was able to save enough money to purchase property, including the location at 119 Dearborn Street (now occupied by the Boston Store) where he set up a large merchant tailoring establishment, patronized by Chicago "society." Jones's displays in 1850 and 1851 in the *Chicago Daily Journal* and the *Chicago Directory* reveal that he understood that advertising pays.

> JOHN JONES. Clothes, Dresses, Repairer. Gentlemen, I take this method of informing you that I may be found at all business hours at my shop, 119 Dearborn Street, East side between Washington and Madison, ready and willing to do all work in my line that you may think proper to favor me with, in the best manner possible. I have all kinds of trimming for repairing gentlemen's clothes. Bring on your clothes gents, and have them cleaned and repaired. . . . Remember, garments left with me are in responsible hands. I am permanently located at 119 Dearborn Street.
>
> Yours for work, J. Jones.

H. O. Wagoner, another Negro citizen, stands out prominently in connection with John Brown's last visit to Chicago, and is credited by one biographer with sheltering and feeding the eleven Missouri slaves during their short stay in the city. Born in Maryland in 1816, Wagoner came to Galena in 1835, learned to set type, and for several years worked as a compositor on the *Northwest Gazette and Galena Advertiser*, a tri-weekly "big paper." He left Galena to go to Canada, but after three years came back to settle in Chicago, where he worked for the *Western Citizen*. He had been engaged in anti-slavery and Underground Railroad since 1835. Quitting the printing trade in 1847, he engaged in several kinds of business and in 1858 owned a milling business valued at $7,000. Acquainted with Frederick Douglass as well as John Brown, Wagoner was invited in a letter from Brown to participate in the secret meeting attended by Douglass. Duty to his family impelled Wagoner to decline the invitation, and in 1860, his fortune impaired by two fires and other vicissitudes, he moved to Denver. In 1861, however, he was back in Chicago, where he joined the Union Army as assistant to a sutler. Later, when Negroes were admitted to the armed forces, he secured a commission to recruit for the 29th Illinois colored troops, and was later engaged by Governor Yates to recruit refugees and contrabands in Mississippi.

After the war, Wagoner returned to Denver where he subsequently held various state and county jobs. He served on the committee to welcome General Grant on his last visit to Denver. In 1887 he is said to have possessed property worth $20,000.

The year 1856 saw the birth of the Republican Party at the state anti-Nebraska convention in Bloomington, where Abraham Lincoln raised his voice firmly against further extension of slavery. Although the new party—composed of Abolitionists, Free Democrats and Democrats—was unsuccessful in national elections, many victories were recorded in congressional districts and for state offices. In the same year a convention of the Negro citizens of Illinois met at Springfield to petition for the rights of Negroes in the state. John Jones was one of the most active participants. The following year another legal victory was scored when it was decided that the laws of other states recognizing slavery could not affect the condition of a fugitive in Illinois. The defeat of pro-slavery forces in Kansas further cheered the abolitionists, while the Dred Scott decision spurred them to increased effort which expressed itself concretely in the building and strengthening of the Republican Party.

The catastrophe predicted by John Brown descended on the nation in 1861. The Negroes of Illinois, not admitted as combatants until two years later, aided the northern forces in every way they could. Only a few months before the firing on Sumter, Negroes meeting in Chicago in February 1861 had been urged to gain their liberties "by the use of their strong right arms." It was not until 1863 that these willing arms were utilized, but they then gave a good account of themselves despite the discrimination practiced against them even in uniform.

During the first years of the war the situation of Negroes in Illinois was not noticeably improved, but with the defeat of the Democratic majority in the state elections of 1864 the state rallied to the support of the national administration. In that year, too, John Jones published his forceful pamphlet, *The Black Laws of Illinois and a Few Reasons Why They Should Be Repealed*. The booklet was an eloquent plea for full citizenship rights for the Negro, reviewed by his condition under the Black Laws, and urged that they be abolished. Jones addressed one adroit argument to the law makers, most of whom were men of property:

> You ought to, and must, repeal those Black Laws for the sake of your own interest, to mention no higher motives. As matters now stand, you cannot prove by us that this or that man (if white) ran into a valuable wagon load of merchandise and destroyed it; therefore you are liable to lose hundreds of dollars any day if your wagons are driven by colored men, and you know they are, in great numbers.

Jones was referring to the inability of the Negro to testify in court against a white man under the existing Black Laws. He noted that he was paying taxes on $30,000, yet could not vote, and reminded the legislature that the Negro inhabitants of Illinois numbered 7,000. He predicted that petitions requesting repeal of the Black Laws would be presented to them "this winter from all parts of your state . . . signed by your most respected and financial citizens." During the debate on repeal, early in 1865, state senator Green expressed his willingness to vote for a special act enfranchising Jones himself, for whom he entertained respect and kind feelings, but not the entire race.

John Jones made speeches, wrote articles, circulated his pamphlet, and led in the organization of Negro and white groups in every part of the state. He lobbied throughout the session of the legislature considering the proposed repeal. The progress made was indicated by the *Chicago Tribune* in its issue of January 16, 1865:

> Petitions continue to pour into the General Assembly from all parts of the State for the repeal of the infamous Black Laws and of other laws upon our statute books placing disabilities upon the black race in the State. The petitions are signed by a large number of every leading man of the State, very many of whom, four years ago, voted against their being stricken from the statute books of Illinois. These Black Laws will be repealed—there is no doubt of it.

The final vote came late in January. The Senate voted 13 to 10 for repeal; the House 49 to 30. The Negroes and all other friends of liberty were overjoyed. Church bells rang; many glasses were lifted in toasts to the success of the campaign. John Jones lighted the fuse of the cannon which at the state capitol boomed the blast of victory.

The movement for liberation of the Negroes did not halt with the repeal of the Black Laws. The legislature went on to endorse the federal amendments granting suffrage to the race, which in Illinois alone had put 1,811 soldiers in the field to preserve the Union. Illinois was the first state to ratify the 13th Amendment, one day after Congress voted to submit the resolution to the legislatures of the various states. The 14th and 15th Amendments were passed with equal speed. As the 1860s closed, the basic laws of the land declared the Negro free and equal. It was the culmination of a long and bitter struggle by Negroes and their white co-workers.

In 1866, a committee headed by Frederick Douglass and including John Jones as a member called on President Andrew Johnson to urge suffrage for freedmen. The committee feared that Johnson, who was said to favor colonizing the race abroad, would not favor the expansion of progressive legislation for Negro rights unless he was subjected to pressure.

John Jones's fortune had grown steadily since his arrival in Chicago. In 1871, just before the big fire, it was estimated at close to $100,000. He was by far the most affluent Negro in Illinois and one of the wealthiest in the country. The great fire reduced the sum of his possessions to some extent, but still left him a rich man.

Shortly after the fire, Jones was proposed for the Cook County Board of Commissioners, short term, by a non-partisan "Fireproof" ticket and was elected practically without opposition. He was re-elected for a three-year term in 1872, but in 1875 he was defeated along with some other commissioners for alleged participation in a conspiracy. When the case came to trial, however, Jones was acquitted, there being no evidence against him.[2] He was one of the first of his race in the North to win an elective office of importance, and the first in Illinois. Following his defeat in 1875, another colored county commissioner was not elected again for nearly twenty years. During his incumbency, Jones was active in the fight against separate schools for the children of the two races, an issue not settled by law until 1874. He donated the site of Jones School, named in his honor, at Harrison Street and Plymouth Court.

In 1875, the Jones family celebrated three decades in Chicago by a reception in their home lasting all night and day. Many noted men and women of both races came to pay their respects to Illinois's leading colored citizen, and the affair also took on the nature of a celebration of the passage of the Federal Civil Rights Act, signed by President Grant a few days before.

CHAPTER SIX

The *Chicago Tribune* wrote of the occasion:

During all of yesterday afternoon there was a continuous throng of visitors at his (Jones's) house by those acquaintances of his earlier years who have stood by him for the past thirty years. In the evening the house was brilliantly illuminated and given over to the younger friends. The parlors presented a beautiful picture. The mirrors were entwined with wreaths of evergreen; the mantels were ornamented with camellias, roses and orange blossoms. Over the center doors of the double parlors was the beautiful inscription, artistically worked in wax, "God Bless Our Home"; over the engraving of the signing of the emancipation proclamation in the rear parlor was the ever endearing motto, "Home Sweet Home." On the right of the front room against the snow white walls were the engravings of Mr. Lincoln, John Brown, and President Grant, surrounded by those of Mr. Chase, Mr. Sumner, Horace Greeley and Joshua R. Giddings. On the left were the large oil paintings of the host and his family.

The *Tribune* also revealed that Jones had provided for the occasion:

. . . a splendid quadrille orchestra, and while he with his happy humor entertained his gentlemen friends, his daughter Mrs. Lee, with ease and grace, marshaled the young people who desired to enter into the terpsichorean pleasures and, under the spirited strains of inspiring music, they tripped the light fantastic until a late hour in the night.

John Jones reviewed the times through which he had passed since entering the state and said it hardly seemed possible that ten years earlier no black or mulatto person was permitted to reside in Illinois unless he had a certificate of freedom, and then only by giving bond with approved security that he would not become a charge upon the community in which he resided. Unless a Negro could produce the necessary document, he would be hunted down and driven from the free state of Illinois. Jones expressed his opinion that the Black Laws had been in large part responsible for the extreme poverty of most of Illinois's Negro citizens. Until their repeal, the black man had no standing in the state: he could not accumulate property and had no inducement to be either industrious or saving. Now, Jones said, the laws were gone but their effects lingered on.

The few remaining years of the life of Illinois's most honored colored citizen were spent quietly in the house on Ray Street, where Frederick Douglass, when in town, and other friends of Jones's more vigorous years were hospitably received and entertained. Since his name was not mentioned in newspaper accounts, it is improbable that Douglass attended the thirty year anniversary party, but Jones had in all probability heard the great orator lecture on John Brown in Farewell Hall a few weeks earlier and entertained him at his home.[3] Possibly the last time Jones and Douglass reminisced about the stirring past and discussed the current problems of the race was in February 1877 when Douglass delivered an address in Chicago. The following month he assumed his duties as United States Marshal for the District of Columbia. Jones continued his liberal donations to charitable institutions and other philanthropies; during his lifetime much of his large fortune went to aid those not so fortunately situated. He died May 27, 1879, after a long illness. The next day his body was carried to Graceland Cemetery, followed by "an immense concourse of friends and well-known citizens."

John Jones was buried in the family plot at the cemetery, in the heart of the great wooded burial park just west of the chapel. The lot is marked by a tall, weather-beaten dark granite tombstone, bearing the names of Jones and members of his family resting beneath. A short distance to the south stands the tomb of John's old friend, Freer. To the north is the grave of Timothy Webster who, with Allen Pinkerton and Kate Warn, safely guarded President Lincoln from assassination at his first inaugural. A little farther north rises the imposing monument marking the grave of Pinkerton, who "sympathized with, protected and defended slaves, and labored earnestly for their freedom." The celebrated detective survived Jones, his friend and co-worker in the cause of freedom, by five years.

John Jones's life bridged two eras. Born in the midst of slavery, he lived to see the Negro raised to legal citizenship. His role in shaping and influencing events during this turbulent period was a significant one.

CHAPTER SIX

7. Leave a Summer Land Behind

There are two drafts of this chapter, both written by Jack Conroy, which can be found in the IWP papers at the Harsh Research Collection. The version that appears here is a significantly shorter draft with comments made in Conroy's handwriting that have been incorporated by the editor.

> When came these dusky legions,
> Braving the wintry wind?
> For our snow-bound, icy regions
> These fleeing, dusky legions
> Leave a summer land behind.
>
> They fly from the land that bore them,
> As the Hebrews fled from Nile;
> From the heavy burthens o'er them;
> From the unpaid tasks before them;
> From a serfdom base and vile.
> —"Exode" by W. H. Stillwell in the
>   *Chicago Inter Ocean*, March 12, 1881

As the spring of 1880 wore on, Democratic Senator Daniel W. Voorhees of Indiana, chairman of the committee investigating the phenomenal Negro exodus from the South, announced that he was weary and dissatisfied with the whole proceedings. The *Chicago Evening Journal*, viewing Voorhees's labors with a critical eye, remarked that the Senator's disgust was understandable, since much of the testimony had repudiated the Democrats' contention that the Republicans had sponsored the importation of southern Negroes into Indiana and other northern states in order to gain political control. "He first turned pale," the *Evening Journal* pursued, "when Mr. Adams from Louisiana was subjected to the inquisitorial interrogation point. Adams recited the circumstances of outrage after outrage of which he knew personally, in which colored people had been murdered, wounded, whipped, and some of them hanged, including people of both sexes, and even children. . . . It was this evidence that made Voorhees sick, and he has since lost all interest in the investigation." One witness had said succinctly: "If I vote the Republican ticket, I wakes up next morning in a graveyard."

Politicians, sociologists, planters, and many others aired their opinions before the committee. Andrew Currie, mayor of Shreveport, Louisiana, testified that most of the colored people of the South, with the exception of a disgruntled minority numbering less than one per cent of the total population, were contented and prosperous, and there was no cause for an industrious and law-abiding Negro to emigrate. "Here," sarcastically remarked the *Chicago Evening Journal*, "was a witness after Dan Voorhees's own heart."

Less agreeable to the "Tall Sycamore of Wabash" was the evidence offered by a slight, light colored and gray haired yet agile Negro who was clasped under his arm a fat scrapbook filled with newspaper clippings. He vigorously denied that the Republicans were responsible for the exodus, particularly not the one to Kansas. "I am the Moses of the colored exodus," he boasted, "the whole cause of the Kansas migration."

The scrapbook, the contents of which he was unable to read, recorded the exploits of Benjamin "Pap" Singleton, born a slave in Nashville in 1809, trained as a carpenter and cabinet maker. He had been "sold a dozen times" and each time ran away and made his way back to Tennessee. Then he felt the call of free soil. After three abortive attempts, he reached Canada by the way of the Underground Railroad. With emancipation, he returned to Tennessee and disillusionment. Unregenerated rebels, smarting from their recent chastisement, had regained power with the Democratic Party, and the Negroes— regarded by many as the cause of it all—were punished in innumerable ways. Jailed for petty offenses, they often found themselves farmed out to the same planters who had formerly owned them and their status, if anything, worse than under legal slavery. They were denied the educational and social facilities they had been led to expect, harried by the Ku Klux Klan, and discriminated against in general. Contract farming kept the Negro tenants hopelessly in debt from one year to the next, since they were obliged to procure all their supplies from a commissary maintained by the planter, who chalked up goods at exorbitant prices, such as 60 cents a pound for bacon, 30 cents a pound for sugar, and 35 cents a yard for calico.

Singleton believed that the Negroes would fare better if they segregated themselves in some new territory. He formed the Tennessee Real Estate and Homestead Association for the purpose of settling ex-slaves on subsistence farms, but Tennessee land proved to be too high and the atmosphere there too charged with racial prejudice. "The whites had the lands and the sense an' the blacks had nothin' but their freedom, an' it was jest like a dream to them," he said later.[1]

After he had discarded Tennessee as unsuited for Negro colonization, "Pap," after considerable investigation, decided upon Kansas, state of "Old John Brown." The idea of emigration to Kansas fired the imaginations of even the most illiterate peasants of the Deep South, for the song "John Brown's Body" and the story of the fiery old abolitionist's martyrdom at Harpers' Ferry were known to all. "Pap" formed various colonies in Kansas and boasted late in life that he had led 82,000 Negroes out of the South. This figure, however, is generally believed to be greatly exaggerated.

The people of Kansas, though for the most part favorably disposed toward the "exodusters," could not easily accommodate all of them, and "Pap" Singleton began to think of other refuges. He visited Indiana and Illinois, not only to spy out the land for colonization sites, but to campaign for Garfield, Republican candidate for president. Indiana had already received a number of Negro pilgrims, and little response was aroused in Illinois. "Pap" later credited himself with winning the two states for Garfield, maintaining that he had visited Democratic chieftains and threatened to lead 250,000 Negroes up from the South unless Indiana and Illinois were found in the Republican column. The alarmed Democrats, "Pap" claimed, stayed away from the polls, and the desired result was obtained.

A few rebuffs were not enough to daunt a seasoned warrior like "Pap." He had been spreading the gospel of emigration for more than a decade, spending $600 of his own money for circulars which he had managed to dispatch to every remote corner of the South. Some were carried abroad by itinerant preachers; railroad porters and steamboat hands distributed others. Unlettered though he was, "Pap" was a forceful and pungent speaker and often voiced his distrust of and contempt for "educated" Negroes and politicians. Following his fruitless visit to Illinois, he told a St. Louis *Post-Dispatch* reporter (who evidently embellished the recital somewhat):

> The colored race is ignorant and altogether too simple, and invests too much confidence in Professor Tom Cat, or some of the imported slippery chaps from Washington, Oberlin, Chicago or scores of places whence are sent intriguing reverends, deputy doorkeepers, military darkeys or teachers, to go often around the corrals and see that not an appearance of a hole exists through which the captives within can escape or even see through.

As time went on the colonization movement took on the character of a fraternal order or a religious body. Numerous local branches conducted meetings, and especially composed songs such as "The Land That Gives Birth to Freedom" added fervor to the proceedings. Churches, halls, and schoolhouses echoed to these words:

> We have held meetings to ourselves to see if we can't plan some way to live.
>> "Marching along, yes, we are marching along.
>> To Kansas City we are bound."
> We have Mr. Singleton for our president. He will go on before us and lead
>> us through.
>> Marching along, etc.
> For Tennessee is a hard slavery state, and we find no friends in that country.
>> Marching along, etc.
> We want peaceful homes and quiet firesides; no one to disturb us or turn us out.
>> Marching along, etc.

The settlers of Nicodemus, one of the several colonies planted by Singleton, sang:

> Nicodemus was a slave of African birth,
> And was bought for a bag full of gold,
>
> He was reckoned a part of the salt of the earth,
> But he died years ago, very old.
>
> Chorus:
>> Good time coming, good time coming,
>> Long, long time on the way;
>> Run and tell Elijah to hurry up Pomp
>> To meet us under the cottonwood tree,

In the great Solomon Valley,
At the first break of day.

"Pap" Singleton's good news about "Sunny Kansas" spread farther and had more effect than he had anticipated. Emigrants not only from Tennessee and Kentucky but from the uttermost recesses of the South swarmed to the state, many of them pausing en route in Cairo, East St. Louis, or other points in Illinois. Though both Negroes and whites tried to keep them moving on to their original destination and formed organizations for that purpose, not a few tarried or made their way to Chicago. The plight of destitute "exodusters" on the bleak Kansas plains soon excited national concern. Though he was constrained to advise Negroes to stay away from Kansas (both Kansas and southern papers, each for reasons of their own, gladly giving prominence to his counsels) "Pap" still joined issue with opponents of the migration such as Frederick Douglass and Ex-Lieutenant Governor P. B. S. Pinchback of Louisiana.

Until he died in Topeka in 1892 at the age of 83, "Pap" grappled persistently with the problem of race colonization. He had considered Liberia and Canada, and—intrigued by a newspaper's suggestion that the Island of Cyprus might be a likely spot—headed thither to investigate, but ran out of funds when he reached St. Louis. He organized the United Transatlantic Society, designed to foster colonization in Africa and elsewhere, but during its several years of existence the society accomplished little more than to pass resolutions favoring "Negro national existence."

The Democratic majority of the senate exodus committee, in submitting its final report, stuck to its original contention that the mass migration of southern Negroes had been engineered by the Republicans for political reasons and by the railroads in search of passenger business. Senator William Windom submitted a Republican minority report, and the *Chicago Evening Journal* observed:

> It is barely possible that the Democrats may learn one lesson from this investigation, and that is that the North is still a Canaan for the oppressed and outraged race, and that, unless they should be accorded better treatment by the Democratic ex-slaveholders, the cotton, corn and rice fields of the South will in time become dreary and unfruitful wastes.

Southerners who had wished merely to chastise the Negroes and "put them in their places" began to realize that the *Journal*'s lugubrious prophecy indeed might be fulfilled. Not only plantations but skilled artisans were heading north in an increasing tide. Both force and persuasion were employed to convince the Negro that the South was his true homeland, and even Negro leaders such as Frederick Douglass were alarmed at the prospect. Douglass maintained that the Negro had been too impatient, that he had not given Democracy enough time to reassert itself in the South, and that he should stand by to assist in the process. The *Chicago Inter Ocean* inquired of Mr. Douglass why he had not remained in the South as an example for his persecuted race.

Professor Richard T. Greener, Dean of the Law School of Howard University and later National Secretary of the Emigration Aid Society, said to a reporter from the *New York Herald*:

> Before the War the Negroes in the Southern cities and larger towns were the carpenters, bricklayers, stonemasons, and, in some instances, manufacturers on a small scale. Send

him (the Negro) West, and open up to him the life of an agricultural laborer, a small farmer, a worker in the mines or on the great lines of railways, and you will soon find out what a steady, cheerful worker he is, and what a peaceful citizen and desirable acquisition he will become. . . . In pursuit of freedom years ago we endured the cold of Canada, the rigor of the Northwest and of New England. I see no reason to fear the effect of any climate on our race now. . . .

The Port Gibson (Mississippi) *Reveille* demanded that all those who encouraged the exodus should be "dealt with as are other incendiaries outside the law," while the Wilmington (North Carolina) *Star* reproached the northern backers of the movement for unwarranted meddling. The Macon (Georgia) *Sun*, though deprecating faintly the flogging of a woman by Mississippi vigilantes searching for Prince Johnson, charged with "trying to induce the Negroes to emigrate to Kansas," added: "If the Negro Johnson is guilty as charged, of trying to influence Negroes to abandon their crops, he should be drummed out of the country."

Those friends of the exodus who placed reliance upon more direct measures were not passive. General Thomas W. Conway, an active advocate of migration, announced in St. Louis that if steamboat companies, influenced by southern interests, continued to refuse transportation to Negroes desiring to leave the South, he and his associates planned to charter a boat and to proceed down stream, using firearms if necessary, to deliver out of the land of bondage those waiting at river ports. Several hundred Negroes were reported to have armed themselves near Caroline and Leoti landings, Mississippi, and proclaimed their determination to confiscate the first passing steamboat and to compel it to carry them as far as possible toward Kansas.

More articulate Negroes throughout the nation seriously and collectively considered the migration and its effects. Henry Adams, a Union Army veteran, was instrumental in calling the New Orleans Colored Convention in April 1879. Adams, like "Pap" Singleton, was illiterate, but a man of energy, courage and ability. Returning to Louisiana in 1869 with an honorable discharge from the Union Army, he was deeply agitated by the treatment being accorded his "liberated" people. His first step was to organize a committee whose members, at one time totaling five hundred, journeyed to every locality in the South to survey conditions. The New Orleans convention met to deliberate over these findings, and adopted a resolution recommending "organized and systematic emigration."

The National Colored Convention assembled in Nashville the next month, and resolved: ". . . That it is the sense of this conference that migration of colored people to those States and Territories where they can enjoy all the rights which are guaranteed by the laws and Constitution of the United States, and enforced by the executive departments of such States and Territories, should be encouraged, and we ask of the Congress of the United States an appropriation of $500,000 to aid in the removal of our people from the South."

Though the Southern press and public officials professed to see in the exodus a temporary and not extremely significant phenomenon, planters and civic leaders organized a convention of both white and Negro citizens which met in Vicksburg, Mississippi, May 6, 1879, to discuss means of regulating the migration. The more militant delegates of both races were out-talked and out-voted by a controlling element of Southerners intent upon keeping on hand a stable and docile reservoir of labor. Little more than speech-making and a few timid resolutions purporting to reaffirm certain rights of the colored citizenry resulted from the conclave.

Even before the Civil War, Negroes—most of them fugitive slaves—had been making their way to Oklahoma, where they were in general made welcome by the Indians. Oklahoma continued to be a favorite destination for migrants, and the 1879 exodus brought a marked increase in numbers. As in Kansas, stories of suffering among newcomers were current. As late as April 28, 1891, travelers arriving from the Indian Territory spoke of Negroes from Oklahoma begging for something to eat. One newspaper account, referring to the Oklahoma migrants, said:

> Their condition is said to be something pathetic. They were deluded into coming to Oklahoma last fall in large numbers, and have found none of the good things promised them—no work, no government rations, nothing to afford them a chance to earn an honest penny. Instead, they soon saw starvation at their door and are trying to make their way back to their former homes in Tennessee, Georgia, Mississippi and other Southern states.[2]

In Oklahoma, and in a lesser degree in Kansas, there has been considerable intermarriage between Negroes and Indians. Oklahoma Negroes with Indian tribal designations as surnames are not uncommon today—for example, "Kiowa."

The migration of Negroes to Illinois during the great exodus was more or less overshadowed by the spectacular events in Kansas and the spotlight thrown upon Indiana by the Senate exodus committee. Nevertheless, a considerable number of "exodusters" entered the state and remained there. Some of them had deliberately abandoned their original intention of settling in Kansas, others had been left stranded and were obliged to make the best of it.

On April 1, 1876, three years before the exodus had reached its peak, the East St. Louis *Gazette* noted:

> The colored immigrants, numbering fifty souls, who were left by the emigrant agents from Kansas in East St. Louis are still here, and no doubt are suffering for the want of food and proper housing. Mr. J. B. Lovingston has notified the city authorities that, in his opinion, the Cairo short line railroad company, who brought them here, can be compelled to take them back to Cairo. Some of the colored people wish to go back to Nashville, Tennessee.[3]

The Negro population of Illinois nearly quadrupled in the decade 1860–70, rising from 7,628 to 28,762. From 1870, when the exodus began to get under way, until 1880, when it reached its summit, the numbers increased to slightly less than 50,000. During the fifty years from 1850 to the turn of the century, the Negro population of Chicago (often designated as a "hotbed of abolition" by antebellum Southern newspapers) multiplied nearly one hundred times, 323 to 30,150, while the colored population of the entire state had multiplied only fifteen times. Nevertheless, not a few prosperous Chicago Negroes were loath to welcome uncouth and impoverished newcomers from the Deep South, anticipating damage to their own status in the community. At the same time, newspapers in the agricultural districts printed invitations to Negro farm hands. As early as January 8, 1862, the *Chicago Times* observed editorially:

> We are not advocates of the introduction of Negroes into Illinois, but if they introduced themselves, or if the abolitionists introduce them, we are advocates of compelling them to labor. The most productive labor to which they can be put is that of cultivating cotton and tobacco wherever in the state those products can be cultivated. From all we can learn

CHAPTER SEVEN

in that regard, cotton cannot be successfully cultivated except with cheaper labor than white labor, and the only cheaper labor is Negro labor.

The *Quincy Herald* (October 8, 1862) reported a typical incident of the troublous war days when unconfirmed rumors and alarms spread space. News reached Quincy that "The Knights of the Black Circle" were bringing in a steamboat load of Negro contrabands from Cairo. Irish and German working men, frequently competitors of the Negro laborers, gathered on the bank to repel the invasion. "Fortunately, no steamship loaded with Negroes arrived," concluded the *Herald*, "or we apprehend there would have been trouble in landing the cargo."

Though he was forced to bear the brunt of indignation, the Negro in almost every instance was a helpless pawn. The Peoria *Daily Transcript* noted (February 23, 1863):

It is said that Negroes are being carried through southern Illinois from Missouri to Kentucky. They are slaves sent out of Missouri to save them to continued servitude, the exodus being caused by the contemplated emancipation measures of the state. Isn't it a little singular that we don't hear a lisp from the copperheads about this "invasion" of Illinois—this bringing of Negroes within our state limits? If those blacks were only passing through Illinois as fugitives, intent on finding a refuge and freedom in Canada, every hound of a copperhead in Illinois would be on their tracks.

Soon after "Pap" Singleton's circulars and persuasion had begun to work efficiently, harrowing reports of suffering among the Kansas "exodusters" reached Illinois. "Would it not be wise," the *Chicago Inter Ocean* suggested (April 11, 1879), "for the churches of Chicago to move in the benevolent work of aiding the colored people who are fleeing from Southern oppression to homes upon our Western prairies?"

The churches responded. The Chicago branch of the Emigration Aid Society arranged meetings and collected funds. An ex-slave, described as the prototype of Harriet Beecher Stowe's Uncle Tom, lectured at the Emmanuel M.E. church for the benefit of a Kansas "exoduster" colony. The *Chicago Inter Ocean* solicited contributions, and listed among other donations $19.17 from the churches of Peotone, Illinois; John Deere, Moline manufacturer of agricultural implements, sent $100 and expressed his fear that the exodus might be "carried too far" and thus "result to the disadvantage of all concerned"; Col. Robert Ingersoll offered $1,000 to the fund. Railroad and express companies agreed to transport relief supplies free of charge.

The despairing cry of the "exodusters" reached across the sea. Sympathizers in London sent 50,000 pounds of goods, $8,000 in cash, and the *London Times* commented:

What is most to be desired is the quiet but firm interposition of the central government to insure the Negro protection and equal justice. The time seems to have come when this task must be undertaken more boldly; and it is to be hoped no political exigencies will interfere with so plain a duty.

Elizabeth L. Comstock, Quaker Missionary, wrote from Kansas to a Chicago friend:

The latest horrible case of mutilation and amputation that we have heard on good authority is this: A respectable colored man came here last spring, worked hard, earned enough to buy a lot, build a cottage, and save $100, and then returned to bring his wife and family.

The brutal Regulators seized him, cut off both his hands, and threw them into his wife's lap, saying, "Now go to Kansas to work."

Mr. Comstock also praised the "good work" being done in Kansas by Sojourner Truth.

P. D. Armour, packer, went out to see for himself, and on his return told of a visit to Wyandotte, Kansas.

> Here, he said, is where the refugees are crowded to the number of nearly 2,000 . . . They cannot exist there, for the town is poor. The churches, private houses, and halls were full, and many of them had to lie out on the docks over Sunday without shelter . . . I talked with a great many of them and was surprised at their intelligence. I asked them where they thought they were going. They said only North to escape persecution . . . They had no idea that they were going to a land of plenty or idleness, but simply to a land of freedom.

So impressed was Mr. Armour that within a short time he had collected $1,200 from the following firms: Armour, Dole & Co., $200; Armour & Co., $200; Field, Leiter & Co, $200; N. K. Fairbank & Co., $100; and a number of others, $50 each.

Though assistance poured in from everywhere, the situation of the "exodusters" remained critical for some time to come. On January 15, 1880, the *Chicago Inter Ocean* inquired:

> Will the government and the people of the land let them (the "exodusters") starve to death in the sight of plenty, even while the press is teeming with the denunciations of England's inhumanity toward the Irish poor? If they were white men, nobody doubts that aid would soon reach them. New Orleans had five deaths from yellow fever, and the demands were so pressing that the $10,000 was at once placed at the disposal of her authorities by telegraph from Washington. We poured money and luxuries into stricken Memphis, and even the government found the constitutional right to appropriate $800,000 for a Board of Health, with tents and government rations. It is true there was some difference. A man dying with yellow fever might infect his neighbor, but a "frozen nigger" is only out of the way.

Despite such demands for federal assistance and the actual introduction of several bills in Congress, relief remained on a voluntary basis, much of it marshaled by the Emigration Aid Society and distributed by the Kansas Freedman's Relief Association. Horatio N. Rust of Chicago was particularly active in soliciting and forwarding money, food, and clothing. To him John Brown Jr. wrote (April 20, 1879) from Put-in-Bay Island, Ohio:

> . . . . It seems to me of importance that these people be aided to reach lands. And be helped until they can help themselves on lands that are opened to homestead entry, or that can be obtained cheaply. . . .
>
> The Northwest can furnish lands of the richest soil in quantity sufficient to meet any probable demand for many years to come—can receive the entire Negro population of the South, if these should leave, and yet have room for the poor whites of the South, and the emigrating poverty-stricken people of the Old World; and all these would find their homes too widely separated if each family were located on every quarter-section of the really desirable land found here. . . .
>
> If we would gladly see the higher qualities of the American citizens of African descent brought out in this country or in any other, we must, in my humble opinion, help him to get a foothold where lands are good and cheap, in a latitude where the climate, instead

of inviting to habits of indolence and lack of thought, will on the other hand be an ever-present stimulus, urging him and his children on to better conditions and a higher life.[4]

Gradually the Kansas "exodusters" receded from public scrutiny. Some of them gave up and emigrated elsewhere, others struggled and gained a foothold, some even achieved a measure of prosperity.

The *Chicago Evening Journal* reported (February 7, 1881) on the status of the immigrants to Indiana discussed a year earlier by the senate exodus committee:

> The thousands of Negroes who went to Indiana a year ago from North Carolina and Virginia have been absorbed, and are distributed all over the state. The resident Negroes supplied them with clothing, furnished them temporarily with food, and found homes for them in the farming districts. Their labor was needed, and they are doing well. They are paying their own way, except in the matter of public taxes, and they are pretty well contented, though the cold weather is a trial to them. They thrive on the "hog and hominy" that is the staple diet of the rural districts, and add to it many luxuries in the form of nuts, rabbits, coons and squirrels. They are social in their habits, and fond alike of dancing, religious meetings and political discussions. Their children go to school, and the next generation will have larger wants, and also a larger capacity for supplying them.

Unfortunately, the cheery sequel to migration pictured by the *Evening Journal* was not a universal one. Not only the new arrivals but citizens who had been respected and valued members of their communities for years learned that the spirit of intolerance and prejudice did not die so easily. On the night of August 14, 1908, Mrs. Mabel Hallam, a white woman of Springfield, reported that she had been dragged from her bed and raped by a Negro. George Richardson, a Negro who had been working nearby, was charged with the crime and identified by Mrs. Hallam as her assailant. Richardson, born in the city and described as "a man above the ordinary intelligence," who talked "with great sincerity and earnestness," contradicted Mrs. Hallam's story. A mob, clamoring for the blood of Richardson as well as that of a Negro tramp and drug addict jailed shortly before for fatally wounding a white man, besieged the jail. When members of the mob realized that the prisoners had been spirited away, they vented their fury upon the restaurant and automobile of Harry Loper, white, who apparently had assisted the authorities. The shop of Scott Burton, Negro barber, was demolished and the proprietor dragged by the neck through the streets, mutilated, and burned. The torch was applied to a block of Negro hovels, while more practical rioters seized the opportunity to loot a number of stores.[5]

Rioting continued throughout the next day and night, and the Springfield correspondent of the *Chicago Inter Ocean* reported:

> A whole brigade of militia is powerless to cope with the mob of mad men, who have turned this peaceful little city into a veritable hell. Fiction contains no scenes to rival this inferno. The mob's thirst for blood knows no bounds.

On the second day, William Donegan, 84, known as a friend of Lincoln, a substantial citizen who had lived in Springfield for fifty years and owned half the block upon which his house stood, was set upon and hanged from a tree across the street from his home. Militiamen intervened and cut the aged man down, but he died the next day. Mr. Donegan's only offense seems to have been that for thirty years he had been married to a white woman, a circumstance which previously had not excited animosity. On the night before, Eugene W. Chafin, Prohibition Party candidate for president of the United States, had interrupted a stump speech to befriend an intended victim by pretending that he had a revolver in his pocket and allowing the fugitive to escape while he held the mob at bay.

When the tumult subsided, it was found that in addition to the two Negroes lynched and the four white men killed during the disorders, seventy-nine persons had been injured and several blocks of Negro homes razed by fire. The City of Springfield, under a state law holding the community responsible for destruction of property resulting from mob violence, was burdened with judgments totaling $39,000. Hundreds of Negroes fled the city during and immediately after the riot, and the *Chicago Tribune* estimated that within two days between 150 and 200 had made their way to Chicago. "Those who had friends here promptly sought their homes, where they were warmly welcomed," the *Tribune* continued. "Others crowded into colored lodging houses or left on early trains for other places." It was estimated that 200 refugees from Springfield had arrived in St. Louis, Missouri, while twice that number had escaped to Alton and East St. Louis. Southern newspapers took advantage of the opportunity to invite the Negroes to return to the more congenial atmosphere of the South, but few heeded the summons.

A grand jury investigation completely exonerated Richardson when Mrs. Hallam confessed that her assailant had been a white man whose identity she refused to divulge. Ironically enough, the victims of lynching and arson were further penalized for their enforced participation in the riot. The Springfield correspondent of the *Chicago Tribune* noted:

> Forty or fifty Negroes now in the employ of the various city departments will be discharged. Many of them are faithful, honest men of long service, but they themselves realize that they may revive the mob rule if they remain, especially on the police force.

Though both mob victims were industrious, well-behaved and respected property owners, apologists for the rioters chose to attribute the disorders to the presence of Negro criminal elements and the immunity granted them by vote-seeking politicians. The *Chicago Tribune*, with a long-standing reputation as a defender of Negro rights, marked a departure from its established custom in commenting on the affair. Under the caption "Dens of Sin Wiped Out" the paper expressed its conviction that "one good thing" had resulted from the burning of the Negro district, and went on:

> The houses of this black belt were hovels. Whites and blacks lived together. Children ran through the streets of this miserable settlement who knew not their parents. Their hair indicated one race and their fair skin the other.
>
> The worst grades of whiskey and gin were served in the barrooms. Drug stores thrived on the sale of cocaine and other drugs. Along Cocaine Alley huts of deepest squalor were the hiding places of the drug fiends. Sandwiched in between these dens were white resorts where the lowest forms of depravity existed.

CHAPTER SEVEN

8. Rising

The most recent draft of this chapter was found in the Jack Conroy papers at the Newberry Library. It was written by Arna Bontemps. There is an earlier draft at Syracuse University. In the IWP papers, there is also an important thirteen-page essay titled "Americanization" by Fenton Johnson dated April 15, 1940, that was used as source material. Much of the background for this chapter was collected by education scholar Alonzo Bowling, who worked on an IWP study titled "History of Negro Education in Illinois."

In January 1825 the Illinois Legislature enacted a law providing that common schools be established in each county of the state. These schools were to be open and free to every class of white citizens between the ages of five and twenty-one years, but it was not until the year 1841 that consideration was given Negroes. In that year colored citizens in one Illinois community were allowed to withdraw assessments they had paid into the school fund. Negroes were counted, however, when time came to apportion the State funds, and by this maneuver the township in question received more than an equal share. If the free people of color had been allowed to use their share of the State fund, plus what they had personally contributed, they might have been able to make progress in the education of their young. But this did not happen.

In the city of Chicago no discrimination was shown against Negro children in the public schools till 1863, but in February of that year the following provision was written into the city charter:

> It shall be the duty of the common Council to provide one or more schools for the instruction of Negro and Mulatto children, to be kept in a separate building to be provided for that purpose, at which colored pupils between the ages of five and twenty-one years old, residing in every school District in said city, shall be allowed to attend; hereafter it shall not be lawful for such pupils to attend any public school in the city of Chicago at which white children are taught, after a school for the instruction of Negro and Mulatto children has been provided.

Accordingly, the council passed an order establishing a separate school for colored children. The school was conducted in a rented building at the corner of Taylor Street and Fourth Avenue. It continued until April 1865, when the segregation provision was repealed by the City Council—thanks to a gradual softening of the harsh feeling which had formerly prevailed.

Meanwhile, Miss Rebecca Elliott came to Peoria from Cincinnati in 1860 and opened a school for Negro children. Miss Elliott's school was conducted in a small frame building erected by a family of Turners. Located on Washington Street, it became the first "Turner Hall" in Peoria. In 1859 the building was sold to the Negro population, moved to Chestnut Street, and used for many years as both church and schoolhouse. The old building finally became a tenement house.

The next school for Negro children of Peoria was located at the head of Franklin Street on a piece of ground claimed by the city. This school house was built about the time of the Civil War and was taught by a Miss Duffer, a woman of Irish extraction, remembered as a good teacher. Miss Duffer returned to Ireland eventually, and her duties were taken over by Miss Houghtailing. Later generations of Peoria children have attended mixed public schools.

The school issue provoked warm skirmishes in Alexander County of Southern Illinois. In 1850 the American Mission Society sent a Miss McBride, a white woman, to the district to teach Negro children. Because of her manifest talents white citizens tried to secure Miss McBride's services for their own school. When she refused to desert the colored people, she was run out of the community and R. C. Tolford, another white teacher, was sent to replace her. But Mr. Tolford was a stern man, and many colored parents refused to send their children to him. Instead, they encouraged a Mr. Kennedy to open a private school, and those whose parents could afford to pay one dollar a month for tuition were enrolled.

The first public school for Negroes in Cairo was started in 1853 in a one-room frame building. The teacher in charge was a terror. He is remembered for his quaint habit of bumping the students' heads against a wall when they were disorderly. Young girls were afraid to attend his school. During his administration the enrollment dropped considerably. Eventually the over-zealous pedagogue was asked to resign.

During this colorful era several churches in Alexander County conducted daily classes in which readin', writin' and 'rithmetic were taught. One of the largest of these church schools was the one in the Hardshell Baptist Church on Tenth and Cedar Street, Cairo, where the Reverend Shire served both as pastor and teacher. The church was later burned by white people of the neighborhood.

Meanwhile white schools of Alexander County were making rapid progress; they erected many new buildings, including a beautiful new high school. Observing that the Negroes had no high school, Rev. Nelson Ricks, founder of one of the oldest churches in Cairo, led a throng of Negroes down Washington Avenue to the white high school and endeavored to force the teachers to enroll the colored children. This effort failed to get the children into the school, but it did bring action on the part of the Board of Education. J. C. Lewis was brought to the city to start a high school for the Negro children of Alexander County.[1]

It is enough to say of Lewis that he was a production of Berea College—a school founded in Kentucky by the crusading southern abolitionist John G. Fee, a school in which the brotherhood of man was both taught and practiced, a school open to colored and white alike. Under the guidance of J. C. Lewis, Alexander County opened its first high school

CHAPTER EIGHT

for Negroes; all private schools promptly closed. In 1868 State Superintendent of Public Instruction Newton Bateman announced that,

> all the school-going children of the state, without distinction shall be entitled to share in such provisions of the free school system. Nor need anyone be scared by the phantom of the blended colors in the same school room. The question of co-attendance, or separate school is an entirely separate and distinct one, and may safely be left to be determined by the respective districts and communities to suit themselves. In many places there will be one school for all, and in others there will be separate schools. That is a matter of but little importance, and one which need not and cannot be regulated by legislation. Only drive the spirit of caste from its intrenchments [*sic*] in the Statues, giving equal educational rights under the law, and the consequences will take care of themselves.

It was easier said than done. In October 1870 School District No. 2 of Champaign held a meeting to consider the question of admitting colored children into the public schools. One of the colored speakers vainly protested the right of the meeting to take a vote to determine whether Negro children should be excluded from the schools.

> The law knows no color, and there is no use talking, we are determined to insist upon our rights. . . .

The vote, cast by ballot, resulted in excluding colored children from the school by eighty-five to five. After this action the colored people met and passed a series of resolutions to the effect that they *did* have a right to send their children to the public schools:

> . . . our children were turned away from the school in District No. 2 on the third day of October, A.D. 1870, and as believe this to be an act in defiance of the constitutional laws of this State, we resolve to test this act before the Circuit Court of the District, and if justice cannot be obtained there, we will then appeal to the Supreme Court of the United States.

In October 1870 the *Champaign Gazette* editorialized on "The Colored People and the Public Schools":

> . . . when the question they raise is viewed abstractly, we cannot help but say: the child of every American citizen has an undoubted right to the benefits of the free school system. Our colored citizens demand and abstract rights, but in point of fact, would their children not be better off, less hampered and embarrassed by invidious comparisons in a school established for their special benefit, than in the public school room? If prompted by the welfare of their children, they will admit the point; if guided by common sense, they will accept the offer of the direction and lend every assistance to the establishment of a first-class school for the colored children of the city.
>
> Some of them may say: "This would be a reflection upon us." Not a bit of it. No more than the building up here of churches for colored people is a reflection upon the whites; no more than a Methodist Church is a reflection upon the Baptists; no more than a German school is a reflection upon the Irish; no more than an institution for the education of men exclusively is a reflection upon the honor of the young women. . . . [2]

The State constitution of 1870 provided for a free school system whereby "all children of this State shall receive a good common school education." According to the *Chicago*

Daily Inter Ocean, this actually intensified the mixed school controversy. Superintendent Bateman gave his opinion in a biennial report for 1869–70:

> Prejudice and caste will be the two antagonistic forces involved. The great majority of the colored scholastic population remaining unprovided for, the legislature enacted a law requiring boards of education to provide a sufficient number of schools and equal education for all youth in the State. It soon transpired that school boards persistently misconstrued this law, and often virtually excluded Negroes by rendering them inferior. Sometimes they openly refused the blacks admittance to the schools under any circumstances.

In his report for 1873 the Superintendent recommended "more adequate penalties, and surer and speedier modes of redress" in such cases. A law of 1874 prohibited all school officers from excluding either directly or indirectly any child from the public schools on account of color. The penalty fixed was a fine

> not less than $5 nor more than $100 for each offense. A penalty of $25 is provided for any person who shall by threats, menace, or intimidation prevent any colored child entitled to attend a public school in the State from attendance.[3]

The *Chicago Evening American*, while relating the provisions of the bill, stated that the Negroes had this right before, in theory, that in many districts it was actually enjoyed,

> . . . but wherever the old Democratic prejudice of color is dominant, the children of Negroes have been excluded from public schools, especially in Southern Illinois.

The *Daily Inter-Ocean* summarized the controversy on April 6, 1874. It held that the Illinois Constitutional Convention, a predominately Democratic body, might have excluded from the Constitution any provision repugnant to its ideas:

> . . . yet this Democratic party not only failed to insist upon separate schools for white and blacks, but it adopted a section on education which is susceptible of only one construction, namely, providing for mixed schools. It is as follows: "The General Assembly shall provide a thorough and efficient system of schools, whereby all children of this State shall receive a good common school education."

During debate on the above section it was moved that the word *children* be stricken out and the word *persons* be inserted in its stead. To the *Daily Inter Ocean* this seemed significant.

> . . . In the entire discussion on this motion it was assumed and not disputed that the substitution of "persons" for "children" would *admit African Adults to the common schools*, and it was argued that it would be a hardship on counties where there was a large number of adult colored persons to compel such counties to educate them. So the Democratic Constitutional Convention in 1870 agreed to the proposition of mixed schools without a protest or a dissenting voice!

Yet,

> . . . between the time of the promulgation of the Constitution and the assembling of the last State Legislature, four years had elapsed, and during this lapse of time, the Democratic party renewed its ancient horror and hate of Negro equality.

Colored children had been excluded from the common schools of the Southern section of the State; it became necessary to provide for their education. Accordingly the following law was enacted:

"That all directors of schools, boards of education, or other school officers whose duty it now is, or may hereafter be, to provide in their respective jurisdictions schools for the education of all children between the ages of 6 and 21 years, are prohibited from excluding, directly or indirectly, any such schools on account of color of such child."

The re-action was terrific.

The bill for this act was assailed by Democrats with all the bitterness of ante-bellum times. The proposition to elevate colored children by educating them was regarded as equivalent to a proposition to degrade white children. The Senate, on the day of the debate, presented a scene of turbulence where cautious Democrats tried in vain to save from disgraceful utterances the hot heads of the party. It was not, however, pretended that the proposed act would be in violation of the Constitution, and so the fact that the Democrats of Illinois had completely changed front on the question of mixed schools since 1870, became apparent. . . . [4]

In 1874 the State Superintendent of Public Instruction reported that many teachers had taken colored children out of their grades and classes and placed them in a separate room under separate teachers, thus depriving them of the benefits to be derived from the graded system. Where the number of Negro children was small, they were likely to be excluded altogether, by one means or another.

In October 1873, the School Board of Springfield decided to strike the word "white" from the regulations of the city schools and to admit all children, without regard to color or previous condition, into the city schools. The *Chicago Tribune* applauded warmly.

. . . It is probable that some children will be withdrawn by the over-nice, but they will no doubt be returned again when the parents find out in what age we are living.

In September 1882, the question of mixed public schools exploded in East St. Louis. A riot occurred; schools were closed there, and there were many fights.[5]

Meanwhile in Quincy the Board of Education divided the city into eight districts and set apart one school for Negroes only. The case was tested in court, where it was ruled that the Board of Education had no power to establish separate schools. In Upper Alton a similar test was made in 1886, when a resolution excluding all Negro children from white elementary schools was passed by the board. Again the court ruled that such an exclusion of children on account of color was illegal.

The school of law on 1889 stated that any school officer who excluded a child on account of color should be fined on conviction. In spite of such laws, separate schools were erected and colored children were turned away from the white schools. The *Daily Inter Ocean* took the political position that in many of the Southern countries:

. . . There is still too much of the old Adam of Kentucky, Virginia, North Carolina, and Tennessee among the original settlers and their descendants to admit colored children to the same schools with the whites. Galesburg, Rockford, Chicago and others of the most refined communities of the entire state distribute these children through all the ward schools and high schools. Nobody seems to notice or object to this, any more than a highborn southern lady objects to sitting along-side of her colored driver in the family carry-all, or to allow a wench as black as the coal-scuttle to nurse her lily white babe. . . . Neither teacher nor pupils can have the ambition to accomplish what they would were not the impregnable wall of caste erected directly across the common school section and the highway of public education.[6]

A further reflection of the mixed schools controversy was the strike of pupils at the Farron School in November 1902; the trouble was attributed to attacks by the white children on colored.[7]

In 1895 Ferdinand L. Barnett, editor of the *Conservator*, denounced the efforts of Rev. J. P. Odean to collect funds for the erection of a manual training school for colored children of Chicago. He feared that the plan would help to establish a color line in the city.

Later in the same year a delegation of Chicago colored citizens protested to the assistant superintendent of schools against actions by the principal of the Coleman school which they charged were an attempt to draw the color line.

However, in the autumn of 1901 just the type of school that editor Barnett had disapproved of and Rev. Odean had advocated was opened at Eldorado, eight miles north of Harrisburg. Another clergyman, Rev. J. D. Alston secured $1,600 through subscriptions for the erection of a trades school "on the same principle as the Booker Washington school in the South." The school, sponsored by the Cuba Libre Industrial Association, was directed by the churchman who had made possible the enterprise.

Northwestern University was the scene of a tempest following its refusal to admit two colored girls to the dormitories.[8] In 1905 the scene shifted to the University of Chicago, where a southern white student waiter refused to serve a colored student. Two years later there was an uproar in Snell Hall because a room was assigned to a Negro student. A few days later the *Chicago Daily Inter Ocean* reported a "juvenile race war was in the Earle and Copernicus School districts on Chicago's South Side, because of transfers of white pupils from the former school to the latter, where the colored children were in the majority.

In 1907 southern white students of the University of Chicago objected to eating in Hutchinson Commons, the university dining hall, with colored students; whereupon school authorities announced that no segregation should be permitted and that the Negroes were entitled to the same privileges as whites. But that same year the sensational case of Cecilia Johnson exploded on the campus. The beautiful, talented and popular graduate student, Miss Johnson, was quickly disowned by the members of her sorority when they discovered that she was colored and the cousin of "Mushmouth" Johnson, Negro gambling king. One of her white sorors was quoted by the *Chicago Tribune* as saying that she thought Cecilia Johnson a fine girl, and without intent to deceive, but "of course we would have never taken her in if we had known more about her."[9]

The other side of the story is a record of scholastic achievement against great odds. In July 1876, McLean County newspapers were writing about Rosanna P. Lindsay, their first Negro high school graduate. Miss Lindsay was said to have maintained herself well throughout the course at the State Normal School, "and her closing exercise was very creditable."[10] In June 1877, it became evident that the *Chicago Tribune* had overlooked the item, for it carried an editorial offering its own "first" colored high school graduate in Illinois:

In a class of twenty-eight at the Springfield High School, Gertrude Wright, the first colored graduate of an Illinois school, stands third.[11]

Someone at the Princeton High School promptly put the record straight, however:

The Princeton High School graduated in the class of 1873 Miss E. A. Lindsay, a colored girl, who came here from Peoria, and took the full course of study in our high school. We think ours was the first high school in the state to graduate a colored girl. Miss Lindsay is now teaching with success in Louisville, KY.[12]

In 1894, Ida Platt was admitted to the Illinois Bar. In their astonishment, commentators may have exaggerated when they proclaimed her not only one of the most remarkable women of the day, but of the century. She was graduated from the Chicago College of Law in June 1894. Speaking of her, one reporter noted that:

In order to pass this institution a student must have a standing of at least 85 marks out of every possible 100. . . . Miss Platt went beyond that, standing 96. Her success contradicts Professor Abbott of the Northwestern University Law Department, who recently stated that "women are not a success as law students."[13]

Miss Platt later took an active part in the fight for women's rights.

In June 1895 Quinn Chapel paid its respects to twenty-one-year-old Winter Woods, recently graduated with honors from Beloit College.[14] G. Wellington McClure became the first colored graduate of Lewis Institute in 1901 and won praise for his scholarship.[15] Three years later Florence Davis topped them all:

Having outstripped all her ninety-three classmates and ranking highest in her class, Florence Davis, colored, will be valedictorian of the South Division High School graduation class this year. While there is disapproval among the unsuccessful classmates of the girl, it is said that no open objection will be made to the present arrangement of Principal Smith to permit the girl to deliver the class oration.[16]

J. Ernest Wilkins was elected to Phi Beta Kappa at the University of Illinois in 1918. In 1940 J. Ernest Wilkins, Jr., a member of the same honorary scholastic society, was graduated from the University of Chicago at the age of sixteen. The following year he acquired a Master's degree and promptly went to work on a doctorate in applied mathematics, concentrating on the calculus of variations. By the fall of 1942 he had finished his work in Chicago and was headed for the Institute of Advanced Study in Princeton, New Jersey, to sit at the feet of Albert Einstein. Meanwhile, two younger brothers, John and Julian, had each entered the University of Wisconsin at fourteen, and both seemed undismayed by the challenge of the older brother's record.

In December 1932, Professor Paul A. Witty of Northwestern University tested a group of Negro children in Chicago. He reported the discovery of a nine-year-old girl with an I.Q. of 200. Statistics indicate that the chances of attaining an I.Q. of 200 or above are one in 100,000,000.

The discovery of this little Negro girl suggested to some observers that the range of intelligence among Negroes runs just as high as it does among other racial groups. Others noted that in view of the depressing effect of poor environment and poor school facilities upon I.Q., it seemed of more than passing significance that the little girl was discovered in Chicago, where she had benefitted by school facilities considerably above the average for the country as a whole.[17]

Yet, thanks to migration from the South, the Negro communities of Illinois continue to show a high rate of illiteracy. Census records for 1930 indicated that in Chicago this rate was higher for Negroes than for any other ethnic group except the foreign born. There was, however, no apparent inclination on their part to be satisfied with this status.

Chicago Negroes were ceaselessly reminding their city officials that school districts had been gerrymandered to their disadvantage, that virtual segregation had been effected by this maneuver, and that schools in the Negro neighborhoods were hopelessly overcrowded—most of them being forced to run two and three shifts daily, while other communities continued to offer full sessions to their youngsters. They welcomed no statement of the case that failed to show the inequalities of the situation as it applied to them. An even stronger demonstration of this will to rise were the accounts of their own efforts against handicaps.

When "Captain" John Robinson died in 1919 at the age of ninety, he was still illiterate. Born a slave, he had witnessed the execution of John Brown and had been deeply affected by the spectacle. His interest ran to children, though he had none of his own. When he noticed that East St. Louis made no provision for the education of Negro children, he personally escorted about a dozen of them to white schools, including the Catholic. To everybody's surprise, the children were admitted. Today as a result, there are seven grade schools and one high school for Negroes in East St. Louis, and all of them observe the 22nd of September each year in honor of "Captain" Robinson, ex-slave. His townsfolk have given him a life-sized monument.[18]

"Grandma" Maria Vance of Danville is another example. In 1901, when "Grandma" Vance was 91, she learned to read "without spectacles." The story of her unusual achievement gained added poignancy when it was learned that the old woman had been the one who packed the belongings of Abraham Lincoln and Mrs. Lincoln when they were leaving Springfield for the White House.[19]

9. Churches

This chapter draft was found at the Newberry Library. It was written by an IWP worker who was only ever listed as "E. Diehl." It was condensed and significantly rewritten from a much longer seventy-nine-page essay titled "Churches" by George Coleman Moore, also located at Newberry. Source material at the Harsh Research Collection includes extensive notes on St. Clair Drake's WPA study Churches and Voluntary Associations in the Chicago Negro Community.

The establishment of Negro churches in Illinois dates from the late thirties of the nineteenth century, with the formation of religious bodies in Brooklyn, near East St. Louis, and Jacksonville. Which town was the first to boast a colored church is uncertain, for while Quinn Chapel at Brooklyn is generally credited as the initial institution (as also the first west of the Alleghenies), founded June 1839, there is evidence that in 1837 two Baptist clerics had organized a church at Jacksonville. The famous Quinn Chapel, Chicago—a branch of the African Methodist order like the church of the same name in Brooklyn—was the first Negro congregation in the northern city, being established in 1844. Which of the three bodies was the first to erect a church structure is not known, although it is a matter of record that Quinn in Chicago built its first home in 1847.

While there was no formal Negro church organization in Illinois until the late thirties, there doubtless had been religious practice of one sort and another among the members of the race, who in 1820 numbered but fourteen hundred, most of them in the southern part of the state. Earlier, in the South, they and their forebears had found consolation in the primitive "churches" approved by the plantation owners; subsequently in Illinois the race—two-thirds still in servitude at the time of adoption of the first constitution—continued to find, or a least seek, easement of its heavy burden in some form of religious service: camp meeting, house prayer meeting, or other group activity having as its motive divine worship. The lack of numbers of the race and the oppressive treatment accorded them held back creation of formally organized religious groups with church edifices, during the first three or four decades of the century; but with the swing to abolitionism within the state, paralleled by a rapid decrease of numbers in servitude and equally increasing ingress of colored migrants from the South, such groups and buildings began to appear.

The Quinn Chapels of both Brooklyn and Chicago were named for an early Negro churchman who is one of the outstanding figures in the history of the growth and development of formal religion among the members of his race, not only in Illinois but in the United States. William Paul Quinn, born in Calcutta, India, of Negro and Hindu parentage, singlehandedly organized most of the African Methodist Episcopal churches in Ohio, western Pennsylvania, Michigan, Indiana, and Illinois in the short space of ten years. Via Gibraltar and England, Quinn arrived in New York in 1831, having fled the wrath of a father incensed at the interest in western religious ideas of his son. Shortly after his arrival in this country, the future bishop was converted to the Methodist Episcopalian faith at New Hope, Maryland, and sometime later secured a license to preach. Joining the Philadelphia Conference in 1834, he drew the assignment to organize a circuit that comprised the first of the African Methodist churches, and Quinn was its first rider; making his rounds from 1834 to 1836, he also engaged in the dangerous business of assisting fugitive slaves to northern territory, winning the reputation among abolitionists as one of the most skillful slave smugglers. At the general conference of the African Methodist Episcopal Church in Philadelphia in 1836, Quinn was commissioned to "go West and build up the church." The great number of denominational congregations he organized indicates the measure of his labors. The daring abolitionist-preacher, about 1838, made his headquarters in Richmond, Indiana, where he founded Bethel African Methodist Church. Along with the Quakers of the neighborhood, Quinn took an active part in the work of the Underground Railroad and on several occasions risked his life directing runaway slaves to Canada. Stories abound attesting the manifold accomplishments of the energetic organizer, ranging from perspicacity in business to prowess in physical combat.

One striking story about Quinn relates to his activity in the vicinity of East St. Louis. Because of the rampant anti-Negro feeling in St. Louis, across the Mississippi, no colored religious services were permitted within the boundaries of the city. But the indomitable Quinn, ferried across the river to the Illinois side by a St. Louis friend, first attracted a crowd on the Missouri bank by singing "Steal Away" and then addressed his remote audience by use of a black kettle that threw his voice across the waters to the faithful.

In 1844 at the general conference, again in Pennsylvania, Quinn, only forty-four years old, was made a bishop of the African Methodist Episcopal Church. One of his first administrative acts was to send Reverend George Johnson to Chicago to form a Methodist Society.

Following the establishment of Quinn Chapel, Brooklyn (called Brooklyn Chapel until renamed for the bishop about 1887), it was not until 1846 that the next standard church of importance in the southern part of the state was organized and built; this was Ward Chapel, A.M.E., in Peoria. In Quincy in 1859 the African Methodists organized Bethel A.M.E. Church; it began its existence as a small mission and could not afford a minister until 1863, when Reverend William Black assumed the office. In 1865 at Mound City was established the African Methodist Church; meeting over an abandoned saloon, they soon had a membership of nineteen, and by 1922 the congregation of over one hundred was able to erect a new stucco building. African Methodist took an active part in community life, sometimes awarding scholarships to Wilberforce University in Ohio.

In 1865 at Galesburg, Second Baptist Church was organized by twelve persons under the leadership of Reverend Jackson of Jacksonville; by 1875 the membership numbered ninety. One of the leading church personalities of the time, Reverend Richard de Baptiste, served as pastor from 1886 to 1890.[1] During the period, the Baptists had a strong hold on the colored people of St. Clair County and managed to support Belleville Baptist Church, Lebanon Church, Brooklyn Baptist Church, and Mount Zion Church, the last located three miles north of O'Fallon. The growing Negro population of this county had its inception in the large number of slaves brought to the vicinity by early white settlers from Virginia, Kentucky, and the West Indies. The First Baptist Church, Quincy, was organized in 1884, and in 1888 Union Baptist Church opened its doors.

At Cairo, Morning Star Free Will Baptist Church was founded under the leadership of Reverend I. Crumpton in 1898; its modest beginning was in an old carpenter shop, but in 1902 it purchased two lots and erected a frame building. The church was soon famous for its successful revival meetings.[2]

Lake Chapel Colored Methodist Episcopal Church, Mound City, was established under a brush arbor in 1899; the six members sat on planks in the open, the pulpit rested on the ground and a wobbly table was used to lay the Bible on. The little band was persistent and sincere; and with twenty-five members in 1905 they were able to meet in their own frame church on the hardroad.

The white press, observing the growth and development of Negro churches in the state, frequently devoted space to their activities. Although some of the papers poked fun at the antics of the more unrestrained worshipers, others of sympathetic bent reported in respectful fashion major occurrences within the new field; the following from the *Chicago Evening Journal* of September 8, 1874, is an example:

> The colored people of the Wood River Association have been enjoying their thirty-sixth annual convention for the past week in Galesburg, Illinois. The enthusiasm characteristic of this people was visible throughout the exercises.[3]

Writing further of Negro church activities in Galesburg, the *Journal* stated, March 3, 1881: "There is a large number of colored people in the educational city of Galesburg. . . . They have three churches, and pulpits are filled with colored clergymen of culture and refinement."[4] But even sympathetic journals sometimes adopted a facetious tone when treating the frenzy displayed on occasion by certain black Christians.

Although the Baptists and African Methodists were the leading rivals in the field, the Colored Methodists in 1875 offered strong competition introducing a program of church activity previously untried. Instead of appealing principally to the emotions, they now offered cultural fare in an attempt to recruit to the fold. Noting this new phase, the *Chicago Evening Journal* reported March 10, 1875:

> The young people connected with the Colored Methodist Church Society, in this city Aurora, gave a concert last evening at their church, which was considered by those in attendance to be one of the best given here during the winter. In this society are a number of most excellent singers.

But despite this new approach to the religious idea, the old time camp meeting still flourished; the *Chicago Inter-Ocean* reported such a gathering, August 9, 1886:

> The colored people are holding a camp meeting at Centralia in the fair grounds, and are attracting a large number of people. The Illinois Central ran an excursion from Vandalia,

bringing down five coachloads. Visiting divines have come from St. Louis, Chicago, Indianapolis, and other places, and are ably assisted by the Rev. Tobia Monor, of this city. An admission fee of ten cents is being charged at the gate. A similar camp meeting is also being held at Salem, this county.[5]

The many newspaper stories of the time anent Negro church activity reveal the steady growth of religious organization among the colored citizens of the state, both as regards the establishment of congregations and building of church edifices and the creation of denominational associations. The Baptists and African Methodists, as noted above, were leading orders. Some measure of the activity of the latter is disclosed in the following report in the *Chicago Leader*, March 18, 1897:

The African Methodists of Illinois are to build a church at Springfield in memory of Abraham Lincoln. It will be named the Abraham Lincoln Memorial Church and will cost $8,000. There will be three memorial windows. The center one will be dedicated to Lincoln and the two smaller to Frederick Douglass and John Brown. In the memorial room are to be kept slavery relics of every description . . . pictures of all the abolitionist leaders, an auction block, the Lovejoy printing press, the rope with was used in the hanging of John Brown, and whatever else can be gathered.[6]

With such a goodly number of churches and church associations it is not surprising that the general religious movement developed numerous memorable leaders. One of the outstanding personalities of the period was the noted woman evangelist, Amanda Smith, who devoted a lifetime of toil to building the church, not only in Illinois but in most parts of the civilized world. Upon her death in 1915 at the age of seventy-eight, the *Chicago Daily News* published on March 5 a brief notice outlining her career. Born in slavery, she had carried the message of Christianity to far off Africa and India. Burial was at the orphanage named for her, at Harvey, a suburb of Chicago; the colored children's industrial school had been founded with contributions she had gathered in the course of her missionary work, and the children of the institution sang "Mother's Prayer" at the last sad rite.[7]

In the north, at Chicago, Quinn Chapel, begun in 1844, was formally organized in 1847 by the famous bishop and given his name. First services were held in a storefront on Madison near State Street, and were conducted by Madison Patterson, assisted by Reverend A. T. Hall, first licensed Negro preacher in Chicago. In the course of the struggle for a permanent residence, Quinn Chapel lost two buildings through fires, moved eight times, and has had thirty-four changes of pastors. Chief among extra-religious activities of Quinn, before the Civil War, was the abolitionist movement; the church played a vital role in the work of the Underground Railroad, and is credited with secreting thousands of fugitives passing through Chicago on their way to Canada. The church itself maintained a station on its premises. Reverend George W. Johnson, pastor of Quinn Chapel, called in October 1850 a large meeting of the colored citizens at his church to organize a Liberation Association. This conference raised on the spot twenty dollars, which was dispatched to General W. L. Chapin, confined to prison in Maryland for helping slaves to escape from bondage. Quinn was the tenth church erected in Chicago, and many notable movements had their inception at the historic institution, including those resulting in Provident Hospital, Young Men's Christian Association, and the Old Folk's Home. The *Chicago Inter-Ocean* noted in 1902 that Quinn operated successfully a kindergarten, reading-room, library men's club,

CHAPTER NINE

women's club, penny savings bank, and employment bureau—indicating that the trend toward activities other than purely religious, begun in 1875, had extended considerably.

Quinn Chapel in Chicago also enjoys the distinction of being the root from which a number of other churches sprang. The first branch was Bethel A.M.E. Church, probably the most important congregation to leave the chapel; its organization was a result of overcrowding, and its members continued on the most amicable of terms with the mother church, as evidenced by their welcome of Quinn adherents to Bethel's auditorium when the chapel was destroyed by the great fire of 1871. Bethel's establishment, first as a mission in 1862, was approved by Bishop Quinn, who formally organized it in May of that year, appointing Reverend John B. Dawson as pastor. In 1874 when plans for the building of the Polk Street Station were being consummated, church-owned property, on which the church stood, was needed by the railroad people for the terminal; aided by H. H. Kohlsatt, editor of the *Inter-Ocean*, Bethel succeeded in getting $41,500 for its land, after an initial offer of $15,000. In the winter of 1890, Bethel entered into negotiations with Reverend [George W. Gaines to merge—Ed.] the two churches into the now great Bethel Church. The following summer the church erected the present building at a cost of $10,500.

Some of the leading ministers of the Negro race in the country have pastured at Bethel, including Reverend Reverdy C. Ransom, who attracted to the church persons who desired intellect in the pulpit, and Reverend A. J. Carey, Sr., who collected more money for the church than any two pastors who had preceded him.

Bethel was the home church of "Aunt" Jane Allen, a well-known character of the community whom Fenton Johnson, noted Chicago Negro poet, made the subject of a poem.[8] When at the church, which was often, she always sat in the "Amen Corner." A deeply religious woman and ardent church goer, Aunt Jane for many years busied herself peddling aprons. She was not strictly loyal to Bethel and A.M.E. faith, for on days when any Baptist church held communion or a baptism she was on hand. In 1915 while attending Bethel Church, the old lady arose and shouted, "Chillun, my chariot is descendin.'" Shortly thereafter she departed this life.

The second group to split from Quinn organized St. Stephen's A.M.E. Church; this third African Methodist Episcopal church in Chicago was founded 1869, and was located in the West Lake Street area. In 1897 another group broke away from Quinn Chapel to form St. Mary's Church. In 1900 the more progressive members split from Bethel, because of differences over church and community problems, and set up Institutional Baptist Church. However, the African Methodist Episcopal Church had grown to such size by 1893 that it was able to hold a huge national congress in Washington Hall in September, with delegates representing all parts of the United States.

Institutional Baptist, immediately after establishment, launched a broad program of social service work, being the first Negro church in the city to initiate a day nursery, a mother's club, an employment agency, and a print shop for the benefit of members. Cooperating with the new church, whose social service program was patterned after that of Hull House, were Jane Addams, Mary McDowell, Bishop Fellows, and members of the wealthy Swift family.

The Baptists seem to have taken the lead early in establishing churches, and down through the years managed to maintain their grip on the Negro community. The first church of the denomination in Chicago was Zoar Baptist, organized in April 1953, with eleven members; it was an outgrowth of Xenia Baptist, a congregation of three, who first met in 1850. The congregation of Zoar, numbering sixty in 1856, lead by Chicago's most notable Negro citizen, John Jones, decided to call a minister. Selected for the job was Reverend H. H. Hawkins, pastor of the colored Baptist Church in Chatham, Canada. Following a period of complete harmony in which the members steadily built up the church, the controversial problem of slave marriage and ritual of foot-washing split the membership seriously; and in 1860 a small group withdrew to form another church, Mount Zion, which was located in a store on Clark Street near Harrison. The next year, however, pastors of the two churches proposed a merger, which was carried through and resulted in the formation of the famous Olivet Baptist Church.

Olivet, out of which so many other churches were to grow, began services in the Bedina Place Baptist Church; the first pastor, Reverend J. F. Boulden, served two years. Richard de Baptiste came to Olivet in 1863, and erected a brick building on Fourth Street between Polk and Taylor Streets at a cost of $18,000. De Baptiste was also the moving spirit in the organization of the colored convention in 1869 to fight for civil rights in Illinois. Subsequently, Olivet moved a number of times. In 1886 with a membership of over 1,500 it had the largest colored congregation in the city, and also no doubt in the state. While the church is justly noted for its illustrious record, serious disagreements arose at times within the organization which led to splits and the establishment of other churches.

Preceding the first division, the Illinois Baptists State Convention in 1865, noting the numbers of Negroes migrating to Illinois, urged upon its functionaries energetic measures to recruit as many of the incoming persons as possible.

> Let them not be tempted to organize churches on the basis of color rather than of Christian faith. Let not Baptists be driven to walk disorderly by joining organizations whose doctrines and practice are unscriptural. Let them know that all Baptists . . . are regarded by us as brethren, and are welcome to all the privileges of membership with us.

The first church to branch off from Olivet—and one of greater community influence perhaps than the mother body—was Bethesda; the split occurred in 1882 when certain members insisted in vain that Reverend John Thomas continue the practice of blessing infants and recognize the young people's organization within the church as a Christian Endeavor society. Other churches established as a result of further disagreements within Olivet congregation were Salem Baptist, 1898, Berean Baptist, 1900, and Ebenezer Baptist Church, 1902.

The success of Bethesda was due in large part to the wisdom of leading members who favored moving to the far south side; a Jewish synagogue was purchased, some years after Bethesda's formation, at a large price at 53rd and Michigan, but the expenditure was proved justified when soon the southward trek of the colored population set in and the church location became the very center of the Negro district. Bethesda also initiated dramatics, was in the front line of action when community problems arose, and conducted daily classes in reading, writing, and arithmetic to eradicate the illiteracy of its older members. Moreover, the church was a leading factor in the Baptist General Association, which cooperated with the American Baptist Mission Union to send missionaries to the Congo country.

Berean Baptist also became an important community institution, and its history is highlighted by the work of its first, energetic pastor, Reverend W. S. Bradden, who when refused

CHAPTER NINE

admittance to the Baptists Ministers' Association informed the members of that body that he would live "to eat the goose that ate the grass off the graves of each of them."[9] In 1914 Reverend Bradden was still an active minister, while every one of the preachers who repulsed him had gone to his maker. Despite the handicap of non-recognition, Bradden and his faithful followers succeeded in building an important church; lead by the pastor himself the members made house-to-house contacts recruiting more communicants, and in June 1903 were able to lay the cornerstone of their first church structure at 4838 Dearborn Street.

Ebenezer Baptist Church soon after its formation distinguished itself by a colorful opening ceremony, described by an observer as follows:

> They immediately procured an old church house at 35th and Dearborn Street and set sail and marched in. It was a grand sight to see "Pap" (affectionate name for the pastor) heading that mighty procession riding a fine and noble looking white horse with Bob Berry's Brass Band. . . . [10]

Other Baptist churches founded during the period were Calvary Baptist, later Providence, established 1886; Hermon Baptist Church, on the north side of the city, 1887; St. John's Baptist Church on Federal Street, 1900; and Burning Bush Baptist Church where, in 1904, a social settlement was opened.

Many other churches saw birth at the time whose classification is difficult to determine. Of these the Christian Society Church at 25th Street and Indiana Avenue is outstanding. In addition, numerous camp meetings were still being held in the open; one was noted in the *Chicago Inter-Ocean*, September 9, 1900:

> "God's prize fighter has come to town," that is the way the Rev. "Dr." J. L. Griffin of Texas announces his arrival in Chicago. He declares he can knock out the devil in twenty rounds. His texts are all war-like: "Samson Slaying Thousands with the Jaw Bone of an Ass," "Moses Leading 3,000,000 Out of Egypt," "A Wicked Man Praying in Hell," "David in Battle with a Man Ten Feet High" are a few samples.

Several Negro churches of the time owed their founding to social conditions within certain white churches having mixed congregations. Apparently some colored communicants were dissatisfied with the restrictions placed upon their participation in church affairs and voluntarily asked for letters of dismissal to form churches wherein they could be free to become integral parts of the organization. Such attitude led to the founding of Providence Baptist Church, for example, the members of which withdrew from the white Union Baptist Church. However, more articulate groups strenuously objected to anything suggesting discrimination in church activities. Such a group in 1895 took issue with remarks made by Reverend Johnston Meyers, pastor of Immanuel Baptist Church, characterizing the Nordic churchman, in a resolution adopted at a large mass meeting, as "a minister who draws invidious distinction between the white and colored converts of his own church," and his sermon which inspired the mass meeting, as a "shameful utterance" exposing Reverend Meyers "to the just contempt of all fair-minded people."

An unusual type of church service, instituted in 1905 by Reverend Richard R. Wright, was conducted at Trinity Mission in the heart of the colored settlement on 18th Street, where a sort of relief station for poor working-class members was maintained. Indigents could obtain food and clothing, advice and counsel, and enjoy recreational facilities at the mission. Wright struggled hard to keep the service going, declining three professorships at Negro colleges while he worked in Chicago as porter, messenger, and unskilled laborer, preaching and teaching all day at the mission on Sunday.

Another preacher of the period distinguished for earnestness and liberality was Reverend Bird Wilkins, pastor for a short time of Bethesda about 1887. His tenure of office was short, due to differences arising out of church policy. A good picture of the activity he desired to introduce is contained in the following statement issued by Wilkins upon resigning:

> I believe in the fatherly kindness of God. The old idea of God of vengeance ready to burn up the world in hell-fire, is opposed to common sense, and abhorrent to me. I no longer endorse the doctrine of the trinity. My belief is that the Bible has a divine and human line of thought running through it; there is a great deal of good in the Bible; and a great deal that is the entire opposite. I am also a free believer in open Communion . . . that a Methodist, Presbyterian, Catholic, or a member of any denomination, is entitled to the sacrament at my hands as well as a Baptist. . . . I preached a sermon on "Socialism" some three weeks ago which caused a great stir in my church. . . . I am a liberal Christian with a leaning toward Unitarianism. I am going to stay in Chicago and build a large church to be known as Liberty Temple. . . . Here the liberal minded people of all denominations will be gathered, and I intend to show Chicago and the world a new sight—an advancing and progressing colored congregation.

The Baptists and the African Methodists early became the two denominations to which the Negro flocked in greatest numbers, but other churches also figure in the religious history of the colored people in Illinois. The Catholic, Protestant Episcopal, white Methodist Episcopal, African Episcopal, Colored Methodist, Colored Presbyterian, and Congregational were some of the denominations that competed for communicants. The first colored Catholic church in Chicago was St. Monica's, dedicated early in 1894. Father Augustine Tolton, born of slave parents in Missouri and the first colored priest in the United States, was appointed to lead the flock. A congregation of forty-five established the first Episcopalian church in Chicago, in 1879, St. Thomas on Indiana Avenue. Members of the white Methodist Episcopal Church, evidently alarmed at the size of their Negro group, sought to provide separate services for colored communicants, and organized St. Mark M.E. Church in 1895. St. Luke Mission, on Thirty-fifth Street, was established in 1912, and later developed into South Park M.E. Church. The African Episcopalians were also active, founding the Hyde Park Episcopalian Church shortly after the turn of the century. The organization started nearly a decade earlier as a literary club, composed mainly of waiters in hotels in the district. In 1907 St. Paul Colored Methodist Church began as a small mission in a storefront at 4008 State Street. Colored Presbyterians formed a club in 1887 among migrants from Tennessee, Kentucky, Ohio, and Canada, and the next year established Grace Presbyterian in a storefront at 3233 State Street. The colored Congregationalists in 1889 held services in homes of members, but in a short time organized Lincoln Congregational Church and met in quarters at 31st and Wabash.

The Negro church organizations named above include some of the more important that were established and grew in the period covered; however those named are but a fraction of the scores, indeed hundreds, founded before the Great Migration. The picture

CHAPTER NINE

presented purports to give only a sketch of the development of formal religious practice by the race in the state. Organization began in those centers where colored people lived in greatest numbers and where the least opposition was offered to their desire for some form of social activity. Formerly encouraged in the South, religious service was the immediate form to hand; and formal church organization, once begun, was carried forward apace by many energetic and eloquent clerics, whose number increased rapidly. The Baptists and Methodists were in the lead from the beginning; and innovations later were introduced that kept the church an attraction for the masses of the race. Other denominations also competed for communicants, and the camp meeting continued to draw many interested Negroes to services in the open. Missions—mainly in Chicago—were a feature in the life of the church, toward the end of the period; and along with this service there appeared pastors of a liberal bent and nonsecular outlook, adumbrating a tendency which was to manifest itself more strongly and widely in the post-war period.

In the nearly eighty years from the date of establishment of the first Negro church in Illinois, religion was without rival as the leading force and attraction in the life of the race in the state.

10. Soldiers

There are two drafts of this chapter, one at the Harsh Research Collection and the most recent at the Newberry Library. The more recent version that appears here was written by Arna Bontemps. Corrections made in Jack Conroy's handwriting have been incorporated by the editor. In the IWP papers, there are also two earlier essays of significance, a ten-page essay by Edward Joseph, "The Negro Soldier," and a fifty-four-page essay by George Coleman Moore, "Soldiers: 1865–1913."

One night a band of young copperheads met John Henry, a colored man, and asked: "What side are you on?"

John Henry replied truthfully: "I'm for President Lincoln and the government of the United States."

"You might expect that from a d——d nigger," the ruffians commented and administered a beating.

Ten minutes later a detective halted the man who was still sore from the mistreatment he had received at the hands of the copperheads.

"What side are you on?" the detective asked.

The Negro, half-frightened, replied: "I'm for Jeff Davis and the Confederate States of America."

At this John Henry was immediately placed under arrest, but after explanation he was promptly released.

He had walked a block or two from the jail when a man stopped him and asked the same question: "What side are you on?"

This time the victim of so much questioning straightened up and looking the stranger squarely in the face said: "You tell me what side you're on, Mister, and I'll tell you what side I'm on."

So characterizes the Chicago of the 1860s.

George W. Williams, writing about the Negro, discloses the fact that Illinois provided 1,811 soldiers during the Civil War; however, Champaign's *Union and Gazette* states,

. . . of the colored men enlisted in the war, Illinois raised one thousand one hundred and eleven. . . .

The correct number was perhaps an average between the two figures; downstate Quincy alone is said to have raised 903 of these men.

Congress was appealed to decide whether or not Negroes were to fight; after long months of pro and con debate an act was passed which required that Negroes be paid ten dollars per month, with three dollars deducted for clothing while white soldiers received thirteen dollars per month in addition to their uniforms.

In a further discussion on the Civil War, Williams states that—

The Negro soldier had to run the gauntlet of the persecuting hate of white Northern troops, and if captured, endure the most barbarous treatment of the rebels, without a protest on the part of the government—for at least nearly a year. Hooted at, jeered, and stoned in the streets of Northern cities as they marched to the front to fight for the Union; scoffed at and abused by white troops under the flag of a common country, there was little of a consoling or inspiring nature in the experience of Negro soldiers.

"But," the writer adds, "here was a war about the Negro, a war that was to declare him forever bond, or forever free."

Judge Advocate Joseph Holt in an official letter to Secretary of War Stanton, August 20, 1863, rendered this decision:

The obligation of all persons—irrespective of creed or color—to bear arms, if physically capable of doing so, in defense of the Government under which they live and by which they are protected, is one that is universally acknowledged and enforced. Corresponding to this obligation is the duty resting on those charged with the administration of the military service, whenever the public safety may demand it.

Out of such conflicts arose a hero—H. O. Wagoner, friend of Frederick Douglass and John Brown, confidant of John Jones, and trusted worker in the Underground Railway.

Wagoner had come to Illinois from Colorado as early as 1839, settling at Galena. When announcement came that colored men were to be inducted into the armed forces of the nation, Governor John Albion Andrew of Massachusetts commissioned him to recruit for the Fifth Cavalry of that state. His outstanding services there brought national attention to his work. So impressed was the Illinois governor, Richard Yates, that he too commissioned Wagoner to go down to Mississippi and recruit refugees and contrabands under act of Congress, and Order Number 227 of the War Department.

Under Wagoner's direction the Negro personnel of Civil War forces in Illinois increased and swelled the Union armies. For his faithful and distinguished efforts general Grant sent Wagoner a personal letter of recommendation, dated September 1, 1865. That letter and another one sent him from Paris, France concerning his son, Henry, who died at Lyons, France, while acting as consul there are still held as souvenirs of the great soldier.

Not much is recorded about the experiences of Illinois Negro soldiers in the Union army. The story of Guthrie Walker may, however, be typical. Guthrie, the brother of John T. Walker, a Glencoe expressman, hailed from Kentucky. He was a private in a Civil War regiment, perhaps a loyal Kentucky outfit.

Once when his regiment was on one of those grueling engagements the Civil War boys spoke of lightly as a "skirmish," the commandant issued orders that no one serving under him was to eat or drink anything until the skirmish was over, his theory being that a man fights better when he is hungry and thirsty.

For over twenty-four hours Guthrie fought hard, without a morsel of food or a drop of water. The pangs of hunger did not annoy him; he had been accustomed to such. But thirst almost maddened him. And to render it worse one of those light showers of rain, so characteristic of Dixie, fell. "Water, water everywhere and not a drop to drink." The air being surcharged with the heat of gunshot, all throats were parched for lack of moisture.

"Fall to! Pursue the enemy through the north thicket!" came the order.

Guthrie fell into line and started running, his bayonet fixed. He and his comrades pushed through the thickets, when lo! a miracle—A puddle of water that seemed to Guthrie like the river Jordan—cool, refreshing water rained down from the heavens. Surely God loves his children.

Guthrie stopped to drink or rather to lap water in the Gideon fashion. He took one long draught and then his eyes were suddenly arrested. Just before him, lying in the puddle was the body of a dead dog. Guthrie blinked for a moment and then decided not to let a dead dog stand between him and the quenching of his terrible thirst. He drank until he was satisfied and then continued in "the pursuit of the enemy."

Another survival is the following:

During the late twenties an aged colored man, garbed in the blue of the Union army, was in much evidence around 59th and State Streets. Accosting any colored person he reminded him, "I fought for your freedom." That was the signal for a donation of at least a quarter, despite pensions, the G.A.R. boys had to live, and tobacco during the late twenties was almost a luxury for some pensioners.

Once at a little storefront church Baptist "covenant" meeting, the elderly veteran spoke:

> I remember the terrors of slavery. I was sold out of my mother's arms when I was less than three years old. I hated slavery and vowed that if the Lord should be with me I would avenge that forced parting from my mother.
>
> War came. I heard it was a war for freedom, for the freedom of the black man. At night I stole from the plantation and ran to the Union camp, placing myself under the protection of Mr. Lincoln's soldiers. . . . In time I was able to enlist, to carry a musket and to pump lead into the bodies of the slave-holders . . . always remembering how I was sold out of my mother's arms. I don't know how many rebels I killed and I don't care . . . for the Lord says, "Inasmuch as ye do it unto the least of these, my little ones, ye do it unto me." I was killing rebels, for the Lord's sake.

The military history of the Negro in Illinois is substantially that of the Eighth Regiment, Illinois National Guard, the only regiment in the United States service whose entire personnel—officers and men—is of African ancestry. While the Eighth is, and has been since first organized, the major organization of colored men in the United States, it was not by any means the first colored military body in Illinois.[1]

Shortly after the great Chicago fire of 1871 the unofficial Hannibal Guards were formed and flourished for many years. This semi-military group was to give way to later a group called the Cadets, also an unofficial military organization. After a while as the Old Sixteenth which became a full-fledged member of the state militia, it successively was known as the Ninth battalion, the Eight Regiment, and in World War II—the 184th Field Artillery.

The Hannibal Zouaves represented the first attempt at formal organization of a military unit, in reality the Zouaves were only semi-military with no official organization. They constantly agitated for acceptance in the state guards but due to the fact that this organization placed more emphasis upon social activities than on military affairs, this was never considered. Oftentimes the daily press took cognizance of such affairs:

> The Hannibal Zouaves (colored) Captain R. B. Moore, will give a grand military entertainment at Burlington Hall, on next Monday evening, August 2nd. The entertainment will consist of drills, speaking, sham battles, cotillions, etc., and a supper. The proceeds will go for buying arms for the company.[2]

Like the Zouaves, the Cadets carried on the social tradition begun by the Old Sixteenth. A news item relates,

> A grand entertainment for the benefit of Company B. Sixteenth Battalion, I.N.G. was given at the exposition building last evening. The Summer Guards of St. Louis were in the city on a visit, and of course, there was a great time generally among the colored population. After a competitive drill in which the Chicago Company compared very favorably with the St. Louis organization, there was a ball at which a large number of ladies and gentlemen tarried well into the small retreating hours of the night.[3]

Different, however, is the case of the Chicago Rifles, an organization of Negroes formed as a result of the enactment of a Militia Law by the state legislature, May 14, 1877. This body was known officially as the 16th Battalion. The Biennial Report of the Adjutant-General for January 1878 stated in part that,

> . . . during 1877 the Division (Illinois State Militia) was organized into 3 Brigades of Regiments of infantry, 1 Battalion of Calvalry, etc. The Sixteenth (colored) Battalion under command of Major Theodore C. Hubbard, Chicago, composed of Companies A and B of Chicago, Clark County Guards of Marshall, and Cumberland of Greenup. There were 11 officers and 106 enlisted men. The Battalion served as part of the First Brigade.

As Negroes in the state grew in numbers and in power their leaders believed it essential that the race should be prepared to take its full part in the maintenance and defense of the nation. Accordingly, a mass meeting was held in old Central Hall at Twenty-second and Wabash Avenue May 5, 1890, for the avowed purpose of organizing a Negro unit of the Illinois National Guard.

Two weeks later it was agreed that the organization be known as the Ninth Infantry Battalion. Immediately, the officers set about obtaining uniforms for the men and to provide a drum and bugle corps. Drilling of the battalion proceeded steadily and satisfactorily. Thereafter, application was made for enrollment in the state militia, but was denied by Governor Joe Fifer on the ground that no appropriation had been made by the legislature for such an organization. Thus the matter rested for a couple of years.

John C. Buckner, major in the Ninth Battalion, was elected a state representative in 1894. Major Buckner used his political strength and influence in the state legislature to create a vacancy in the state militia together with an appropriation for its maintenance.

Such a stir on the part of Major Buckner caused much sensation in military circles; press, public officials, and military authorities expressed themselves freely, and sympathetically. One editorial carried the following opinion:

Why should Adjutant General Orendoff refuse to admit a battalion of colored troops to the Illinois National Guard? It has been more than thirty years since the United States government recognized the colored man as having the same right to serve his country in the army as the white man and there has ever since been a regiment of colored troops in the regular United States army. More than that, the colored regiment stationed at Missoula, Montana had the honor of special mention from the War Department for excellent service in the great railroad strike last summer, and the Inspector General of the Department of Dakota published an order complimenting that regiment as the best disciplined in the department.

General Orendoff admitted the Hibernian Rifles to the National Guard, although it was organized as a church battalion and was protested. The colored battalion will not be a class group, but will be made up of U.S. and Illinois citizens. The only difference in it and other battalions will be one of color, and State and National statues decree that Negroes are citizens to be accorded all rights of citizenship just as the whites are.[4]

Another Chicago newspaper carried this article:

After considerable efforts for a number of years the four colored military companies of Chicago have affected a half entrance into the National Guards of Illinois. They had a bill passed by the Legislature increasing the companies of the state militia to eighty-eight. It will give them a chance if the Governor signs it. The Buckner Bill was a rider to the regular bill for the regular military appropriations and although obnoxious was sufficiently strong to carry.

There is not so much objection to the companies themselves or their color as there is to the way they seek to obtain admission. Col. Henry L. Turner in an interview last night said:

"I had not heard of the passage of the Buckner's bill but as it was taken on the appropriation bill, it is not at all wonderful that it passed. While I personally have no prejudice against the colored companies or any company that seeks admission into the guards, I do object to have them force the issue strictly on a race basis. It is the objection I had to the Hibernian Rifles. We want men to come in as soldiers not as companies of this or that order or this or that race. Of course colored men would not be permitted to the first Regiment."[5]

The Buckner rider finally passed the law-making body and was subsequently signed by the governor. The measure provided for both, a battalion on and an appropriation for its maintenance. Shortly afterwards the battalion was muster into state service, and was attached to the First Infantry, Illinois National Guard, as the Ninth Battalion.

T. W. Goode, in his history of the Eighth Regiment, states:

. . . when the president of the United States urged upon by emergencies and respect for his country's pride and honor, issued a call on the 23rd day of April, 1889, for 125,000 volunteer soldiers to reinforce the regular army of the United States, it was then the military organization known and recognized as the Ninth Battalion militia proffered their services and were among the first of their country's men to offer themselves and their lives, if necessary, for the cause of humanity, honor and liberty. Though their services were not accepted on account of prejudice and lack of confidence in the colored brother, his oft-heard cry was "give us a chance; give us a leadership."[6]

According to rumors, Major Buckner, who had figured prominently in state military affairs, was to become the object of many schemes to blemish his record. In 1895 when the Italians of Spring Valley, Illinois, rioted against colored miners, the *Chicago Tribune* stated that

there was some wild talk about turning out the Ninth Battalion under arms, but it is due to the good judgment of its officers to say that at no time did they encourage such an idea. Major Buckner, the Commandant of the force, stoutly asserted . . . that he would only order his command out at a call from the Governor of the State through the proper military channels.

Governor Tanner sought to investigate the matter. Reporting the results of the probe the *Tribune* stated,

The Governor's investigation was a roaring farce. . . . The investigation took the form of a love fest without the presence of the colored brothers. Representative Buckner came with the Governor's envoys. He said: "This matter is going to be settled for once and for all times. The colored people are peaceable and should have their rights if it takes the Federal Troops to secure them, I am going to Seatonvile (site of the trouble) to stay with them until they get their rights."

The Ninth Battalion had been participating in camp maneuvers downstate when an order from Buckner's superior officer advised a return trip of the unit to Chicago. When Buckner's men arrived at the depot they learned that inferior, dirty cars had been reserved for them. Buckner refused to permit his men to ride in the unclean coaches. Colonel Smith of the adjutant general's headquarters was contacted, and proper protest lodged.

Colonel Smith journeyed to the station to inspect the coaches, declared them fit, and commanded the troops to proceed according to instructions. However, Buckner would not yield his position and instead threatened to negotiate with another railroad company. Only after Smith had ordered that the car be swept and drinking water be provided did Buckner agree to make the return trip.

As a result of this incident Major Buckner was summoned to appear before a court-martial to answer to charges of insubordination, conduct pre-judicial to morale of the militia, and refusal to carry out orders of a superior officer. In recording the affair the *Illinois State Journal* expressed the following article:

But for the fact that Major John C. Buckner rode to Chicago from Springfield in an ordinary coach last Saturday, the major would today be without a command. And but for the good nature of Assistant Adjutant General Smith he would not be a major anyhow. And even as matters stand it is not safe to make a pool on Major Buckner retaining the title which his position in the guard gives him.

Major Buckner's refusal to ride home on the cars provided for himself and his men, amounted to a breach of discipline. At the time he was fuming about the depot platform, declaring that he would never permit his men to go back to their homes in the cars, there was a sword hanging over his head that would shorn him of his rank if Colonel Smith had been in the proper humor to let it fall. For Colonel Smith had authority from Governor Tanner to make a common, everyday civilian out of Major Buckner and put another man in his place.

. . . The Governor was in a barber's chair when the information concerning the trouble was brought to him. He made inquiry to Kearn whether Buckner's complaint about the cars was well founded and the information that he received was that the coaches were better ones than he had been in the habit of riding in down to his Southern Illinois apple farm. 'Then,' said the governor, 'remove Buckner and put in a man who is willing to obey the orders of the department.'

On the strength of this, the orders were made out but the kindly and conservative nature of Colonel Smith stood between the business-like determination of the governor and the unruly major, and it did not become necessary to serve them.

Major Buckner's trial was held in secret sessions at Chicago, November 9, 1897, and it was ruled that,

> Under the sentence of the court, Major will not be recognized as an officer of the Illinois National Guard for a period of six months from this date, and no official military inter-courses will be permitted with him during this period.
>
> (signed)
> John R. Tanner
> Governor and Commander-in-Chief

The *Chicago Record* on May 13, 1898, carried the following announcement:

> Maj. John C. Buckner's letter to Gov. Tanner finally severing his connection with the 9th Battalion was made public last night. Buckner thanked the chief executive for reinstating him but says business reasons prevent him from continuing at the head of the battalion.[7]

It was just after the sinking of the battleship "Maine" that John R. Marshall vowed, "I'm going to Governor Tanner to see if he will organize a regiment of Negro soldiers." Four years after Buckner was elected to the Illinois legislature, Marshall was promoted to major in command of the Ninth Battalion. A news article dated April 27, 1898, carried the following facts:

> Capt. John R. Marshall of the 9th Battalion (colored) left the city last night for Springfield to lay before Gov. Tanner the temporary organization of a twelve-company regiment and to urge the Commander-in-Chief to call out the 9th for war service. . . .

Captain Marshall was accompanied by Robert R. Jackson, Frank Dennison, E. H. Wright, S. B. Turner, Rep. R. C. Randall, and Rev. J. W. Thomas. Governor Tanner assured the delegation that he would comply with their wishes, and that "every officer of the regiment will be a colored man."

Thus encouraged the work of organizing and recruiting was soon completed. The old Ninth Battalion of Illinois was mustered into service as the Eighth Illinois National Guard, and now comprised 1,295 men and forty-six officers. All parts of the state were represented. Chicago led with 700 men; 120 came from Cairo; a full company from Quincy, almost a company from Springfield. Mound City, Metropolis, and Litchfield furnished smaller contingents.

CHAPTER TEN

Six of the officers of the regiment were lawyers, ten were college graduates, several had served in the regular army as non-commissioned officers and all had had public school education. Most of them had been born and bred in Illinois and were "accustomed to the full exercise of their rights as citizens." Subsequent events proved that "in character and intelligence the official element of the Eighth was about up to the standard of the volunteer army."

Considerable rivalry was evinced by the several candidates for honor of heading the regiment. Many a citizen expected Major Buckner to become the Regiment's first colonel; rumors circulated that Charles Young, the only Negro graduate of West Point, would get the post; several of Chicago's leading white military men had their hats in the ring.

Much to the surprise of all was the elevation of Major John R. Marshall to the position of colonel in command of the Eighth Illinois Volunteer Infantry on July 23, 1898. This distinguished Marshall as the first colored man to wear the silver eagles denoting a colonel's rank in the United States Army. Governor Tanner said he chose Marshall to head the regiment because he was, "the best loved, the gamest and by far the most progressive military commander anywhere in Illinois."[8]

Though he was born a slave in Alexandria, Virginia, in 1859, John R. Marshall was the son of Representative Andrew Marshall (white) who was in turn son of John Marshall, renowned Supreme Court justice, and one of the signers of the Constitution of the United States.[9] Colonel Marshall's maternal aunt, Jane Brent, was said to have been a descendant of Pocahontas. He received his first military training in the Alexandria schools where he was graduated in 1874 with the highest honors of any pupil in the state of Virginia; for this scholastic attainment he was granted a free course in military training at Hampton Institute. He afterwards learned the bricklayer's trade and assisted in constructing the State Department building, Pennsylvania Avenue and 17th Street, Washington, D.C.

Marshall came to Chicago in 1880; he quit his trade in 1893 and accepted a political post in the county clerk's office where he was employed until the beginning of the Spanish-American War. It is difficult to speak of the soldiers of any race without paying some respect to their women folk—soldiers also. Miss Essie Arnold, a niece of Mrs. Marshall, was reared by the colonel and his wife. Red-headed, vivacious, smartly dressed Essie was toasted and known as "The Daughter of the Eighth Regiment." Essie too came from Alexandria, Virginia; her folks owned a farm on the spot where the Congressional Library stands. It was Essie who raised $2,000 for trees to be placed along Giles Avenue to glorify the Eighth Regiment Armory.[10]

While the War Department discouraged volunteering by colored men at the outset of the Spanish-American War, circumstances caused a change in this attitude. Yellow fever and other tropical diseases took a heavy toll of the white troops in Cuba. Medical testimony to the comparative immunity of Negroes resulted in the formation of ten regiments of "immunes." Of the ten, four were composed of colored men. These were the Seventh, Eighth, Ninth and Tenth U.S. Volunteer Infantries; all with the exception of the Eighth were officered by white men. The Eighth Regiment, 1,300 strong, was sworn into the U.S. Government service on July 13, 1898, by Major Ballou of the U.S. Army.

In Illinois the Eighth, through Colonel Marshall, requested Governor Tanner to muster them for the fight in Cuba. Governor Tanner accepted the offer and transmitted the same to Washington where President McKinley expressed jubilation over the offer. Immediately,

Governor Tanner ordered the Eighth Regiment, then at Camp Tanner, to be in readiness to leave for Santiago, replacing the First Illinois at the front.

When the order from the Commander-in-Chief came through to the Eighth at Camp Tanner, the *Chicago Tribune* reported:

> Strange as it may seem, the men, who realizing the dreadful conditions existing at Santiago, manifest no fear of the fever and accept the situation without a murmur. There were expressions of "That's what we enlisted for" from all sides.

The Eighth left from Camp Tanner on the journey to Cuba August 8, 1898. Most of the cities along the route of travel turned out in large numbers to cheer the bravery of the black troopers.

By September 6, 1898, Governor Tanner received word from Colonel Marshall stating that the troops had arrived safely and all was well. A local daily newspaper published one letter to the governor,

> Sir: I have the honor to inform you that the Eighth Illinois Infantry, United States Volunteers, is stationed at San Luis, and we are getting along nicely. A good many of the men are sick with malarial fever, but none have the yellow fever yet. . . .
> The water is bad and the surgeon cannot get any ice. We have about thirty in the hospital. . . . No one is complaining. We are proud to be here to represent Illinois. . . . I think we will add glory to our race and honor to you, who sent us. I assure you that you have the thanks of every man in the regiment.
> . . your obedient servant,
> John R. Marshall, Colonel
> Eighth Regiment Volunteers.

Major Robert Jackson was sent with a detachment of the guard to Palma Soriona to preserve order between Spaniards and Cubans. Major Jackson handled the situation so well that both belligerents came to admire him. Years afterwards when the Major "Bob" sat in the lobby of the legislature building in Springfield (he was state representative for a number of years), he delighted in reflecting—

> When I was in Cuba back in '98 I was given a detachment of Eighth Regiment boys and sent to an inland town to take charge of it in the military occupation fashion. We had to clean up the town of malaria and yellow fever and cholera and other pests and pestilences.
> I was head man in the town and the natives considered me to be their temporary mayor. They would wine and dine me . . . nothing was too good for the old mayor.
> And the senoritas—Oh, those pretty Cuban senoritas!—Would place their beautiful heads on my shoulders and purr, "Oh, Senor Alcade, won't you stay with us forever? You're so brave, Senor Alcade!
> If left to me I would, believe me, gentlemen. I hated the day when I received orders from the superior command to evacuate . . . those senoritas were so tempting.

One evening forty years after the events in Cuba, Essie was busily preparing to attend a party; a plumber interrupted by calling to fix a leak in the old Marshall homestead at Calumet Avenue and 36th Street; while examining the job an old envelope fell from out of the nowhere. The envelope contained a batch of letters addressed to the colonel; excerpts from these letters were the following:

Sept. 13, 1898
Col. John R. Marshall

Dear Sir:
You and your regiment are, without doubt, undergoing the privations and hardships incident to a soldier's life, emphasized, in this case, by the fact of the unhealthy clime in which you are stationed. The eyes of your race and the country are upon you and your regiment. So far you have done your whole duty as American citizen soldiers and patriots. I have an abiding confidence in you as Colonel, in your officers, and the rank and file of your regiment.

I am keeping close watch of your doings, because of the fact that yours is the only and full regiment of Afro-American soldiers ever sent to war.

(signed) John Tanner, Governor

Springfield, Ill.
Sept. 22, 1898
Col. John R. Marshall

Dear Sir:
The 6th Illinois has just returned from Porto Rico [sic], and reports that they have no potatoes during their stay of several weeks on the Island, so that it would appear the troops are all being treated alike in this matter.

(signed) J. Mack Tanner, Sec'y
to the Governor

Springfield, Ill.
Oct. 17, 1898

My dear Colonel:
. . . You and your command stand well at the White House, and the President said that the happiest moment of his life was when he received the telegram from Gov. Tanner informing him that you and your men were ready for duty at Santiago.

(signed) Jasper N. Reese
Adjutant General

After the war the regiment returned to the States amid great applause and excitement. In Chicago twenty-three year old Nellie Anderson, 213 West 42nd Street, was discharged in the West 54th Street Police Court on the morning of September 2, 1898. Nellie had been arrested on charges of disorderly conduct. Detective Curry of the "tenderloin" precinct had arrested the woman at 8 o'clock in the morning for kissing men on Sixth Avenue. When asked if the charge was true Nellie replied:

"It certainly is, your honor, I not only kissed but I hugged two men at Sixth Avenue and Thirty-first street, but they were both soldiers, and they were in uniform."

"Were they tanned and browned up? Were they from the Seventy-first Regiment?" asked Magistrate Pool.

"They were tanned all right," the prisoner replied, "but they were from the Eighth Regiment. I'd be glad to kiss a Seventy-first man, but there are other heroes in the town."

"Was your only motive in greeting these men so affectionately to show your appreciation of the fact that they had returned home safe and sound from the dangers of camp?" was the next question.

"That was my only purpose," declared Nellie. She was discharged.

The President of the United States sent for Colonel Marshall to have luncheon with himself and Charles Dawes who was then Controller of Currency. The president tried to persuade Marshall to accept a position in the Philippines, but the colonel had one ambition to fulfill, to build an armory for the Eighth Regiment. A few months later a Washington newspaper carried the following article:

Through the efforts of Col. J. R. Marshall of Chicago, the Legislature of Illinois has been induced to appropriate $100,000 for the Eighth Regiment Armory.

When the Colonel got so persistent in his asking the appropriation of $100,000, one of the senators asked him did we have the least idea how much money he was asking for, and he said, "Yes Sir. I learned that at Hampton 30 years ago. Why, I am asking for one million dimes or two million nickels." This humor was so great it made the whole senate laugh and they said, "Well, any man who knows how many dimes and nickels there are off-handedly, as do you, deserves the money, and we will give it to you for your hall."

Colonel Marshall was the only Negro on the governor's staff, and he was an honorary member of the St. Louis Country Club. He was to go to that city to dedicate the Illinois building during the St. Louis Fair. The following letter from Lieutenant C. Sidney Haight was received by Colonel Marshall on July 12, 1902:

Col. J. R. Marshall

Dear Sir:
Kindly inform me whether your regiment is colored. Col. Culp, who recently died, failed to inform me of this fact, and if this is the case you will see how necessary it will be to make some special arrangements for your accommodation. Would you be willing to bring your own tents and cooking outfit, and occupy a site that has been provided for your organization of the size of your regiment?

Very truly yours,

(signed) C. S. Haight,
1st Lieut. 4th Cov. U.S.A.
Military Attache

The answer:

Lieut. C. S. Haight
4th United States Cavalry
St. Louis, Mo.

Dear Sir: I have the honor to acknowledge the receipt of your communication of the 23rd, and in reply to same will state that the Eighth Infantry of which I have the honor to command is a colored regiment and Colonel Culp was informed of that fact at the time that I made the arrangements. We do not ask more, and would not accept less than what is provided for other military organizations, and to relieve you of any dilemma which you may have fallen into by being the successor of Col. Culp, I herewith cancel our engagement at the St. Louis Exposition . . . and will issue the order to my command to-day.

Very truly yours

(signed) John R. Marshall
Colonel Eighth Infantry,
Ill, M.N.G.

A few days later newspapers carried the following headline:

AS A RESULT OF HIS CORRESPONDENCE WITH THE COL. OF THE EIGHTH ILL. REGIMENT SUG-
GESTING SEGREGATION OF BLACK TROOPS AT FAIR, GENERAL BATES ADVISES HIM TO QUIT.

President Roosevelt has given another illustration of his regard for the Negro and as a result of this friendship Lieut. C. S. Haight of the Fourth United States Cavalry has tendered his resignation as military aid to President Francis. The resignation has been accepted by the Board of Directors, and Lieut. Haight will join his regiment in the near future. . . .

By 1900 the Chicago Negro community had re-established itself so well after the siege of war that it could sponsor a gala celebration as the one described in the following article:

The First Regiment Armory rocked and swayed with ragtime music last night for the celebration of the greatest entertainment by colored talent in the city. ARMANT'S famous colored orchestra fairly carried the dancers off their feet with its bursts of staccato harmonies.

Colored men and women dressed in the height of fashion swayed and swirled and glided over the waxed floor in the maze of the ragmalia cotillion. Mingling with them were other figures dressed in the most fantastic costumes. One dark woman whose face had been liberally plastered with some cosmetics looked absolutely green under the electric light. But generally they were quite pretty and one or two handsome.

It was evident from the conversation and bearing of the spectators that they were generally of the select circles of the colored society. . . .

With each trip to Texas, Negro officers and men experienced trouble and embarrassment. In 1911, *Inter Ocean* published the following article:

Because Colonel John R. Marshall, senior of the eleven officers of the Illinois National Guard, now attending the school of instruction at San Antonio, Texas, is a Negro, an embarrassing situation had developed in military circles in that city, and word was received in Chicago last night that relations between Colonel Marshall and his fellow officers are becoming more strained every hour.

It is the custom of the war department to hold a school of instruction for military officers once a year, to which a proportionate number of officers from each State are invited. Illinois quota this year was eleven. They were selected by Gov. Deneen, and the list was headed by Colonel Marshall, in command of the Eighth Infantry, colored. Necessarily there is much social life where the "schools" are held, and the advent of the colored Colonel in San Antonio is causing much comment.

Usually each National Guard officer or each body is assigned to some of the division officers of the Federal Army for entertainment and instruction. But no one has yet been found who is willing to accept the assignment to extend these courtesies to Colonel Marshall.

Again in 1916, trouble brewed because the white soldiers failed to salute officers of the Eighth Infantry while they were in Texas. Stated the *Chicago Defender*, Negro weekly:

> The lot of our soldiers . . . is not a pleasant one. Although they wear the uniform of the United States they are barred from all places of amusement, saloons refuse to serve them while the taunting remarks from the white soldiers and the citizens sting them. . . . The white soldiers will not salute superior officers if they are colored. This is a grave offense in the army, and it would seem strange to any land to have one class of men who have no redress in such cases.[11]

The article goes on to quote the *Daily Northwestern*, published in Oshkosh, Wisconsin, which gives a clear view of the situation. A letter from its correspondent who was with the Wisconsin regiment at the front reads:

> There is no use in moralizing about this fact, there are regulars and a large majority of state troops that *hate* to see a Negro in a uniform. . . . I was standing at the head of the car line . . . when a colored Captain of the Eighth and a white regular from a regular company met nearly in front of me. The white man failed to salute the Negro officer and the latter stopped him and asked him if his failure to salute was intentional and the white officer's answer was that he would salute the uniform if he (colored) hung it on the post . . . taking them man for man, they have been as orderly as the whites. . . .

Concerning the regiment's contemplated trip to that state in 1919 the *Defender* announced that:

> Illinois has always felt proud of the Eighth Regiment and also knows that the Regiment is capable of taking care of itself. They won't molest the Texans but Texans must not molest them.

Once again the "Eighth" was to hold itself in readiness for the call of war; this time the conflict was to be against our Gulf Coast neighbors, the Mexicans. Colonel John R. Marshall early began drilling and training men for possible duty on the Southern border. A sudden change in administration was effected at the armory, but the new commander, Colonel Franklin A. Denison, continued the war effort:

> Colonel Franklin A. Denison commanding the regiment has taken advantage of the "war fever" and is using it to enlist men. Last Sunday morning he assigned several friends and officers to speak at churches in the city. . . .
> Secretary of the War Garrison sent word to Adj. General Dickson of the Illinois mobilization, and Springfield, Col. A. Denison, Monday night communicated this message to his staff officers.[12]

A few days after Colonel Denison began recruiting, word reached the city that plans for a new regiment home for the Eighth was being rapidly pushed ahead. The *Chicago Defender* reported:

> The 8th Infantry will have for its home one of the most imposing structures in Chicago. This became an assured fact when Colonel Franklin Denison conferred with Governor Dunne. The Governor signed the plans for the new Colonel.
> The building will be erected at 35th Street and Forest Avenue. The ground covered will

CHAPTER TEN

be 5,000 square feet. There is every known convenience to perfect the soldiers in ways of modern warfare and physical training. The swimming pool and gymnasium will be along a most improved plan.

Other features will be rifle range, main drill hall, banquet hall, two reception halls, ladies and gentlemen's reception halls, smoking parlors, dining room, kitchen, sanitary barber shops and bowling alleys.

This is the first time in the history of the United States the race has been so honored. . . .[13]

The regiment was steadily increasing its numbers and eventually orders were received to report to their home base preparatory to moving to the border for duty. Daily newspapers reflected the sentiments of the populace regarding Negro troops. The following item is a typical example:

From 35th Street down Michigan Avenue to Grant Park a real old-fashioned Negro jubilee was held last night to speed Col. Franklin Denison's Eighth Infantry on its way to Springfield—the last of Chicago's regiments to leave.

Two thousand men, women, and pickininies marched beside the soldiers, and even in the ranks all the way from the armory to Grant Park, and thousands of others poured downtown in street cars.

"Heah is de boys waht goin to bring Villa's head," shouted a fat man with a shiny face round as the moon, when the procession neared the Auditorium Hotel.

. . . and the band struck up "Dixie." The crowds stringing along beside the band, let out a roar that bodes ill for the Mexicans should the Eighth be given a chance to avenge the wiping out of two troops of the Tenth Calvary.

Inside the Armory men were kissing wives, sweethearts and sisters, and those who had no relatives present, kissed the other men's relatives for good measure.

Sgt. Robinson of Company A, who was on guard duty at the door, reached into the crowd and pulled out Geraldine Randall, dressed in pink and blue and wearing a blue-ribboned bonnet.

"Come heah gal," he said. I don't know yo' name but I got to bus you just once. My wife couldn't come down but I got to tell somebody goodbye."

The girl grinned and gave him as hearty smack as he bestowed.

As the Regiment swung down Michigan Ave. the nested choir of Trinity Church came out on the steps and sang "America."[14]

As was characteristic of the Eighth, the regiment is said to have done a good job on the border and conducted itself well. The boys returned to their native Chicago early in November 1916, and were given a "grand home-coming reception." According to the *Defender*,

The Eighth Illinois Infantry, Colonel Franklin A. Denison commanding . . . returned from the border Saturday morning . . . the regiment was disbanded after a buffet luncheon was served and speeches by prominent men were made.

. . . The line of the march was through all of the principle streets in the loop and back to the Armory.

Employees of the Marshall Field store surged out and gave them a rousing welcome as the band struck up "There'll Be a Hot Time in the Old Town Tonight," as did the City Hall employees as the regiment passed.[15]

The Mexican skirmish only served as a workout to warm up the soldiers for a REAL war—World War I. The spirit of the people was well expressed in the following article:

The war spirit of Chicago's Negroes was voiced yesterday in Bethel Church.

Resolutions were adopted urging the President and Congress to be unwavering in dealing with Germany and promised the support of all Negro citizens of Chicago.

At every mention of the word "war" the audience stood up and waved flags and cheered. That the church body itself wanted war—war that stood for the "shedding of blood to wipe out the sins among nations," was indicated in the invocation by the Reverend Doctor W.D. Cook, pastor of Bethel.

Never has the patriotism of the Negro been questioned. When our country seeks out spies and traitors, it never comes to the door of the colored man. His loyalty and devotion will always be unquestioned.

"From Bunker Hill to Carrizal our blood has been shed for our country's cause," said Doctor Allen A. Wesley, chairman of the meeting. "Our greatest heroes are military men. We name our children after them."

Negroes in their zeal to swell the rolls of the Eighth invented novel methods of recruiting. Taking cognizance of this feature the *Tribune* reported:

It was a gala afternoon in the vicinity of 35th Street and Forest Ave. yesterday. The regimental band of the 8th Regiment Illinois Infantry was tuning up. In the sunlight they came and dense crowds gathered and applauded. Bandmaster James B. Tucker swung his baton—bam! "da-da-de-da, da-de-da-a-a-a."

The crowd swung from side to side in involuntary rhythm. . . . On the window sills the beauties of Forest Ave. tapped their knuckles as they watched their men with adoring eyes. Down the street went the band and swerved and came back to the armory. And a dozen glory inspired boys rushed in and enlisted.

Fifty recruits were "rugged" in during the day. Had the band included a trap drum the regiment could have gotten twice as many recruits. Although not yet called to service, there have been over 200 enlistments in the last five days.

"If we were called to service there should be a rush of 200 men inside an hour," said Capt. Lewis.[16]

On April 6, 1917, when the United States formally declared war on Germany, the Eighth was one of the first to be ordered overseas. On July 25, 1917, the regiment, under the command of Colonel Franklin A. Denison, was ordered to join the American Expeditionary Forces and became known as the 370th Infantry, attached to the Thirty-forth, Thirty-sixth, and Fifty-ninth French divisions.

According to Addie W. Hunton and Kathryn M. Johnson, the regiment landed at Brest on April 6, 1918, and after spending three days at Camp Pontanezen, took a train and went to the town of Grand Villars and here—

they . . . were reorganized according to the French regulations, and in fact became French soldiers in every respect except their uniforms; they were even furnished with French food, and chefs to teach them how to prepare it most economically.

With the Negro troops in France, Oct. 20, 1918—Some writer once said that the only pure folklore we have in the United States are the old time melodies and camp meetings songs of the southern Negro. One starts thinking the proposition over as the line of colored doughboys swings down the sycamore lined roadways of France, in the dusk of the evening, singing in that quavering, strident, half moaning voice that surely has the elements of both primitiveness and originality.

"It's Me, O Lawd, Standing in the Need of Prayer" . . . the high-pitched voice of the leader and the harmonious tones of the chorus as they give the refrain in organ-like tones.

It has a swing to it that cannot be described without the notes. Lieutenant Sonny (white), a Plattsburg and Harvard man who has charge of this company told me he couldn't possibly have a finer lot of soldiers under him than these Negro boys. He encouraged them to use their plantation songs and kept them at it for months until they had no fear of Hun, nor death, nor anything in the world if only their hearts can give voice to the stirring melodies.[17]

The writer tells a story of a group of soldiers singing the above named song when they were fired upon by a Hun plane and all of them seeking the shelter of their trench except one who became excited and ran across the field with a shovel over his head, singing at every jump, "It's me, it's me O'Lord."

> Give roast beef hot,
> Give roast beef cold,
> Give roast beef ninety days old.
> Give you a sour wine,
> Then a slice of bread,
> You hear taps blow,
> You hunt for bed.
> Give navy beans hot,
> Give navy beans cold,
> Give navy beans ninety days old.
> Give you fat meat,
> Think it is sweet,
> Go back after seconds,
> Get more'n can eat,
> Give white potatoes hot,
> Give white potatoes cold,
> Give white potatoes, jackets and all,
> Give you sour wine,
> Then slice of bread,
> Hear taps blow,
> You hunt for bed.

The words were written by a colored boy; though the meter and music were primitive, the song became very popular about mess time. "Somehow they do manage to make real melody out of it."

It is this continual singing for every task the day through that makes the colored boys the most cheerful soldiers of all the American Expeditionary Forces. They are gluttons for work all through the S.O.S. zone, and the war machine doubtless would get clogged up many times were it not for the black boys. . . .

The colored boys are great fighters. . . . They do take pardonable pride . . . in the fact that Mistah Johnson, a colored boy, was the First American soldier in France to be decorated for extraordinary bravery under fire.

It is not an uncommon sight to see a crowd of white doughboys around a piano in some "Y" or Red Cross hut, singing to beat the band, with a colored jazz band expert pounding the stuffing out of the piano. . . . Many a bleak and drab day of privation and suffering is made a bit brighter by the humor that comes spontaneously to the lips of the "bronze boys."

How this will work out after the war no one can foresee, of course. A few may insist that they be treated with the same consideration that the French people show them, but on the whole I don't think there will be a serious development along this line.

The Negro soldiers, for the most part, are not thinking of social equality, but they are thinking very hard of a little cable message that came across the other day. It was to the effect that the United States government intended to throw open land reservations for the soldiers who have served in France.

A very intelligent view of the situation was expressed to me the other day by Henry M. Collins, a colored chaplain, who has about 8,000 Negro soldiers to minister to. Collins was an A.M.E. pastor in Tacoma, Washington, at the outbreak of the war. He is a graduate of Fisk University and the theological school of Wilberforce University. He is a man of great charm and refinement and of a profound education.

He entertains no illusions as to the question of social equality, but sees in this war a new day dawning for the colored race in America.[18]

In May 1918, Addie W. Hunton and Kathryn M. Johnson joined up with the Eighth Illinois Infantry Regiment and found themselves overseas in France during YMCA work. The two women made day-by-day accounts of Negro troops all over the country.

. . . Our soldiers often told us of signs on YMCA huts which read "No Negroes Allowed," and sometimes other signs would designate the hours when colored men could be served. . . .

Sometimes even when there were no such signs, service to colored soldiers would be refused. One such soldier . . . came across a YMCA hut, went in and asked them to sell him a package of cakes, they refused to sell it to him under the plea that they did not serve Negroes.

We feel that special emphasis should be given the 370th Infantry, because it was the only regiment that crossed the sea with a full quote of colored officers, made a splendid record for bravery, received numerous individual citations for conspicuous and meritorious conduct, and returned with a full quote of colored officers with the exception of a colonel, one captain, and one second lieutenant.

When the regiment had served eleven months in France where it distinguished itself and was decorated by the American French government, it returned to America and arrived in New York on February 9, 1919.

According to reports the following comprised a resume of casualties and citations:

Killed in Action	90
Died of wounds	53
Wounded	370
Captured	1
Distinguished Service Crosses	22
Distinguished Service Medals	22
Divisional Croix De Guerre	12

Regimental Croix De Guerre   1
Army Croix De Guerre   Co. "C"

The regiment was finally mustered out of the National Army and was reorganized on April 11, 1919, under the command of Colonel Otis S. Duncan, and on August 26, 1921, the Eighth Regiment, Illinois National Guard, was given federal recognition.

The years 1918 to December 1941 may be termed "Peacetime," but during this period the Eighth from time to time showed the nation that she was yet alive. In August 1928, the Sangamon post of the American Legion elected Colonel Otis B. Duncan one of the sixteen delegates to the Illinois State Convention of the American Legion, held in Chicago. Sangamon post at that time boasted a membership of about 1,600. On April 16, 1932, the regiment and friends mourned the death of Brigadier General Franklin A. Denison (at that time, the only race officer to hold such a position). The following year found nine hundred officers and enlisted men of the regiment leaving for their two-week encampment at Camp Grant.

Colonel Spencer Dickerson, commander of the unit, will head the rank.

In August 1935, Colonel W. Warfield the new commander

demonstrated outstanding strategical military knowledge when he led his famous regiment in the combined field maneuvers which lasted from August 11 to 14. . . . Because of millions of grasshoppers found in this area, the men unanimously named the camp "Hopperville."[19]

In February 1939, Colonel William J. Warfield, "who commands Chicago's 8th Regiment, has been signally honored in the state legislature by appointment as chairman of the Military Affairs Committee of the House of Representatives."[20]

In September of the same year it was announced by the War Department that the Eighth Regiment—

will become the 184th Field Artillery Regiment effective September 15, 1940.

Camp Grant, Illinois-November 9, 1940.

Training effective only for actual combat, forced the Eighth Infantry outgrown of the "fighting Eighth" of World War fame when on Sunday they began seven days of extensive battle training at Camp Grant.

It also marked the first time in Twenty years the 8th Infantry has been called into an extra training period and followed an emergency order from the War Department.[21]

It was around 1939 that the Associated Negro Press, and the two leading Negro magazines, *Opportunity* and *Crisis*, began open warfare anent the Negro's place in military affairs. In February 1939 *Crisis* advised the public that—

Hundreds of millions of dollars are to be spent making the United States ready for any emergency. One item is to be the expansion of the air force, with the training of as many as 20,000 men in aviation at selected centers. What part is the Negro American to have in this program of national defense?

The article concludes:

In the navy, Negroes may serve their country only as mess attendants. The doors of the naval academy at Annapolis have been barred much more tightly than those at West Point.

There is no good reason why we should have no Negro aviators or generals or admirals.

. . . We want all the hard barriers in the armed services of the nation taken down. We want to fly and fight for our country. We want no bars in any branch of the army, navy or air corps. Let us see some Negro cadets in training and let the enlistment offices for other branches open to our men and boys.[22]

In another article of the same edition the audience was reminded of the fact that—

Every tenth man in America's World War Armies was a Negro: 400,000 out of 4,000,000 were Negroes.

"If a person is of African descent, tear off the corner" was a sentence at the bottom of over 10,000,000 registration blanks sent to those who registered for the draft.

In March of the same year *Crisis* called attention to the fact that—

When the war started the question arose whether or not to give Negroes commissions as officers. There was already one Negro Colonel in the Army, Colonel Charles Young, class of 1889 West Point. Colonel Young should have been made a General but to get around all questions the government retired him from active duty, the excuse being physical unfitness. Thus a white man became commander of the 92nd Division.

Judging from prevailing Jim Crow practices in the armed forces of the United States today, the next war—if we have another—will see the same gross maltreatment of the Negro soldier as seen in the World War.[23]

In May 1940 *Opportunity* published an article titled "The Negro at War":

If America should enter the Second World War we hope that she will permit her Negro citizens to bear their burdens and assume their responsibilities without the humiliation and insult which was theirs, particularly in the armed forces of the Nation, during the last World War. The treatment accorded the Negro soldier in France, and to lesser extent in America, constitutes a shameful chapter in American history. It is without parallel in the military annals of any country in the world.

Nowhere is racial prejudice more entrenched than in the Army and Navy of the United States. . . . Negroes may not enter the air corps, the artillery, or the signal corps of the United States Army. And in the Navy the Negro may aspire to no grade other than mess attendant. . . .

Negro youth is entitled to an opportunity to enlist in the Army and Navy, in every branch of the service. The obligation to offer one's life for one's country should be free from the dispiriting humiliation of racial prejudice.[24]

In June 1940, the *Pittsburgh Courier*, a Negro weekly, stated that—

The United States army must cease being a white man's army and become a citizen's army; the American people wish it.[25]

In December 1941, the President of the United States, Franklin D. Roosevelt, declared this nation is a state of war, World War II. On Wednesday, April 8, 1942, the *Chicago Tribune* carried the following article:

NAVY TO ACCEPT NEGRO RECRUITES FOR ACTIVE DUTY
Marine and Coast Guard Doors Also Opened.
Washington, D.C., April 7 (AP)

The Navy department announced today that Negro volunteers would be accepted for enlistment for general service as reservists in the navy, marine corps, and coast guard, with recruiting soon to get under way.

... small warships such as destroyers or patrol craft eventually may be manned with Negro crews commanded by white petty officers and commissioned officers.

Negroes will get the same ratings and pay as white enlisted men and may be assigned to a variety of duties, including a special Negro outfit in the marines, employment in navy yards, and work on construction crews.

In commenting on this decision of the United States Navy Department, Lucius Harper, prominent Negro newspaper man, in his *Chicago Defender* column, titled "Dustin' Off the News," said,

this action brought to a close the black man's fight of some 80 years to be included in all branches of the defense forces of this nation.

11. Business

There are several drafts of this chapter. The most recent that appears here was written by Jack Conroy and found at Newberry Library. There is a twenty-page essay and a four-page chapter fragment in the IWP papers with corrections made in Conroy's handwriting. There is also an earlier version labeled "Business 2nd draft" in Arna Bontemps's handwriting at the Newberry Library with IWP worker Mathilde Bunton's name listed on the front page as the author. Bunton did much of the original research on this topic.

In 1837, three of the seventy-seven Negroes included in Chicago's population of 4,170 were business men. Lewis Isabel, the first Negro barber in Illinois, came to the state in 1824, and to Chicago fourteen years later. Abram Hall, an itinerant preacher, who opened a shop in 1844, is reputed to be the first Negro barber to own his business. John Johnson was another barber of the time; the Chicago Public Library is said to have developed from the library and reading room conducted by the Young Men's Association above his shop. In the forties, Ambrose Jackson was the first restaurant operator of his race. In 1845, John Jones became the city's first Negro merchant tailor.

By 1843, the Negro population of Chicago had decreased to sixty-five, including four in business: a saloon keeper, a bath house operator, and two barbers. Harry Knight owned the largest stables in the city in 1852, and John Collins became Chicago's first Negro decorator. Thornton Ellsworth maintained a fruit business. Ison Artis hauled from the lake in his wagon water which he sold for eight cents a barrel. Jary Gray in 1856 opened the first hair store downtown, while Israel Bunch was running a transfer business. Reuben Collins in 1857 became the first confectioner, and J. B. Dawson, for whom Dawson Avenue was named, owned a large grocery store in addition to a real estate business. Platt Place is named for Jacob F. Platt, first lumber dealer. Isaac Atkinson in 1859 ran a stage bus line rivaling Parmalee's.

There were 1,500 Negroes in the city in 1860, and thirty-two of these were engaged in business. There were sixteen hairdressers, five barbers, four draymen, three butchers, one hotel keeper, one blacksmith, and one whitewasher. Mrs. Joe Stanley in 1862 employed five girls in her hair-dressing establishment. J. O. Grant and his wife opened "The Break of Day," an all-night lunch room, in 1868.

Negro business suffered in the "panic" years of 1867, 1873, and 1876, with many ventures failing. One of the outstanding successes of the following years was Charles H. Smiley, who arrived in 1885, and became one of the city's foremost caterers. Smiley first worked as a janitor, serving dinners and parties in his spare time. Then he went into the catering business for himself. He prided himself upon his complete service; as caterer for a wedding he prepared to supply the wedding cake, floral decorations, canopies, pillows, ribbons, kneeling altars, and even ushers. He announced that he would also deliver invitations and guard wedding presents. In 1907, Booker T. Washington said of him:

> He possessed assets more valuable than mere money. He had a resolute character, good powers of observation, ambition and brains.[1]

Chicago's first Negro millionaire was William Henry Lee, publisher. Earlier a partner of F. C. Laird, Lee became sole owner of the business in 1887. Lee's employees were white, and it was not generally known that he was a Negro. When he died in 1913, Chicago papers revealed his race. Eli Bates was a prosperous contemporary of Lee. Owner of a fleet of trucks, he accumulated a fortune which he invested in the "Bates Block" on South State Street. His exclusive apartment house, for white tenants only, was viewed with admiration by many visitors to the Columbian Exposition. It was equipped with steam heat and elevator service and was guarded by a doorman.[2]

It was also during this period that the first Negro businessmen's association was formed. The Chicago *Daily Inter Ocean* announced in 1880:

> The colored men of this city who are doing business for themselves held a meeting yesterday at 4 o'clock at the store of Johnson and Hoagland. The object of the meeting was to form an association to be known as the Colored Business Men's Association. After a general talk over matters pertaining to the proposed society and the appointment of several committees, they adjourned to meet next Monday, Aug. 30, at No. 198 Fourth Avenue, at 4 o'clock, for the purpose of completing the organization.[3]

In 1885 there were 110 businesses in Chicago owned and operated by Negroes in twenty-seven fields. Fourteen of these were service establishments, thirty-one barber shops, fourteen restaurants, twelve "sample" rooms (combination liquor stores and saloons), eight dressmaking shops, and seven expressing companies. John Maxwell opened the first Negro undertaking parlor.

H. C. Haynes arrived in Chicago in 1896 with two old razors, which he traded at a profit as the beginning of a flourishing business in barber's supplies. He was soon known as the "king of the razor sellers," and started the manufacture of a razor strop he had patented. The strop became so popular throughout the nation, and even in England and Germany. The German Kaiser's barber is said to have used a Haynes strop.[4]

Another enterprising manufacturer was A. C. Howard, born a slave in Mississippi. While working for the Pullman Company out of Chicago, he invested $180 in materials with which to manufacture shoe blacking. His first scales were two tin cans tied to a stick and made to balance. Howard peddled his polish to street bootblacks and railroad porters. Later he sold to all parts of the United States, and received orders from Mexico for as much as 70,000 boxes at a time.

Mrs. Annie M. Pope Turnbo-Malone, originator of the Poro beauty products and founder of Poro College, in 1900 used a small rear room in a cottage in Lovejoy, pioneer all-Negro village, as her first workshop. Two years later she moved to St. Louis, just across the Mississippi, to take advantage of the Louisiana Purchase Exposition. Poro Beauty College and a world-wide distribution of Poro products resulted from her efforts.[5]

Chicago's pioneer Negro banker was Jesse Binga, who opened his bank in 1908 after a career as a Pullman porter, huckster and peddler, and realtor. Other early Negro bankers were R. W. Hunter and A. W. Woodfolk.

From 1905 to 1908, Negro business in Chicago suffered a decline of 34.5%. The depression of 1907 took its toll, and newcomers from southern Europe were taking over many of the businesses formerly considered Negro enterprises, such as barbering and shoe shining. In 1912, Dr. George Cleveland Hall became president of a Chicago branch of the National Negro Business League, organized nationally by Booker T. Washington. Negro business had catered largely to the white public, but with the World War and the attendant great migration increasing the Negro population, a new market was created.

Shortly after the war, J. A. "Billboard" Jackson, special representative of the Essolence Company, and Albom Holsey of Tuskegee endeavored to publicize the fact that ten million Negroes represented a very profitable market. However, it was in 1932 when a white advertising firm of Chicago published the pamphlet, *The Negro Market*, that the concept became fully accepted. In this pamphlet the authors inferred that they knew the idiosyncrasies of the Negro and hence knew exactly how to reach successfully his pocketbook. The foreword points out:

> No merchandise picture is complete without an accurate knowledge of the living conditions of the buyers to whom the appeal is to be made. The purpose of this booklet is to give you a graphic pictorial idea of the living conditions of approximately one-tenth of our population—a market actually larger, by far, than the entire Dominion of Canada. This market must be capably understood and appealed to on its own terms if the millions of colored people comprising it are to be successfully courted as buyers.

During the migration thousands of southern Negroes sold their homesteads, withdrew all their savings from banks, stockings, or old mattresses, came to Chicago with these sums of money, and banked them. Because the hustle and bustle of the loop was frightening to these newcomers, the two Negro banks, centrally located, and easily reached by foot, became their repository.

The purchasing power of the Chicago Negro in 1929 is indicated by the combined resources of the Binga State Bank and the Douglass National Bank, which totaled almost four million dollars. In that year, when there were twenty-one Negro banks in the country with combined resources of $11,000,000, these two Chicago banks held thirty-six percent of the combined resources of all Negro banks in the United States.

It has been estimated by the Chicago Urban League that Chicago Negroes spent $39,000,000 in 1931. Eleven million was spent on groceries and vegetables, seven million on meat, a little over two million on milk, butter and eggs, over four million on wearing apparel, nearly two and a half million on shoes and overshoes, a little less than a million on millinery and haberdashery, over a quarter of a million on laundry and cleaning, and twelve million on furniture.

The depression beginning in 1929 dealt a severe blow to Negro establishments, many of them of recent origin and less prepared for the shock than older firms. Toward the end of 1929 it became evident that the Binga State Bank was nearing collapse and President Binga sought to stave off disaster by borrowing from Anthony Overton of the Douglass National Bank, but the terms were not acceptable. Binga then turned to Samuel Insull, who had assisted him before. Insull, however, was himself involved in difficulties and could not supply the requisite cash. In desperation, Binga then appealed to Melvin Traylor, chairman of the Board of Directors of the First National Bank of Chicago, who referred him to Edward Brown, first vice-president.

Binga later told a reporter from the Baltimore *Afro-American*:

> When I went to Brown he derided me, saying, "Why, you are no banker." I had known his father. The words hurt and confused me. I replied, "Your daddy would not have said that." The interview ended with Brown taking a position against me and (he) blocked every effort I made afterward to save the bank.

Binga's subsequent attempt to form a national bank led him into legal difficulties culminating in a prison sentence. The Douglass National Bank, heavily involved in real estate and insurance investments, closed its doors shortly after the Binga Bank succumbed.

A Negro politician has declared:

> I think we bury more money in the ground than any other group of people. We have the old-fashioned belief in elaborate funerals.

Be that as it may, Chicago Negro undertakers (in recent years "morticians") have prospered and built elaborate "funeral homes" with ornate chapels, electric organs, cushioned seats and soft lights. Expensive stream-lined hearses smoothly bear the dead to cemeteries which, too, are often "going" concerns. A case in point is Burr Oak Cemetery, maintained by the Supreme Liberty Life Insurance Company. Burial associations also do a thriving business. At one time some of the regular insurance companies considered Negroes as a poor risk, and the burial associations, guaranteeing a proper funeral for a small sum each week, developed in consequence.

Although they had many Negro policyholders, insurance companies for a long time seemed loath to employ members of the race, even in the minor category of collector. Resentment aroused by this practice helped along several insurance companies founded by and employing Negroes, the first of these being the Underwriters Mutual Life Insurance Company organized in 1918. The Liberty Life Insurance Company, in 1942 operating in nine states other than Illinois, followed in 1919. Between 1919 and 1927 many small industrial companies operated for brief periods. In 1942, four all-Negro insurance companies survived: Supreme Liberty Life, Victory Mutual Life, Unity Mutual, and Protective Mutual.

In 1942, there were more than 2,600 business concerns owned and operated by Negroes in Chicago. About 60% of these were service enterprises. The first ten varieties—comprising 75% of all Negro owned businesses were beauty parlors, grocery stores, barber shops, restaurants, tailors and cleaners, express and moving, auto repairers and garages, taverns, undertakers, and shoe repair shops. Approximately 35% of these were retail establishments.

Negro beauty parlors in Chicago numbered more than 1,500 in 1942. One of the first was opened in 1918 by Mrs. Marjorie Joyner, a Moler Beauty School graduate. Later she attended the Madam C. J. Walker School and became an agent for the Walker preparations, selling them throughout the United States, in South America, and the West Indies. Other South Side beauty training schools are the Apex, the Dimples, and Poro College, the last being a branch of the main Poro enterprises at St. Louis.

Negro restaurateurs have ranged from the operators of small hot dog stands and chile "parlors" to the proprietors of well-appointed dining rooms, catering primarily to professional and business men, such as Morris' Restaurant and the Palm Tavern. The "Chicken Shack" has been a typical development of the South Side, the best-known being the one founded by Ernie Henderson, and generally supposed to the scene of an episode in Richard Wright's novel and play *Native Son*. Mr. Henderson has indicated the genesis and progress of his venture:

> I started my business in 1930. I got the idea from a number of successful barbecue establishments: more people eat fried chicken than barbecue. I naturally thought it would be a wise investment. I started in a basement; I cooked the chicken myself. I advertised "The Best Fried Chicken in Town," and later had the name copyrighted. I soon had to hire a boy to deliver chicken on his bicycle; in four months I had quite a trade. Business got better and better; I enlarged the place, hired a cashier and bought a delivery car. In 1933, I bought the whole building.[6]

Some business men have managed a more or less gradual transition from "shady" enterprises to respectable commerce. A monumental instance of this trend was marked by the opening of the Ben Franklin Department Store by the Jones Brothers, policy magnates. Throngs crowded the streets for the ceremony, Champion Joe Louis was there to voice a few words of approval, and Bill "Bojangles" Robinson executed some of his intricate dance steps. Sociologist Horace Cayton, after surveying the comely brown-skinned maidens serving as clerks, said:

> I don't know the guy who hired the girls, but I think he picked them rather than hired them, because they sure are nice looking.

Then in less jocose mood he went on:

> The only unpleasant looks that I noticed came from some of the white officials of the South Center and Neisner (white owned and operated department stores) who stood in their doorways and looked upon the crowd with an unchallenging expression. . . . I think that this was one of the greatest events in the history of Chicago, a pace setting event for modern Negro business. I pray to God this will inspire some other Negroes who have money to open a real modernistic business place of their own.

The former owner of a chicken shack and barbecue stand has said:

> There is also one other thing in favor of those who have made their money from gambling or policy. The men who have run these places are the ones that have taken the lead in the business world. There is the Jonas Brothers' five and ten cent store; there is Dan Gaines' Ford Agency. There is also King Cole, owner of the Metropolitan Funeral Home.

A number of Negroes have successfully operated manufacturing establishments in Chicago. G. J. Washington, shirt maker, grossed $48,000 in 1932, Marshall Field, Rothschild, and the Boston Store being among his customers. Dr. E. A. Welters manufactures a tooth powder bearing his name. Two casket factories are operated by Negroes, while Paul E. Johnson manufactures physio-therapy equipment, including ultra-violet lamps and diathermy machines.

Colored taxicab companies, under the impetus of competition, have developed a kind of zoning system without legal sanction. The usual fee is ten cents for any ride between 31st and 67th on South Parkway; if a passenger wishes to leave the Parkway the sum becomes fifteen cents. Enterprising drivers also carry a number of riders picked up at various points and delivered at different destinations, a survival of "jitneying."[7]

Representing a more colorful though less general form of business is the proprietor of the Incense Book Store, who has protested:

> I do no "spookus" work. I am not a healer. Whenever people come to me for medical service or legal counsel, I refer them to a good physician or lawyer.

The Incense Book Store sells "guaranteed" policy numbers, lucky roots and herbs, as well as dream books and "holy" candles and incense. Listed among the lucky oils sold are magnet, lover's, attraction, crucifixion, holy bath, concentration, altar, spirit, success, seventh heaven, and compelling. A novelty and occult shop offers these sachet powders: uncrossing power, success, protection, attracting, commanding, lodestone, hi-john conqueror, dressing, fast luck, confusion, lover's, and holy. Another shop advertises:

SPECIAL TO NUMBER PLAYERS:
Are your dreams unlucky to you?
Do the gigs you get from your dreams split out?
Do others catch on your dreams when you fail to play them?
Do you have trouble remembering your dreams?
If so, you should read the 70th Psalm and use
MYSTIC DREAM INCENSE, 15¢–25¢

12. Work

There are two drafts of this chapter written by Jack Conroy. An earlier draft with footnotes is located in Conroy's papers at the Newberry Library. The version used here is a draft found at Syracuse University in which Conroy has integrated the footnotes, eliminated sections, and included additional material.

> WANTED: A man or boy who understands how to cook. A colored man would be preferred, to whom 20 dollars per month would be given and if found to be valuable the wages would increase.

This advertisement published in the *Illinois State Register and People's Advocate* in 1838 indicates one of the few occupations which Negroes at the time were considered capable of practicing.

Even after the Civil War, colored persons for the most part were restricted to the field of domestic and personal service—as butler, coachman, maid, cook, housekeeper, valet, or janitor. Negroes occasionally conducted businesses, were employed as skilled artisans, and successfully pursued professions, but the greater number of the race gainfully employed were found in the occupations named above, in agricultural work, and at unskilled labor.

The tasks at which Negroes were employed were a reflection of the limited opportunities afforded members of the race earlier in the South and of the fierce competition they met in the North when they attempted to invade fields other than those to which they were attached to by tradition. Few of those who below the Mason-Dixon line had mastered trades—and a surprising number were skilled workmen—migrated until several decades after the Civil War.

The continued influx of colored domestics, however, was noted by the *Chicago Times* in 1862:

> The large importation of Negroes, mulattoes, and other lighter shades of the servile tribe, threaten, if continued, to revolutionize the labor market in Chicago. It is a very convenient thing to have a Negro in the house. . . . He comes in so handily to fix things up generally; and can be got for little or no pay and will displace a class of help which is held in greater contempt by the employer than is the Negro.

In 1864 the *Times*, commenting on the animosity with which white ship loaders greeted Negro longshoremen, said:

A number of Negroes settled in the state of Illinois. Their labor could be secured much cheaper than the whites,' so the Negro labor replaced the jobs formerly held by the white shoremen at the lumber dock of C. Mears & Co. at the foot of Kinzie Street at the light-house. When the employer failed to discharge the Negroes about three or four hundred men called to force them out. The employer received no word of the gathering and the Negroes fled before the mob appeared. Except for speaking no trouble resulted.

That Negroes, many of them newly emancipated, were not willing to work for any wage, is attested by an item in the *Cairo Daily Democrat* in 1866:

The Negroes engaged in the dirt pit, outside of the level, struck yesterday for higher wages. They have been receiving $1.75 per day, and want $2.00. In consequence, the dirt cars have stopped running, and the street filling has, for the time being, been discontinued. There is little doubt that the Messrs, Foxx, Howard & Co. will speedily satisfy their employees, and resume work.

In many of the larger cities of the North, and notably in Chicago, colored waiters in hotels and restaurants were dominant, and in several instances conducted strikes for higher wages or against objectionable conditions. One walkout occurred in the Palmer House in 1875, and the *Chicago Daily Inter Ocean* said of the rebels:

Some of them became so demonstrative as to require the assistance of the police in quieting them.

In 1874, growing tension between white miners and imported colored workers in the southern part of Illinois was indicated by the posting of a "notis to black legs and negroes" warning them to leave the Barnett mines in Clay County.

. . . between this and Saturday nite or abide by the consequences. Woe to the bosses is found. By order of 500 men.

Later in the year, the *Cairo Bulletin* urgently called "the attention of Governor Beveridge and the Republican party of this State . . . to the deplorable condition of affairs in Southern Illinois." It was reported that business concerns and citizens of Anna, Union County, had "received notice that they must discharge all the Negroes in their employ and send the Negroes out of the county or suffer the consequences." These threats were attributed to the Ku Klux Klan.

It has been contended that much of the bitter labor conflict between white and black workers might have been avoided had the National Labor Congress, meeting in Chicago in 1867, decided to organize both instead of laying over to the next session the question of organization among Negroes. The order declined rapidly in the following years, as did the National Labor Union, an independent Negro organization formed in 1870. Although some colored workers were admitted to the Knights of Labor, which disavowed racial prejudice, the great mass remained aloof. The Industrial Workers of the World, organized in 1905, made a special appeal to Negroes, but few heeded.

A Colored Men's Convention which assembled in Springfield in 1885 passed resolutions favoring free trade and the liberation of Ireland. Civil Rights and the problems of the Negro jobseeker, however, were the principal topics. One delegate (named Smith) said:

> There is no greater question the people have to deal with than this question. It is whether the seven million colored people of this country shall prove a source of strength or weakness. If of strength, it is good; if of weakness, it is evil. It is far better to educate men and women than to educate them and deprive them of opportunity to exercise their facilities. We can find colored graduates of schools and colleges serving in club rooms, thrown into immoral associations which must contaminate them. Our young men can obtain employment in some lines, but those lines are dangerous to their morals, preventing the building and blossoming of high noble and patriotic purposes in their hearts. Result: they feel that they are aliens in their own land, doomed to a life of drudgery, and hence they will feel a lack of interest in the welfare of the country. Shut our young men out of the factories and throw them into brothels and club rooms, and you dwarf their manhood and ruin their morals. It is as a plant transplanted, a rose turned into a thorn. You keep a man from rising from the position of a menial or serf, keep him always in temptation and adverse circumstances. In short, you can't grow a good citizen by keeping him in the worst position in society. The interests of the colored people today are not with any political party, but with the great laboring masses of the country. If we would only form an alliance with them, the door of every factory would open as if touched by a magician's wand.

Following the appointment of Chicago's first Negro policeman in 1876, others managed to obtain from time to time political jobs increasing in number and importance. In 1882, John Welsey Terry was promoted for foreman of the ironing and fitting department of the Chicago West Division Street Car Company shops. In 1886, he was chosen by his Knights of Labor lodge to represent it on a committee endeavoring to settle a strike at the stockyards. E. P. Smith, a bridge tender at Van Buren Street, was removed from his position in 1887, and a protest meeting developed. Commissioner of Public Works Swift told a *Daily Inter Ocean* reporter:

> I don't believe there is any indignation. Why, we've had this office full of colored brethren protesting against Smith's holding the place, and they put it about right when they said that a colored man had no business being a Democrat. . . . There is no race prejudice about it. . . .

While there were isolated instances of advancement or entry into new fields, Negroes were being supplanted in other lines of endeavor. As early as 1888 the *New York Sun* commented on the forcing out of northern Negroes from occupations formerly considered their particular province, such as those of barber, waiter, coachman, and whitewasher. The Chicago *Daily Inter Ocean* requested the opinion of Ferdinand L. Barnett, prominent Negro attorney and editor of Chicago, and he replied:

> I think the statements are materially correct. . . . The fact is the colored man is shut out of all the great middle class of employment. He must either find his way into the professions, if possible, or accept a position of humble servitude. The trades, the mercantile branches, are practically closed to the colored man. . . . It is undoubtedly on account of his color.

In March 1887, more than one hundred Negroes arrived in Peoria to take the place of striking white miners. The *Chicago Evening Journal* observed:

Outside a few of the more skilled and organized trades, if a body of workmen generate sufficient temerity to ask for less hours or an advance in wages, the Goliath in command has only to utter the magical word "Negroes" to drive them back into the ruts in fear and trembling for their positions.

Despite threats and violence, Negro workers continued to invade new territory. In 1893, Negro quarrymen were involved in a strike on the drainage canal between Lemont and Romeo, and a month later white workers in the village of Sandoval protested against the hiring of two Negro carpenters. Later in the same year, the *Daily Inter Ocean* called attention to the employment in Chicago of two Negro newsstand operators, one a man and the other a woman, by the Union News Company.

Apparently not profiting by the errors of its predecessors, American Railway Union in 1894 wrote into its constitution a clause limiting membership to "railway employees born of white parents," despite opposition by President Eugene V. Debs and more than a few delegates. Colored workers promptly formed the Anti-Strikers' Railroad Union. Later that year great numbers of Negroes and newly arrived Polish immigrants were secured to break the stockyards strike. Though the first Negro stockyards workers—two men—had been hired in 1881, colored workers were not conspicuous for several years. Many more were taken on in 1904 to break the largest strike the yards had known. It has been estimated that 10,000 Negroes were then working at the stockyards. However, after each strike most of the Negroes were displaced by defeated workmen returning to their jobs.

The Negro's role in Illinois employment is indicated by 1890 census figures. Those engaged in domestic and personal services—10,865 men and 4,061 women—still were in the majority, while agriculture, fishing and mining occupied 4,323 men and 134 women. Trades and transportation engaged 1,994 men and 41 women; manufacturing and mechanical occupations, 1,603 and 361. Listed as professionals were only 486 men and 118 women. Forty percent of the Negro population of Illinois was employed.

In 1895, the *Chicago Tribune* reported the formation of a union by the colored printers and journalists of the city,

... the first of its kind in the world. ... It is called the National Afro-American Typographical Association. Delegates were present from Indianapolis and the southern states.

While northern Negroes were demanding the right to join labor unions, coal companies of southern Illinois continued to import as strikebreakers Negroes who had only the vaguest notions as to the purposes and practices of labor unions. The Spring Valley massacre of 1895 occurred when striking white miners—most Italian immigrants—were displaced by Negro newcomers and retaliated with violence.[1] Again in 1898 a coal company at Virden installed 300 Alabama Negroes, and 75 armed guards to protect them, in the place of employees who had walked out in protest against the company's refusal to recognize the terms of an agreement between the Illinois Coal Operators' Association and the union. In the ensuing riot, ten miners and six guards were killed and about 30 persons injured.

Although generally excluded from labor unions, most Negro workers were inclined toward solidarity with their fellows, white and black. In 1901, the Latrobe Steel and Coupler Company found difficulty in applying the usual formula for overcoming the obstinacy of striking workers. Commenting on the company's declaration that it has abandoned its plan to substitute Negroes for the dissenters, the Chicago *Daily Inter Ocean* said:

While General Manager G. Weortsen gave out a statement that the company had been actuated by a desire to avoid possible bloodshed . . ., the Negroes themselves revolted when the true state affairs was pointed out to them, and absolutely refused to work for the firm under any circumstances. Out on the open prairie . . . the five coaches, baggage car, and caboose which brought the 312 Negroes from Birmingham, Alabama, were stalled yesterday. Without food or water, the condition of the Negroes was pitiful, and their denunciation of the company was loud and bitter.

A delegation from the Chicago Federation of Labor had visited the emigrants, and one of the speakers appealed to them:

Do you want to enslave us now and bring us to a condition worse than your forefathers were in before Lincoln said they must be free? My father died on the battlefield fighting for the freedom of your race, and I believe he purchased my right to talk to you. Go back to your homes from whence you came and let the word go forth to the world that the black man refused to degrade his white brother. . . .

Though the Negroes responded to this plea, its eloquence may be less inspiring when consideration is given to an item appearing in the *Daily Inter Ocean* a year later:

No matter how expert a colored man may be, it is said that it is next to impossible for him to secure membership in a union in Chicago. Not being a member of the union, he can get no work at his trade . . . and is compelled to act as a porter, a waiter, a bootblack, or a laborer at much less wages.

In 1902, the Chicago Federation of Musicians held an agitated discussion concerning fifty Negro musicians who had formed a club and applied for admittance to the union. According to the *Chicago Daily Inter Ocean*, some members favored the granting of a separate charter to the applicants. Thus the newcomers would be segregated, while the union could not be accused of "drawing the color line." At the same time, the separate union would be entitled to representation in the Chicago Federation of Labor. Some time later the Federation refused to seat delegates from a local union of colored laborers. The president of the Hodcarriers' and Building Laborers' Executive Council maintained that the group had been sponsored by contractors and politicians intent upon breaking up his organization. He declared that his own local, No. 4, had 900 Negro members, a great majority of them preferring to remain in a mixed local. George Brown, an advocate of the separate local, attempted to explain the position of his group. But the president of the Executive Council called up an anti-separationist, who said:

My face is just as black as Mr. Brown's, but I don't want to be in a union composed entirely of colored men. I would like to be like Booker T. Washington, and dine with the President. It is not Mr. Brown of his movement, but Mr. Jones, the colored politician. Don't fool with Victor Falkeman, the leader of the Contractor's Council, who would like to have a union of colored men working at odds with the regular union. I belong to Local No. 4, which is an Irish union, and I want to stay there. Any time you separate yourself from the Irish you'll get the worst of it. They're the men who have raised the laborers' wages in this city, and that is what I am looking to!

The separationists at length agreed to remain in local 4, but they had won a concession when they marched as a body at the head of the Hodcarriers' division of the Labor Day parade, bearing the banner of the local. They agreed to carry "transparencies reading that they are satisfied to be under the same banner as the white laborers." They were preceded by a band composed of Negro members of the Musicians' Union, who had been granted a charter.

The dilemma of the labor leaders was to continue for some time. Unorganized Negroes were prone to become strikebreakers, sometimes from resentment at being barred from union membership but more often from lack of knowledge as to the purpose of trade unionism. During the 1904 stockyards strike, labor leaders John Fitzpatrick and William Russell wired Booker T. Washington at Tuskegee:

> Organized labor of Chicago, representing 250,000 men and women of all races, respectfully request you to address a mass meeting of colored people on the subject "Should Negroes Become Strike Breakers?"

Maintaining that "the labor movement has done more than any other influence to eliminate race prejudice," Fitzpatrick declared:

> Colored men have been admitted to our union on an equality with white men; in fact, should a union refuse Negroes admission, it could not hold a charter from the American Federation of Labor.

In 1906, the Franklin County Trades Council issued a call for a mass meeting of labor and farm bodies "to effect an organization of all labor organizations into one labor union." In the summons the organizers of the meeting said:

> We recognize that the interests of all classes of labor are identical, regardless of occupation, nationality, religion or color, for a wrong done to one is a wrong done to all.

Racial prejudice was not effectively exorcised by these pronouncements, however. In 1910, a Chicago minister asked that "the unions give a square deal to Negroes by admitting them to membership," and called attention to the oath of initiation in the American Federation of Labor:

> I promise never to discriminate against a fellow worker on account of color, creed or nationality.

13. Iola

The chapter that appears below was written by Jack Conroy and found in his papers at the Newberry Library. Corrections in Conroy's handwriting have been incorporated by the editor. An earlier draft is located in the IWP papers.

Almost ten years after ratification of the Thirteenth Amendment, the *Chicago Evening Journal* noted:

> In calculating the features of the "war of the races" in the South, it would be well to remember that white men, and not the Negroes, have charge of the telegraph wires and dispatches. Some of the white dispatches are black with lies, and though highly colored, do not favor the blacks.

Evidence of white control of the printed word was not confined to the South. Illinois newspapers adhering to the Democratic Party almost invariably treated the Negro with undisguised hostility, while even the Republican press ordinarily regarded all his activities as likely subjects for heavy-handed humor. Especially favored were items tending to fortify legends relating to the Negro's appetite for watermelon and chicken, his reliance upon the razor as a weapon, the thickness of his skull (accounting for his miraculous escapes from injury), his fondness for gaudy colors and fantastic attire, his inordinate fear of ghosts, and his extraordinary speed in retreat from danger were especially favored.

While attention was centered upon those unfortunate enough to become involved with the police, the most eminent colored people were not immune to ridicule and abuse. As early as April 9, 1862, the *Chicago Times* published under the caption "The Irrepressible Nigger vs. History," a complaint from a reader who had attended a lecture by Wendell Phillips, and, as he put it, "[had] heard his elaborate eulogy upon that distinguished 'darkey' of San Domingo, Touissant L'Ouverture." "As Mr. Phillips has made the irrepressible nigger his special study for many years," the correspondent contended, "he ought to be well informed in every particular that concerns this interesting race." He then disputed two minor historical points brought up by the celebrated orator, and concluded, "These may suffice to show how much confidence may be placed in a man who evidently reads history only to exalt and glorify the African race."

Later in the year, the *Times* commented at length upon the thieving indolent habits and general unreliability of the many "contrabands" in the city. One of these, the paper said, had been hired by a man who "had no great faith in her capabilities," and assigned her to the simple task of sweeping out the bedrooms. The *Times* went on:

> She did it with a vengeance. A bottle of pure tokay, kept convenient for sudden attacks of night sickness, first attracted her attention, and its contents were quickly abstracted to the amount of about a pint. She then started downstairs, with a vase in one hand and a gold watch in the other; but, slipping, reached the bottom sooner than intended, smashing her cargo into smithereens, and cutting herself severely.

Another *Times* story referred to " . . . one of those hideous gorillas with which the city is infested" and his arraignment in police court with two white women who lived with him. "Fond hearts were rudely torn at the sad prospects of separation," the *Times* concluded, "when in addition to their fines the magistrate shut up the women for thirty days each."

Politically sympathetic newspapers, such as the *Chicago Inter Ocean*, could not resist punning at the expense of Negroes. This item appeared November 18, 1874:

> Abraham White, who is BLACK, ungallantly assaulted Lizzie Black, who is WHITE, and was fined $25.00 by Justice Boyden yesterday morning, which had the effect of rendering Abraham White, black, blue, and Lizzie Black, white, happy.

The *Chicago Evening Journal*, on May 20 of the same year, quipped:

> A Danbury little darkey refused to go to church 'kase he didn't want to look like a huckleberry in a pan of milk.

And a short time later:

> A Louisville Negro fell asleep on the top of a high building and rolled off. He didn't complain of the fall—and never will.

This 1879 fashion note appeared in the *Inter Ocean*:

> "Bandana" dresses do not "take" very well with cultivated and refined women, but colored lady help go into raptures over them.

On April 29, 1875, the *Evening Journal* printed an article entitled "A Brutal Darkey," reading in part:

> Silas Morrissey, a darkey as black as ink, was on the war path last night, and went to the home of Mary Lewis, a saddle-colored female who resides on Pacific Avenue, and demanded accommodations for the night. The woman offered him a pallet on the floor, but that did not suit the African. On being refused anything better, he seized her by the wool and beat her until she was black and blue. . . .

To the 1893 World's Columbian Exposition in Chicago came Ida. B. Wells, a young Negro woman who had commented frequently and with point on the prevailing attitude of the white press toward her race. Already she had attained a reputation as a journalist and crusader against lynching. While attending the exposition, she collaborated with Frederick Douglass, I. Garland Penn, and Ferdinand L. Barnett on writing a booklet recording the

Ida B. Wells, 1930. (Vivian G. Harsh Research Collection
of Afro-American History and Literature, Chicago
Public Library, Richard Durham Papers 023)

achievements of American Negroes and refuting the false impressions created by most of the newspapers.

Ida B. Wells was born in Holly Springs, Mississippi, four years after the close of the Civil War. When she was fourteen and a student at Rust College, a Freedman's Aid Society school in the village, both her parents were stricken with yellow fever, and she found herself burdened with the support of four younger children. She not only discharged this obligation, but managed to continue classes at Rust. Later she spent a summer at Fisk University, where she contributed to the school publication. After teaching at a rural school for a time, she won an appointment near Memphis and shortly afterward one in the city. She began to write steadily for the *Living Way,* a local Negro paper.

After six years in the classroom, during which her work appeared in many Negro publications under the pseudonym "Iola," Miss Wells forsook teaching to become half-owner and editor of the Memphis *Free Speech*.

In 1891 her fellow journalist, I. Garland Penn, saluted Ida B. Wells:

> Decidedly, "Iola" is a great success in journalism. . . . She is popular with all the journalists of Afro-American connections, as will be seen by her election as assistant secretary of the National Afro-American Press Convention, at Louisville, two years ago, and her unanimous election as secretary of the recent Press Convention, which met at Washington, March 4, 1889.

In May 1892, three young Negro business men of Memphis were lynched, and *Free Speech* charged that disgruntled white competitors had instigated the deed. So telling were the paper's denunciations, that one dark night a crowd of hoodlums descended upon the plant, demolished the press and office, and chased the editor from town.

Undaunted, she arrived in New York and resumed her condemnation of lynching, writing for the *New York Age*, which had published her work before she fled from Memphis. Publisher T. Thomas Fortune described her as "one of the few of our women who handle a goose-quill, with diamond points, as easily as any man in newspaper work." "If 'Iola' were a man," Mr. Fortune continued, "she would be a humming independent in politics. She has plenty of nerve, and is as sharp as a steel trap." Shortly after her arrival in New York, "Iola" established a lasting friendship with the elderly Frederick Douglass. She published also *The Red Book*, said to be the first authentic record of lynching in America and became associated with Monroe Trotter, Harvard graduate, and some time editor of *New York Age*, in the National Equal Rights League.

The Woman's Loyal Union presented Miss Wells with a gold pen, symbolizing her journalistic achievements, and a purse of $700 to finance a lecture tour in Great Britain. Late in 1892, she sailed for London in response to an invitation from the Anti-Caste Society of Great Britain. Her lectures evoked a tremendous response, and the press and churches of the British Isles resounded with outcries against lynching. "Iola" left England in 1893 to attend the World's Columbian Exposition.

One of the journalists who collaborated with Ida B. Wells on the World's Fair booklet was Ferdinand L. Barnett, a graduate in law from Northwestern University. Barnett had founded in 1878 Illinois's first Negro newspaper, *The Conservator*. Later in the year, he relinquished the editorship to Reverend Richard de Baptiste, founder of Mt. Olivet Baptist Church, who announced that the aim of the paper would be to "discuss in a fair and liberal spirit those questions that agitate and cause an honest opinion among citizens, whose aims are alike patriotic."

In 1881, Barnett was working for the Evanston *Right Way*, and participated in the first independent organization of Negro newspapers, the Colored Press Association, held in the Chicago offices of *The Conservator*. The convention was presided over by John Q. Adams of the Louisville, Kentucky, *Bulletin*, later publisher of the *Chicago Appeal*. Begun in St. Paul, Minnesota, as the *Western Appeal*, the paper moved to Chicago in 1888.

In 1882 W. S. Scott had launched the *Cairo Gazette*, believed to be the first Negro daily in the United States, in connection with a weekly which he had established previously. The ambitious venture struggled through six months before it gave up.

Ida B. Wells continued her work as a journalist during her visit to Chicago in 1893. Commissioned by the Chicago *Inter Ocean* to investigate a recent lynching, she published a report tending to prove the innocence of the Negro victim. She organized the Ida B. Wells Club, first Negro organization of its kinds in the city, and headed it until her death. Its example led to the formation of many other colored women's clubs, and, finally, their amalgamation in the Federation of Colored Women's Clubs. In subsequent years, Miss Wells organized young people's and women's clubs not only in Chicago but in Louisville, a number of eastern cities, and elsewhere. The Chicago organization bearing her name was instrumental in establishing the first Negro orchestra in the city, opened the first kindergarten for children of the district, and became a charter member of the Cook County Women's Clubs, thus dealing a blow to the color line.

When she returned to England in 1894, Ida B. Wells found that sixteen branches of the Society for the Recognition of the Brotherhood of Man had been organized in Great Britain as a result of her previous visit, and a monthly magazine, *Fraternity*, was being issued in London. Her former successes on the lecture platform were eclipsed, and once again her activities created intense interest in the United States. The *Chicago Inter Ocean* noted:

> It may not be pleasant for Americans to know that the *London Chronicle* and other great English dailies have taken up the cause of Miss Ida Wells, the young colored woman who is now lecturing in England.

The Colored Men's Republican League of Chicago adopted this resolution:

> Whereas: Miss Ida Wells, now in England, deserves the compliments of 8,000,000 of our people in the United States for her unexaggerated statements of lynchings of colored people in the states, therefore, be it resolved, voicing these views of 8,000,000 and paying $264,000,000 in taxes, we do send Miss Wells, our representative, our sincere compliments and approval.

This pleasure was not shared by Southern newspapers and others who gave tacit or open approval to the subjugation of the Negro. Later in the year, the *Inter Ocean* observed:

> The eloquent Negro girl, Ida Wells, who was forced to go to London to obtain a hearing for the tragic story of the wrongs of her race in the South, is now gravely notified by the *Memphis Confederate Appeal* that he has "intensified the bitterness of race prejudice and disarmed the whites who are contending against the prevalence of lynching."

So greatly were certain opposition elements in the United States concerned over Miss Wells's revelations, according to the *New York Tribune*, that they dispatched agents to England to counteract her influence. Their efforts, however, ended in ignominious failure. T. Thomas Fortune sent notices to all branches of the Afro-American League throughout the United States to hold mass meetings to endorse Miss Wells's campaign. She maintained an average schedule of ten addresses a week. A British clergyman said that "nothing since the days of *Uncle Tom's Cabin* has taken such a hold in England as the anti-lynching crusade."

Ida B. Wells returned to the United States in July 1894, to command huge audiences in New York City. Only twenty-five years of age, she was recognized as the most implacable and effective enemy of mob rule. She told a New York gathering:

Our work has only begun; our race—hereditary bondsmen—must strike the blow if they would be free. I have been endeavoring to tell the whole truth. I have been banished from my home for this alone. An English lady who had seen for herself the condition of our people in the South, and seeing the hopelessness of our ever arousing public opinion in the North, asked me a few days after a colored man was burned alive at Paris, Texas, February 1893, to come to England to arouse a moral sentiment in England against these revolting cruelties practiced by barbarous whites. The British people took with incredulity my statements that colored men were roasted or lynched in broad daylight, very frequently with the sanction of officers of the law; and looked askance at statements that half grown boys shot bullets into hanging bodies and after cutting of toes and fingers of the dead or dying carried them about as trophies. They could easily have believed such atrocities of cannibals or heathens, but not of the American people, and in the land of the brave and the home of the free.

But when I showed them photographs of such scenes, the newspaper reports and the reports of searching investigations on the subject, they accepted the evidence of their senses against their wills. As soon as they were positively convinced resolutions were passed asking the American people to put away from them such shame and degradation.

Anti-Lynching Leagues formed in many American cities raised funds to keep Miss Wells in the field. After a tour of the middle west, she found larger audiences than before awaiting her in New York. She was described as:

A quiet, demure . . . Negro girl, who to prove a point quotes great writers with an ease which makes it apparent that larger questions even than the one on which she discoursed last night have occupied her leisure hours. Her voice was not strong enough to be heard by everybody present, but all who did hear her simple narrative appeared to be convinced. She has not a trace of accent that one is accustomed to associate with Negroes.

On March 14, 1895, the *Chicago Inter Ocean*, praising the good work accomplished by Ida B. Wells, went on to say:

But in San Francisco Bishop Goodsell denounced her thirty years' experience, her statistics showing that most lynchings take place on no or insufficient evidence of guilt, to say that "extenuating circumstances" excused lynching because "a strong example was necessary to protect the purity of white women in the black belt."

The paper characterized the bishop as "a disgrace to the Methodist Church."

At one of Miss Wells's lectures in Rochester, New York, an irate Texan arose to ask the speaker why Negroes did not leave the South if they didn't like the treatment they received there. Susan B. Anthony, a member of the audience, "heatedly reproached the Texas and ably supported Miss Wells." At Kansas City, Missouri, an acrimonious debate was precipitate in a meeting of the Protestant Ministers' Alliance when a resolution endorsing Ida B. Wells and her anti-lynching campaign was introduced. Rev. S. M. Neel, described as a "southerner," opposed the resolution with such vehemence that it eventually was tabled.

Miss Wells continued to write for the Negro press, including the *Conservator*, in which Ferdinand L. Barnett retained an interest. She knew that a strong, independent Negro press was highly desirable. In a letter to the *Chicago Inter Ocean* she said:

... Is not the North by its seeming acquiescence as responsible morally as the South is criminally for the awful lynching record of the past thirteen years? When I was first driven from Memphis, Tenn., and sought a hearing in the North to tell what the Negro knew, from actual experience, of the lynching mania, and refute the foul slander that all the Northern papers were publishing, without question, about Negro assaults against white women, not a newspaper to which I made application would print the Negro side of this question. . . .

In the meantime the interest of Ferdinand L. Barnett in the young crusader whom he had met at the World's Columbian Exposition had intensified to such a degree that he asked her to marry him, his first wife having died seven years before. Miss Wells accepted, and their wedding at Bethel Church in Chicago on June 27, 1895, was an important social event, the bridegroom being a prominent member of the Chicago bar, and the bride well known for her lectures, her social work, and her contributions to the *Daily Inter Ocean*, *The Conservator*, and other publications.

Henceforth the Barnetts figured in almost every Illinois battle against racial injustice. They have been described as "representative of the more militant body of Negro opinion long before that body acquired a leader in Dr. W. E. B. Du Bois."

The Illinois Negro had had little opportunity to enjoy the guarantees of the 13th, 14th, and 15th Amendments to the federal Constitution or the national civil rights act of 1875. Aside from being segregated in schools, Negroes had been refused service in restaurants, admittance to places of amusement and hotels, the right to live in certain sections in towns and cities, membership in trade unions, and entrance to and use of public accommodations. The Ku Klux Klan was particularly active in the southern counties of Illinois during the seventies.

One of the earliest cases of color discrimination in a public conveyance to be contested occurred in 1869 when Anna Williams, a Rockford woman, was awarded damages to the amount of $200.00 from the Chicago and Northwestern Railway Company after a brakeman excluded her from the "ladies car," for which she possessed a ticket. Late in the eighties, a Mrs. Baylies successfully prosecuted a theater proprietor who had declined to admit her.

Perhaps discrimination in restaurants, bars, and soda fountains was and is the most common form practiced against Negro citizens. Throughout the nineties, the press carried stories from all parts of the state concerning action brought by Negroes because of trouble in eating places. When Abraham Green sued a Bloomington drug store in 1894 under the state civil rights act, he discovered that his claim for damages because of refusal of service was invalid, since the state act did not specifically name drug stores. The Associated Cycling Clubs in 1893 reaffirmed an earlier decision barring Negro riders from participation in the Pullman road race that year. Two years later Samuel Elliot received a judgment for $100 from the Tattersall skating rink after he had been refused admittance because of his race.

In 1894, Mrs. A. M. Curtis, "a woman of culture and beauty," was threatened with ejection from her Chicago home when the landlord discovered that she had Negro blood in her veins, despite the fact that "when the lease was made she presented letters of endorsement from P. D. Armour, Moses Handy, and Judge Kohlsaat."

The political Equality League in 1903 asked Mrs. Barnett to address its members on "The Colored Woman, Her Past, Present and Future." The speaker, as was her custom, presented a realistic picture of her race's plight, pointed out that "there was little employment for the Negro, and the average Negro scarcely exceeded the domestic scale." Her white hearers responded with expressions of sympathy.

"My heart goes out to the colored race," said one. "Let us remember that when we say a thing against one Negro we say it against all."

"Our treatment of colored people is our national disgrace," another put in.

To these well-wishers, Mrs. Barnett replied quietly: "We ask only that the door of opportunity be opened to us."

In 1908 Mrs. Barnett organized the Negro Fellowship League, serving as its president. One of the league's major achievements was a mass protest against the Chicago production of Thomas Dixon's anti-Negro play, "The Sins of the Fathers." With the establishment of the National Association for the Advancement of Colored People, Mrs. Barnett earned a position as one of its leaders. Indeed, her long fight against lynching and discrimination has been credited with supplying a powerful impetus toward the association's organization.

In 1909 Ida B. Wells-Barnett took a leading part in the campaign to prevent Governor Charles S. Deneen's reinstatement of the sheriff of Alexander County, following that official's negligence in connection with the lynching of a Negro there. The sheriff was not reinstated, and since that day no other lynching has occurred in Illinois, though there have been several race riots.

Ferdinand L. Barnett, in a newspaper report of his wedding, was credited with being "half owner of the *Conservator*, the second oldest colored newspaper in the world." He became more and more preoccupied, however, with politics and the defense of Negroes in the courts. In 1896 he was appointed assistant state's attorney for Cook County, the first Negro to hold the position. In 1906, he was defeated for judge of the municipal court by a very narrow margin, his friend charging that he had been "counted out."

Another journalist who gradually forsook his profession for the pursuit of politics was Sheadrick B. ("Sandbag") Turner, who had founded the *State Capital* in Springfield in 1886 and the *Springfield Chronicle* in 1893. The former publication was designated by I. Garland Penn, author of *The Afro-American Press* (1891), as the foremost race organ west of the Ohio River and the recognized voice of the Negro in Illinois. Turner established the *Illinois Idea* in Chicago in 1898, its slogan being "Justice is what we advocate—More we do not ask—Less will not content us." He transferred his editorial duties to his wife in 1910, and in 1914 won a seat in the state legislature. Thereafter, he was elected several times, his last term beginning in 1926. The *Illinois Idea* espoused the cause of the Republican Party until its suspension in 1927.

Ida B. Wells-Barnett was appointed adult probation officer in 1913, the first of her race. Two years later she was elected vice-president of the Chicago branch of the National Independent Equal Rights League. In 1917, the League sent her to Washington to present to the President of the United States and to Congress a memorial asking that lynching be made a crime under federal law and to protest against segregation of Negro workers in government service. The organization also designated her as its representative at the 1919 peace conference in Paris.

Long a friend of Jane Addams, Mrs. Barnett directed her energies toward the creation of social centers similar to Hull House in the Negro districts. She was selected as a trustee of the Amanda Smith Industrial School for Girls at Harvey. Deeply agitated by the 1919 Chicago race riots, she advocated a committee of "the best men and women of both . . . races to devise ways and means for the protection of the Negro and the discouragement of race prejudice."

Approaching age did not diminish perceptibly Ida B. Wells-Barnett's zest for the prosecution of social reform measures. She attacked vice conditions, the housing situation, and new evidences of discrimination from the lecture platform and in newspaper articles, notably in the Chicago *Defender*. She contemplated and even announced her candidacy for the state senate. But her seemingly inexhaustible energy spent itself at last, and she died on March 25, 1931, at the age of sixty-two, after an illness of only two days. The writer of an obituary article in the *Defender* remembered her as " . . . elegant, striking and always well groomed, . . . regal, though somewhat intolerant and impulsive."

When the federal government planned a low-rent housing project for Chicago's South Side, South Parkway Gardens was the tentative name selected. The Ida B. Wells Club, the Federated Women's Clubs and other organizations advocated so vigorously the naming of the development after the crusader whose pen and voice had been silenced by death a few years before that the housing authority acquiesced. Construction was delayed, and a strong protest movement demanding completion of the Ida B. Wells homes gained momentum. Dedication ceremonies were held October 27, 1940. St. Clair Drake has said:

> The issue which probably united the largest number of Negroes in 1937–1938 was the fight to secure immediate construction of the Ida B. Wells Housing Project. A militant Negro woman's name (heritage of the 1900s) becomes the rallying cry for social action.

14. The Migrants Keep Coming

This chapter was written by Jack Conroy, who first planned to conduct a study of the black migration when he joined the Illinois Writers' Project. The most recent version that appears here was found at Syracuse University. There is an earlier draft in the IWP papers titled "The Great Migration," with the name of E. Diehl on the front page. It also includes comments in Arna Bontemps's handwriting.

Two lanky Negro youths, their overalls powdered with the red dust of a Georgia road, paused at a street corner to listen to their friends and neighbors discussing Kaiser Bill, the Battle of the Marne, the boll weevil, "doodlum," and other matters interesting to a Saturday afternoon street corner crowd in a small town of the Georgia farming country.

"Why n't y'all get outa this whole mess?" one of the youths inquired. "Go Nawth where you can make big money and live like a man besides."

"How you gonna go?" one of the elder sharecroppers inquired mockingly. "Ride Shank's Mare?"

"Don't have to. Don't even have to ride a freight. A Chicago labor agent's gonna be in town today. Carry all the hands he can get up there free and on the cushions. Stockyards in Chicago's cryin' for fifty thousand men to take the place of them foreigners they used to hire. Listen to this, what I got out of a Chicago paper for colored folks called the *Defender*.

He fished a creased newspaper clipping from his pocket and began to read:

Some are coming on the passenger,
Some are coming on the freight,
Others will be found walking,
For none will have time to wait.

A deputy pushed through the crowd and laid his hand on the boy's shoulder.

"Reckon you'd better come with me, son," he said. "The sheriff wants to see you."

"What for? Ain't done nothin' but read a little old poem."

"That's just it! Got orders to arrest all you colored boys I ketch readin' poetry out of that *Chicago Defender*. Been a lot of that stuff read and it's raisin' hell all over the South. Hand's leaving the plow right in the field and runnin' away from their honest debts to traipse

North. You'll likely be charged with 'inciting to riot in the city, county, and throughout the State of Georgia.' Yes sir, son, looks like you're bound for the prison farm."

As in the seventies, when "Pap" Singleton had cried "Let my people go!" to the Pharaohs of the South and led thousands of Negro pilgrims to the plains of Kansas, news of a better land lying to the north began to spread more generally shortly after the outbreak of the first World War. The *Chicago Defender*, most energetic purveyor of the good tidings, published articles and poems inviting immigrants North. Referring to southern opponents of the migration who urged that the Negro was better off where he was, the *Defender* said:

> We'd like to oblige these unselfish (?) souls and remain slaves in the South, but to other sections of the country we have said, as the song goes: "I hear you calling me," and boarded the train singing "Goodbye to Dixie-Land."

Since the mass exodus of Singleton's day, the northward movement has slackened considerably. In 1910, almost fifty years after Abraham Lincoln had pronounced the slaves "thence forward and forever free," 89% of the freedmen remained in the South, some of them from choice or inertia, others because of necessity imposed by debt and other restrictions. One million Negroes were living in the North; 109,000 in Illinois, more than half of these in Chicago.

Complicating the problems of reconstruction in the South, the boll weevil, an insect migrant from Mexico, had invaded Texas in 1892. Armed with its sharp proboscis for puncturing tender young cotton bolls, it ranged northward and eastward at a speed reaching 160 miles annually, leaving behind it thousands of wilted and devastated cotton fields. Consequently, the World War, which cut off the supply of European immigrant labor, was at first an indirect blessing by impoverished planters who could no longer command credit with which to operate. Northern factories needed laborers, and the southern Negroes needed work. Labor agents appeared with enticing offers of wages doubling and even trebling the local scale.

Not only was the southern Negro's economic position insecure, but he was still deprived of most of the civil rights guaranteed him by the Fourteenth Amendment. Mob violence had not been curbed to any appreciable extent. The *Atlanta Constitution* observed:

> While mob violence and the falsehood which has been that foundation constitutes, perhaps, a strong factor in the migration of the Negroes, there is scarcely a doubt that the educational feature enters into it. . . . We have proceeded upon the theory that education would, in his own mind, carry the Negro beyond his sphere; that it would give him a higher idea of himself and make of him a poorer and less satisfactory workman. That is nonsense. . . .

Many southerners who had professed to see in the Negro a liability rather than an asset to the economy of the region, took alarm as the migration assumed tidal proportions. This movement was more or less leaderless, and spontaneous; there was no "Moses" comparable to "Pap" Singleton directing it. Nevertheless, as in Singleton's time, it looked as though nobody would be left to till the fields and do the hard work. The Birmingham *Age-Herald* pointed out that:

> It is not the riff-raff of the race, the worthless Negroes, who are leaving in such large numbers. There are, to be sure, many poor Negroes among them who have little more than

the clothes on their backs, but others have property and good positions which they are sacrificing in order to get away at the first opportunity. The entire Negro population of the South seems to be deeply affected. The fact that many Negroes who went North without sufficient funds and without clothing to keep them warm have suffered severely and have died in large numbers has not checked the tide leaving the South. It was expected that the Negroes would come back sorry that they ever left, but comparatively few have returned.

Deriding this belated repentance and concern, the *Defender* continued its series of hortatory poems bearing titles such as "Northward Bound," "Farewell," "We're Good and Gone," and "Bound for the Promised Land." So effective was its propaganda in the South, that possession of a copy of the paper was sometimes grounds for imprisonment.

The fact that the southern planters and manufacturers sought to hamper the activities of labor agents sent South to recruit workers only served to convince the skeptical that there must be something to the reports of high wages and better living conditions. Clubs of migrants secured special rates from the railroads, or traveled free on passes supplied by agents. The Illinois Central Railroad alone is credited with having transported tens of thousands of colored plantation hands to Illinois, principally to Chicago. Chicago was known to all. It was the big town by the lake from which the mail order catalogues came, and thus vaguely associated in the minds of hinterland folks with everything desirable but hitherto unattainable.

The movement to Chicago attained huge proportions two years before the United States entered the World War and continued almost without recession for a year or two after it ended. The *Chicago Tribune* reported on March 4, 1917, that 2,000 or more Negroes from Tennessee, Alabama, Louisiana, and Georgia had arrived in the city with the preceding two days, and that 10,000 more were expected before the first of April. Attorney Beauregard F. Mosley and the Appomattox Club were said to have rushed agents south to warn prospective migrants that accommodations were overtaxed. Meanwhile, a persistent rumor that the stockyards would require 50,000 new workers within a short period had penetrated to the uttermost regions of the South. The tide increased rather than diminished. When short-handed stockyard firms offered to provide a minimum of one week's food and housing for the new arrivals, the Appomattox Club and other organizations halted their campaign of dissuasion. Chief of Police Schuetler delegated Lieutenant John Hawkins, a Negro, to the job of assisting the newcomers in adjusting themselves to city ways and in avoiding the pitfalls besetting the greenhorn everywhere.

May 15, 1917, was designated by rumor as a definite date for the "Great Northern Drive." A southern woman wrote Robert S. Abbott of the *Defender*:

> I read about the Great Northern Drive to take place May 15th on Thursday and now I can hear so many people speaking of an excursion to the North and on the 15th of May for $3.00. My husband is in the North already working, and he wants us to come up in May, so I want to know if it is true about the excursion. I am getting ready and oh so many others also, and we want to know is it true so we can be in the Drive.

Securely established Negro citizens were perturbed by the avalanche of their rustic brethren whose manners and personal appearance were not always as prepossessing as they might be. Carl Sandburg has related a typical incident:

At Michigan and 31st Street a colored woman (here two months from Alabama) walks along the street with her bare footed children. Suddenly a colored man steps out of a big limousine and speaks to the mother and children, "We don't do this up here. It isn't good for us colored folks to send our children out on the streets like this. We're all working together to do the best we can. One thing we're particular about is the way we take the little ones out on the street. They ought to look as if they're washed clean all over, and they ought to have shoes and stockings and hats and clean shirts on. Now you go home and see to that. If you haven't got the money to do it, come and see me. Here is my card." He hands her the card of a banker and real estate man.

The Chicago Urban League since 1916 has made the housing and employment of Negro migrants its chief concern. The newcomers themselves, homesick for familiar speech, faces, and scenes, banded into social and fraternal clubs representative of various states and localities from which they had emigrated. There were the Alabama Club, the Mississippi Club, the Vicksburg Club, the Louisiana Club, the Arkansas Club, to mention a few. Some of these organizations have survived. In 1937, a member of the Natchez Club said:

> It was organized mainly to get the Natchez members together. There are a lot of people here from Natchez that don't know each other. We sent all of the people cards that we knew telling them to invite others that they knew about. We knew some that others didn't know and they knew some that we didn't know. We had about fifty at our first meeting. If you are married to a person from Natchez, you are in that branch. The older people are in another. It is all the Natchez Club, but we have different chapters.

Chicago was not the only Illinois city to receive a large number of Negro migrants from the South. The industries of East St. Louis began to feel the pinch of labor shortage and to attract a fresh supply of workmen by means of advertisements, labor agents, and kindred methods. The grapevine telegraph, in the use of which Negroes had developed amazing proficiency during slavery, helped to spread the word. Soon every train arriving in East St. Louis brought colored job seekers.

Less than two years before the city was to be visited by a great catastrophe involving a racial clash, the *East St. Louis Journal* (October 19, 1915) commented on the hanging of Joe DeBerry, a Negro at Murphysboro. The ceremony had been made a gala occasion, with more than a thousand witnesses created temporary "deputies." Upon hearing of the circumstances, Governor Dunne wired Sheriff James A. White that the affair was a "scandal and disgrace to the state" and requested that Elston Scott, another Negro scheduled for hanging the following Friday, be dispatched with "decorum, decency, and privacy." On the 2nd of November the *Journal* noted reprovingly:

> Murphysboro seems to gloat over the brutal Negro hanging pulled off a few weeks ago. The movies in that place were showing the uncivilized scene and the exhibitions were crowded. Foreign-missionary activities ought to be somewhat diverted to Murphysboro.

On May 25, 1917, the *Journal* discoursed editorially on the "Negro Influx Problem" and pointed out that "thousands have come into East St. Louis . . . and they are still coming." While East St. Louis was agitated at the invasion, southern planters were complaining that fields which might supply food and clothing for soldiers and civilians were lying fallow because most of the able-bodied laborers had fled north. The *Journal* concluded:

But they are here in East St. Louis, and the problem must be met in a humane and patriotic spirit. Settlements and abodes should be provided for them. In order to avoid friction, our officials, civic and business organizations should take hold of the matter, and, in co-operation with colored church pastors and other Negro leaders work out a plan that will be satisfactory to all, and maintain good relations.

The "humane and patriotic spirit" was destined to be manifested in peculiar ways. Mayor Mollman exerted pressure on railroad agents and exacted a promise that they would no longer encourage or, indeed, permit the importation of Negroes. Representatives of organized labor presented their protests. Nearby Belleville warned "strange Negroes" that they must not stop in that city, and Mayor Duvall assigned patrolmen to the railroad stations with instructions to chase away all "undesirables."

The familiar devices employed to harry "undesirables" were used by East St. Louis authorities. "Vagrancy" and "loitering" charges, arrest for "suspicious conduct" might be anticipated by any Negro—and particularly one new in town—regardless of his behavior or financial status. Minor "incidents" between the two races multiplied. One was precipitated by the apprehension of William Engram, a Negro, by patrolman Thomas Gebhardt, who repaired with his prisoner to Thomas Boston's saloon, his intention being, he said later, to call for additional help to conduct Engram to police headquarters, there to book him for "spitting on the sidewalk." Gebhardt had been followed by several Negroes who were incensed at the plain evidence of discrimination, since spitting on the sidewalk certainly was not uncommon, nor were any others save Negroes jailed for it. Boston, described as "well known as a politician," ordered the crowd around his door to disperse, and when it did not comply as quickly as he wished, shot and critically wounded George Lee, Negro.

East St. Louis has been called a "satellite" city, most of its prominent business men and industrialists preferring to make their homes in St. Louis, Missouri, across the Mississippi River. Politicians and police authorities have been charged with winking at prostitution, gambling, and other lawlessness, since these activities prove a profitable source of revenue. "Black Valley," a section of dilapidated shacks in close proximity to the City Hall, became one of the most renowned vice districts in the world. The industrialists who had invited Negro laborers to the city were inclined to be indifferent toward their housing, social, moral, and educational problems.

It has been estimated that between 10,000 and 12,000 colored workers from the South flocked to East St. Louis and its neighboring St. Clair County industrial communities from the autumn of 1916 to the spring of 1917. Some of these, labor leaders asserted, were imported as strikebreakers.

On May 28, 1917, a rumor that a white man had been slain by a Negro was circulated widely, and a white mob made the rounds to assault a number of Negroes, beating some of them severely.

These events were climaxed on the night of July 1st, when one or two automobiles—witnesses do not agree as to the number—careened wildly through streets inhabited by Negroes, the occupants of the machines peppering dwellings with bullets. Surmising that the Negroes might be organizing for retaliation, policemen drove to the neighborhood—ostensibly for the purpose of preserving order. Whatever ensued, the result was that a group of Negroes fired on the automobile, killing one policeman and fatally wounding another.

The Migrants Keep Coming

Throughout the next two days, the city was ruled by a mob which killed, burned, and pillaged at will. Militiamen summoned to quell the disturbance fraternized with the rioters, and even assisted them. White women and children participated in acts of almost incredible cruelty. Colonel Tripp, commanding the five companies of Illinois National Guards sent to the scene, secluded himself in the City Hall. When asked why he was not active in command of his men, he is said to have retorted: "The President never goes out of *his* office."[1]

By Independence Day the disorders had abated, after fearful carnage and destruction of property totaling almost $400,000. The exact number of dead will never be known. Estimates range from fifty to several hundred. A congressional investigation committee severely criticized the municipal and military authorities for their conduct, but commended Assistant Attorney General Middlekauf, in charge of the subsequent prosecutions, for showing "neither fear nor favor." Eleven Negroes, but only eight white men were sentenced to the state penitentiary, and the committee reported:

> The additional white men have been sentenced to prison terms, fourteen white men have been given jail sentences, twenty seven white men, including the former night chief of police and three policemen, have pleaded guilty to rioting and have been punished.

Dr. LeRoy A. Bundy was indicted with fourteen other Negroes for the murder of the policeman slain on the night of July 1st. On testimony of white witnesses who declared that they had seen armed Negroes in the vicinity of his home on the night in question, Dr. Bundy was sentenced to life in prison. In 1920, however, the Illinois Supreme Court reversed the decision.

Oscar Leonard, superintendent of the Jewish Educational and Charitable Association of St. Louis, in an article published in *Survey*, compared the riots to Russian pogroms directed against the Jews. He said:

> ... I went in the company of a young Russian Jew, a sculptor who had witnessed and bears the marks of more than one anti-Jewish riot in his native land. He told me when he viewed the blocks of burned houses that the Russian "Black Hundreds" could take lessons in pogrom making from the whites of East St. Louis. The Russians at least, he said, gave the Jews a chance to run while they were trying to murder them. The whites in East St. Louis fired the homes of black folk and either did not allow them to leave the burning houses or shot them the moment they dared attempt to escape the flames.

Mr. Leonard interviewed observers who testified that a great number of Negroes were burned alive in their homes and consequently were not counted among the dead. Some expressed their conviction that a hundred or more perished in the flames consuming a deserted theater where they had sought sanctuary from the mob's fury. Mr. Leonard went on:

> Thrifty black folk, who were doing their bit (to win the World War) by raising vegetables, were murdered. I saw ruins of their homes, into which had gone the labor and savings of years. The little thrift gardens had escaped the flames, and the orderly rows where seeds had been planted gave the plots the appearance of miniature grave yards.

More than 6,000 refugees fled from the state of Abraham Lincoln across the river to Missouri, a former slave state. John Schmoll, Director of Public Welfare in St. Louis, complained that the East St. Louis authorities were disposing of their problem by sending their homeless Negroes across to the St. Louis municipal lodging house. The St. Louis *Globe-Democrat* noted:

> Throughout the day, truckload after truckload of Negroes with baggage, luggage and household goods continued to arrive at the lodging house. The four-story building packed to the roof, the crowd overflowed on the street, and across to the City Hall lawn.

A poll conducted among the 4,000 temporarily quartered in the lodging house revealed that less than 15% were willing to return to the South, though governmental and private agencies in more than a dozen cities—including Atlanta, New Orleans, Louisville, and Mobile—had invited the wayfarers back home to protection and jobs.

As on other occasions, the absence of the Negro workers at once made itself felt. The East St. Louis manager of the Swift Packing Co. reported that 300 of the 700 Negroes normally working in the plant had left their jobs and that it might be necessary to close down. The general manager of the Armour Company added:

> We have lost more than 100 Negroes, most of them hard-working men who were as glad to get the good wages as we were to pay them. Continued terrorizing of Negro laborers will drive many more of them away. We are working as fast as we can on contracts for the United States army and navy, and if a considerable portion of our force is driven out of the city it will interfere with the most important of all war munitions—the food.

The manager of the Morris plant stressed the fact that the 150 men who had left his employ were not come-lately "ficaters," but solid citizens. "The 'ficaters' don't mind a little thing like a riot," he said, "but these men with families and homes do not feel like taking chances of being assaulted on their way to and from work."

The day after Independence Day the *East St. Louis Journal* disclosed that:

> Chamber of Commerce members and business leaders, at a meeting today, behind closed doors, discussed the advisability of bringing the Negro laborers back to East St. Louis. They took up the question of how they were to be housed and protected when they arrived....

While a large number of refugees fled to St. Louis, many departed for Chicago and other Illinois cities. Brooklyn, all-Negro community near East St. Louis, extended its hospitality to more than 500. Laid out on paper by white men in 1837, Brooklyn is said to have been settled first in 1858 by slaves who had escaped across the Mississippi from Missouri. Here they were joined by other fugitives and later by freedmen. Brooklyn was incorporated in 1874, but because of the possibility of confusion with another community with a somewhat similar name, the post office was named Lovejoy, in honor of Elijah Lovejoy, the abolitionist editor. The city government was managed by white people until 1910. Since then it has been controlled exclusively by Negroes.

On May 30, two months before the East St. Louis riot, the *Chicago Tribune* had commented on the growing race tension and recurring "incidents" in East St. Louis and elsewhere:

They say down South that "niggers are all right in their place," but where is that place? South? At Memphis, Tennessee, a Negro was recently burned alive. North? At East St. Louis, Illinois, Negroes are mobbed beaten and run out of town. We taunt the South with race prejudice when it burns a "bad nigger," but just see how we Northerners detest even "good niggers." The real race prejudice is ours. Our very philanthropists betray it. They say to a black man, "God bless you, good bye," whereas the South says, "—you, come here!" Or put it this way: The Northerner is a great friend of the Negro, but not of a Negro; the Southerner is a great friend of a Negro, but not of the Negro.

The migrants kept coming to Chicago. Within the decade following 1910, the Negro population increased from 44,103 to 109,458. As a consequence, the Negro community began bursting its bonds. More than 90% of the migrants settled on the South Side. First the newcomers found homes in areas of established Negro residence, principally west of Indiana Avenue, east of Wentworth, south of Twelfth Street, and north of Fifty-fifth, but before long they were forced to seek living room in sections previously inhabited exclusively by whites. It has been estimated that 50,000 Negroes, a majority of them fresh from the South, came to Chicago within an eighteen-month period after the first of January 1916. Chicago figured as a distribution center, too, a large number of the migrants proceeding directly or after stops of various lengths to Detroit and other industrial centers.

The all-Negro village of Robbins, named after an enterprising realtor who platted the town on marsh meadowland within twenty-five miles of Chicago's loop, grew along with Chicago, and was incorporated in 1917. Robbins (population in 1940, 1,200) accommodated victims of the depression beginning in 1930. The unemployed erected their ramshackle huts built of miscellaneous salvaged materials alongside the neat cottages of earlier settlers.

The problem of helping rural Negroes readjust themselves to city ways was tackled energetically by the Chicago Urban League, by churches, and other organizations. Numerous complaints relating to the uncouth behavior and appearance of recently arrived Negro workers in street cars and other public places were constantly aired in the *Defender*, with appeals to the offenders to conduct themselves in a manner reflecting credit on their race. The North did not quite live up to its reputation for equality of opportunity and lack of prejudice. Some white people disputed the right of colored citizens to the use of beaches, playgrounds, and other public facilities.

On Sunday, July 27, 1919, Eugene Williams, a Negro youth, floated on a raft across an imaginary line dividing the 29th Street Lake Michigan beach into white and colored sections. Soon afterward, a number of Negro men approached white patrolman Daniel Callahan and asked him to arrest George Steuben, white, who they said had pelted young Williams with stones until he fell, unconscious, into the water. Negroes later charged that Officer Callahan not only rejected their petition, but prevented rescuers from helping Williams, who drowned. Upon being attacked by the incensed Negroes, Callahan enlisted the support of white men and boys on the beach, and the battle was on.[2]

Throughout the night the occurrence on the beach was the chief topic of conversation on the South Side. Widespread skirmishes between the two races took place. White men and boys stopped street cars and attacked colored passengers, while Negroes retaliated with similar action. The members of so-called "athletic clubs," white teenage boys (mostly of

Irish ancestry) recruited by ward politicians for political purposes, ranged through the Negro district with revolvers, clubs, and other weapons, shooting and beating indiscriminately every Negro or group of Negroes unequal in size. "Ragen's Colts" was the best-known of these organizations, others being "The Hamburgers," "Our Flag," and "The Sparklers."

The Negroes fought back with telling effect. The first general riot call since the 1887 Haymarket riot rallied nearly 2,000 policemen to pacify the area, but they failed to restore order. Wild rumors dispensed by newspapers and individuals helped to keep the fires of animosity alight. It was said that a Negro had telephoned a dealer in firearms to order $3,000 worth of revolvers, shotguns, rifles, and ammunition, saying he would be after the goods with a truck. He never appeared. Other stories told of the looting of South State Street pawnshops by rioters in search of shotguns and revolvers. Alderman Joseph McDonough returned from the riot area in a state of alarm, warning that the Negroes possessed enough ammunition for "years of guerilla warfare." The chief of police detailed sixty detectives armed with rifles to the task of guarding the city hall, explaining that he feared an assault in force by Negroes.

Five days of disorder ensued during which a large force of state militia arrived. The death toll of the riot officially has been placed at 22 Negroes and 16 whites, while more than 500 people are known to have been injured in varying degrees. The actual number of fatalities probably was much larger. Persistent legend had it that the fetid waters of "Bubbly Creek," a sewerage ditch near the stockyards, concealed the bodies of innumerable slain Negroes, estimates ranging from scores to hundreds.

Representatives of 47 business and philanthropic organizations, called together by the Chicago Association Commerce, passed a resolution urging Governor Lowden to appoint a committee "to study the psychological and economical causes underlying conditions resulting in the present race riot and to make some recommendations as will tend to prevent a recurrence of such conditions in the future." The Governor responded by creating the Chicago Race Commission, composed of six colored and six white citizens, which published a voluminous report as a result of its investigations.

Shortly before Mayor Thompson admitted the inability of city police to cope with the situation and requested the help of state troops, a delegation of Negro citizens including Alderman R. R. "Fighting Bob" Jackson, Dr. A. J. Carey, Rev. L. K. Williams, Ferdinand L. Barnett, and Col. F. A. Denison, called on the mayor to complain of police indifference toward or complicity with white law breakers. Attorney Beauregard F. Moseley, at a meeting of Negro business and professional men in the Idlewild Hotel, expressed his opinion, according to newspaper reports, that Negroes from the South had been responsible for a lot of the trouble, and reminded his hearers that "this is a white man's country." The *Chicago Tribune* quotes him as saying:

> Some of us forget that the white man has given us freedom, the right to vote, to live on terms of equality with them, to be paid well for our work, and to receive other benefits. Now if the white man should decide that the black man has proved he is not fit to have the right to vote, that right might be taken away. We might also find it difficult to receive other favors to which we have been accustomed, and then what would happen to us.

The *Chicago Tribune* editorialized:

Chicago is disgraced and dishonored. Its head is bloodied and bowed, bloodied by crime and bowed in shame. Its reputation is besmirched. Its fame tarnished for years.

President Woodrow Wilson issued in the columns of *The Nation* "An Appeal to America Not Yet Written" concerning the Chicago riot and one which had occurred in Washington on July 19. The president said in part:

> The evidence at hand points not only to a failure of the civil authorities to act promptly and so prevent loss of life; it goes to prove that in each case the white race was the aggressor. This makes the matter infinitely worse; it casts a stain upon everyone of the majority group in our land. It is the more censurable because our Negro troops are but just back from no little share in carrying out our cause and our flag to victory. As they stood by the majority, so must and should the majority stand by them with true Christianity.[3]

Though the post-war years brought a slackening of the demand for laborers and finally an acute depression, the trend of migration was toward and not away from Illinois, and particularly toward Chicago. During the depression years of 1930 to 1935, the number of white farm operators in the southern states increased by 264,047 (11.3%) while the Negro farmers decreased 65,940 (7.5%). In 1930, the colored population of Illinois numbered 328,974, slightly more than 4% of the total. Ninety-two percent were residents of urban centers. Chicago and East St. Louis was 11,536, Cairo and Evanston each had nearly 5,000, and Springfield and Peoria 3,000 each. While 24 counties had more than 1,000 Negro residents, sixteen had less than ten, and no Negroes were living in Cumberland, Mason, or Moultrie counties. There are no counties in the state, however, where Negroes have never lived. Cairo, principal point of entry both for the "contrabands" of Civil War days and for the succeeding migrations, contained the largest percentage of Negro population—34%.

Rev. Harold M. Kingsley has said that the Negro is a "fringe" worker—the last hired and the first fired. "His jubilant singing . . . when migrating to the North changed to a minor key, and, disillusioned, he faced facts."

In an effort to halt the movement of indigent migrants to Illinois, the legislature passed in 1939 a law requiring recipients of relief to prove three years' continuous residence in one of the 1,455 governmental units of the state. In the fall of that year, it was discovered that about 4% of all relief clients had lived in their local units less than the specified time. Negroes comprised about 20% of these. Cook County, with 35% of all the cases in this category, counted Negroes as 80% of the total.

On August 19, 1940, Mayor Edward J. Kelly of Chicago, testifying at the Chicago hearings of a congressional committee investigating the interstate migration of destitute citizens, referred to the three-year residence law, and said:

> I think three years is too long. I know of many instances where it has been a real hardship. I can cite one case of a young colored man who came here thinking that he could get work, or get relief. Of course, he was not recognized. He became a highwayman. He shot a policeman. The policeman shot him. He got 199 years in the penitentiary. It does not seem to me as though there was anything else for that man to do. He was starving. He could not get anything. He finished up with 199 years.

To these hearings Horace R. Cayton, director of the Good Shepherd Community Center, submitted a paper dealing with Negro migration, while Howard David Gould and Frayser

T. Lane represented the Chicago Urban League. Mr. Cayton expressed his opinion that any increase in Negro population must be coming from migration, since " . . . the rate of natural increase for the foreign-born white was 10.4% and the native white 7.6%, the Negro was increasing at a decreasing rate—that is, negative 2.9%." Mr. Gould agreed that this situation had been true from 1933 to 1937, but pointed out that beginning in 1939 a small natural increase had made itself apparent.

Ishmael P. Flory, organizer of the Chicago Council of the National Negro Congress, called the attention of the committee "to the plight of at least 8,000,000 white and colored citizens of the South who suffer under a system of debt slavery which had its counterpart only in the feudal system of the Dark Ages," and continued:

> Here on Chicago's South Side, we have thousands of Negroes who have fled from the South to escape the burden of debt slavery. More arrive each month, so that it is estimated that at least 50,000 Negroes here—one-sixth of the colored population—have no regular place of abode, begging their meals at back doors and on the streets, sleeping in parks, hallways, or on the floors of already overcrowded apartments.

Three modern slave-catchers from Oglethorpe County, Georgia, notorious for its peonage system, came to grief in their attempt to return Otis and Dock Woods and Solomon McCannon to Sandy Cross Plantation near Lexington, Georgia. William Toliver Cunningham, owner of the plantation, arrived in Chicago in September 1939, accompanied by his attorney Hamilton McWhorter, and a deputy sheriff. Enlisting the aid of Cook County Deputy Sheriff Keenan, McWhorter succeeded in having the three Negroes arrested for the theft of two bushels of corn in 1935. The tenants had remained on the plantation a year after the alleged theft, the charge being brought against them only after they had departed for the North. While in Chicago, McWhorter also made an effort to apprehend Clyde Smith, Ella Smith, and Edward Raines, Negro refugees from Oglethorpe County, but failed because he had no warrant.

Though he did manage to have Otis and Dock Woods and Soloman McCannon lodged in jail, McWhorter's plea for extradition to Georgia was denied by Governor Henry Horner. Moreover, through the efforts of Col. William Henry Huff of the Abolish Peonage Committee and several allied organizations, Cunningham and McWhorter were indicted by a federal grand jury for "conspiracy to retain and hold Negroes in a condition of peonage and slavery." In January 1942, the United States Supreme Court in a unanimous decision voided the Georgia debt law.

At the Chicago hearings of the committee investigating migration, the chairman read into the record a portion of an article by Jonathan Daniels published in *The Nation*:

> But I am glad the migrants moved, even to brutal murder in Chicago, mass violence in California. This business back of Bigger Thomas, this business which drove the Joads, is not a migrant problem. The migrants are only the messengers, carrying both news and shame to the whole land. California did not like it, and Chicago is not entirely pleased about it. . . . What I fear now is that in California and Chicago, New York, and Detroit, the war abroad will pull all our home memories down. I am grateful to Congressmen and novelists and playwrights, to everyone who keeps these people under our eyes. The only answer will come from uninterrupted attention. They will not stop starving or moving because they are forgotten.

15. The Exodus Train

The most recent draft of this chapter was written by Joseph Bougere and dated May 22, 1942. It was found at the Newberry Library with minor comments in the handwriting of Jack Conroy that have been incorporated by the editor. A copy of the same draft was also found in the IWP papers without Conroy's corrections.

The Great Migration reached flood tide by 1917. The *Chicago Defender* received thousands of letters out of the Deep South, as did the Chicago Urban League, the organization to which the paper usually referred prospective migrants inquiring about employment. A Birmingham staff correspondent of the *Defender* wrote early in February:

> The members of the Race in this section of the country are way ahead of the leaders who are just now considering the advisability of going north to better their conditions. The leaders among the churches, ministers, and bishops are telling the cause for leaving, but they are too late. Thousands have left for the North and thousands are still leaving and a million will leave with the Great Northern Drive on May 15, 1917. The maltreatment of the whites toward members of our Race is the sole cause of the exodus. It is the general belief here that its God's plan and hand and that through His Providence the Race will be helpful.

At the same time the paper urged from Chicago:

> The *Defender* invites all to come north. Plenty of room for the good, sober, industrious men and women. Plenty of work. For those who will not work, the jails will take care of you. When you have served your 90 days at hard labor, you will then learn how to work. Anywhere in God's country is better than the southland. Don't let the crackers fool you. Cast the yoke from around your neck. See the light, when you have crossed the Ohio River, breathe fresh air and say, "Why didn't I come before."[1]

The legend of the Great Northern Drive spread rapidly months before the appointed date, May 15, 1917. The Birmingham staff correspondent on March 10:

> The Great Northern Drive spoken of by the *Chicago Defender* is taking place long before the time set by the paper. They are leaving here by the thousands. The Birmingham *Age-*

Herald is trying to make light of so many leaving but they seem to have the *Defender* tonic in their system and are heading north.

A month earlier the Savannah correspondent had said:

The word has been passed along from father to son, from mother to daughter, brother to brother and sister to sister, prepare for the day is coming. This spring a general movement will be started northward by millions of members of the Race from all over the south. It is expected before that time, however, that thousands will have left despite the fact that many educated men of the Race who have hid behind the clock of school teachers and ministers of the gospel aided by the publicity of their acts given them by the white press, have tried to scare them with the cold weather gag. Not only this but some of the more trifling kind took advantage of free transportation given by railroads and other industries, went north without desiring to work, and found out that there was no white men in that section of the country who would give him money to battle on Jim or John, has come back with some excuse. These fellows are "good niggers" and find their names in print the day following their arrival back home.

Letters requesting information about the Great Northern Drive flooded the *Defender* office for months. Anxiety and even desperation pervaded many of them. One from New Orleans read:

I reads your paper and I am asking about the drive of May the 15. We want more understanding about it for there is a great many of us that wants to come and the depot agent never given us any satisfaction when we ask for they don't want us to leave. Please put in your paper Saturday, just what time the train will be here, and the fare so we can be there on time. Many women are wanting to come. They are hard working women, the white folks tell us we have to have plenty of money to come north, if this is right let us know, also let us know where the train is going to stop.

Often it was planned that the breadwinner go first to the "Promise Land." A letter from a Mobile woman read:

I was reading in your paper about the colored race and I seen in it where cars would be here for the 15th of May. Will you be so kind as to let me know where they are going to stop so my husband and children can get on. We have been living in this hole for years, and with a family we can hardly live. My husband can leave first and then we can come later when he gets a good job. If the cars are not going to stop here let me know and my husband will meet the cars where ever you say. Let me know at once so he can get ready.

A New Orleans woman wrote:

Please sir will you kindly tell me what is meant by the Great Northern Drive to take place May 15, on Tuesday. It is a rumor all over town to be ready for the 15th of May to go in the drive. The paper said the first drive was to be the 10th of February. My husband is in the north already preparing for the family but hearing that the excursion will be $6.00 from here north and having a large family I could profit by it if it is true. Do please write at once and tell me of this excursion to leave the south. Nearly the whole of the south is ready for the drive. Please write at once. We are sick to get out of the south.

The exodus was helped along by such poems as "Farewell—We're Good and Gone," by W. E. Dancer, "poet and humorist" as well as "a graduate of Tuskegee Institute, State Grand Master of the Mosaic Templars of American of Florida Jurisdiction and author of the famous concert book *Today and Yistidy*." Here are a few verses as they appeared in the *Defender*:

> You talk erbout er race can stand
> Just anything dat come;
> An' one dat's had fum head ter feet,
> What patty give de drum;
> Dis Negro race been shot an' burned,
> And things too bad ter tell;
> Day nachly tried ter make us b'lieve
> We all was born fer-well,
> But anyhow dis thing done changed,
> And goodbye sho's you born;
> You need not say it's cold up North,
> For "Bud" we're good and gone.
>
> We nursed you south once, white you fought,
> Ter keep us bound in chains,
> We stood your whip an' patarolls
> And worked while racked with pains:
> We ate your ash cakes, peas and milk,
> While you ate toast and broth;
> But thank de Lord de time has come
> We'll help you cut dis cloth;
> You've had a chance ter treat us right,
> But no, you went rite on
> And classed us wid the lower brutes,
> And now we're good and gone.
>
> It's not to mix up wid you folks,
> We nachly love our own,
> And can live always side by side,
> An' leave de rest alone;
> But, let us feel dat we are free,
> To work, an' walk, an' talk;
> An' vote an' ride jest where we please,
> An' we will never balk;
> But us done tried you up an' down
> An' been struck by your thorn,
> So now you do the best you ken:
> Fer we're good and gone.
>
> It's true we love de south all right
> But, yes we love God too;
> An' when he comes ter help us out
> What's left fer us to do?
> You dare us to dispute your books,

Let dem be right or wrong;
What cotton dem 'boll weevils' leave,
You take dat rat er long;
Den comes de North wid high wages
Sayin' 'Come on up de horn'
An' den you think we'll stay down here
Not you,—Good bye we're gone.

William Crosse contributed "The Land of Hope":

I've watched the trains as they disappeared
Behind the clouds of smoke,
Carrying the crowds of working men
To the land of hope,
Working hard on southern soil,
Some one softly spoke;
'Toil and toil and toil and toil,
And yet I'm always broke.'

On the farms I've labored hard,
And never missed a day;
With wife and children by my side
We journeyed on our way.
But now the year is passed and gone,
And every penny spent,
And all my little food supplies
Were taken 'way for rent.

Yes, we are going to the north!
I don't care what state,
Just so I cross the Dixon Line,
From this southern land of hate,
Lynched and burned and shot and hung,
And not a word is said.
No law whatever to protect—
It's just a 'nigger' dead.

Go on, dear brother; you'll ne'er regret;
Just trust in God; pray for the best,
And at the end You're sure to find
"Happiness will be thine."

"Farewell—We're Good and Gone," "Bound for the Promise Land," and "bound to the land of Hope" were slogans often chalked on the sides of special trains carrying exodusters. In many instances, local authorities tried to divert or halt the emigrants. The *Defender*, after reporting the addition in Memphis of two eighty-foot steel coaches to the Chicago train in order to accommodate exodusters, printed the text of a telegram just dispatched:

THIS IS TO NOTIFY BRAVE CHIEF OF POLICE PERRY THAT THE *CHICAGO DEFENDER* HAS
MORE THAN 10,000 SUBSCRIBERS IN THE CITY OF MEMPHIS WHO GET THEIR PAPERS DIRECT
THROUGH THE UNITED STATES MAIL, AND TO ACCOMPLISH HIS PURPOSE OF PREVENTING

A Tennessee friend of the *Defender* sent in a two-column item from the *Memphis Commercial Appeal*, commenting:

. . . . [T]his is a purported interview . . . with a Jackson, Mississippi, Negro whose sole relation to the article, I have not the slightest doubt, is his name, the *Appeal* supplying the thoughts and words. . . . What a pity it is that such Negroes, the most annoying and mischievous type of "white folks" niggers cannot be smothered outright, whenever in times like these, they land or sell their aid to the persecutors of the race.[3]

W. Allison Sweeney scanned the article, and demurred slightly:

Nay, nay, Mr. Correspondent; not quite so sweeping, please; hold your horses; check up a trifle. . . . [T]hey're a devilish annoying type of "nigger" and I am with you to the extent of choking and smothering them ALMOST to extinction . . . but not quite for that. Don't you see THAT would be murder! Cruel, picayunish murder. The killing as it were of a stink bug with a sledge hammer.

Considering the interviewee, described by the *Commercial Appeal* as "a well informed and observant Negro lawyer and physician," Mr. Sweeney went on:

Viewing him simply as a sporadic growth, an unsightly wart and excrescence disfiguring, but in not so much as a feather's weight halting, the mighty march and onward sweep of our brethren in the southland to the northland, let us as briefly as possible glance him over, even though incidentally we "run him through" in our quest to ascertain through his coached and edited effort why the Negro should remain in the south and avoid the north.

Mr. Sweeney then divided the "marrow and Kernel" of the interview into "exhibits," appending caustic and pertinent comment to each. "Exhibit No. 3" read:

I admit that conditions here are not all they might be, but they are not that anywhere. It is very largely with every man, though, to make his conditions, to a great extent, what he would have them, and is but the quintessence of the spectacle of weakness and unmanliness most pitiable to see a man spending a lifetime ever seeking the line of least resistance, making himself a wanderer upon the face of the earth, looking for a soft spot.

Mr. Sweeney exclaimed:

Magnanimous man: Disciple combined of Esculapius and Lycurgus! He admits, learned (?) renegade that he is, that: Conditions there "are" not all they might be. . . . For the love of mike, what would I not forego to write on this sheet of virgin paper the words I'd like to shout at THAT MAN. . . . WHAT CHANCE HAS THE BLACK MAN IN THE SOUTH TO CHANGE CONDITIONS? WHAT CHANCE HAS HE EVER HAD? WILL HE EVER HAVE? It is unbelievable that a butterfly could light in hell and not scorch its wings. Or a canary OCCUPY a cage with a cat and ESCAPE devourment?

"Exhibit No. 4" was couched in lyrical terms:

HERE in the balmy and beautiful southland where everything in nature blends in such perfect harmony to make live everything that one could ask, where the sun shines all the 365 days in a year; where our soil is as fertile as the far-famed valley of the River Nile.

This apparently, was almost too much for Mr. Sweeney and he retorted:

Balmy and beautiful southland, eh? Balmy and yet so often its breezes have been putrid with the smell of BURNING FLESH. Beautiful and yet so often its skies have been darkened with the smoke of burning houses. . . . The thousands of murdered black men whose cries long ago were still, whose bones long since were dust, are beyond the possibility of Noise Makers of Harmony disturbers; theirs is a silence which will continue 'till the DAWN OF THE GREAT JUBILEE. Dead! THEY SPEAK NO MORE. DEAD! TROUBLE NO MORE. . . . GONE FOREVER.

Mr. Sweeney concluded:

If deductions drawn from the exhibit noted are complimentary—helpful to the cause of this Negro propagandist—"To what base use may we come, Horatio?"—he's welcome to the same; but I warn him, and in doing so I LAUGH in his face; I KICK that part of his anatomy that is looking west while his face looks east. As well might he attempt to dig up the Gulf of Mexico in a teaspoon as stop this mighty avalanche marching—can't you hear its tread?—sweeping northward to a NEWER and more significant emancipation.
STOP IT? STOP IT?? STOP IT????
WHY, NIGAH, HIT'S GOD'S WORK. . . . IT'S GOD'S WORK. . . . STOP IT? OH, GEE AN' SECH AS YOU BE. . . . . . . !

And the mighty avalanche *did* continue to move northward. A letter from Mobile, Alabama read:

We have a club of 108 good men who wants work we are willing to go north or west but we are not able to pay rail road fare. Can you help us come, or get us work we will pay you out of our salary or you can take it yourself. Hope to hear from you at once.

A Natchez man, "having a wife and mother to support," wrote to express his "greatest desire . . . to leave for a better place," and went on:

I can write short stories all of which portrays negro character but no burlesque and can also write poems, have for a gift for cartooning but have never learned the technicalities of comic drawing. Would like to know if you can use one or two short stories in serial form in your great paper they are very interesting and would furnish good reading matter. By this means I could probably leave here in short and thus come into possession of better employment enabling me to take up my drawing which I like best.

This letter came from Rome, Georgia:

I've just read your ad in the *Defender* on getting employment. So I will now ask you to do the best for me. Now Mr. _____ I am not a tramp by any means I am high class church man and business man. I am the Daddy of the Transfer Business in this city, and carried it for ten years. Seven years ago I sold out to a white concern.
I prefer a job in a Retail Furniture Store if I can be placed. I'll now name a few things

that I can do. Viz I can repair and finish furniture. I am an expert packer and crater of furniture. I pack China, cut glass & silverware. I can enamel grain and paint furniture, and repair violins, guitars & mandolins, and I am a first class umbrella-man. I can do anything that can be done to an umbrella and parasol. I can manage a transfer business. I know all about shipping H.H. Goods & Furniture, and can make out bills of lading and write tags for the same.

    If you can place me in any of these trades it will be O.K.

The desire for better educational facilities, either for themselves or for their children, actuated the writers of many letters. One from West Palm Beach, Florida, read:

While reading the *Defender* I saw where you needed laborers in Chicago. I have children and I lost my wife a few years ago. I would like to properly educate them. I am a barber by trade, and have been barbering for twenty years. I have saved enough for our fare. If I could make more money in Chicago, I will come where they can get a good education. I am a church man and don't drink whiskey.

A resident of the same city wrote:

I saw your advertisement in the *Defender* for laborers. I am a young man and want to finish school. I want to look out for me a job working mornings or evenings. I would like to get a job in a private family so I could continue taking piano lessons. I can do everything around the house but drive and can learn that quick. Send me the name of the best high school in Chicago. How is the Wendell Phillips College? I have finished the grammar school. I can not come before the middle of June.

This letter came from Alexandria, Louisiana:

I am planning on leaving this place about May 11 for Chicago and wants to know everything about the town. My job for the past eight years was with the Armour Packing Co., of this place. I know all about the office and what goes on in a packing company. I am doing the smoking in this company now. I am 36 years old and have a wife and two children. I have been here all my life and would like to go somewhere I could educate my children so they could be of service to themselves when they gets older, and I can't do it here. I will pay you for your trouble if you can get me a job with any of the big packing companies there, if not I will accept any job you can get.

There were hundreds of responses to such advertisements as these printed in a single issue of the *Defender*:

Advertisement
$3.60 Per Day
Can be made in a Steel Foundry in Minnesota by strong, healthy, steady men. Open only to men living in Chicago. Apply at the Chicago Urban League—Chicago League on Urban Conditions Among Negroes.
3303 S. State St.
Chicago, Illinois

Wanted
25 Young Men as Bus Boys and Porters
Salary $8.00 a Week and Board

John R. Thompson Restaurant
314 S. State St.
(Call between 7 and 8 A.M. Ask for Mr. Brown)

Wanted
25 Girls—for Dish Washing
Salary $7.00 a Week and Board
Apply—John R. Thompson Restaurants
314 S. State St.
(Call between 6 and 8 A.M. Ask for Mr. Brown)

Wanted
2 Young Men
6243 Halsted St. and 1581 Milwaukee Avenue
Salary $8.00 and meals
Thompson

Wanted
10 Moulders—Must be experienced.
$4.40 to $5.05 per day
Write—B.F.R. Defender Office, Chicago, Illinois

Employment Agencies offering a wide variety of jobs to exodusters flourished. One of them advertised in the *Defender*:

Advertisement
No Job, No Pay. . . . No Job, No Pay. . . . No Job, No Pay. . . . No Job, No Pay. . . .

Women	Men
Kitchen Help	Elevator Boys
Maids	Bus Boys
Cafeterias	Chauffeurs
House Girls	Janitors
Laundresses	Porters
Day's Work	Chefs
Married Couples to work together	Pantry Boys
Entertainers	Kitchen Men
Musicians	Mechanical Trades
Stenographers	Laborers
Solicitors	Molders
Pantry Girls	Waiters
Waitresses	Bell Boys
Cooks	Butlers
	Stewards
	Bldg. Helpers

A.B.C. Employment Agency
4750 S. State St.
Come in and fill out your application with this office.
No Charge to register. . . . No charge to register—No fee charged for any position.
Attention new-comers and persons from the South.

Professional and business men often followed or accompanied their departing clients. Many preachers led their entire flocks north and established their churches anew, usually in vacant storerooms. A *Defender* reporter interviewed Rev. R. H. Harmon, who had arrived with his wife and 28 members of his congregation in a carload of exodusters from Harrisburg, Mississippi, and other southern points. Rev. Harmon said:

> I am working at my trade. I have saved enough to bring my wife and four children and some of my congregation. We are here for keeps. They say that we are fools to leave the warm country, and how our people are dying in the east. Well, I for one am glad that they had the privilege of dying a natural death there. That is much better than the rope and the torch. I will take my chance with the northern winter.

Most of the preachers toiled each week day at some other job, putting aside their work clothes to occupy the pulpit on Sundays or for "prayer meetings" and other occasions, such as the protracted "revival" services held nightly.

A great number of less daring preachers nevertheless were perturbed at the course of events. One of these wrote from Newborn, Alabama:

> We desire to know if you are in a position to put us in touch with a reliable firm or private family that desires to employ two women; one is a school teacher in the public schools of this country and the other is a high school pupil. The teacher has a mother and sisters to care for and she is forced to seek employment elsewhere, because wages are so low. The high school pupil is able to work in a private family.
>
> Wages are terrible here. A grown man is forced to work for 50 cents a day. Sometimes he may earn 75 cents for all kinds of work. Here a man is only able to get a peck of meal and from three to four pounds of bacon a week, and he is treated as a slave. As leaders we are powerless for we dare not to resent such or even show disapproval. Only a few days ago over 1,000 men and women left here for the north and the west. The white man says that we all can't go but he doesn't raise our pay. As a minister of the Methodist Episcopal Church I am on the verge of starvation simply because of the above conditions. I shall be glad to know if I could be of any real service to you as director of your society. Thanking you in advance for an early reply, and for any suggestions that you may have and be able to do for us.

From Greenville, Mississippi, came this letter:

> Please inform me as to whether there is employment for colored insurance agents by company as industrial writers, sick and accident and death in a company that handles colored agents, in Chicago or suburban towns. Please see whether the supt. of a company could use a live reliable agent. I am planning on moving to Illinois. This is confidential. I have been working for 15 years as an agent in an insurance company.

There were similar appeals from barbers, automobile mechanics, school teachers and others who had been left stranded by the exodus.

A Greenwood, Mississippi, woman sent this inquiry:

> I noticed in the *Defender* about receiving some information from you about positions up there or rather work and I am very anxious to know what the chances are for business men. I am very anxious to leave the south on account of my children but my husband

doesn't seem to think that he can succeed there in business, he is a merchant and also knows the barber trade. What are the chances in either? Some of our folks down here have the idea that the northern movement means nothing to anybody but those who go out and labor by the day. I am willing to work myself to get a start. Tell me what we could really do. I will do most anything to get our family out of Bam. Please let this be confidential.[4]

The *Defender* maintained its role as the friend and advisor of the exodusters after they had settled in the city. However, an impatient correspondent, "Constant Reader," addressed columnist "Wise Old Owl" early in March 1917, to administer a mild rebuke:

Myself and a party of friends have been wondering why you remained asleep all winter while such a thing as the "exodus" has been going on. Haven't you anything at all to say, or are you waiting for warm weather?

"Wise Old Owl," frankly confessing that the communication had aroused him from "a long winter's sleep," went on to say:

While the foregoing letter does not specify any exact part of the so-called exodus in which I should focus particular attention the first thing that comes to my mind after opening both eyes in a befitting and characteristic manner, was to look into what should be an important phase of the situation viz how to do, what to do and where to do it, after arriving from the south.

The columnist then proceeded to "elucidate what should prove as interest—a theory generally as it should prove a warning to the unwary—not to say the unsophisticated." After discussing desirable objectives and outlining the civil rights to be demanded in the North, "Wise Old Owl" concluded:

But it must be remembered that these rights are not to be abused and the rules governing them are the same for white and members of the Race alike. Be clean, ladies and gentlemen; water is cheap and deportment should be a discount; avoid loud talking, and boisterous laughter on street cars and in public places; keep away from the buffet flats like you duck a small-pox sign; help starve out the gypsy fortune-teller—they are conducting an illegal practice and there is a gang of them every day in the police courts for thieving and don't show your ignorance by entrusting your money with anybody without a proper receipt for same, and then only with responsible people. In thinking all this over and while praising the Lord for your deliverance from the bloody zone in the south where the lynch-billies are supreme, remember and deal only with your own race and shop where A MEMBER OF THE RACE IS EMPLOYED. If you do these things you will be doing yourself and your people an inestimable good and at the same time you will be pleasing the WISE OLD OWL as he deserves for the worrying he is doing about your welfare.

The *Defender* did not relax its vigilance. An item published a few weeks later struck a grim note:

The *Chicago Defender* wishes to impress firmly upon the minds of the newcomers to carry an identification card in their pockets all the time. If you are a newcomer and your family are still in the south, carry their name and address and your nearest relative's name on you at all times. In case of accident we may be able to notify them. Twenty deaths and accidents occurred last month and the bodies of these persons are still at the County Morgue, unidentified.

In May the paper found it necessary to repeat some of the advice offered by "Wise Old Owl."

Laboring men who have been placed at shops and factories are urged to appear on the street cars and in public places in clean decent clothes. They can leave their working clothes where they work, and put on better ones when they leave. In the north a man is usually judged by the clothes he wears, how clean they are and they have cars and elevated roads to keep themselves clean going to and from work. It is different here in the north. In the south they don't care how they dress, here they make it a practice to look as well in the week as they do on Sunday. We have seen a number of southern women wearing boudoir caps. They don't seem to know when to wear them. Don't wear them on the street and on the cars. They are to be worn in the house with a kimona. Also wear your kimonas in the house.[5]

The *Defender* warned against "scheming preachers and labor agents getting rich off newcomers," the latter "charging them a dollar a month for the entire year." That fee, the paper said, was "outrageous" and asserted that "half of those sent do not know anything about the work or what they are going for, and consequently there is a breach between labor and the employer, who is dissatisfied with his new laborers and gets a grudge against all members of the Race." The *Defender* also condemned "scheming preachers through this section of country and the east, who for 50 cents and a dollar find one a job. You go to the place where they want no labor, but your money is gone." Censure was directed at twenty men who had declined "to leave the 'bright lights' of the city and 'State Street'" to accept out of town jobs procured for them by the one to which newly arrived jobseekers should turn. Though it stoutly championed the cause of "the hard working man, the steady fellow with a family, who has come north to be able to associate with the whites on an equal basis," the paper was not inclined to coddle idlers. In one issue it complained:

With conditions more promising than at any time in the history of the city, a *Defender* reporter found many loafers hanging around the pool rooms near 31st and 35th on State Street. When asked if they wanted work, they shook their heads in the negative. The bright lights are attracting them strongly. They care not how they live or where they stay. It is only a question of time before these people, poorly clad, without proper food, will succumb to the white plague. In addition to the foregoing there is another class that depends on gambling for a living, and they imbibe too freely of whiskey. The police are gradually cleaning up this sort, and the judges are getting severe. This class we do not want here, and the better element of the city will do all they can to see that those who do not behave themselves will be handled by the proper authorities.

Though the *Defender* urged courtesy and respect for the rights of others, it did not advocate servility. Working men were admonished:

Quit calling the foremen "boss." Leave that word dropped in the Ohio River. Also captain, general, and major. We call people up here, Mister This and Mister That. When your payday comes, take it home. Depend on your work to keep you in a job and not the dollar or two you have been used to slipping the foreman. Cut that out. If you are working for $18.00 keep it. Your employer pays the foreman much more than you, and if he has got to graft let him go to the employer. If you can't stay because you don't pay, quit and go somewhere else, or go in person to your employer and complain.

When you get among white workmen, treat them as you want them to treat you—AS A MAN—not as his inferior. Keep your hand off your hat when you pass men in and around the shop or plant. There is no law that requires you to tip your hat to a man because he is white.

The South missed the exodusters and sought to restrain them first by blandishments and minor concessions, and then, if necessary, by force. Even in the North, the refugees were not always safe. The *Defender* reported a typical case:

Southern kidnapers made a bold and successful raid on Chicago citizenship Saturday when in broad daylight a sheriff from Miss., went to the railroad yards at 18th St. and with the help of Chicago police "captured" a man named James Halley, and in less than two hours had this man handcuffed and on a train bound for Holly Springs, Miss., to stand trial for selling a pint of whiskey, make a penitentiary offense for the purpose of establishing a new form of slavery in the south and setting forth a complicated condition of affairs in the state which the Race has started to fight in order to protect its own citizens from illegal kidnapping.

Attorney Ferdinand L. Barnett interested himself in these kidnappings, ordinarily effected with the assistance of Chicago police. Another exoduster was saved from extradition on the charge of having "insulted a white woman in Memphis" when his wife summoned Barnett in time for the attorney to procure a write of habeas corpus. The southern officers prudently refrained from pressing their charges in court, and departed without their intended victim. The *Defender* ran this notice.

Attention New Comers:
IF THE POLICE ATTEMPT TO MOLEST YOU AND YOU ARE NOT GUILTY, OR IF YOU GET IN TROUBLE, SEND FOR ONE OF THE FOLLOWING LAWYERS.
F.L. Barnett—184 W. Washington Street
Ellis and Westbrooks—3000 S. State Street

Enterprising advertisers sometimes profited from the *Defender*'s insistent warnings to gullible exodusters who might fall prey to city slickers. The State Theater offered a motion picture entitled "Beware of Strangers," exposing "methods of blackmailing and facts about clairvoyants," and "endorsed by the United States Department of Justice." Directed to the attention of "New Comers from Southland," an advertisement read:

Little did Hinton Clabagh think when he brought to justice a blackmailing syndicate preying on the unsuspecting public that he was laying the network of a moving picture. An eight-reel play exposing the organizations of crooks and showing how they operate. It is not the proper food for juvenile minds so children must stay at home. The subject is of paramount interest and is worth seeing. Selig made this a worthwhile picture and not one of those fly-by-night things. Its moral is "beware of strangers."

No matter how suave, sweet or smiling Mr. Stranger may be do not entrust in him either yourself or your money. If you do you are liable to get blackmailed or go to jail. This and the reason why are pointed out in this film. The cast includes Fritzi Brunett, Thomas Santschi, Jack Richardson, Bessie Eyeton.

Whatever might befall them, few of the exodusters even contemplated a return to the South. Sparrell Scott wrote for the *Defender*:

"When I Return to the Southland It Will Be"

When lions eat grass like oxen,
And an angle worm swallows a whale,
And a terrapin knits a woolen sock,
And a hare is outrun by a snail.

When serpents walk like men,
And doodle-bugs leap like frogs,
When grasshoppers feed on hens,
And feathers grow on hogs.

When tom cats swim in the air,
And elephants roost in the trees,
When insects in summer are rare,
And snuff can't make you sneeze.

When fish live on dry land,
When mules on velocipedes ride,
And foxes lay eggs in the sand,
And women take dress to no pride.

When a German drinks no beer,
And girls deck in plumes for a dime,
When billy goats butt from the rear,
And treason is no longer a crime.

When the mocking bird brays like an ass,
And limburger smells like cologne,
When plowshares are made of glass,
And the heart of true lovers are stone.

When ideas grow on trees,
And wool on cast iron rams,
I then may return to the South,
But I'll travel then in a box.

A churchwoman who had heeded the call of the "Promise Land" sent back this report to her church sisters:

My Dear Sisters:
   I was agreeably surprised to hear from you and to hear from my home. I am well and thankful to be in a city with no lynching and no beating. The weather was a great surprise to me. I got there just in time for one of the greatest revivals in the history of my life—over 500 joined the church. We had a holy ghost shower. You know I like to run wild at the services . . . it snows here and even the churches are crowded and we had to stand up last night. The people are rushing here by the thousands, and I know that if you come here

and rent a big house you can get all the roomers you want. I am not keeping house yet I am living with my brother. I can get you a nice place to live until you get your own house. The houses are so pretty, we has a nice place. I am very busy I work at the Swift Packing Co., in the sausage department. My daughter and I work at the same place. We get $1.50 a day, and the hours are not so long, before you know it, it is time to go home. I am so thankful the Lord has been so good to me. Work is plenty here, and we don't loaf we are glad to work. Remember me to Mrs. C. and T. and tell all the children I am praying for them. Hurry up and come to Chicago it is wonderful. I hope I see your face before I die.

Pray for me I am heaven bound. Let me know if you are coming soon as I will meet you at the railroad and bring you to my house, and what a good time we will have thanking God and going to church.

And enclosed was this special greeting and request:

Dear _____:

How are you. I am fine the family is well to. I am working and have been since I left. I make $90.00 a month with ease. Hello to all the people of my home town. I am saving my money, and have joined the K of P up here. Send me five gallons of country syrup. Love to all yours in Christ.

16. Slave Market

This chapter was reconstructed from two drafts at the Newberry Library. The first draft is a twenty-two-page essay written by E. Diehl, as determined from a footnote with the initials "E. D." Jack Conroy rewrote the chapter, eliminating the footnotes and shortening it to nine pages, although the first page is missing. The earlier draft was used to make up for the missing first page in the version that appears here. Corrections by Conroy on his draft were also incorporated by the editor.

In the Spring of 1938 the passerby in 16th Street between Avers and Keeler, a half dozen miles southwest of Chicago's Loop, could observe a curious scene, reminiscent of ante-bellum days in the South. Local white housewives and agents of others residing in distant neighborhoods searched up and down the thoroughfare among the gathered Negro women domestics for the best and cheapest workers, bidding for their services much as southern blacks had been appraised on the block before emancipation. The average price offered for a long, hard day's work was between a dollar and a half and two dollars. The forenoon was the busy time, brisk bargaining taking place in the street with the arrival and departure of scores of employers and employees. Some of the Negro women—ranging in age from the very young to the very old—held out for better pay; others were borne off by successful bidders.

The "Slave Market," as this unique labor exchange was called, attracted hundreds of unorganized, needy Negro women long after the back of the depression was supposed to have been broken and after collective bargaining had been written into national law. The "black bourse" however was about this time beginning to be invaded by labor organizers, stimulated to the task by examples of sisters and brothers in other fields opened a few years earlier by formation of the Committee for Industrial Organization. One such young woman, mingling with the crowd of job seekers, was approached by a young housewife, come to shop in the open-air domestic labor market.

"You looking for work?"

"Yes. How much do you pay and what do you want done?"

"What do you care what I want done as long as you're working. You want work, don't you? I'll pay you $1.75."

"I want $3.00."

"You'll never get it—nobody pays $3.00, pooh!"

A prim, aggressive, elderly Negro woman who had been listening, said: "Yes, they do too; if they want their work done they'll pay for it."

"For $3.00 I'll do my work myself," retorted the housewife.

"Well, if you don't want to pay for it you'll have to do it yourself."

The would-be employer turned again to the young organizer. "Come on, you want work?"

"No; I'll wait."

"You'll be waiting all day." A number of housewives expressed their solidarity with their exacerbated sister by sympathetic, meaningful laughter. One said: "They sound like a union." They all laughed again.

All morning the bargaining went on, the young woman organizer and a colleague circulating among the domestics, urging them to hold up the price of their labor and taking names and addresses for the Domestic Workers' Association, begun some years earlier but as yet unknown to the majority of colored housekeepers.

This "slave market" in a Chicago street in 1938 revealed the low economic status of the race three-quarters of a century after emancipation. Encouraged to migrate to the North during World War I to produce the goods needed to insure American victory in 1918, the Negro entered many industries previously closed to him and contributed largely to the success of our arms. Yet prejudice and discrimination against him continued, on the part both of employers—except when they could use him as a strikebreaker—and of union officials of the American Federation of Labor. Discrimination by the latter played a large part in instigating the attack on colored workers at East St. Louis in 1917. In May of that year, hundreds of "labor sympathizers," including sixty representatives of the Central Body of Trade and Labor Unionists, met in the city hall auditorium and protested the influx from the South and the hiring of the migrants by East St. Louis industrial concerns. One representative "suggested that if the manufacturing plants did not stop hiring the Negroes and importing them into the city that the city officials should notify them that they would no longer be given police and fire protection."

The bloody riots that followed were due as much to the attitude of the union leaders as any other factor in the situation. The Negroes in many instances were not taking the jobs of whites: packers and officials of the Aluminum Ore Company states that "the work which the Negroes have been doing . . . the white laborers refuse to do at any price." Union officials, finding the Negro a stubborn competitor and potent strikebreaker, at last decided—as scores of times before—to admit him to membership. Colored ministers announced the lifting of the color ban and urged Negroes to join at a mass meeting in April 1919.

However, in the same year occurred the memorable riots in Chicago, their roots in economic strife traceable to exclusion also. Three years earlier, the Pullman Car Cleaners' strike had been broken by Negro men and women, and after the strike large numbers of them were kept on the payroll, displacing white workers. In the summer of 1919 there were only three hundred Negroes employed at the Corn Products Refining Company at Argo when the plant went on strike. Nine hundred Negroes were used to break the strike, and when the conflict was over five hundred of them were retained, some on jobs which up to that time were performed by white labor only. Many Negroes entered the semi-skilled fields in steel during the great strike of 1919. At the stockyards, although colored workers had been admitted to the Amalgamated Meat Cutters and Butcher Workmen of the World after their successful strikebreaking in 1904, great numbers of Negroes (comprising over 70 percent of the total working force in 1918) remained unorganized. The International Ladies Garment Workers Union also discriminated against colored workers until the latter showed their strength in defeating the strike of the unionists, after which union officials made special efforts to enlist Negro members.

The governor's commission on race relations in its report on the causes of the Chicago race riots of 1919 stated that Negroes

> . . . are denied opportunity with whites for advancement and promotion where they are employed. . . . There is much fair talk on the part of trade union leaders about the absence of color discrimination. . . . In spite of the resolutions at national conferences, the local branches are subject to the same popular prejudices as other groups in the community. . . .

At the same time that the migrants were meeting with resistance and violence calculated to exclude them from or drive them out of entire areas of the labor field, they succeeded in entering many new occupations. Colored molders were being hired, shipping clerks were engaged in warehouses, and taxi and automobile companies were accepting Negro labor. The Northwestern Railroad Company employed a number of ex-soldiers (not as porters), and the Peoples Gas Company and the Commonwealth Edison Company hired a small number of the race for the first time.

The governor's commission noted that while it appeared that the Negroes' strike-breaking activities were directed against the white worker

> . . . they were in fact desperate acts of opportunism in the struggle for the economic security of an entire national group, and did not, in the main, spring from any disloyalty to labor's code of honor.

The large percentage of Negroes (30 percent of the total) employed in the Chicago stockyards even after the war was attributed to the employers' "fear of trade unionism and labor difficulties." Most of the Negroes were still outside the union. In 1922, southern Negroes were imported to break a strike in the southern Illinois mine fields.

Before 1925, when the Brotherhood of Sleeping Car Porters began, organizing of—or the attempt to organize—Negroes had been sporadic and on a small scale. Few unions welcomed them to full membership. Although the constitutions of only eight American Federation of Labor international unions and four unaffiliated railway brotherhoods specifically barred colored members, twenty-four additional unions (all A.F. of L.) effectually excluded Negroes by requiring that membership be predicated on terms of apprenticeship ranging from three to five years. By the simple expedient of not permitting Negroes to enroll as apprentices, it was possible to exclude them completely.

The only important unions admitting Negroes to white locals on terms of complete equality—even permitting them to hold high office—were the Amalgamated Meat Cutters and Butcher Workmen, Hod Carriers, Flat Janitors, and Ladies Garment Workers. In addition, two labor organizations which not only admitted Negroes but made special efforts to enroll them were the Industrial Workers of the World (with a very small membership in the Chicago area) and the Amalgamated Clothing Workers of America. The latter's experience in 1917 accounted for the eagerness to recruit colored workers thereafter on terms of full equality. In that year Negro women were instrumental in breaking a strike called by the latter union.

Of the dozen unions which excluded Negroes by constitutional stipulations, all but one were in the transportation field or a contributory occupation. In protest, a group of Negroes in 1815 organized the Railway Men's International Benevolent Industrial Association, which admitted all railway men regardless of craft. It had in Chicago a membership of 1,200, divided in seventeen locals.

The successful organization of sleeping car porters after 1925 marked the first mass movement of the type among the race. The brotherhood held its first annual convention in Chicago in September 1929; M. P. Webster, president of the Chicago local, said:

> Negroes have long been organizing religiously, fraternally, socially and every other way but economically. They have feared they would lose out on their jobs if they organized, but in fact they have lost out on jobs because they were unorganized and lacked even a spokesman to say they did not want to be supplanted. They said the American Federation of Labor wouldn't admit us, but it has admitted us.

A few months earlier, the *Chicago Daily News* had commented on the activities of president Michael J. Kelly of the Cook County Wage Earner's League, also leader of the butchers and meat cutters, who had been busy on the South Side for some time, "with the hope of eventually organizing all Negro labor." The paper went on:

> Already the fruits of this work, in line with the dictum of President William Green of the American Federation of Labor for doubling the membership of the A.F. of L. in 1929, are shown in a score of Negro unions in flourishing condition. Among them are the plasterers, painters, janitors, meat cutters, and so on—all of them separate locals affiliated in the several district councils of their respective trades and in the Chicago Building Council.

Despite the advantages gained by organization and wider employment, the Negro in the latter twenties was still the hardest pressed economically of any major racial group. In 1927, 47 percent of Negro mothers were working for wages, as compared to 18 percent of mothers of white families. Moreover, the colored women were principally employed in arduous types of personal and domestic services: 31 of a total of 41 were engaged in day work or in laundries and restaurants. In 108 families, 175 employed children were contributing to the family income. Further indication of the need of supplementary income was the large proportion of roomers and boarders in the homes of Negro families.

Even before the depression following the stock market crash of 1929, the dark future facing Negro high school and college graduates was a constant subject of discussion, white firms operating in all-Negro neighborhoods aroused resentment by maintaining a staff of white employees. Rallying behind the slogan of a Chicago Negro newspaper—"Don't spend your money where you can't work"—colored leaders and civic, church, and social organizations put into effect a plan to boycott and picket business houses refusing to hire Negroes. Many white business men capitulated at once, employed Negro workers, and inserted advertisements in the Negro papers emphasizing their approval of the great job campaign. Others refused to accede and were subject to picketing. Considerable rioting and violence occurred during the picketing of chain stores, but diehards eventually were compelled to accept the new order and install Negro employees.

With the arrival of the C.I.O. in Illinois in 1935, both white and black organizers directed a special appeal to Negro workers. The majority of colored workers, being unskilled, came within the assumed jurisdiction of the industrial organizers, and were urged to join a union proscribing discrimination. The C.I.O. made considerable progress in organizing Negroes in the steel, packing, and other industries. The American Federation of Labor began to seek Negro members.

A notable contest was that over the Negro's affiliation at International Harvester in June 1941, when both union bodies bid for his vote in a National Labor Relations Board election. Each faction ran a full-page advertisement in the *Chicago Defender*. The A.F. of L. boasted of a membership in the plant of 4,768 and declared that "90% of the Negro workers in McCormick have signed up with the A.F. of L. and have pledged their vote to the A.F. of L. on June 18."

The C.I.O. countered:

> Every Negro, man, woman and child in America knows, or should know, the record of the A.F. of L. toward Negroes. It is a record shot through with JIM CROW. More than 20 A.F. of L. unions Jim Crow Negro workers. If the A.F. of L. wins at Harvester, it will be no different.

The C.I.O. won the election.

The year before the Illinois State Commission on the Condition of the Urban Population had been told at its hearing in East St. Louis that ". . . unions affiliated with the American Federation of Labor generally bar Negroes, but that unions affiliated with the Congress of Industrial Organizations admit Negroes."[1] Exclusion by the A.F. of L. was said to be particularly apparent in the building trades, with the exception of the hod carriers' union and the common laborers' union.

The commission's report called attention to even more serious discrimination:

> In most industries receiving national defense contracts Negroes are generally being denied work, in spite of the fact that the Federal Government has stated expressly that there shall be no discrimination in employment because of race, creed, or color.

The investigating body further declared:

> There are many fields of employment from which Negroes are completely barred and denied any opportunity to enter and compete with other workers. Department stores (except where Negroes serve as porters or menials), banks, brokerage houses, and most insurance companies are among the most flagrant. Yet, many Negroes are training for and are capable of filling many classes of positions in these fields.
>
> Public utilities in the State which employ over 75,000 workers refuse employment to Negroes. . . .
>
> Negroes have been increasingly employed in the public service, but still there are a few state departments and many local governmental bodies which do not give employment to colored citizens. There have been complaints without due results.
>
> There is available, as is evidenced by the registration figures of the Illinois State Em-

ployment Service, a wide and varied supply of positions, but, it appears, the agency is able to place Negroes, for the most part, only in domestic service and unskilled jobs.

Many trade unions in the state bar Negroes from membership by constitutional, ritual, or customary practice. These bars have practically eliminated Negroes from many fields of employment, and made it impossible for them to secure training and apprenticeship in these occupations. . . .

Most trade union officials in unions which bar Negroes are equivocal and evasive in presenting reasons for refusal to admit Negroes. Often they aver that Negroes and whites cannot work harmoniously together. . . .

Your commission is forced . . . to conclude that employers and union officials must bear the major responsibility for the discrimination against Negroes rather than the employees and union members themselves. The employers and union officials apparently have deep-seated prejudiced against Negroes, are indifferent to the employment of them, lack knowledge concerning their abilities, have false beliefs about the possibility of harmonious working relations between colored and white employees, are subject to unwarranted fears of economic loss, or lack the courage of their convictions.

Taking cognizance of numerous complaints, the President's Committee on Fair Employment Practices, headed by Mark Ethridge, conducted a hearing in Chicago early in 1942. Testimony tended to substantiate the allegations of the state commission, though not a few firms maintained that they practiced no discrimination and some progress was noted.

The Chicago Urban League, which since the Great Migration has taken an active role in industrial affairs as they relate to the Negro, gave a more optimistic report in 1942. The industrial department of the league had persuaded 76 firms to begin employing them in skilled and technical positions. Howard D. Gould, industrial secretary, stated that 222 of 332 firms visited had never employed Negroes in any capacity.

17. Professions

There is a nineteen-page version of this chapter in the IWP papers with Mathilde Bunton's name on it, but it is choppily written and has several errors. It includes a note in Arna Bontemps's handwriting, "Reduce to about 6 pages." A later four-page chapter draft was found in both the IWP papers and in Bontemps's papers, although it appears unfinished. The shorter draft by Bontemps is the one that appears here. Although originally called "47th Street" in the book outline, the two chapter drafts are titled "Professions." In the source material, there is a large amount of research compiled on saloons, policy kings, herb doctors, prostitution, and other illegitimate businesses—some of which was moved to other chapters, and some was not used.

I. C. Harris's *Colored Men's Professional and Business Directory of Chicago*, published in 1885, records the presence of one teacher, four physicians, and eight lawyers. One of the physicians was a woman. Apparently, no Negro dentists, librarians, or social service workers had yet appeared.

In 1886, Samuel T. Jacobs obtained a transfer for his daughter from the Keith School to the Raymond School upon complaining that a Negro teacher had been placed in Keith. The *Chicago Daily Inter Ocean* commented:

> It should not have been made a precedent. It stands a precedent. Denial to the next man who objects to having his ignorant white child taught by a competent colored teacher will savor of injustice, now that the prayer of the first man has been granted. The schools of Chicago are open to black and white, yellow and brown children. All races are eligible to the office of teacher. We regard the action of the Board of Education as ill-advised. There must be no color line in the schools.

The next year Mollie Hudson was appointed a cadet, or practice teacher, in the Jones School, from which she had graduated and where she won the approval of the principal. She served as a cadet in the same school until 1890, when she received her full certificate and replaced a teacher on leave. Appointment of Negro teachers became more general when the great migration brought a tremendous increase in the colored population. In 1920, several Negro teachers were teaching successfully in predominately white schools, but as the areas of Negro residence became more definitely established, most colored teachers were concentrated in those districts. In 1930, there were 531 white teachers in all all-Negro schools and 272 (or 33.9%) Negro teachers. Ten years later there were 350 Negro teachers.

When Wendell Phillips High School opened in 1904, all its fourteen teachers were white. A Negro teacher was added in 1920, and in 1930 twenty-three of fifty-seven teachers were Negroes. In 1940, however, Negroes numbered but twelve in a faculty of seventy-five. At the same time, Du Sable High School, with an all-Negro student body of 2,800 had 137 teachers with only thirty-seven regular and seven temporary colored teachers. In 1940, too, Maudelle Bousfield, after twelve years as principal of Keith Elementary School, was installed as principal of Wendell Phillips High School.

In 1942, librarians at Wendell Phillips, Du Sable, and Medill High Schools were colored, and several Negroes were attached to the staff of the Chicago Public Library. Vivian Harsh, librarian of the George Cleveland Hall branch, in 1931 was granted a fellowship by the Julius Rosenwald Fund enabling her to complete a study of libraries in eastern cities. Charlemae Rollins, stationed at Hall Branch, compiled a pamphlet, *We Live Together*, which has been used extensively as a bibliography of children's literature. Miss Rollins has achieved prominence as a story teller, touring the schools and hospitals.

Early workers in the field of social service include Dixie Brooks, Faith Jefferson Jones, and Bernice McIntosh. Zephyr Holman Stewart has served as a medical social worker at Provident Hospital, while Daisy Fauntleroy of the Court of Domestic Relations, Mildred Henson of the United Charities, and Lillian Summers of the Ida B. Wells housing unit have performed similar functions.

Dr. James Hall, who was an interne at Provident Hospital in 1897–98, has said that there were nine Negro physicians in the city then, and observed:

> The doctors in those early years ofttimes became discouraged because they feared that there were too many here for the small population. Of course, that period preceded the great migration.

In 1916, 200 Negro physicians formed the Cook County Physician's Society, and organization of the Lincoln Dental Society followed shortly afterward.

Dr. Ida Nelson Rollins of Chicago has maintained that she was the first woman dentist in the United States, having graduated from the dental school of the University of Michigan in 1890. One of Dr. Rollins's favorite stories is that concerning the very dark-skinned man who came to her office rejoicing that he could at last fulfill a life-long ambition to have a gold crown placed over one of his front teeth. The dentist advised porcelain, but the patient insisted upon gold. Ten years later, having been nicknamed "Goldie," the man returned and asked Dr. Rollins to remove the gold crown. "I've become educated," he explained.

In 1942, there were more Negro lawyers in Chicago than in any other city in the United States. Of the 150 registered, 100 or more belonged to the Cook County Bar Association, formed because of the refusal of white lawyers to admit Negroes to the Chicago Bar Association.

18. Health

There are two early drafts of this chapter in the IWP papers, the earlier of the two with Mathilde Bunton's name on it. The version used here is a third draft that was re-written by Arna Bontemps, copies of which are located at both Newberry Library and Syracuse University. Although this chapter includes a lengthy discussion of Provident Hospital, noticeably absent is any mention of its controversial relationship with the University of Chicago.

One bottle of Holland gin, eight pounds of prunes, one bucket of ice cream, four bars of laundry soap, one washboard, one clothes basket, two sponges, one rolling pin, eight pounds of feathers, one pair of crutches, and a steam atomizer were included among the donations to Chicago's first Negro hospital. In a public acknowledgement the hospital signified its need of rubber sheets, ice bags, syringes, shoes, stockings, brandy, plasters, and old linen.[1]

Dr. Daniel Williams, young Negro physician, had called a mass meeting the year before (in 1890) to consider the need of a hospital for "the sick poor among the colored people and all people regardless of race or creed . . . and also to furnish to colored young women an opportunity of becoming trained nurses."[2] Dr. Williams enlisted the support of a number of white philanthropists, including Herman H. Kohlsaat, George M. Pullman, Marshall Field, Arthur Meeker (vice president of Armour Company, who promised to send all colored accident cases from the company to the hospital), Cyrus McCormick, and Potter Palmer. In 1891, Provident Hospital opened with thirteen beds and the first training school for Negro nurses in the United States. During its first year of operation it cared for 189 patients, 154 of whom were Negroes.

On a July night in 1893, Provident received its most extraordinary case, and Dr. Williams performed what has been called the first successful operation on the human heart. George Cotton, a sailor, had been stabbed in a tavern brawl, the knife entering his heart. With "a score or more of surgeons . . . present in the interest of science," Dr. Williams sawed through two of the patient's ribs, removed them, and laid the heart bare. He closed the cut. Cotton recovered, and in 1942 was said to be pursuing his trade as an interior decorator in Pittsburgh, Pennsylvania.[3]

Dr. Austin M. Curtis, Provident's first interne, worked with Dr. Williams daily; after their medical labors the two scrubbed the floors and walls of the operating room. Dr. Curtis became the first colored man to serve on the medical board of the Cook County Hospital. Later, he succeeded Dr. Williams as Chief-of-Staff at Freedmen Hospital, Washington, D.C., Dr. George Cleveland Hall headed the Provident staff when Dr. Williams departed for his position in Washington.

During Dr. Hall's administration, the hospital was moved to its second home at 36th and Dearborn St. A new department, the Provident Clinic, was added, and in 1899 Nathan L. Freer erected the Esther Freer Home for Nurses as a memorial to his mother.

In 1929, the late Julius Rosenwald became interested in Provident and, together with Edwin R. Embree, Dr. Franklin C. McLean, Dr. George C. Hall, and Alfred K. Stern, sponsored a complete reorganization of the hospital. The financial goal was set at $3,000,000. The Rockefeller Foundation subscribed the income from a $1,000,000 fund for medical education of Negro physicians; $500,000 was subscribed by the Huber Fund of New York; $250,000 by the Julius Rosenwald Fund. The balance, $1,200,000, was to be raised by public subscription.

The subscription campaign was opened with a dinner at the Palmer House. Among those present were Hugh S. Cumming of the United States Public Health Service and Dr. Frank Billings, who officiated as host. At a later dinner given by Samuel B. Insull at the Blackstone Hotel, $414,500 was subscribed within twenty minutes. The Public Health Institute gave $100,000, while Richard T. Crane, Jr., and Max Epstein each donated $50,000.[4]

The major portion of the amount raised was spent to purchase equipment and to remodel the old lying-in hospital at 426 E. 51st Street so extensively that it became one of the outstanding Negro hospitals of the country. A smaller sum was used to provide a teaching-research fund at the University of Chicago.

In 1933, when the Provident Hospital and Training School moved into its third and present home, Julius Rosenwald described the institution as the greatest project for the American Negro since Lincoln's Emancipation Proclamation.

Its alliance with the University of Chicago established Provident as a recognized educational center, gaining the hospital standing as a teaching institution, the only one in America where Negroes may take accredited post-graduate training. In 1937, the American College of Surgeons, strictest rating body in the United States, gave Provident unqualified approval for graduate training in general surgery, the only Negro hospital anywhere so rated, thus placing the institution on a level in this respect with Billings, Passavant, and Northwestern University hospitals.

The Social Services Department of Provident is affiliated with the important social agencies of Chicago. In 1940, 94% of the 5,337 patients registering in the department were "co-operative" cases. Here patients are referred to the proper clinics and hospitals. For example, tuberculosis patients are sent to the Municipal Tuberculosis Dispensary, while relief clients are referred to the proper agencies.

Provident's Max Epstein Clinic is the third largest in the entire Chicago area and grants more emergency service than any other of the city's hospitals except Cook County Hospital, world's largest. The Cancer Clinic, established in 1938, was made possible by a substantial gift of money for the purchase of radium being used in conjunction with the deep ex-ray machine installed in 1935.

The Allergy Clinic, one of the few in Chicago, has special facilities for treating such ailments as hay fever and asthma. Another of the clinics is equipped with a flexible gastroscope, a recently developed instrument used to detect stomach and intestine disorders defying diagnosis by other methods. Dr. Leonidas Berry has used it extensively.

Provident has installed a special pneumonia service. Through the co-operation of Billings Hospital, the institution has been able to supply without charge the life-giving serum so necessary to successful treatment.

According to the hospital report,

> This was especially important on the South Side because the economic condition of many sufferers in the community prevented paying up to $200 for this serum, the proper administration of which often means the difference between life and death.

The children's wards are equipped with three pneumonia boxes, and two fully-equipped oxygen-attached incubators.

The American Medical Association has approved Provident for seven residents: one each in surgery; medicine; pediatrics; obstetrics; eye, ear, nose and throat; pathology; and radiology. Three residents have received certificates from the American Board of Ophthalmology, two in general surgery, and one from the American Board of Dermatology.

In 1933, Dr. Roscoe C. Giles, one of the two residents in general surgery, was the first Negro member of the American Board of Surgery. Since then his colleague at Provident, Dr. Carl Roberts, has been admitted.

Other outstanding members of Provident's staff are:

> Dr. Taft Raines, instructor at the Loyola University medical school.
> Dr. George Schrophear, known for outstanding work with the fluoroscope.
> Dr. Walter Grant, kidney specialist.
> Dr. Benjamin W. Anthony of the University of Chicago's division of roentgenology.
> Dr. Ulysses G. Dailey, heart specialist.
> Dr. Theodore K. Lawless, one of the country's foremost dermatologists.

According to the *Chicago Tribune*, Dr. Lawless

> . . . cured one boy in the East of leishmaniasis who had been mistakenly treated for tuberculosis of the skin for more than a year; and a South Side physician who had been treating a patient for syphilia was so surprised he fainted when Dr. Lawless informed him the patient had leprosy.

In 1942, there were less than a dozen hospitals in Chicago willing to admit Negroes, even to private rooms, while even fewer have ward facilities. Including the 165 beds in Provident Hospital, only one-fortieth of the 10,116 beds in voluntary hospitals could be occupied by Negroes, though they constituted one-seventh of the total population.

During 1939, there were 704 deaths due to tuberculosis among Chicago's estimated 250,000 Negro population, while there were 1,139 in a white population estimated at 3,300,000. Thus, the death rate per 100,000 stood at 281.7 for the Negroes and only 34 for the whites.

A pioneer worker and one of the organizers of a health program for Chicago Negroes is Dr. A. Wilberforce Williams, heart specialist, who served as an attending physician at the South Side Municipal Tuberculosis Dispensary, and in 1926 became a supervisor of the Chicago Municipal Tuberculosis Sanitarium Survey.

Believing that no home is safe until all homes are safe, the Chicago Tuberculosis Institute established in 1934 a department of Negro Health Education. Its program consists of lectures, films, health literature, exhibits and tuberculin testing of high school students. The 1939 report of the department showed that the following projects had been carried out.

Through community projects:

Conducting a campaign among underprivileged groups in the area from 30th to 40th Sts. and State St. to Wentworth Ave., and from 35th to 39th Sts. and South Parkway to Cottage Grove Ave. House to house visits by field workers were made, and speakers addressed various groups.

Through field house activities:

Classes in Madden Park, Union Park, and Washington Park were held for groups of all ages. Health talks were supplemented by motion pictures.

Through clinic service:

Physical examinations given by N.Y.A. and W.P.A. workers consisted of Wasserman tests, tuberculin tests, and general examination and x-ray of all positive tuberculin reaction. Reports with suggestions for treatment were made for private doctors and clinics.

Through club activities:

Health talks, moving pictures and literature to voluntary organizations.

Dr. James Lowell Hall, supervisor of clinics and chairman of the Department of Medicine of Provident, formed a special committee of Negro and white physicians and social workers to solve the problem of proper hospitalization of tuberculosis patients. Since its beginning Provident has been greatly concerned about tuberculosis, and though it has been the custom for the hospital to refer active cases to special clinics, it has found it necessary to provide care for many of them.

Dr. John B. West, who became Provident's medical director in 1941, had grappled with the tuberculosis question in New York. *Time* magazine has said of him:

Head of the bustling Central Harlem Health Center . . . is young Dr. John Baldwin West. Dr. West often marches into theaters, churches, basements, schools, apartment houses, exhorting Harlemites to visit the Health Center for x-rays, Wasserman tests, infant care. In the last three years, Dr. West and his staff of 200 have x-rayed 250,000 people, have lowered the infant mortality rate from 100 per 1,000 to 52, the maternal mortality rate from 18 to 5. Over 500 patients a day visit a venereal disease clinic in the Center.

Dr. West was the first of his race to occupy the position of assistant bureau chief for the Chicago Board of Health.

Much of the ill-health among Chicago Negroes has been attributed to their low economic status. Dr. Richard R. Wright has said:

Sickness is one of the very fruitful causes of poverty. But is also often a result as well as a cause of poverty.

19. Houses

There are three drafts of this chapter in the IWP papers, one thirty-two pages long, another forty-nine pages, and a twenty-page version that appears here. All drafts were written by Joseph Bougere, with significant comments by Arna Bontemps which included grammatical changes as well as suggestions for cutting sections.

When Chicago was incorporated in 1837, the entire population was housed in fewer than 400 dwellings, and most of them were mere shanties. Some Negro-owned property was included in this reckoning. The amount is uncertain, but ten years later there were at least ten Negroes with holdings in the city. Their property was located on Madison, Clark, Lake, and Harrison Streets, and on Fifth Avenue. When the Fugitive Slave Law was passed in 1850, some of these property owners fled to Canada, selling their holdings at less than actual value.

At the time this law was passed, Chicago's Negro community numbered 323 persons. Ten years later, just before the outbreak of the Civil War, the number was 958.[1] A small settlement had been established between Clark and State Streets near Harrison. This was not a colored neighborhood; Negroes lived side by side with whites in friendly association. Smaller groups were scattered throughout the city. Unhampered by restrictive covenants or threats of violence, they bought property as far south as Thirty-Third Street. The career of John Jones is an example of how an enterprising Negro might rise to the property-owning class at the time; he accumulated land and buildings to the estimated value of $150,000 in the early seventies.

In John Jones's heyday most of Chicago's colored citizens lived between Monroe and Sixteenth Streets, Lake Michigan and the Chicago River, already a shabby section. The total population of the city had increased from 109,000 in 1860 to 290,000 in 1870, and the black population increased to 3,696 persons. After the destructive fires of 1871 and 1874, the Negro community moved southward to Twenty-Second Street and westward across the Chicago River. Some scattered out into other parts of the city, one small group settling in the neighborhood of Fifty-first and Dearborn. There were 8,480 Negroes in Chicago in 1880, and by 1884 approximately one thousand more had migrated to the city. They represented 1 percent of the city's population in 1885, and their community continued to expand southward from the central business district.

By 1890, Chicago had become the second largest city in America, and its Negro population totaled 14,271. They were still scattered over the city, but the area in which they were most numerous extended from the edge of the "Loop" southward to Thirty-fifth Street. The western boundary was Wentworth Avenue and the eastern, State Street. This community was closest to the vice district, however, and when families became financially prosperous, they moved to the more desirable neighborhoods east of State Street and south of Thirty-Fifth.

In 1892 Congress authorized and financed a survey of slum areas in a number of large cities, including Chicago. The investigation, to determine occupations, incomes, and sanitary and other conditions, placed the slum population of Chicago at 1.30 percent, that for the Negro population of the city at 5.69 percent.

Yet there were several prominent Chicago colored men who owned fine property during the nineties. Edward Morris, the lawyer, owned a building at Twenty-Seventh and Dearborn Streets, a building which attracted much attention during the Columbian Exposition. Eli Bates mortgaged property across from the Polk Street depot and erected a building at Thirty-Seventh and State Streets. The Bates Building too, was considered a show place at the time of the fair. Obviously a few Chicago Negroes shared the gaiety of the "Gay Nineties."

Most of the families who came to Chicago between 1900 and 1910 were from the border states. They represented a cultured and industrious type of southern Negro, and they raised the percentage of home ownership of their race. A Chicago Negro went into the real estate business in 1908.

The fight to wipe out the vice district adjacent to the Negro community began in the nineties. It gained strength in the following decade. In 1909 the campaign reached full tilt. That was the year in which the great evangelist "Gypsy" Smith stormed the area. However, the crushing of the "Levee" did not completely rid the colored neighborhood of vice conditions.

By 1910 a small number of colored families had settled as far south as Sixty-Fourth Street, in Woodlawn, and a few Negroes were living as far east as Vincennes Avenue. No serious attempts had been previously made to restrict them to designated boundaries, but the Springfield riot of 1908 cast the shadow of coming events in the state. The squalor in which the colored citizens of the capital lived was later seen as a contributing factor leading to the trouble. Reports of widespread violation of the Tenement House Code were made public, whereupon the Chicago School of Civics and Philanthropy prepared a survey of ventilation, sleeping quarters, and sanitary conditions in two Negro neighborhoods of the city in 1911–1912.

The normal increase of the Negro population in Chicago was disrupted by the great migration. The trickle of Negroes from the South became a flood during the First World War. Most of the newcomers crowded into the congested district between Twenty-Second Street and Thirty-Ninth, between Wentworth on the west and Wabash Avenue on the east. Scattered groups got as far east as Cottage Grove Avenue, but the majority of the newcomers moved into the deteriorated section near the old vice district. Houses unfit for human habitation became their homes; the new arrivals had no other choice. A few migrants settled in "Little Italy," a poor Italian section on the near North Side. A somewhat larger number moved into dilapidated houses on the near West Side, formerly a Jewish neighborhood, and this became the second largest Negro district of pre-war days. Like the near North Side area, it had a low percentage of home ownership and a high percentage of delinquency.

When the pressure of the influx increased, a number of urbanized Negro families moved out to Woodlawn. A group of servants, employed by the professors of a theological seminary on the outskirts of the city, established the suburban community of Morgan Park. Some settled on the far southwest side in Englewood. Among these groups the percentage of property owners was high. Still other colored families settled in Ravenswood, South Chicago, Ogden Park, Burnside, Oakwood, and on Lake Park Avenue.

When the United States entered the war in 1917, building was halted. A housing shortage resulted. White communities began to complain of "encroachments"; white realtors, unable to supply demands of whites for homes, moved to curb the expansion of the Negro community. They argued that Negro occupancy depreciated property values. Arrangements were made to keep certain sections of the South Side "lily white." At the same time many realtors discovered a questionable means of making big profits by renting to Negroes at exorbitant rates. An earlier investigation by the University of Chicago had disclosed that Bohemians and Poles were paying $8.50 per week for certain apartments and Jews $10.50, while Negroes were charged $12 to $12.50 per week for similar quarters in dilapidated houses bordering the vice district. Rents to colored tenants were now increased from 5 to 30 percent. In some cases the newcomers paid $40 per unit for apartments that had been formerly rented to whites for $20.

The Negro migrants were not always received cordially. When two Negro families moved into a flat building previously occupied by whites, about one hundred school boys rained the structure with stones. This occurred in February of 1917. Other clashes took place as the Negroes continued to push southward. Bombings became frequent. Twenty-four occurred between July 1, 1917 and July 27, 1919. During the next two years there were fifty-eight. Two Negroes were killed, a number of persons injured. The damage to property was estimated at more than a million dollars.[2]

Violent resistance to colored expansion continued after the riots of 1919. In 1922 the *Chicago Defender* declared:

> North Shore residents are greatly stirred over the news that the immediate establishment of a colony of several hundred homes along the "Gold Coast" in the vicinity of Evanston is being contemplated for members of the race by the real estate firm of Rankin, Wilson and Pegues.

White arsonists, incensed over the purchase of a church by a colored congregation, in a former all-white neighborhood, set fire to the structure in 1924. The damage amounted to $250,000. In 1925 a bomb was thrown into a church purchased by Negroes at Fifty-Third Street and Michigan Avenue; the building had formerly housed a Jewish congregation. Attacks continued against Negro families moving southward to escape the congestion and squalor of the overcrowded northern section of the old colored district.

Meanwhile the Department of Public Welfare revealed in 1925 that native whites were paying $20 to $25 per month for unheated flats; foreign-born whites were paying $15 to $20, while Negroes were being charged $25 to $30. The median rental for heated apartments in white communities was from $55 to $60 per month; in Negro areas rentals ranged from $65 to $70. Moreover, many of the houses occupied by Negroes at these rates were greatly inferior to the lower rental houses in white neighborhoods.

Chicago as a whole suffered greatly during the depression which began in 1929, but the Unemployment Census of 1931 declared that "there were no areas in the city which were harder hit than the sections inhabited by colored people." Many Negroes who lived on the South Side moved over into the even more deteriorated neighborhoods of the West Side because of reduced incomes. Those already living on the West Side adjusted themselves to an even lower standard of living. Thus the depression, plus continued migrations from the South, tended to aggravate the already acute problem of housing for Negros in the city. The construction of the Michigan Boulevard Garden Apartments in 1929 was one remedial attempt, financed by Julius Rosenwald to test the practicability of private investment in housing for Negroes. The apartments accommodated 417 families; they were modern in construction and warmed by a central oil-heating system; but the rents were high and the enterprise did not benefit families in the lower income brackets.

The depression was graphically reflected in the Chicago housing situation. Finding rents hard to collect, many owners agreed to condemnation and demolition of rundown houses as the cheapest way out. The consequent loss of living units in the sections resulted in further doubling-up of dislodged families. Between August 11 and October 31, 1931, the Renter's Court in Chicago heard 2,185 eviction cases, 831 of them involving Negroes. The Welfare Committee found whole families leading a nomad existence, sleeping in city parks; small children were "tied-up like bundles of newspapers against the cold."

In 1930 militant Negroes joined neighborhood Unemployed Councils, said to have been led by Communists. Meetings were held in Washington Park on the South Side, meetings at which plans to "do something" were proposed. These groups resisted evictions by putting the furniture of the dispossessed back into their former homes as soon as the bailiffs had departed; in some cases officers were vigorously restrained from even beginning the job. A young Negro radical, active participant in these scrapes, reported on behalf of his organization:

> We put hundreds of families back into their homes. Sometimes we put them back before the law had taken all the furniture out. Occasionally bloody fights ensued. We used to have night and day meetings in Washington Park. The men who put the furniture back into homes were composed of whites and Negroes. We started out by putting Negroes back into their homes but the practice later spread to white neighborhoods. After relief was organized, the fight was carried to the relief stations.[3]

The climax of this resistance occurred August 3, 1931, when the police stopped a group of Negroes and one or two whites attempting to put the possessions of a 72-year-old colored woman back into her house. Three Negroes were killed, three more wounded. Several bystanders were also shot. The *Chicago Tribune* reported: "Reds Riot; Three Slain by Police—South Side Crowds Attack Squads in Eviction Row—City Acts to Avert New

Outbreaks." Mayor Anton J. Cermak, out of the city at the time, instructed the chief bailiff to halt all eviction orders. He promised that upon his return he would arrange to give aid to those evicted in the future.

The Councils of the Unemployed clamored for a moratorium on all evictions, and the colored ministers of the city launched a fight against "Communist propaganda." The following statement by members of the Negro clergy appeared in the *Tribune*:

> "The Communists are signing up our people by the thousands. They guarantee that, if any member of the party is evicted, the vigilance committee will replace his furniture in his home."
>
> "They call it a rent strike. . . . They charge a dollar dues and get members from among the unemployed. At the rate they are going, not a landlord in our district will be able to collect rents before long."
>
> ". . . when put out of one dwelling, [they] look around the block for the nearest vacant flat, break the locks and move in."
>
> "Although they are without lights, gas, or water, the squatters remain in their new quarters until evicted again."

The press aided in heightening the hysteria that had seized many South Siders. It was claimed that "the Reds who have been holding daily meetings in Washington Park . . . have been instructed by lenders in Moscow to resist efforts of their landlords to put them out for non-payment of rent." The mayor was reputed to have requested the governor to "send money or bullets."[4] Realtors and property owners in the Negro community were especially alarmed. Many of them refused to pay taxes to the city. As soon as the tenseness of the situation subsided, the bailiff's office resumed the practice of serving eviction writs, and the Unemployed Councils renewed their efforts to frustrate the evictions. As late as 1933 the League of Struggle for Negro Rights moved the furniture of an evicted colored family back into the home.

Rentals continued to be high in Negro communities. In 1932 a comprehensive survey of housing revealed that in the most deteriorated section of the South Side Negroes were paying from $20 to $32.50 per month for a flat.[5] Better places in the same area, east of State Street, rented for about $37.50 a month. Some flats over State Street stores were renting for $40 a month. Rentals in the one-time aristocratic northern section along Michigan Avenue ranged from $50 upwards. On South Parkway steam-heated apartments rented for $60 and better. Flats in the more exclusive southern end of the Negro area, not long vacated by whites, were rented for from $65 to $85 a month. "Buffet flats" in the district just east of South Parkway in the center of the Negro neighborhood rented for $75 and $80 a month. These, however, were not houses in good repair in all cases. Vice lords were merely being charged more because of their lucrative business.

In 1938 Robert C. Weaver, special assistant to the administrator of the United States Housing Authority, made an address at the convention of the Eastern Regional Conference of the National Negro Congress in which he said: "In Chicago, the average number of occupants for a Negro dwelling is twice as great as that for the general population." At that time more than 80 percent of Chicago's black population was clustered in an area seven and one-half miles long and from one-half mile to a mile and one-half wide. The northern part of this area, which housed most of the city's Negroes at the time of the great migration, was still noticeably dilapidated; it had continued to be the first stopping place for poor Negroes from the tenant farms of the South. The gaiety that once abounded in this community had faded. A survey worker in the area observed:

> The exterior appearance of this old graystone mansion is deceiving. Viewed from the street it appears to be in fair condition; but once inside the large, dirty hallway, one is confronted with the typical state of disrepair that characterizes most of the houses in this area.
>
> The rottening stairway that leads to the second floor is very unstable, and one not so strong of heart might be tempted to descend several times before completing the precarious ascent.
>
> The apartments are in an advanced stage of deterioration, and not one of the rooms is fit for human habitation. Plaster is falling off of the walls and ceiling in many places exposing the unsound wooden framework. The air blows through the defective windows with so much freedom that one has to look several times to be reassured that they are not open.

The worker found Hattie Hawkins, a middle-aged widow who was "on charity," living in a small cubicle (converted "kitchenette") with her two adolescent sons.

> . . . There is a single and double bed in the overcrowded room. Each has a very dirty, and much worn mattress and equally dirty cotton blankets. The floor is bare, and there are no curtains, shades, or draperies. The windows are dirty and greasy. In one corner is a little dirty oil stove which is "out of commission." In another corner, a little flat-top trunk in which beans, sugar, salt port and other staples are kept. A greasy kerosene lamp rests on a small, rickety table. Dirty clothing is in evidence everywhere on the backs of the unsteady chairs.

The mother explained in a tired, worn out voice:

> The baby boy and I sleep in the double bed and Willie, my oldest boy, sleeps by himself. I hates to live like this, but I can't do any better. . . .
>
> Willie doesn't go to school now nowhere. He wants to but the children laugh at the way he dresses because his clothes are patched. The other boys call him "rag bag." He is a good boy and doesn't run around. . . . He isn't so strong.
>
> I prays all the time, I don't know what I would do if I couldn't pray. I'm trying to hold on but I'm 'bout to give up.

A combination of circumstances were responsible for these conditions. There was very little building construction in Chicago following 1928, and less on the South Side than elsewhere. New business establishments further decreased the number of living units. Demolition, as noted, took its toll. Between 1934 and 1940 twenty-seven hundred dwellings were lost to the Negro community, thanks to the wreckers' bar and pick.

Meanwhile, families forced from their homes were required, because of restrictive covenants—written agreements between white property owners to refuse to sell or lease their buildings to Negroes—to seek new quarters only within the confines of the already crowded area. As Horace Cayton, director of Good Shepherd Community Center, has said: "The Negro's only mobility is within the boundaries of the area of 'concentration.'" In 1930 a member of the Chicago Housing Authority estimated that 80 percent of the city was covered by such covenants.

During the early years of the present century 20 percent of Chicago's Negro population lived in areas where whites constituted 95 percent of the total. The area of greatest concentration was one in which they comprised between 60 and 69 percent of the total. Thirty years later 90 percent of all the Negroes in the city lived in areas in which they constituted more than 50 percent of the total. Covenants have been far more effective than terrorism.

In order to pay exorbitant rentals and at the same time make ends meet, Chicago Negroes were often compelled to rent rooms. In some instances they rented all sleeping rooms and lived in the dining room or parlor. The Negro home without a "Room to Rent" sign was rare.

Such conditions also perpetuated the kitchenette evil. Large buildings and old mansions were divided into numerous one and two-room "apartments." A gas burner in the closet and a sink which doubled as a wash basin provided the "conveniences." Toilet and bath facilities were the poorest features; usually they were located in a hallway, equally accessible to strangers from off the streets. The Chicago Housing Authority, investigating 140 kitchenette buildings, reported that even 6-flat buildings had been cut up to make 161 small apartments. Other buildings had yielded a proportionate number of smaller units. The survey disclosed that the kitchenette was commonly infested with vice and crime, not to mention rats, mice, roaches, and vermin. Proprietors had often violated laws requiring fire escapes and other health and safety measures. There were blocks where 90 percent of the buildings had been converted into such kitchenette apartments. Yet a survey of 78 kitchenette families revealed that 44.9 percent were spending 31 to 50 percent of their income for rent. It further disclosed that these buildings wore out twice as fast as the conventional flat or apartment building.

The Chicago Negro community did not accept the exorbitant rentals without protest. Rent strikes have frequently been threatened. Special committees to hear rental charges have been appointed by the Illinois State Senate and the Chicago City Council. Frayser T. Lane of the Chicago Urban League, called to testify before a combined committee, warned: "It is entirely possible that the whole area will simply sit down," and added that it might be necessary to call out the state militia to cope with the situation. Groups have been organized to resist increased rentals. Foremost among such organizations were the South Side Tenant's League and the Consolidated Tenants' Association.

In 1937 Carl A. Hansberry and Harry H. Pace, Negroes, purchased houses in Washington Park Subdivision. They were instructed to move by court order. The State Supreme Court, to which they appealed, sustained the lower court. However, the United States Supreme Court reversed the state tribunal in 1941. A *Defender* headline joyfully proclaimed: "Hansberry Decision Opens 500 New Homes to Race." The majority of the houses were in excellent condition and rentals had ranged from $55 to $85, a few even higher. As soon as Negroes came in, rents were increased from 25 to 50 percent.

The Chicago housing situation has generally been representative of conditions throughout the state. Even greater prejudice exists in some cities downstate. Certain towns do not permit Negroes to settle. Herrin is one such town. Negroes who work within its limits must return to Colp at the end of the day. There many of them occupy houses built by the Madison Coal Company, for the first colored miners imported into the state by that concern. On that matter exclusion of Negroes as residents, the mayor of Herrin stated in 1941:

CHAPTER NINETEEN

When the city of Herrin was first settled it was built by a class of people that did not care to mix with Negroes. They wouldn't allow Negroes to live here. Of course there is no written law in this city demanding the Negroes to stay out of this territory. It is merely a custom settled upon this town by the first inhabitants. There could be no law made [under] the Constitution of the United States, proclaiming that the Negro has no right in this city.[6]

The Illinois State Commission on the Condition of the Urban Colored Population found housing conditions for Negroes in the state "shocking" in 1940. Homes in East St. Louis were described as "the worst of any which your Commission investigated." So great was the shortage of houses for colored families that many had built shacks of scrap wood and tin on the "wastelands" where they were forced to live. At Cairo and Mound City, Negroes were living in every section overcrowding, and squalid conditions were noted. An F.H.A. survey of Cairo revealed that four-fifths of the houses occupied by Negroes were substandard. Negroes in Champaign and Urbana lived in segregated districts.

In some instances, because of a shortage of homes and high rentals, Negroes have been forced out of their traditional areas by whites seeking cheaper quarters. In Peoria a number of colored people who owned homes adjacent to an exclusive white suburban community have been subjected to "pressure." In some cities and towns in the southern part of the state Negroes have settled in all-white neighborhoods despite vigorous opposition.

Yet the Negro housing picture in the state is not an entirely drab one. There are a few bright spots. Many Negroes with substantial incomes live in homes comparable to those of middle and upper class whites. A "suburban set" has emerged among the more prosperous Negroes.

Home ownership among Negroes in Chicago has been estimated at 7.4 percent, the percentage being very high in the neighborhoods at the southern extremity of the city. The contract system of buying homes has long been popular with Chicago Negroes. An initial payment of three or four hundred dollars is made, and the balance of the purchase price is paid in monthly installments. Many families buy houses of two flats, occupying one and renting the other. Some colored people have built homes through the assistance of home loan associations.

The Negro's desire for a good home and his willingness to keep it up were substantiated by the report of the Illinois State Commission on the Condition of the Urban Colored Population:

> It has been shown that the race of the occupants has nothing to do with the up-keep of property values. Negroes, as is evidenced by thousands of well-kept properties throughout the State, are as careful, as interested, and as anxious about the preservation of their homes and the neighborhoods in which they live as any other group when given an equal opportunity to develop a stable community life.

The Federal Housing Authority has answered some of the pleas of Negroes for adequate housing facilities. In 1933 the State Housing Act made provisions for the creation of the Illinois State Housing Board to consist of seven members appointed by the governor. This board eliminated many of the obstacles preventing local communities from participating in the program established by the United States Housing Act of 1937. In January 1938 the Chicago Housing Authority leased from the United States Housing Authority the Jane

Addams Houses, the Julia C. Lathrop Homes and the Trumbull Park Homes. All three of these low rent projects accepted some Negro tenants.

In 1941 the Ida B. Wells Homes, a project built expressly for the colored citizens of Chicago, were completed and tenanted. "Wellstown," the area occupied by the project, extends from Thirty-Seventh Street on the north to Thirty-Ninth Street on the south, and from South Parkway to Cottage Grove Avenue. These modern, fireproof, brick and steel structures comprise 1,662 units, 868 in apartment buildings and 794 in row houses and garden apartments. Units consisted from two to six rooms, all equipped with electric refrigerators, modern gas ranges, cupboards, two-party laundry sinks in the kitchen, and built-in bathtubs. There was a central heating plan for all the buildings.

Springfield, East St. Louis, and Peoria provided low rent projects for Negro families, while a project of fifty units in Jacksonville provided thirty apartments for whites and twenty for Negroes.

20. Social Life and Social Uplift

There exists one draft of this chapter, copies of which are held at both Newberry Library and Syracuse University. The copy at Newberry includes one small correction. Both copies have footnotes, but only the draft at Syracuse includes a final page with the list of references. The footnotes have been eliminated by the editor in what appears below. The chapter was written by Arna Bontemps.

In the early days, the swank of the social life in Negro communities was as colorful and as interesting as the era in which it occurred. Various social clubs entertained lavishly and often; individuals gained reputations as entertainers on a grand scale. Receptions, cake-walks, dinner parties and barbeques were common events on the social calendar of the women's clubs, social clubs, lodges and other fraternal organizations.

The appearance in 1879 of the wife of the United States Senator from Mississippi at a reception in Chicago was a social high point of the era. Because of her conspicuous position as bride of the only Negro Senator, there was naturally some speculation as to how she would receive and be received. However, the *Inter Ocean* reported that:

> . . . she made an exceedingly favorable impression upon her callers, and nowhere were people more gracefully or handsomely received. She wore a black velvet robe of Worth and handsome diamonds. Mrs. Bruce has unusual personal beauty. . . . A stranger would suppose she was of Spanish blood.

Apparently, the early social life of Negroes was highly organized and controlled, for in 1892, Mrs. J. Shaw presented her young daughter to Chicago society at Oakland Music Hall, and C. R. Johnson played host to a banquet at which the famous theatrical team of Williams and Walker were the guest of honor in 1896.

This early Chicago was able to afford an exclusive Sionilli (Illinois in reverse) Adelphi Social Club, composed of children from the homes of the elite. W. H. Talley was unofficial host to visitors of note and provided them with lavish entertainment. Because he owned four spirited horses and a fine carriage he was nicknamed "Four Horse Talley."

Sheridan Brusseaux, well-known private detective, often gave expensive dinner parties where the guests received valuable presents such as gold watches, twin blankets, glassware and travelling bags. The Grand Pacific Club, composed of waiters in downtown hotels, were sponsors of outstanding dress balls.

Contemporary with these exclusive affairs of very polite society were the old-fashioned barbeques enjoyed by the "down home" folks.

> An old-time barbecue, such as used to form a merry festival in the South in antebellum days, was advertised to be held in Auburn Park yesterday, between the hours of 11 a.m. and 12 p.m. The object of the old-fashioned feast was to boom the joint interests of Messrs. Cook & Peterson, proprietors of the Auburn House, a World's Fair hotel for colored people, at No. 8045 Winter Street, and the Messrs. Still and Roberts, real estate and renting agents, with an office at No. 3023 Armour Avenue.
>
> . . . Besides the boiled meats (the carcasses of an ox, a sheep and a pig) the bill of fare consisted of hash, corn, Irish and sweet potatoes, pickles, pie, ice cream and cake, bread and butter, tea and coffee. During the afternoon and evening many came to enjoy the feast, and there was dancing in one of the larger rooms of the hotel.

Sometimes the frolicking of gay funsters got them into difficulties as was the case when the *Chicago Inter Ocean* reported:

> While a "cake walk" was in progress at the Swelldom Social Club at No. 1508 Wabash Avenue last night the place was raided by the police. Eighteen women and twenty-five men, all belonging to the best colored society in that part of the town, were presented. Complaint of the cake walk was made by neighbors, and arrival of the officers caused great excitement.

At other times a humorous note was added to the evening's entertainment. On one notable occasion the *Cairo Bulletin* carried this item about a social affair:

> The colored brothers and daughters indulged in a Leap Year party on Thursday night, in a hall on Commercial Avenue, between Seventeenth and Eighteenth Street, took pepper in their'n. The way of it was this. The daughters and brothers were dancing with a hearty good will—right and left, cross over, ladies chain, seeing on the corners and all that, also when the sensitive nose of a "fair black belle," the special favorite of a colored hotel keeper "downtown" spoke sneeze to his nose which sneezed again, then all went on sneezy as a snuff factory. Every last daughter and brother was compelled to sneeze loud and long. The musicians ceased their dulcet strains and sneezed, and every dancer quieted their toes and stayed their heels and—sneezed. The dance sneezed to a close, and the indignant dancers made search for the cause, determined to close its eyes if it walked on two legs. And it did. A man had taken a position in the room above and slyly dusted pepper down upon the heads of the dancers through the store pipe hole, and, of course, they sneezed.

Other social clubs in Chicago were the Danabegy Club, a group of young musicians who gave monthly recitals in Central Music Hall, and the Hannibal Guards, a club of North Side men who staged lavish semi-military parades. Mother Seames formed a Table Tennis Club, and a group of inter-married whites and blacks, who felt they had special problems of their own, organized the Manassa Club. Most of the members of this club lived in the mixed Englewood district of the South Side. They were often criticized as low-brows, by conviction that this was unfair judgment is strengthened by the knowledge that Mr. &

Mrs. Ingley, parents of Harry Anderson, former principal of the Jones School, and Mr. & Mrs. C. Thomas (Thomas was a prominent lawyer) held memberships.

Downstate, East St. Louis had its popular Maceo Club which held most of its meetings and functions in the fashionable Hotel Scot. The *East St. Louis Gazette*, July 29, 1871, announced a "big basket picnic" in the northern part of the Third Ward given by the Negroes of East St. Louis and suburbs "for the benefit of old 'Uncle' Hardy Roberts." Two years earlier the same newspaper had observed:

The colored folks from the other side of the river must have a hankering after the flesh-pots of Egypt at least they have had festivals of different kinds here every week for some time past. Yesterday a number of them marched from the Levee to the East St. Louis park, preceded by a fife and drum. They there enjoyed themselves in different ways until a late hour.

Charity balls were always popular occasions in the Negro community, and benefits were sponsored in behalf of hospitals, old folk and children's homes, scholarship funds and similar worthy causes. The *Inter Ocean* furnished favorable publicity for these affairs:

Colored society is expected to muster in full force at the charity ball to be given Wednesday evening under the direction of Mr. and Mrs. C. H. Smiley at their parlor No. 76 Twenty-Second Street. The event of itself, so complete and elaborate are the arrangements, should secure a large attendance, but the object for which it is give, to aid the funds of the Provident Hospital, is certain to make its patronage the most generous affair yet given by the colored residents.

According to the same newspaper the first annual charity ball held in the auditorium in the downtown area was a gala event:

About 150 couples took part in the grand march, which was led by Major John C. Buckner and Mrs. Irene Lewis, Morris Lewis and Mrs. Fanny Hall Clinton. Colored people from all sides of city, prominent in business and social life, were there, and contributed toward the object for which the ball was given. The dancing programme and the floor were in charge of Chairman N. D. Thompson who had sixteen assistants. It was said $4,000 was raised.

In 1904 a grand Bal Poudre, held in the Coliseum, was reported:

With the orchestra rendering ragtime music and with the calcium light throwing its most powerful beam, Chicago's colored society patrons will tread through the measures of the court quadrible at a bal poudre to be given at the Coliseum on the evening of February 12. . . . The Auditorium minuet will be completely out-classed by its colored supplement when some of the fanciest steps known to the vaudeville stage will be introduced by the natural born dancers.

This was colored aristocracy in its heyday. For a woman to really "belong" she had to hold a membership in the exclusive Tuesday Two Club. This organization was composed of the wives of men who had achieved in business, the professions, or other accepted pursuits. Memberships were by unanimous vote only. Activities of the club were little known to the outsider since no publicity was released. The function of the club was purely social with the emphasis on bridge playing. Members entertained in their homes and no affairs were given to which outsiders were invited. Among the members of the club were: Mrs. Robert. S. Abbott, Mrs. Reginald H. Smith, Mrs. James Allison, Mrs. S. A. T. Watkins, Mrs. Leroy T. Johnson, and Mrs. Theodore Jones.

For the men there remained the Masons and the John Brown Post of the Grand Army of the Republic which scored heavily with Negro society.

The Emancipation Day celebrations began at the time of the announcement of the Proclamation and continued until the turn above. They combined gay festivities with serious speech making. The *Cairo Bulletin* of April 12, 1870, reported a typical Emancipation celebration in all its color and ceremony:

> The city will long live in the memory of the Cairo colored people. Scores of years hence, colored grandfathers will detail to their descendants how the streets of Cairo with a long line of men with badge, regalia, flags and banners and how the city opened with the sound of cannon and closed with music, revelry and mirth. They will tell how thirty-six little colored girls, clothes in white, and wearing wreaths, and red and blue sashes, sat in a highly ornate car, as representatives of the different States, and how in their midst, a handsome colored girl, personating the goddess of Liberty, supported the colors of the country—the whole forming an object that was gazed upon with pride and exultation. They will tell, too, how well dressed, well behaved colored men, numbering nearly a thousand, formed a column in the rear, bearing aloft banners proclaiming the orders to which they belonged; that "Republican Principles" (not the party) shall never live; that "United We Stand, Divided We Fall"; that "All Men Are Created Equal"; and other mottoes suggested by the times and sentiments of the people. All this they will tell and more, but having a word to say ourselves, we will beg "grandfather's" pardon and proceed to say it.
>
> The column, more than half mile in length, moved through the principle streets of the city, drawing crowds to the side walk along the entire line of the march, until, about 3 o'clock P.M., when the vast throng assembled at Washington Hall, and listened to enthusiastic addresses from Messrs. Munn, Bird, and Linegar.

In Chicago, preparations for gigantic celebrations were begun even before the passage of the law. Very often these celebrations were in honor of the emancipation of slaves in the West Indies as well as in the country.

> The coming anniversary of the emancipation of slaves in the West Indies, August 1st, the colored citizens of Cairo will celebrate in an appropriate manner. A grand Barbecue Dinner will be served in Shell's garden, and speeches by well-known orators will be made in the forenoon and afternoon, and a cordial invitation has been extended to the surrounding country.
>
> The best brass band in Southern Illinois has been procured for the occasion.
>
> Invitations have been extended to some of the most talented speakers in the land and favorable answers have been received from most of them. Among the speakers solicited to speak on the occasion are: Hon. Fred Douglass, of Washington; Gov. Pinchback, of Louisiana; Hon. J. H. Obleey; Hon. D. J. Linegar; and J. J. Bird, Esq. of Cairo.[1]

The following year in Chicago, the *Inter Ocean* paid a pleasing compliment to the Negro population:

> The colored people of the city went out yesterday to Bremer's Grove, to celebrate the first of August, which is their Fourth of July, being the anniversary of the abolition of slavery

in the West Indian Islands. There was a large assemblage; and there was a remarkable peaceful, as well as pleasant, day spent in the beautiful grove. The colored people have a habit in spending their holidays in agreeable way. They have in fact a habit of doing a good many things (this among them) that might be a moral lesson to some nationalities that take a particular pride in being national. For one thing, they can gather an immense crowd, go out in to the country, and enjoy themselves without having a fight. Another thing, they can come in from a picnic without getting drunk. Once more, they can assemble in a hall after the thrilling experience of the day, and the enthusiasm of a national celebration and join in a dance without getting turbulent. [2]

The next year another joyous anniversary was celebrated:

Emancipation Day was celebrated yesterday, by as it would seem, the whole population of the city in a grand picnic excursion over the Lake Shore Road to Colehour, Michigan. A train of seventeen closely packed cars went out at 11 o'clock, and the regular later trains took large numbers more. Indeed, all day long the Grand Union Depot at the head of La Salle Street was a gay scene. Dianah's yellow sash and Sambo's lavender cravat fluttered in every corridor, and the old Aunties and their happy looking escorts by no means yielded to the younger ones in bright picturesque dress. Unmistakably all were having a splendid time yesterday, as well as those who took in the picnic and the east shore.[3]

Even inclement weather could not dampen the spirits of the Emancipation Day celebration at Harrisburg 1883.

The colored people had a rather gloomy Wednesday for their celebration. There was but little rain, yet it looked like rain throughout the day. There were quite a number of colored people in town and at the fair grounds, most of whom were residents of our county. There was some disappointment on account of not getting excursion trains to run from Cairo and Carmi, where a large number of colored folks were expected from. A large sprinkling of pale faces were on the grounds and patronized the tables freely. The barbecued meat was well cooked, and plenty of pig mutton was dished out from noon till night to those who were hungry. There were no disturbances of any kind and all seemed to enjoy the feast. There were no public exercises celebrating the day of freedom outside of the street procession, which was headed by a large four horse wagon decorated with the national colors and loaded with gaily dressed ladies and children.

At Clinton, Illinois, in 1881 the Negroes of that city celebrated the emancipation of the slaves of the United States and the West Indies with a "grand celebration and barbecue." The Hon. W. F. Calhoun, member of the Republican State Central Committee, was the principal speaker. On the same day a similar festival was going on in Central Park in Peoria, Illinois. Meanwhile, Springfield was the scene of a large gathering in 1881 when Negroes from Cincinnati, Louisville, Indianapolis, St. Louis and other cities participated in a parade and a barbecue in one of the parks there. An *Inter Ocean* reporter was among the interested spectators.

A halt was made in front of the old residence of Lincoln, where the band played a dirge and appropriate remarks were made by Dr. Wendeland who resides in the house. In respect to the dead President (Garfield), the flags and vehicles were draped in mourning, and other respectful evidences of grief manifested the feeling among the celebrators. The tomb of Lincoln was visited, and memorial services were held there.[4]

Still another large celebration in Springfield was worthy of public comment:

The thirty-fourth anniversary of the emancipation of southern slaves was appropriately observed here today, at the former home of Abraham Lincoln. Trains from every direction brought colored people.

The largest excursion being 3,000 from St. Louis. A handsome procession was formed and the people went to Washington Park, where addresses were delivered by the Reverend A. H. Roberts of Chicago, the Reverend R. F. Hurley of Springfield, the Reverend P. C. Cooper of Decatur, the Reverend William Burnett and Judge J. J. Bird of Springfield. The crowd then adjourned to Lincoln Memorial Monument at Oak Ridge Cemetery where appropriate services were held.

The day closed with an entertainment tonight at Carpenter's Hall.

In time, the Emancipation Day celebration began to devote more and more attention and energy to the portion of the program following the festivities. Social welfare and social uplift were encouraged. As early as 1887 at Cairo, the celebration included a "dinner and fair," the proceeds which were to be "applied to the support of a free school for the colored children."[5]

The two phases of these early affairs, entertainment and social uplift, were taken over by separate organizations as the anniversary celebrations became a thing of the past. At East St. Louis in 1901 the Maceo Club was formed to participate in local political campaigns to insure a hearing of the Negroes' expectations from the candidate for office. By 1915, the Negro community had become so articulate in their demands that the populace was ready to accept the advent of the National Association for the Advancement of Colored People in its midst as official spokesman. Negroes of East St. Louis found ready white friends, members of the Rotary Club, and began formation of a local branch of the National Urban League also. The League's purpose as stated was to improve industrial and social conditions of the Negro citizen. A specific list of these improvements were issued through the pages of the *East St. Louis Daily Journal*, August 17, 1917, as follows:

1. To emphasize co-operation of agencies doing social work among Negroes.
2. To encourage the training of colored social workers.
3. To help with probation oversight amusement.
4. To organize boys' and girls' club and neighborhood welfare movements.
5. To help with probation oversight delinquents.
6. To investigate and better conditions affecting health, education, housing, employment, and to stabilize and increase the efficiency of Negro labor.

At the close of its first year's work, the League reported many accomplishments. It had sponsored four public celebrations, filled over 300 questionnaires, distributed 49 Christmas baskets to the needy, conducted an evening school for adults, and urged community members to work for their own improvement. Commenting on these accomplishments, the *Journal* stated:

The League has filled an indispensable place in this city through the message of hope it has carried to the masses in their church services and their homes heretofore untouched. . . . In the industrial department service has been rendered to the government in recruiting unskilled labor for cantonments at the close of the War, and in securing better working conditions in the plants.

Among co-operating agencies in the Urban League program were the various churches, social clubs and civic organizations.

Many of the new problems created by the migration were met by agencies specifically organized for that purpose. One such group was the Phyllis Wheatley Woman's Club, which later was to operate the Phyllis Wheatley Home for Working Girls. In 1906, Chicago civic women leaders were shocked into a realization that newly arrived and unattached young girls were faced with serious problems of adjustment. These women purchased a home and surrounded it with a wholesome atmosphere where the girls might live in a healthful and economic way. The Phyllis Wheatley Home was first located at 3530 Forrestville (now Giles) Avenue. Later it moved to 5128 S. Michigan Avenue. The Home offered besides residence quarters and Christian protection, classes in knitting, handicraft, dressmaking, science, dramatics and music, with the view of preparing young girls for advanced positions.[6]

One of the most powerful and influential groups in the state was the Federation of Colored Women's Clubs, which was organized at Boston in 1895 by Mrs. Josephine St. Pierre Ruffin.[7] Mrs. Booker T. Washington served as first president of the national association. The Illinois organization attempted to reach almost every woman in the state. Each one of the affiliated clubs pledged support to some worthy young woman, established kindergartens for children of working mothers, cared for delinquents and dependent youngsters, and invested funds that had been raised to establish a scholarship fund for deserving girl students. Among the institutions receiving aid from the Federation of Colored Women's Clubs are the YMCA; YWCA; Old Folk's Home; Provident Hospital; several day nurseries, all in Chicago; the Lincoln Home in Springfield; Yates Memorial Hospital at Cairo; the Lillian Jamieson Home in Decatur; the Home for Dependent Children at Bloomington; the Woman's Aid Community House at Peoria; and the Iroquois Home for Girls at Evanston.

The Domestic Art Club at Bloomington is another of the Negro woman's civic groups in the state. It was organized in 1915 and has become a potent factor in civic affairs. Often club heads are consulted by city officials on matters of relief and uplift efforts among the Negroes of the town.

The Ida B. Wells Club of Chicago was formed at the close of the World's Fair of 1893. The club advocated real Americanism and fought against discrimination and segregation in any and all forms. The president, Mr. Ida B. Wells-Barnett, was known throughout the land as an enemy and a relentless fighter against the barbarism of lynch law.

The Elizabeth Lindsey Charity Club of Chicago was organized in 1918 principally to welcome strangers to the city and help them to adjust themselves to the new environment. Very often new arrivals were poverty-stricken, and the club provided hospitalization fees, sick relief, and grocery showers; each year it sent out well-stocked Christmas baskets.

So well organized and co-ordinated were the women's clubs that when World War I struck the country they were prepared to integrate into the program of the Red Cross. They knitted, sent boxes of food to entrenched soldiers, and engaged in child welfare work and food conservation activities.

The YWCA was organized in 1914 at the Douglass Center, 3032 Wabash Avenue, where the Chicago Urban League now has headquarters, by a committee of women headed by Mrs. Eva Jennifer. They first located the YWCA building at 3432 Rhodes Avenue and remained there until 1919 when an increased population demanded larger quarters. Then they removed to 3541 Indiana Avenue. Victor Lawson, philanthropist and editor of the *Chicago Daily News*, left a legacy for the South Side association. With this money, in addition to other donations, the present site of the association at 4559 South Parkway was purchased in 1927.[8]

The YWCA has a well-trained staff, utilizing some National Youth Administration and Works Projects Administration employees to aid in carrying out the program. South Parkway Branch is regarded as a model branch and has for a long time been used by local universities as a center for field work.

Activities at the "Y" are arranged to suit the interests of those it accommodates. There is a business girls' club, as well as a club of industrial workers, which have programs of activities including parties, discussions, classes in modern dancing, bridge, and speech. There are interest groups in handicraft, music, dramatics, "stay slim gym," talks on beauty, and travel lectures. They enjoy weekend outings at YWCA Forest Preserves near Glenview, Illinois, and summer vacations at Forest Beach on Lake Michigan. There are nine girl Reserve Clubs associated with the center. The South Parkway Branch also has dormitory rooms for girls and a new feature called the Nook. It is composed of a kitchen, pantry, and social room, where the young ladies can cook a meal for themselves and entertain their friends at lunch or dinner.

Among the prominent women connected with the branch have been Mrs. Bertha Cook, wife of the pastor of Metropolitan Community Church; Mrs. John W. Robinson, wife of the pastor of St. Marks' Methodist Episcopal Church; Mrs. Julia Lawson, Mrs. M. V. B. Mason and Mrs. Ruth Moore.

To meet the problem of the young Negro man, efforts were begun in 1911 to provide a YWCA in the Negro community. A group of interested people held a meeting in Odd Fellows Hall in January of 1911 at 3335 S. State Street, and were able to around enough enthusiasm for the project to interest Wilbur Messer, general secretary and William J. Parker, business manager of the YWCA. Later Julius Rosenwald, philanthropist, offered to donate $25,000 for a building providing an additional $75,000 would be raised.[9] The daily newspaper that often championed the cause of the Negro, the *Inter Ocean*, was generous in granting space for publicity to the campaign. Excerpts from typical releases follow:

Mr. Rosenwald's announcement was received by the cheer of over 1,000 members who attended the dinner, at which Booker T. Washington, president of Tuskeegee University, was the principal speaker and guest of honor. This dinner was given at the auditorium hotel.

Booker T. Washington said in part:

. . . Chicago must face the fact that it has a large and increasing colored population, coming largely from the South which is unused for the most part to life in a large city. When the colored man comes from the South he finds he is face to face with new conditions, as to climate and as to methods of labor. He also finds he is surrounded by increasing temptations. No race under such circumstances, without help and guidance can adjust itself to those new conditions. . . .

Sometimes the question is raised as to why it is necessary in a city like this for the white people to come to the aid of the colored people in so many philanthropic directions. The colored people, since they were freed, unlike many newly freed races have clothed themselves, sheltered themselves, fed themselves without asking aid from the national government. . . .

More in the future than in the past, a city like Chicago, the best element of the two races should come together for consultation, for exchange of thoughts and for mutual effort in upbuilding the community. The worst elements in both races usually get together, and the time has come when the best elements of the two races should learn to work together and know each other.

This movement in Chicago has emphasized the fact that the Negro has consciousness, that he has civic pride and that he will work as enthusiastically as the white man at tasks that assume his citizenship and manhood.[10]

When Booker T. Washington had concluded, Mr. Rosenwald stated his attitude on the race question:

It is the greatest problem we of today must face. The Negro is a part of our commercial, national and social institutions and it is our duty to aid him in his struggle for better things. I believe the movement started by the YMCA is the logical method of doing this.

The Wabash Avenue Department of the YMCA is located in a neighborhood that is changing from a residential to a commercial district, as a result of the expansion of the Negro community. The area is largely deserted and even members are not inclined to return to the premises for recreational purposes. Wabash Branch has had for an operating budget as much as $128,000, but in 1941 the budget was only $85,000. These funds provide organized play and recreation for some 5,000 boys and girls. The "Y" reaches into homes, schools, and churches, giving assistance and helping to make the community a better place in which to live.

Chicago's South Side Negro section suffers from the half-way school system which means that many children are left to roam the streets, or otherwise remain idle and unsupervised in their activities. The YMCA makes a special effort to meet this need by conducting character-building activities and making their program attractive to these youth. Since the organization of this fine YMCA there has come another. It is the Maxwell Street YMCA, located on the West Side of the city. It provides an outlet for the energies of alert youngsters in one of the poorest sections of the city. The Maxwell Street "Y" has been in existence only since 1931, but it is generally agreed that it has done a good piece of work in the community. The fashionable suburb of Evanston also has a Negro YMCA. This Emerson Street Branch serves the small community on the North Shore through the aid of the Federal, State and County relief agencies. Northwestern University cooperates with "Y" officials by providing seven students to assist in the program. These students are paid out of NYA funds.

In 1916, the Chicago Urban League on the Urban Condition of Negroes was formed at Wabash YMCA. Listed as among those present at this important meeting were Mrs. Elizabeth Lindsay Davis, Mrs. Joanna Snowden Porter, A. L. Jackson, Dr. George Cleveland Hall, Miss Edith Abbott, and Miss S. P. Breckenridge. Approval from all sides greeted the advent of the Urban League into community life. Dr. Graham Taylor writing in the *Chicago Daily News* said:

> Not only for the benefit of the Negro population but for the safety and progress of the city as a whole, this League should rally to its equipment and direction, its growth and efficiency, both personal and financial resources adequate to his end. . . .

The League launched into a good-will, educational program which has resulted in many firms employing Negroes. For instance, in 1919–20 the League placed 1,200 colored girls with Sears, Roebuck and Company as stenographers, billers, fillers, typists, and calculating machine operators. It also induced Montgomery Ward and Company to utilize Negro girls in like capacities. This innovation was frankly an experiment, but a highly successful one and shortly afterward, Rand McNally employed 100 girls, Gage Hat Works followed through with jobs for 75, and the Chicago Lamp Company used 250. Chicago's Negro community was hit hard by the depression of 1929. Thousands of men and women, unemployed, hungry, looked to the Urban League for aid. The organization provided shelter for some 200, maintained a feeding station where 1,800 men were given free meals each day, and set up a kitchen for women. The headquarters of this social welfare agency was also used as a clothing distribution center.

The league maintains a department for civic betterment, and for the past twenty years has fought for improved housing conditions, cleaner streets and alleys, for more health centers and recreational facilities. In making a survey of the situation, A. L. Foster says:

> At the present time, Negroes are employed in United Charities, including a district superintendent, two assistant district superintendents, social case workers, stenographer-dictaphone operators and switchboard clerks. A Negro is assistant to the Assistant General Superintendent, and a stenographer is employed in the Inter-City Department. Another organization which early began the use of Negro workers is the Illinois Children's Home and Aid Society. . . . The American Red Cross, the Visiting Nurses Association, the Committee of Fifteen, Juvenile Protective Association—all of these agencies have employed Negroes on their staffs. There are Negro residents in the Abraham Lincoln Center who help to conduct the interracial activities there, and a colored man has for years conducted classes for boys and Northwestern University Settlement, although it is located in the community where no Negroes live. Hull House, University of Chicago Settlement, Eli Bates, Henry Booth House, Association House, and other settlements include Negroes in their programs. Representatives of the Urban League served on the committee which organized the Child Placing Division of the Joint Service Bureau which at present has a Negro supervisor. At present all of the public welfare agencies employ Negroes in various capacities. The Social Service Department of the Cook County Hospital, Municipal Tuberculosis and Infant Welfare stations of the Board of Health, the Juvenile Court, the three specialized municipal courts, namely the Women's Court, the Boy's Court, and the Court of Domestic Relations, and the Cook County Bureau of Public Welfares. . . . Cook County Bureau employs as supervisor of the Blind Pension Department, a Negro and also as supervisors of two of its field offices. The largest number of Negro workers are employed by the Illinois Emergency Relief Commission through its many branches. At one time, the Unemployment Relief Service employed 129 Negro workers, and the Field Service of Cook County Bureau of Public Welfare 179.

These gains made by Negroes are not due to efforts by the league exclusively, but the league has certainly influenced those gains.

The National Association for the Advancement of Colored People grew out of the Niagara Movement initiated by Dr. W. E. B. Du Bois in 1906.[11] It adopted all of the principles of its forerunner and added others of its own:

1. To educate America to accord full rights and privileges to Negroes.
2. To fight injustice in courts when based on race prejudice.
3. To pass protective legislation in State and Nation and defeat discriminatory bills.
4. To secure the vote for Negroes and teach its proper use.
5. To stimulate the cultural life of Negroes.
6. To stop lynching.

Beginning with the Springfield riots in 1908, the NAACP has played, in the opinion of many, the leading role in the fight for equality under the law for Negroes and much more: complete integration into the life and culture of America. After the historic report made on the inhuman nightmare at Springfield by Willoughby Walling, a writer for the contemporary magazine *The Independent*, a committee was immediately formed which operated principally in Chicago. A few years later in 1913, a formal charter was applied for and granted. Since that time a local office of the Association has been maintained intermittently in Chicago until within the last seven or eight years a plan was devised to continue without interruption permanent headquarters in that city.

The all-important and basic law upon which the branch depends for legal support is the Illinois Civil Rights Law passed by the state legislature in 1885. Since the time of its passage the original bill has been extended and strengthened by amendments adopted in 1935 and 1937. According to this law, an establishment of public accommodation guilty of violation of the law shall be declared a public nuisance and subject to abatement. Another law precious to the workers in the NAACP is the act approved by the legislature on June 28, 1919, making it unlawful for operators of public places to publish discriminatory matter against any religious sect, creed, class domination, or nationality. The purpose of the law as it concerns the Negro is to prevent proprietors of restaurants, hotels, resorts, etc. from posting signs such as, "We Do Not Cater to Colored Trade," and "White Persons Only." Signs such as these are, nevertheless, not uncommon in bus stations, restaurants and other public places in southern Illinois.

During the Chicago race riots in 1919–1920, the local NAACP branch conducted independent investigation and furnished information for the grand jury investigating the violence which had occurred. The organization has also conducted a fight against restrictive covenants, which bar Negroes from living in districts bordering the Negro community; it has successfully fought against the extradition of Negroes who would have met certain death had they been returned to the South to indifferent and biased authorities; it has a high percentage of victories in cases involving discriminatory practices in theaters, restaurants and hotels.

As long as there are civil rights problems to be met and solved by Negroes, organizations such as the National Association for the Advancement of Colored People will continue to assume an important role in Negro community life.

In the midst of an economic depression and business recession, Negroes had their heads held high, hope in their hearts, and an optimistic view of the future. They displayed this attitude in the exhibits presented at the National Negro Exposition held in Chicago at the Coliseum during the summer months of 1940. An advertizing circular announcing the opening of the Exposition read in part:

> The American Negro's history since emancipation 75 years ago reads like fiction. Until 1865 held in bondage; men, women and children sold and traded like domestic animals, these people have since then become a vital factor in our national life, contributing invaluably to the culture and industry, the patriotism and valor, the scholarship and faith of the United States of America.
>
> After three-quarters of a century of freedom, it is fitting that the Negro exhibit in colorful pageantry his great achievements. To graphically show the entire world his glorious progress the huge American Negro exposition has been conceived. . . .
>
> In this manner will our peaceful and democratic nation in these days of world strife and chaos, come to know more of its fellow citizens, the black American, and in so doing realize the tremendous part played by Negroes in making our common country the greatest land on the face of the globe.

The social phase of the old Emancipation Day celebration has developed to a point where, today, there are hundreds of social clubs in Chicago. These organizations participate in the multitudinous activities which make up the social life of the community. Negroes dance in modern, air-conditioned ballrooms and in small private club rooms; they take moonlight dance cruises on Lake Michigan, and they go rowing in Washington Park lagoon; they listen to big names at the Regal Theater, the Parkway Ballroom, Bacon's Casino, or the Savoy, and they drop nickels in the big, shiny "vendors" in every corner tavern and lunch room. Negroes gather at swanky formal dinners, chat politely over cocktails or tea, and socialize at chicken, fish or chitterling suppers. They gather together chauvinistically; they also intermingle with their white friends at the movies, at parties and at literary and artistic soirees. Sororities, fraternities, trade unions, church groups, adult, and youth organizations, with their bazaars, formal and sport dances, picnics, parties and meetings, carry on the tradition of "having a good time."

The pattern of social life of the group as a whole is similar to, and at the same time different from, that of the larger community; and the Negro plays, keeping an eye on, yet ignoring, his white neighbors who can use the Loop as their playground.

21. Recreation and Sports

Several drafts of this chapter exist. There are three early drafts in the IWP papers at the Harsh Research Collection, a slightly modified draft at the Newberry Library, and the most recent draft at Syracuse University, which appears here. Like much of the project, authorship was shared, as the IWP drafts indicate they were written by Robert Lucas, the Newberry draft has E. Diehl's name on it, and Arna Bontemps reworked the most recent draft.

More than one thousand spectators witnessed a ten-mile foot race for a $300 purse, which took place in Chicago in 1847. A Canadian, Armstrong, beat the Americans, Gildersleeve and Lewis Isabell; nine years later Isabell, a Negro, represented Cook County at the Alton Convention of Colored Citizens of Illinois.

In 1854, "A skating match took place on the canal at Elmira . . . between Patrick Brown and George Tate, a colored man. Brown won the stakes—$20—with ease, coming out five rods ahead." Time, two minutes eight seconds. $500 changed hands on this occasion.

The *Chicago Evening Journal* on September 8, 1874, announced that "the Napoleons, a colored baseball club of St. Louis, are coming to this city to play the Uniques, also colored, for the colored championship."

Pedestrianism also interested the Negro in the early days of Illinois.

Danville, Ill., February 19 (1879)—On the 7th Inst., G. G. Johnson (colored) of this city, started on a walk of 2,700 quarter miles in as many consecutive quarter hours. He has made 1,183 quarter miles up to tonight, and is confident of completing his task on time. If successful here, it is his intention to enter the Brooklyn match, commencing March 3.

In Chicago in December 1879 another Negro, Albert Pierce, who called himself the "Unknown," finished last in a field of four in a six days' go-as-you-please walking match at McCormick Hall. Pierce completed 259 miles, 2 laps.

Three years later Charles Nickels and James Hallie, colored, engaged in a 100-yard race on the Chicago lake front for a purse of $50. Hallie gained the lead early and won by five feet. He was challenged by Abe W. Williams to run the same distance three weeks later on July 4, 1882.

In the middle nineties, a two-mile race between M. J. Kennedy and Joseph Jordan was the feature of a field day at Union Park, Chicago; $200 a side was wagered. The same day the Chicago Unions and the Edgars, colored baseball teams, played the second of a five-game series at the park.

Cycling appealed to Chicago Negroes. In 1898, a "cycling club composed entirely of colored riders" was organized on the west side in Chicago. "The members include pretty fast men," said the *Chicago Daily News*.

In 1906, a billiard tournament was held at Wiley and Gillespie's Room, 3130 State Street. Six leading colored players of the city met to determine the "colored championship of the Middle West."

One of the teams composing the Chicago Cricket Association was the West Indian Club, an organization of "young men representing the Afro-American race."[1] The Negro club in 1914 took part in a Decoration Day meet with other members of the association: the Pullman, Chicago, Hyde Park, and South Park Clubs.

Negro participation in organized baseball began as early as 1875, when a sportsman named W. S. Peters organized and equipped Chicago's first all-Negro baseball team. Peters called his nine "the Chicago Unions" and secured a field at 75th and Langley, outside the city limits. There the Chicago Unions played until 1894, when the name was changed to the "Chicago Union Giants." The *Daily Inter Ocean* in 1897 said:

> The club . . . stands today the foremost colored organization of its kind in the world. Many of the players, if given the chance, would hold their own in major leagues. Last year the team made a wonderful record, winning one hundred games and losing nineteen.[2]

In 1900, the club was disbanded and the players went to two other teams, the Columbian Giants and the Page Fence Giants. The Columbian Giants had their home field at 37th and Butler, near the present home grounds of the American Giants. The team sponsored by the Page Fence Company was the first Negro nine to meet a major league all-star team.

In 1904, Frank Leland, county commissioner, bought the Columbian Giants and reorganized the club, changing the name to Leland Giants. The team won 122 games in 1905, taking 44 consecutively. The home field was at 79th and Wentworth. In 1907, "Rube" (Andrew Ruber) Foster who had previously played with the team in 1907, returned to Chicago at Leland's request. The next year, when Leland retired, Foster became manager.

Rube Foster and his team were superior. A sports writer for the *Daily Inter Ocean* said in August 1907:

> Talk about the post-season baseball series. The past week has witnessed a contest that exceeded in interest to the people it attracted anything that took place between the White Sox and the Cubs last fall. It was the series between the Leland Giants and Mike Donlin's All-Stars. If you have never seen "Rube" Foster, captain and manager of the Leland Giants, the aggregation of colored ball players that is the pride of the entire population of Dearborn Street, in action you are not qualified to discuss baseball, first degree fan though you may be. . . .
>
> Rube Foster . . . has all the speed of a Rusie, the tricks of a Radburne, and the heady coolness and deliberation of a Cy Young . . . but his color has kept him out of the big leagues.

CHAPTER TWENTY-ONE

The Leland Giants swept the series, giving an exhibition of reckless base running and "performing almost impossible stunts."

Late in 1908, Foster and Attorney Beauregard Moseley purchased the team from Leland, renamed it the American Giants, and gave Foster complete charge. In October 1901, "Rube" succeeded in booking a series of games with the Chicago Cubs, despite Frank Chance's refusal to play against Negroes. Although the Giants lost the series, they won a moral victory, for they hit the best Cub pitchers and had the crowd with them before the contest was over. A pitcher's battle between Foster and Mordecai Brown in which the great Cub hurler eked out a one-to-nothing win, was the high point of the series.

The Giants joined the Chicago City League in 1909, and in 1910 they moved into the old White Sox Park at 39th and Shields, renaming it the American Giants Park. Foster was instrumental in forming the Negro National Baseball League at Kansas City in 1920 and was elected president. He retired in 1926, after winning his last championship for Chicago. The league was reorganized into the National and American Leagues, and in 1932 an annual all-star game was inaugurated; Comiskey Park, home of the Chicago White Sox, is the scene of this yearly contest.

Chicago industrialists in 1917 sought the help of the YMCA in orienting rural Negroes who flocked to their plants during the war migration. Henry R. Crawford of the Wabash Avenue YMCA evolved a plan to combine recreation with the association's training program. Most of the workers involved were interested in baseball, and in April 1917 teams of the Armour, Wilson, and Swift packing companies became the foundation of the Industrial League. Presently other teams joined—Libby, McNeal and Libby, U.S. Quartermasters, Morris and Company, Hammond and Company, and a second team from Armour and Company. Still other teams joined later. From the very first, play was open and democratic in the Industrial League. All workers who wished to enjoy the sport participated on a basis of equality. Some teams were colored, some white, some mixed. They played each other indiscriminately.

In 1927, John C. Day replaced Crawford as commissioner of the Industrial League. Games were held at Thirty-Third and Wentworth from 1919 to 1926, then Washington Park replaced the old site. The organization is credited with improving racial relations as well as providing good baseball at low cost.

In 1917, while the Chicago YMCA was creating the Industrial League, the Bond Avenue YMCA in East St. Louis was also providing recreation to build civilian morale. The *East St. Louis Daily Journal* reported, "The whole colored public is cordially invited to share in every feature of the morning, afternoon and evening exercises," exercises which include drills, games, racing, jumping, wrestling, and boxing.

Prior to 1917, the several Negro church teams—Grace, Quinn, Chapel, Bethel, and Olivet—featured prominently in the Cook County Sunday School League. When the league was reorganized, and the Negro teams segregated, the four teams withdrew from the county organization. With four other church teams they formed the Union Church Athletic Association in 1913. The association sponsors bowling, basketball, tennis and track, as well as baseball for its members.

In 1897, according to the *Daily Inter Ocean*, Chicago boasted "the only football team of colored players in the country," organized by the Columbia Club, "swellest social organization among the young colored men of the city. . . . R. A. J. Shaw, right end, was a substitute quarterback on the Michigan University eleven a few years ago."[3]

Negroes have frequently made good on the football teams of high schools, colleges, and universities in and around Chicago. Shortly after the turn of the century little Sam Ramson, a three-sport man, won lasting acclaim at High Park High. In 1913, Farrell Jones was the only colored young man, stated in the *Chicago Defender*, playing regularly on a high school football team in Chicago that season. He was left end on the Lake High team, lightweight, which won the city championship.[4] Paul Leach of the Chicago *Daily News* included two Negroes in his all-star prep eleven of 1915: Sam Payton and Homer Lewis.[5]

Among outstanding colored college football starts have been Fritz Pollard (and later Fritz Pollard, Jr.), All-American in 1916; and Duke Slater, All-American tackle, who also played with the Chicago Cardinals from 1926 to 1931 and was later appointed assistant commerce commissioner of Illinois. Other Negro football stars include Bernie Jefferson and James Smith of Northwestern, Young and Wheeler of Illinois, and Jack Hart.[6]

The annual game between Wilberforce and Tuskegee Universities at Soldier Field, an importation which has gained favor, began in 1927.

American Negroes have done well in track and field events, and Illinois has had its share of noted performers. One of the earliest was Binga Diamond, University of Chicago quarter-miler. In 1916, at Northwestern University field, Diamond set a track record for the quarter-mile around one turn which has never been equaled.[7] Another great Negro track man was Metcalfe, the Olympic star who started his career at Tilden Tech in Chicago. Miss Tyde Pickett and Sol Butler were other Chicagoans who put new records in the books.

The Prairie Tennis Club, colored organization formed in May 1915, has developed players who have participated in Chicago City Championship matches, in the tourney sponsored by the Walgreen Drug Company, and in the annual championships of the American Tennis Association.[8] More recently an increasing number of Negroes have taken to golfing.

Boxing, too, has had its colorful figures and interesting incidents. In 1891, George Godfrey, heavyweight, was given "a tremendous ovation" when he "gave an excellent exhibition of science and skill" against Jim Phillips at Central Hall in Chicago. Phillips was "outclassed from the very start . . . while Godfrey won the plaudits of the crowd by not taking advantage of his inferior foe." In the preceding week Godfrey had been the guest of honor at a banquet given by the Chicago Hunting and Fishing Club, "composed of the leading colored residents of this city."[9]

In Champaign in 1893, a local pugilist named Speedy and a Chicago unknown, both Negroes, were scheduled to fight in a shed of the Empire Cordage Company. The bout failed to come off. "During the first round the sheriff and his deputies were present. The lights were extinguished and the crowd scattered. Speedy was arrested." The following year "A brutal finish prize-fight took place" at Pecatonica between Cully Ferguson of Rockford and George Dixon of Brooklyn for a $200 side bet. The fight was declared a draw and Ferguson was placed under "$200 bonds not to fight in the county."

Young Peter Jackson, Negro welterweight boxer, in 1901 engaged one Eddie Croake despite the intervention of Governor Richard Yates. The bout, scheduled for Belvidere, was moved to Gilberts, Kane County.

A special train, with 500 on board, reached that little village soon after midnight, and adjourned to a hall where a ring was formed, and the fight commenced. There were no police, save the village marshal, and there was no interference.

Jackson was the winner by a knockout in the twelfth round.

Negro boxers of Chicago have been bright figures in the sports parade since the earliest days. Jack Johnson, after defending the heavyweight championship against Jeffries at Reno in 1910, returned to Chicago to open the ornate Elite Café at 31st and State Streets.[10] Otis Broughton ("Jamaica Kid"), a leading heavyweight, owned and operated a Chicago restaurant.

More than any other Negro, however, Joe Louis captured the fancy of American sports fans. When he entered the United States Army he had defended his heavyweight title twenty times—an almost unbelievable record. Meanwhile, his conduct in the ring and out was cited as a model for the country's youth.

Somewhat less of a model was one Policy Sam who, with the financial assistance of a white man, introduced the game of numbers to Chicago in 1885.[11] A few years later, "Mushmouth" Johnson became interested in the game. With King Foo, a Chinese, as partner he added policy to his operation. For a time the game brought increasing profits to Johnson, but in 1905 an anti-policy law, said to have been sponsored by a competitor and enemy, abolished the lucrative business for a decade. Johnson died in 1907.

Hundreds of policy "stations" have periodically flourished in South Side grocery stores, barber and beauty shops, shoe shine parlors, cigar, magazine, and cleaning establishments. Newly opened stations would sometimes acquaint the public with the activities going on in the back by a sign in the window bearing the notice "All Books," "Gig," "Open," or "4-11-44." In each case the meaning was the same—policy.

Inside each station was a rack with many small pigeonholes containing slips on which appeared the winning numbers of all "pools." A pool was twelve ("one-legged book") or twenty-four numbers ("two-legged book"), from 1 to 78 inclusive. A gig was three numbers, within the given range, selected by the player. If he "saddled" his gig, any two of the three numbers he had drawn would win him ten dollars for the fifteen cents invested.[12]

Policy "wheels" were usually located on upper floors of business buildings; however, one of the largest in the city was situated over a Baptist church on the second floor. In the heyday of policy there were three daily periods of immense activity at the wheels (really rotating kegs); they were the moments preceding the three drawings—a.m., p.m., and midnight. Shortly before drawings, "writers," "riders," players and visitors assembled to watch the procedure. Seventy-nine numbers, wrapped in leather containers, were dropped into the keg and shaken together; a blindfolded person picked out twelve numbers; these were stamped in a column in the order of drawing along the lengthwise margin of a two-by-six such piece of paper. The numbers were then rewrapped and replaced in the keg and shaken, again twelve were drawn, and these were stamped in order down the other margin. (In the case of a one-legged book, the twelve numbers were stamped in order down the center of the slip.) Each wheel had several books. The names of some of the more popular were "Goldfield," "Royal Pal," "Wall Street," "Northshore," "Rio Grande," "Air Plane Mail," "Harlem," "Times Square," "Tia Juana," "Greyhound," "Red Devil," and "Green Dragon."[13]

Thousands of Negroes played policy regularly despite the known odds against them—7,776 to 1. One Negro minister, after unsuccessful attempts to have the game outlawed, advised his congregation: "If you must play policy, saddle your gig." It was occasionally said that operators of wheels could manipulate the drawings; if so, the odds were still greater than most players imagined. Many big hits were made by persons working in the business—a rather suspicious development.

Most policy players were common laborers and relief clients. To assist themselves in their efforts to beat the game they frequently had recourse to dreams, dream books, and spiritualists who purported to be numbers specialists. Such expert advisers sold their knowledge to the policy players for sums ranging from ten cents to a couple of dollars. The dream books interpreted names and phrases in terms of three numbers, or gigs. A player might dream he had seen his dead mother; in the book that was the dead mother row, interpreted as 12-27-29. Perhaps he saw his sweetheart in his dream; 30-47-72 was the winning combination in such a case.

The hundreds of policy stations and the dozens of wheels were owned by a handful of "barons" who composed a syndicate which in turn paid handsomely—or so it was said—for "protection" against "interference." Yet a time came when leading members of the "syndicate" were indicted by the grand jury and the game suspended. But the folklore of policy continued. For example—

A young Negro fresh from the South was standing with a companion on a street-corner in Chicago's Negro district. A well-dressed man drove up in a shining, luxurious Cadillac.

"Who's that?" the young newcomer asked his city friend.

"That's Jones, he's the policy king who owns all the wheels."

"I wouldn't mind bein' Jones," the young visitor commented.

A few moments later another well-dressed Negro drove up in the latest model Buick. "Now who's that?"

"That's Brown. He's pick-up man for Jones."

Again the stranger commented, "I wouldn't mind bein' Brown."

Then, looking across the street, he saw a lean and hungry man, conspicuously ragged, his shoes run down.

"But who's that?"

"That's the man who plays the numbers with Jones."[14]

22. Defender

The black press was to play a central role in the history of African Americans in Illinois. Before the establishment of *The Negro in Illinois*, Horace Cayton supervised a study of the black press, plans for which included a ten-chapter book. Much of the work was carried out by black journalist Henry N. Bacon. This material was folded into a forty-eight-page chapter Arna Bontemps wrote in 1941 under the heading "Newspapers." This draft was significantly condensed for an essay titled "Defender," which appears here. Copies of the chapter are in Jack Conroy's papers at Newberry Library and Bontemps's papers at Syracuse University. A copy of this essay was also sent to *Chicago Defender* editor Lucius Harper with a letter from Bontemps asking him to review it. The envelope it was sent in was marked "Federal Works Agency" with the address of Bontemps's office, 4901 Ellis Avenue, and dated May 11, 1942. It was discovered in the Abbott-Sengstacke papers when they were given to the Harsh Research Collection in 2009. Although focusing heavily on the *Defender*, it is a more recent draft and was therefore chosen as the final version of the chapter on African American newspapers.

Among the out-of-town visitors to the African Congress held in conjunction with the 1893 World's Columbian Exposition was Robert Sengstacke Abbott, almost age 23, principally known as the tenor of the Hampton Quartette, which frequently toured the country. The young man listened to Frederick Douglass's address, "What I Know about Field Slavery," and heard Ida B. Wells, already famous for her anti-lynching crusade throughout the United States and England, tell of the destruction of her Memphis newspaper, *Free Speech*, at the hands of a mob. Abbott also was interested in journalism, and had been learning the printer's trade at Hampton Institute, Virginia.

Abbott enjoyed his World's Fair visit, and in 1897 returned to Chicago with the intention of staying. He was a fully qualified printer, but found that printing firms were reluctant to hire a Negro. He picked up odd jobs and his trade, and took up the study of law in night classes at Kent College of Law, where his closest friend and counselor was Harry Dean, subsequently a sea captain and adventurer. Dean has recounted his somewhat astounding experience in a book, *The Pedro Corino*, written in collaboration with Sterling North.

John R. Marshall (later Colonel Marshall of the Eighth Illinois Infantry), a Hampton graduate, was a Chicago brickmason, and to him Abbott brought a letter of recommendation from General Samuel C. Armstrong, founder of Hampton and at that time its principal. Marshall's circle of acquaintances was large, and included many persons of prominence and authority. The young printer-lawyer benefitted from his association with the popular brickmason, who for years encouraged and actively assisted him in the pursuit of his ambitions.[1]

Edward H. Morris, possibly Chicago's most successful Negro attorney of the period, told Abbott bluntly that he was "a little too dark to make any impressions on the court in Chicago," and advised a debut in a smaller town. The beginner displayed his most hopeful shingle in nearby Gary, Indiana, but it was almost totally ignored by the citizens of that steel-making community.

Giving up his attempt to practice law, Abbott fell back upon his intermittent printing jobs. But he had another idea. The evening of May 6, 1905, found him peddling on the street and from door to door copies of a four-page paper, the *Chicago Defender*, bearing an arrogant sub-title, "The World's Greatest Weekly." The publisher was also editor, business manager, and the entire staff. The editorial desk doubled as a kitchen table in the apartment of Mrs. Henrietta P. Lee on South State Street. Mrs. Lee also proffered the use of her telephone, and the Western Newspaper Union, a printing company specializing in small country weeklies, was persuaded to extend as much as $25 credit. Abbott seldom was able to pay the full amount of the bill at once, but was forced to take out a portion of the edition, sell it, and then return with the proceeds to bail out the remaining copies held in escrow by the printer. Abbott's friend Marshall had introduced him to a foreman in the *Chicago Tribune* engraving plant who arranged a month's credit for engravings. A nightclub proprietor championed the venture, often depositing ten dollars in his cash register subject to the demand of the hard-pressed publisher and editor. When Abbott expressed worry over the obligation thus incurred, the slate was wiped clean by insertion of an advertisement.

Though Abbott continued for some time as sole regular staff member, he enlisted a number of volunteers. Julius N. Avendorph, sports promoter and social figure, wrote about both fields of interest. Tony Langston, a bartender at the Keystone Club, took advantage of his position to gather news about frequenters of the establishment and other tidbits accessible to members of his profession. Alfred Anderson, manager of old Provident Hospital, helped out with editorials, and Dr. A. Wilberforce Williams edited a health column. Recognizing the role of the barber shop as a social center and forum, Abbott called on as many as he could reach to leave papers for sale and to collect items of news, comment, and criticism deposited by customers.

James A. Scott, subsequently appointed assistant state's attorney, had suggested *Defender* as a suitable name for Abbott's new paper, since Negroes of Illinois and the nation were in critical need of a vigorous defender of their rights. A great many of the preceding and contemporary Negro papers had attached themselves to one or the other of the dominant political parties (usually the Republican) and too often had subordinated the battle for justice and equality to political expediency. Abbott resolved to remain rigorously independent and to fight incessantly for Negro rights. His resolute adherence to this policy at length brought him more readers than any other "race" publisher.

After several years of operation on a one-man basis, Abbott engaged as managing editor J. Hocker Smiley, Jr., son of the well-known caterer who had donated a $5,000 scholarship to the University of Chicago. Frank A. Young, a dining car employee, replaced Julius N. Avendorph as sports editor and in 1942 was still on the paper. Louis B. Anderson, a young attorney later elected alderman of the Second Ward, was a frequent contributor. Pon Holley became the first cartoonist. The kitchen table office of the *Defender* gradually occupied the whole room, and overflowed into the dining room. In 1914, a cub reporter, Robert Butler, was added to the staff. Lucius C. Harper went to work in 1916, and has remained in various capacities since then, with the exception of a short transfer to the *Whip* in 1929.

Harper in 1921 created a children's department, "Defender Junior, edited by Bud Billiken." "Bud Billiken" has become an institution, and each year the *Defender* entertains in his name thousands of children at a picnic in Washington Park and sponsors various other events and competitions. "Bungleton Green," first comic strip to appear in a Negro paper, was conceived by Harper in 1921 when he described an old handyman whom he had known in Augusta, Georgia, to cartoonist Leslie L. Rogers, who executed the drawings. The feature at one time occupying a full page in colors was continued by Jay Jackson after Rogers's death.

W. Allison Sweeney, who had been an editor of the *Indianapolis Freeman*, moved to Chicago in 1905 to establish the *Chicago Leader*, which wooed the religious bodies, adhered to the Republican platform, and printed a market and finance column. Despite the energy and resource of its founder, the *Leader* issued its last edition late in 1906. In 1915, Sweeney was enlivening the pages of the *Defender* with his caustic wit. Another acquisition from the *Freeman* was Salem Tutt Whitney, a prominent actor with the Smarter Set Company, who transferred his popular weekly column, "See and Heard While Passing" to the *Defender*.

When the *Defender* outgrew the facilities of the Western Newspaper Union, Abbott made a printing arrangement with the *Chicago Daily Drover's Journal*. A composing room foreman who had worked for the Hearst press persuaded him that his make-up should be more sensational and eye-arresting. Abbott agreed, and before long was being called "the William Randolph Hearst of Negro journalism." It was rumored widely that the paper actually belonged to Hearst. The *Defender* cartoonist had designed a masthead so similar to that of the *Chicago Evening American* that hurried newsstand purchasers often mistook one paper for the other to the disadvantage of the dealer, since the *Defender* sold for five cents and the *Evening American* for two. The Hearst paper filed suit for infringement of copyright, but Abbott forestalled the action by substituting the masthead now used.

The *Defender* achieved national prominence with its vigorous advocacy of the Negro exodus from the South beginning with the First World War and reaching its peak in 1917. Circulation leaped, and Abbott added pages and various improvements. He cultivated a homely, direct style of expression, never "talking down" to his readers, and demanded that his writers follow this policy. The paper became the "bible" and inspiration of southerners yearning toward New Canaan, and the "defender" indeed of those already in the North.[2]

Below the slogan, "American Race Prejudice Must Be Destroyed," every edition of the *Defender* emphasized these points:

The opening up of all trades and trade unions to blacks as well as whites.
Representation in the President's cabinet.

Engineers, firemen and conductors of all American railroads and government controlled industries.

Representation in all departments of the police forces over the entire United States.

Government schools open to all American citizens.

Motormen and conductors on surface, elevated and motor bus lines throughout America.

During the race riots of 1919, the *Daily Drover's Journal*, fearing mob violence, refused to print the *Defender*, and Abbott was forced to bargain with the *Gary Tribune*, whose small presses required two days to turn out an edition of 150,000. Impressed with the desirability of owning his own plant, Abbott moved a year later into his own building on Indiana Avenue, where printing equipment valued at more than $500,000 now turns out the paper.

Before Abbott died in 1940, after an illness lasting eight years, he had the satisfaction of seeing his "World's Greatest Weekly" attain a circulation larger than any other Negro paper. During the exodus, a record of 500,000 is said to have been reached, and a consistently high figure has been maintained.

Since the founder's death, the *Defender* has been managed by a board of directors, including in 1942 John H. Sengstacke, Abbott's nephew; Dr. Metz T. P. Lochard, an editorial writer; and James P. Cashin, an attorney. The militancy fostered by Robert Sengstacke Abbott had not diminished, and the readers were being exhorted to "Remember Pearl Harbor, and Sikeston, too," the latter reference being to a particularly brutal lynching in Missouri.

One of Abbott's earliest competitors, the *Broad Ax*, moved to Chicago from Salt Lake City in 1889. Julius C. Taylor, its editor and publisher, decorated each issue with the numerous likenesses of politicians who, it is said, often enough lent the paper financial aid to escape the uncomplimentary comments of Taylor, who excelled in personal accusations and preacher-baiting. His motto was: "Hew to the line, let the chips fall where they may." The editor was inclined to condemn ministers who mixed politics with religion, and on one occasion said:

> The Negro race is the only race in the world to have their churches turned into political halls for faking preachers and the small-headed base White Republican politicians who contend that they can buy any "darkey preacher and a whole church full of niggers for ten dollars."

As a matter of policy, the *Broad Ax* favored the Democratic Party, but expressed its willingness to print contributions from "Republicans, infidels, or any one else . . . so long as their language is proper and the responsibility fixed." Aside from its pungent editorial style, the paper is notable as the first in Chicago to attack the tradition demanding of Negroes full and unquestioning loyalty to the Republican Party. The *Broad Ax* ended its hectic career in 1927.

The *Illinois Chronicle* was founded in 1912 by Williams A. Neighbors, formerly a realtor and banker. Policy and management were in the hands of A. N. Fields, formerly editor of *Western Opinion*, and he was followed by Carey W. Lewis, who remained in charge until 1915, when the paper suspended. Like the *Defender*, the *Chronicle* advocated independence in politics, though ordinarily favoring Democratic candidates.

The *Springfield Conservator*, which began publication in 1911, often carries more advertising than other reading matter, and the same is true of the *Springfield Chronicle*, established in 1936, not a continuation of "Sand Bag" Turner's paper of similar name.

Jacob R. Tipper, a grocer, launched the *Chicago Enterprise* in 1917. The *Enterprise* became the *Chicago World* in 1925, having grown from a four-page hand-printed sheet to an eight-column, sixteen-page newspaper carrying an unusual amount of neighborhood advertising. A circulation of 25,000 has been reached. The *World* announces as its platform:

> Fight against the words Negro, Nigger, and Negress. Use your buying power as you use your ballot. Spend your money in your own community. Married women should not be made to work. Teach your dollar sense. Cut down on southern representation in Congress. Don't spend your money where you can't work.

The last slogan was the battle cry around which another journal of the period waged an effective community crusade. The *Chicago Whip*, founded in 1919, conducted in 1929–30 a job campaign resulting in the employment of thousands of Negro men and women in manufacturing plants, stores, and offices.[3] Not only neighborhood merchants but corporations and chain stores capitulated and hired Negroes for the first time. The *Whip* was first established by William C. Linton, who enlisted the aid of two law graduates from Yale, Joseph Dandrige Bibb and Arthur Clement MacNeal. One of the *Whip*'s first targets was the Metropolitan Insurance Company, which had many Negro policyholders but no Negro collectors. When the company declined to change its attitude, Negro insurance companies profited by the acquisition of many policyholders who had quit the Metropolitan. Though its circulation was at one time estimated at more than 16,000 and its insistence upon jobs for Negroes brought it considerable popularity, the *Whip* was boycotted by most of the business men and corporations it had condemned for their exclusion of Negro employees. Advertising was hard to get, and a raise in price from two cents to five cents drove customers away, thus failing to increase revenue appreciably. The *Whip* suspended in 1932, but was revived in 1939 by Joseph D. Bibb, who reminded his readers: "This is the great fighting paper now famous all over the world for its great campaign for jobs in Chicago. It created 3,000 jobs." The new *Whip*, however, closed its doors less than three months after it had opened them. Bibb joined the staff of the new *Chicago Sun* in 1941, while his co-editor on the old *Whip*, A. C. MacNeal, was managing editor of the *Defender*.

The *Chicago Bee* was established in 1925 by Anthony Overton, formerly a municipal court judge in Kansas. In Chicago, he organized the Douglass National Bank and was the dominant spirit in the formation of the Victory Life Insurance Company. During its best years, the *Bee* sold 35,000 copies or more, nearly half of these outside Chicago. Sponsoring community betterment and church attendance, independent in politics, and scrupulously avoiding sensationalism, it is the favorite newspaper of conservative elements.

H. George Davenport, a roving sign painter, arrived in Chicago sometime during the depression of the thirties and began to write acrimonious comment for the Negro press, principally the *World*. Editors often rejected or censored his forthright pronouncements, and in 1936 Davenport, an adept craftsman whose business motto, "I Made Signs Before I Could Talk," was somewhat justified, investing his savings in a personal mouthpiece, *Dynamite*. The tabloid-sized journal usually ran four pages, though sometimes it had eight. From 1,000 to 5,000 copies were printed weekly, and distributed free. While readers enjoyed Davenport's fulminations against prominent individuals and organizations, they successfully resisted his attempt to make them pay two cents a copy for *Dynamite*, and free distribution was resumed. Eight evils were sentenced to death under a front page caption: "This Vicious Circle Must Go." Listed were organized vice, racial discrimination, restrictive covenants, unfair business and professional men, false race leaders, unfair labor unions, brutal police, and rent hogs.

Announcing that *Dynamite* would "blast everything that stands in the path of the Negro and his progress," Davenport expressed his determination to "use the power of the press in the same sense as dynamite is used in getting what we think rightfully belongs to me." The militant sign painter was forced by lack of capital to suspend *Dynamite* for six months in 1937, but managed to re-enter the arena early 1938. When the Negro Labor Relations League was formed for the purpose of directing the jobs-for-Negroes movement, *Dynamite* supported it with characteristic gusto. The League, while it welcomed and acknowledged Davenport's potent propaganda, was embarrassed by some of his utterances. *Dynamite* frequently charged that Jewish merchants on the South Side were foremost in the exploitation of Negro citizens. Advertisers were inclined to shun the pugnacious tabloid, readers would not pay for the privilege of reading it, and late in 1938 it ceased publication.

The *Chicago Daily Bulletin* appeared in 1927, and seemed to be enjoying moderate prosperity when it ran a story concerning a "policy" hit which, the paper alleged, the gambling lords had refused to pay off. The *Daily Bulletin* succumbed in the course of litigation instigated by powerful interests backing the "policy" syndicate, having lived seven months. The *Chicago Times*, also a daily, lasted one month in the summer of 1927. The next attempt at a daily was made ten years later by Gus Ivory (publisher of the magazine *Flash*). His *Daily Mirror* struggled through a few months. The *Pittsburgh Courier* in 1938 began a special Chicago edition.

The great majority of Illinois Negro newspapers have been published in Chicago, have been weeklies, and, with a few exceptions, have been short-lived. Of those operating in 1942, only the *Chicago Defender* and the Springfield *Conservator* were established prior to 1925. Outside of Chicago, a score or more of Negro newspapers have appeared from time to time. Aside from the Chicago papers, most of the Negro journals in 1942 were linked with political activity, stressed community news, and depended upon local advertising.

The need for independent Negro newsgathering agency impelled the organization in 1919 of the Associated Negro Press in Chicago by Claude Barnett and Nahum D. Brascher. The Chicago agency supplies the Negro press of the nation with interpretations of the news, affords many special syndicate features, and maintains paid correspondents in all-important centers of Negro residence.

23. Politics

There are two drafts of this chapter, one an early draft by Mathilde Bunton, and the other a more recent version that appears here, written by Jack Conroy. Both drafts were found in the IWP papers at the Harsh Research Collection and in Jack Conroy's papers at the Newberry Library.

On September 8, 1865, the *Peoria Daily National Democrat* inquired:

> This is the question to be answered at the coming elections, whether white men shall govern America, or whether it shall be ruled by Negroes. Shall Africans or Caucasians rule?

On the eve of the election the same paper exhorted its readers to

> . . . show by your vote that you will now and forever oppose Negro equality, and its legitimate results. . . . Do this so that your children shall never blush at being compelled to say that the proud County of Peoria voted in favor of Negro equality.

Five years later the *Cairo Bulletin* reported that a United States marshal at Mound City had rounded up two hundred Negroes and herded them to the polls with the grim warning: "Death to the Negro who scratches the ticket!"[1] The "ticket" was the Republican, and it was charged that the federal officer informed the election officials that his authority was superior to state law.

Early in 1867, the *Peoria Daily Transcript* observed:

> . . . The time is not far distant when the Democratic Party will be forced to beg for Negro votes. It will then set up the cry that they were always of that way of thinking and that while they were oppressing the colored race, it was their highest ambition to make them free and bestow upon them the right of suffrage. We predict that in less than six years, there will not be a Democratic journal of any standing in the northern states but will be on the universal suffrage plan.

Having been given the right to vote by federal and state constitutions, Illinois Negroes began to organize for political action about five years after the close of the Civil War. As the *Cairo Bulletin* put it:

They adhered with great tenacity to the party which had given them their freedom and the ballot.

Though George White had been appointed town crier of Chicago in 1837 and John Jones, a popular business man of Chicago had been elected as a Cook County Commissioner in 1871, the Negro voters of Cairo in 1873 for the first time in Illinois demonstrated the effect of organization on a racial basis.

They rallied around I. I. Bird and elected him to the second best office in the city, that of police magistrate. Commenting on the election, the Democratic *Cairo Bulletin* complained:

> Negro voters were bought and sold like sheep. Some of them sell these votes with the same nonchalance that they do their garden truck or cord wood. To such creatures the ballot is a blessing. Isn't it.

The following year Bird was chosen as one of the two delegates to the Republican State Convention, while another Negro, Warren Wims, was elected as an alternate.

In 1876 John W. E. Thomas, a Chicago grocer who had lost his business in the great fire and conducted a private school, was elected to the Illinois House of Representatives. Since the colored population of the city was less than 7,000 and Thomas polled 11,532 votes, he must have been favored by a number of white voters. Thomas was re-elected in 1882 and 1884. Since 1882 there has been at least one Negro member of each legislature, though for thirty-two years no more than one was elected.

On December 6, 1881, the *Chicago Inter Ocean* noted:

> Mr. Esau Sherman, a pure-blooded African, once a slave, has been elected a member of the City Council of Nokomis, Illinois, the President of which is a Southern Democrat.

Though there have always been a small number of Negro Democrats in Illinois, their power was negligible for many years. By 1890 the Democratic Party in the South had effectually disenfranchised colored voters. Many disgruntled southern Negroes came to Illinois, and particularly to Chicago, where they took a lively interest in politics. A great many of the refugees were from Alabama, Mississippi, and Louisiana, where, during the Reconstruction era, Negroes had enjoyed suffrage and held office.

In 1896 thirteen colored voters of Quincy formed a Bryan Silver Club, and William Jennings Bryan received a delegation of colored voters at Democratic National Headquarters in the Auditorium Hotel, Chicago. W. T. Scott, spokesman for the delegation, said:

> The Negro should be the last to support either the gold standard or high protective tariff. Having nothing to sell but labor, he is best benefited when the volume of money in circulation is greatest. The high protective tariff discriminates against the Negro because he is not permitted to work in these protected industries.

Mr. Bryan replied that he "considered it a healthy sign when colored men who have been as a mess Republicans rise up and assert that they are thinking for themselves."

White Republican office holders, anxious to retain Negro loyalty, from time to time placed members of the race in appointive positions or supported them for elective offices. In 1888 Edward H. Wright was appointed as clerk and bookkeeper in the Secretary

CHAPTER TWENTY-THREE

of State's office in Springfield. Joseph Medill, Mayor of Chicago, appointed a Negro fire company of nine men in 1872 when the city's first Negro policeman was installed. Between 1891 and 1893, Mayor Hemstead Washburne appointed eleven Negro officers and reinstated two others. Franklin A. Denison became assistant city prosecutor in 1891, and his law partner, S. A. T. Watkins, was assigned to the same position in 1898 by Carter H. Harrison, II, a Democrat.

Carter H. Harrison, the elder, had preceded his son as mayor, and during his administration had given jobs to a number of Negroes. On March 26, 1901, "a young colored lawyer" addressed the Cook County Republican Marching Club to denounce the younger Harrison, and also his father, whom he characterized as "a well-known demagogue and fake." Contending that the son was like the father, the speaker said of the latter:

> Whatever nationality he addressed he claimed to have some of its blood in his veins. He was Irish, German, Scandinavian, Polish, and Bohemian. Even when he addressed colored audiences, he used to say: "I can never forget the health and strength I drank in with the milk of my dear old colored mammy, and when I look in the glass the hair behind my ears looks a little kinky." He was a human mud turtle.

William Hale Thompson, elected mayor in 1915, won the support of an overwhelming majority of Negro voters, and often took occasion to publicly acknowledge their help. He selected as assistant corporation counsels Edward H. Wright, formerly a county commissioner, and Louis B. Anderson and named Rev. Archibald James Carey, a staunch political ally, as chief investigator in the same office. In 1927 Thompson appointed Rev. Carey a city Civil Service Commissioner. Mayor Thompson granted Negroes so many jobs in the City Hall that opponents began to refer to the building as "Uncle Tom's Cabin." At a mass meeting held to commemorate the fiftieth anniversary of the Fifteenth Amendment to the United States Constitution, Bishop Carey declared:

> There are three names which will stand high in American history—Abraham Lincoln, William McKinley, and William Hale Thompson.

Thompson forces elected, along with the mayor, Chicago's first Negro alderman, Oscar DePriest, from the Second Ward. DePriest, regarded as a protégé of state representative John C. Buckner, had been a Cook County Commissioner. Becoming involved in a political scandal, he did not run for alderman in 1917, and was succeeded by Louis B. Anderson, who served for sixteen consecutive years thereafter. In 1918 Major Robert R. Jackson, a veteran of three terms in the Illinois House of Representatives, was elected as the second alderman of the ward. When ward lines were adjusted in 1921, he became alderman of the Third Ward and remained in office for twenty years.

Meanwhile the number of Negroes in the Illinois House of Representatives was steadily increasing to reach a peak of five in 1929. Adelbert H. Roberts, first Negro state senator, was elected in 1924 and defeated in 1934 by William E. King. King previously had been an assistant corporation counsel, assistant state's attorney, state representative, and Republican ward committeeman. This succession, according to Harold G. Gosnell, marks "the typical course of advancement for an able young colored lawyer." King's political career received a setback in 1940, when he was an unsuccessful candidate for United

States congressman from the third district, being defeated by the Democratic incumbent, Arthur W. Mitchell. Mitchell, who had unseated Oscar DePriest in 1934, was the first Negro Democratic congressman. Harold G. Gosnell has said:

> ... In the national field the election was an outstanding event. Several spells had been broken. Northern Democrats had given national recognition to the place of the Negro in their party. The Democratic caucus in the House of Representatives was compelled to admit a Negro. The Republican Party could no longer claim that it had the Negro in its vest pocket.[2]

In 1937 congressman Mitchell, having been denied sleeping car accommodations in the state of Arkansas, filed suit against the Pullman company for discrimination and denial of rights. Ensuing litigation carried the case to the Supreme Court of the United States, which affirmed the right of Negroes as well as other citizens to demand equal accommodations on public carriers. Mitchell's case was vigorously supported by the National Association for the Advancement of Colored People, which has participated in many struggles involving the civil rights of Negroes.

Attorney Earl B. Dickerson often gave legal aid to the NAACP and became the central figure of one of its celebrated cases. Dickerson, in the prosecution of his duties as special assistant attorney general, had occasion to visit Springfield, and applied for accommodations at the Abraham Lincoln Hotel. He was informed that Negroes were not accepted as guests. Suit initiated by Dickerson and the NAACP resulted in an unfavorable decision, and an appeal had not been heard in 1942. Commenting on the case, Dickerson said:

> The situation becomes ironical when one considers that I was refused hotel accommodations in the capitol while representing that attorney general of the state that has a civil rights law designed to protect all citizens against discrimination because of race or color.
>
> But unless the legislators themselves and others of our people begin to demand accommodations at hotels, restaurants, and other public places, there will be no necessity to put teeth in the civil rights law because there will never be any opportunity to demand its enforcement.

Dickerson had been appointed assistant attorney general in 1933, the first Negro under a Democratic administration. Elected a Democratic alderman in the second ward in 1939, Dickerson quickly established a record as a progressive and has been described as a political idealist of the new type as contrasted to the horse-trading old timers. He was an unsuccessful candidate for the Democratic nomination for Congress in the First District in 1942, running without Kelly-Nash support.

Unlike Dickerson, a number of Negro politicians, in common with their white confreres, have been embarrassed by their alleged (or actual) connection with the underworld. The *Chicago Daily Inter Ocean*, April 7, 1901, recorded the passing of one of these underworld political characters, Willis Woodson, described as "monarch of a dive" who had "prospered by his great political pull until he fell out with his protectors." The obituary continued:

> He was frequently in collision with the police, owing to the many shooting and killing affrays which took place in the dive, but his corps of ready-swearing witnesses and his aldermanic backers saved him from serious punishment. In return for this kind of help on the part of alderman, Woodson took an active part in politics. ... He had the disreputables

of the district thoroughly under control, and the count at the primaries, and frequently at the regular election polls, was made as he dictated. . . .

John "Mushmouth" Johnson, a gambler who died in 1907, wielded considerable political power, and is said to have made an arrangement with "Hinky Dink" Kenna and "Bathhouse John" Coughlin in which immunity from raids and prosecution was exchanged for successful efforts toward getting Negroes to register and vote in the desired way. It is said that "Mushmouth" would donate liberally to each side in a mayoralty campaign, on the theory that his business could continue regardless of the outcome.

Oscar DePriest's political career is believed to have been halted in 1917, when he was indicted along with several others for conspiracy to allow gambling resorts and houses of prostitution to operate. Henry "Teenan" Jones, who had moved his gambling establishment from Hyde Park to the Second Ward, confessed that he was head of the "Second Ward gambling syndicate." Though De Priest was acquitted he refrained from standing for reelection as Alderman, evidently fearing the effect of undesirable publicity. In 1929, however, De Priest became the first Illinois Negro member of the United States House of Representatives, retaining his seat until 1934.

Robert T. Motts, a second ward contemporary of "Mushmouth" Johnson, was a patron of the arts as well as a gambling king, being the founder of the Pekin Theater. Motts boasted that he had placed forty Negro women in the recorder's office, and he is credited with effecting the election of Edward Green to the state legislature in 1904.

Daniel M. Jackson, an undertaker who had attended Lincoln University in Pennsylvania, was chiefly known as the operator of a gambling syndicate. He wielded his political power unobtrusively but effectively during the second and third administrations of Mayor Thompson. The Jones Brothers, policy kings of the South Side, switched from the Republican to the Democratic ranks after the defeat of Mayor Thompson in 1931.

Marcus Garvey's Universal Improvement Association attained considerable political influence in Chicago in the twenties, William A. Wallace, an ex-banker who headed the local movement, later becoming a state senator. A number of Garveyites are presumed to have entered the ranks of the Communist Party during the depression, when the Communists carried on a militant campaign among Negroes. In 1937 the Communist Party had less than six thousand members in Illinois, and of these about two thousand were Negroes, ninety percent of them living in Chicago. The extent of Communist political influence cannot be accurately gauged. Certainly, it has not been demonstrated at the polls, since in the 1940 congressional election in the First District the winning candidate, E. King received 30,698, while the Communist candidate's share was included in a scattered vote totaling 442.

24. What Is Africa to Me?

This chapter draft, discovered at Syracuse University in the papers of Arna Bontemps, is the only copy known to exist. The title was taken from Countee Cullen's well-known Harlem Renaissance poem, "Heritage." More than any other, this chapter was collectively written, but the version that appears here was written by Bontemps. Originally, sections on the Moorish American Science Temple and Nation of Islam appeared in the chapter "And Churches," the chapter that follows this one. The material on these two organizations was later moved to the essay that appears below and developed more fully. For this reason, information on them was removed from the chapter "And Churches" to avoid repetition. The reader will recognize how these groups are still discussed here as "cults" and their members referred to as "zealots."

In the March 6, 1894, issue of the *Chicago Inter Ocean*, P. O. Gray addressed a letter to Master Workmen Sovereign of the Knights of Labor, who had complained that the presence of Negroes was impeding the progress of his organization in the South and had expressed a desire to see them sent back to Africa. Mr. Gray said in part:

> That I, a Negro, should be interested in the future success of the race is very natural. Therefore, I take exception to your proposition to deport the Negro back to Africa (as being the best way to solve the Negro question) as being contrary to all international law. There was a day when you preached the universal brotherhood of men. . . . Now, I will suggest an easy solution of the whole trouble—that is, for Mr. Sovereign to accept Negroes into the order in the South. . . . But in case you attempt to force the Negro from the country to make it easy for the K. of L. to continue the inculcation of prejudice and inhumanity, you may run against a greater force than the one you bring to bear upon the Negro. . . .

Three days later, the Chicago Colored Women's Club, meeting at the Tourgee Club (named after Judge Albion W. Tourgee, who has portrayed sympathetically in his *Bricks Without Straw* the lot of southern Negroes under reconstruction), pointed out that Negroes had been residents of this country for 250 years, and were "as much American citizens as anybody." "If this country is too small for the Knights of Labor and the Negro," the club members advised, "then let the Knights leave."

The Knights of Labor were not the first to contemplate the repatriation of Negroes. Before the Revolutionary War, many Quakers, for humanitarian reasons, were manumitting their slaves and casting about for some way to return them to their homeland. As early as 1800, the legislature of Virginia, alarmed at Gabriel Prosser's abortive slave rebellion, had authorized the governor of the state to confer with the President of the United States on the possibility of the colonization of malcontents "dangerous to the peace of society." Free men of color were increasing in number, and, in the opinion of the slaveholders, setting a bad example for Negroes still in bondage. Their insubordination and independent attitudes were irksome to those in power and authority, and it was thought that they would be much less dangerous if settled at a safe distance in Africa. From time to time slaveowners were assailed by qualms of conscience or became convinced that the institution of slavery was economically unsound, and released their bondsmen. Usually, the owners preferred that those freed be sent away.

Thomas Jefferson in 1811 indicated his belief in the desirability of settling American Negroes on the coast of Africa, and in 1814 wrote a letter to Governor Edward Coles of Illinois in which he discussed colonization of Negroes in the West Indies, and particularly in the Negro republic of Santo Domingo. Jefferson was convinced that members of the colored race eventually would drive all white people from the Caribbean Islands.

British foes of the slave traffic, such as William Wilberforce, Thomas Clarkson, and Granville Sharp, took practical steps toward colonization in Africa, and it was mainly due to their efforts that 400 Negroes, principally soldiers and sailors who had fought on the British side in the Revolutionary War, and 60 Europeans were settled on the Sierra Leone peninsula in 1787. The Europeans have been described as "mostly women of abandoned character." Some fugitive slaves who had sought refuge in London were included in the number, and these were joined later by freed slaves from Canada and West Indies.

Paul Cuffee, a New England Negro sailor who had attained some wealth, was the first American to supplement theory with action, and in 1815 deposited at his own expense 38 Negro colonists in Africa. Cuffee's feat is believed to have inspired the formation of the American Colonization Society in 1816, with Henry Clay and Francis Scott Key as officers. This organization established settlements which were bound together in the independent Republic of Liberia in 1847. Joseph Jenkins Roberts, an ex-slave, arrived in the colony in 1829, assembled and trained a force of militiamen, and was appointed governor in 1841. Upon the establishment of the republic, Roberts became its first president.

The colonization scheme was opposed by various forces. Not many slaveowners were willing to part with their black chattel, and the colonization enthusiasts dared not compel free Negroes to quit the United States in the face of the abolitionists' rising protest against expatriation. Most free men of color were as firmly rooted in the national life of America as any other citizens, and they called mass indignation meetings throughout the North in opposition to the African venture. A majority of the emigrants, therefore, were manumitted slaves who had no choice in the matter, their masters for one reason or another desiring to be rid of them.

The British had freed their West Indian slaves in 1838, and there followed considerable emigration to Haiti, Trinidad, and British Guiana. Despite the general unpopularity and seeming ineffectuality of the American Colonization Society, interest in colonization did not die. In 1853, a conclave of Negro leaders took up the problem of emigration, and divided into three factions favoring respectively the Niger Valley in Africa, Central America, and Haiti. Martin R. Delaney, foremost proponent of the first group, journeyed to Africa and negotiated agreements with eight African kings to accept American Negroes. The Haiti faction is credited with directing 2,000 settlers to that country, but only a third of them established permanent residence.

The *Central Illinois Gazette* observed in its August 8, 1858, issue:

> The colored people of this state are beginning to agitate the project of a general colonization to some unoccupied portion of the territories, or elsewhere, to set up for themselves. They have already held several meetings.[1]

The Civil War halted all emigration or even consideration of it for a time. Abraham Lincoln, known as an advocate of colonization, had entertained the idea of sending freedmen to Liberia, but little official action in that direction actually was taken. A legend persists among poor whites of the South to the effect that Lincoln would have had all Negroes out of the country had he been permitted to live.

The American Colonization Society celebrated its fiftieth anniversary in 1897 and announced that it had dispatched during that period 147 ships carrying nearly 12,000 African colonists. Free born among these numbered about 4,500, while approximately 6,000 had been freed on condition that they go to Liberia. A minority of the 344 had freed themselves by self-purchase. The society was not the only one sending colonists to Africa. The Maryland State Colonization Society had founded in 1831 the "Maryland in Africa" colony, which maintained its independence until 1858, when it was incorporated in the governmental structure of Liberia as Maryland County. The Maryland State Colonization Society had transplanted 1,221 colonists while the United States government had returned 6,772 Africans who had been smuggled into America to their native land, deposing them in Liberia.

The bark Azor, chartered by the Liberia Exodus Association, set sail from Charleston, South Carolina, on April 22, 1878, with 250 passengers bound for the Negro republic. Four days after its embarkation the *Chicago Inter Ocean* presented an optimistic prospect:

> The colored people who recently sailed from Charleston, S.C., for Liberia propose to settle at Bopora, situated about 75 miles northeast of Monrovia. The settlement was founded by a colored man from Charleston in 1866, who went to Liberia without funds, and now has a plantation bringing him an annual income of $3,000. By act of the Liberian Congress each head of a family among the emigrants will receive a free grant of 25 acres of land with privileges to occupy as much more as he pleases at 50 cents per acre.

Several years later (May 15, 1885) the *Cleveland Leader* noted:

> When colored people consent to give up their homes and emigrate to Liberia, there must be some justifiable cause. They either expect to do better in a foreign land or else their present situation has become so intolerable as to force them to emigrate.
>
> It is said that there are 700 colored families in North Carolina averaging six persons to a family who contemplate finding homes in Liberia. They have each paid into the treasury of the Emigration Society of Raleigh the sum of $10. A further payment of $15 is to be made, and it is calculated that this sum of $25, together with the aid they will receive from other societies, will secure an outfit and land them at their destination.

Complaints relating to swindling in connection with the colonization movement were found in the newspapers for years. On January 21, 1891, an Atlanta dispatch to the *Chicago Inter Ocean* said:

The excitement among the Negroes over the Liberia colonization scheme being engineered by the United States and Congo National Emigration Steamship Company does not abate. It is estimated that 2,000 Negroes have come to Atlanta from Texas and Mississippi to wait for the promised ship to take them as they expect from Savannah to Africa, and the cold weather of the past few days has found them in such destitution that the city has in many instances been compelled to aid them. There is some talk among those who contributed of bringing the matter before the courts, but as each has paid so little it is not probable that such action will be taken.

Bishop H. M. Turner of the African Methodist Episcopal Church, who had been commissioned by President Lincoln as the first Negro chaplain in the United States Army, became convinced that segregation of a large number of Negroes in Africa would be the best immediate step toward solution of his people's troubles after reaction and Ku Kluxism had displaced the military administrators and "carpetbaggers."

Bishop Turner came to Chicago in 1893 to address the African Congress held as a part of the World's Columbian Exposition and advocated emigration to Liberia. He was opposed by Frederick Douglass, who took a prominent part in the affairs of the Congress.

Two years later (February 11, 1895) the *Chicago Inter Ocean* vouchsafed its faith in Bishop Turner's sincerity, but maintained that his activities had given sharpers and swindlers an opportunity to fleece gullible southern Negroes, and went on:

An association with headquarters at Birmingham has advertised to carry Negroes to Africa for $40 each, the applicants to pay $1 a month until the money is subscribed. The agents of this association have also gone into the districts of Mississippi offering a cut rate transportation and colonial land for from $4 to $7. Many have been taken in by this fraudulent dealing.

The *New York Press* noted on April 14, 1895:

"Africa for the Negro" is being reechoed in the South. No good can come of this emigration. Nothing is said of the fevers and famine to be met on African shores. Douglass's call to stand up in America and fight was a clearer note than Turner's cry to run away to an unknown land. American Negroes should become Americans.

Nevertheless, a small percentage of American Negroes continued to turn to emigration outside the borders of the United States as a way out. Press reports announced in January 1895 that "the Afro-American Labor and Benevolent Association and the Mexican Colonization Company are furnishing free transportation to Mexico." Three months later a tragic sequel was indicated in the *Chicago Inter Ocean*:

A huge swindle was perpetrated on the Negroes who left to populate Mexican land. They were lured there by Negro leaders who were in cahoots with white men to get free labor corps to work a piece of land they had purchased from the Mexican government. The Negroes are being kept by force and are inadequately fed and housed.

What Is Africa to Me?

Eventually, most of the disillusioned homeseekers made their way back to the South.

The Colored Emigration and Commercial Convention, meeting in Chattanooga, Tennessee, in May 1902, passed a resolution requesting Congress to appropriate $50,000,000 to the purpose of colonizing Negroes desiring to quit the United States. Bishop Turner was named as "the leading spirit in the movement. By this time, however, colonizing schemes attracted but faint interest. Negroes dissatisfied in the South usually preferred to try the portion of the United States north of the Mason and Dixon line rather than a foreign land.

On a windy day late in March 1916, a young Negro from Jamaica, destined some years afterward to captivate hundreds of thousands of his racial brethren with his proud assertion that he was "a full-bodied black man," made an inconspicuous entry into New York's Negro colony, Harlem. He was Marcus Garvey, who had been in correspondence with Booker T. Washington on problems pertaining to their common race. Washington, it is said, had urged him to come to the United States. But Washington had died at Tuskegee, and Garvey was alone and all but penniless in a strange land. Previously, he had worked in London for Duse Mohamed Effendi, half-Negro and half-Egyptian writer and scholar. From Effendi, Garvey must have derived some of his "Africa for the Africans" philosophy.

Four years passed before Garvey, as President-General of the Universal Negro Improvement Association (UNIA), issued his eloquent call to "The Beloved and Scattered Millions of the Negro Race." The association was an outgrowth of Garvey's efforts to incorporate a Black Star steamship line for the dual purpose of returning the race leaders and American Negroes to their homeland and of opening commercial relations with the African continent. Garvey contended that Negro scholars, scientists, and industrialists should match wits on African soil with white interlopers and thus regain supremacy.

Rather than seek capital from wealthy Negroes, of whom there were few, Garvey appealed to the masses for small investments. They responded so enthusiastically that he found a movement on his hands. His glorification of the color black, as evidenced by his demands for a Black House as well as a White House, Black Cross nurses, etc., fostered intense nationalistic feeling and revived the "back to Africa" movement on a scale never remotely approached by other evangels of the idea.

The first national convention of the Universal Negro Improvement Association, held in New York City on August 1, 1920, was climaxed by a huge public meeting in Madison Square Garden. The delegates, "representatives of Negroes in all parts of the world," proclaimed their determination to elect "a world leader and a Negro leader of the United States and a provisional president of Africa." They also demanded "a constitution and bill of rights in the nation and of the Negro."

Garvey's UNIA found fertile soil in Chicago. In 1930, membership in the city is said to have totaled 7,500 while branches flourished in East St. Louis, Springfield, Mounds, Alton, Cairo, and other localities. William A. Wallace, later a state senator, gave up a thriving bakery business to head the Chicago movement.[2]

Garvey founded *The Negro World* as a house organ for the UNIA. The weekly, which attained a circulation of 75,000 or more, attacked as misleaders such prominent Negroes as Dr. W. E. B. Du Bois and Robert S. Abbott, of the *Chicago Defender*. Abbott, however, had a potent weapon in his own paper, and he was also skilled in the art of invective and in tough-and-tumble journalistic warfare. When Garvey bought a dilapidated excursion boat, the Yarmouth, and advertised it as the first vessel of the Black Star Line, the *Defender* made a sarcastic comparison to a similar ship purchased by a predecessor of Garvey, "Chief Sam" of Kansas, whose plans for setting up an independent Kingdom in Africa had gone awry, some said because of the antagonism of the British toward the venture, others alleging that "Chief Sam" was a fraud who had collected huge sums solely for his own enjoyment. Garvey held to the latter viewpoint, and filed a libel suit against Abbott demanding a million dollars to repair the damage to his character. Though he won a moral victory and finally was awarded one cent, Garvey was obliged to pay the court expenses.

Before the case was decided, Garvey announced his intention of invading Chicago. He rented the Eighth Regiment Armory and from its platform denounced Abbott more vigorously than before. At the close of the meeting he was arrested for selling stock in the Black Star Steamship Line in violation of the Illinois Blue Sky Law, which governed the sale of stock certificates and shares. Garvey later claimed that the arrest had been engineered by Abbott, who, he said, had arranged to have a detective in the guise of a prospective investor insist upon purchasing stock from the leader of the UNIA in order to incriminate him. Released on bail, Garvey departed from the city, never to return.[3]

The UNIA soon was beset by internal dissension. In 1920 there appeared in Chicago a white man named R. D. Jones, reputed to have been an organizer for the UNIA. With the assistance of a Negro, Grover Cleveland Redding, Jones organized the Abyssinian Movement. Since one of its principal aims was to facilitate the return of Negroes to Africa, not a few of the converts believed the two organizations were identical.[4]

On Sunday, June 20, 1920, Redding, astride a white horse and clad in what was supposed to be the costume of an Abyssinian prince, appeared on East 35th Street, leading a parade of his followers. At Prairie Avenue the procession halted while Redding produced an American flag, poured either liquor or gasoline over it, and set it afire. A Negro policeman rushed up to remonstrate, and was shot down by one of the Abyssinians. In the ensuing riot, a white sailor and a white shopkeeper were killed. Police later rounded up Jones, Redding, and another leader, and all three subsequently were hanged, though Jones tried to save himself by giving information about the movement. He said:

Redding has been sending out propaganda to the Negroes, not only in Chicago, but in other cities. He gives them a blank on which is printed "Star Order of Ethiopian and Ethiopian Missionary to Abyssinia." It is supposed to certify that the signer is in sympathy with our motherland Ethiopia, and henceforth denounces the name of Negro which is given him by another race, and that he is ready at any time to go back to Ethiopia to fill any position for which he is qualified.

During the trial Redding comported himself with a great deal more dignity than his white confederate, and resolutely and unrepentantly addressed the court:

My mission is marked in the Bible. Even if they have captured me, some other leaders will rise up and lead the Ethiopian back to Africa. The Bible says, "So shall the King of Assyria lead away the Egyptian prisoners and the Ethiopian captives, young and old . . . to the shame of Egypt." The Ethiopians do not belong here and should be taken back to their own country. Their time was up in 1919. They came in 1619. The Bible has pointed out that they were to appear in 300 years. The time is up. The burning of the flag last Sunday night by me was a symbol that Abyssinians are not wanted in this country. That was the sign the Bible spoke of.

Though Garvey, to evade legal entanglements and probable imprisonment, returned to Chicago no more after the Eighth Armory incident, his organization in the city and state continued to prosper. It reached its high point in 1925, when Garvey was sent to federal prison on a charge of using the mails to defraud. Thereafter, the UNIA was divided by recurring schisms. As late as 1938, there were six divisions in Chicago: The Garvey Club, Paston Research Society, Division No. 217, Isaiah Morter Division, Division No. 172, and the Peace Movement in Ethiopia.

According to the *Chicago Defender*, Isaiah Morter

> . . . was a wealthy native of British Honduras who died in 1924, leaving $25.00 to his widow and $300,000 to the U.N.I.A. The widow sued. The U.N.I.A. split. Fifteen years later, the courts awarded the money to a faction headed by a New York physician, to Mr. Garvey's great chagrin.

The Peace Movement of Ethiopia was formed originally to help the Ethiopians in the Italo-Ethiopian war of 1935–36, but when the conflict was over, the members, who had in the meantime separated into warring factions, carried on a nationalistic and "Back to Africa" campaign. Though all the Chicago organizations directly descended from the U.N.I.A. boasted a combined membership of less than a thousand members, they united in 1939 to sponsor enthusiastically a proposal by Senator Theodore ("The Man") Bilbo of Mississippi that Negroes desiring to go back to Africa should be speeded on their way with federal assistance. Three hundred lobbyists representing remnants of the Garvey legions proceeded from Chicago to Washington in trucks.

Mrs. M. M. L. Gordon, a Chicago leader of the Peace Movement of Ethiopia, was summoned before federal authorities on August 25, 1941, to answer to a charge of influencing young Negro men against registering for the draft. She denied this allegation, and asserted that the principal object of her organization was to return American Negroes to Liberia. She said that approximately 4,000,000 people were affiliated with the movement, all of them having signed petitions endorsing the Bilbo proposal. Abraham Lincoln and Thomas Jefferson, she pointed out, had recommended similar action. She went on:

> Those men knew the two races couldn't live together. And our race is dying out through amalgamation. There are 8,000,000 mulattoes in the United States now. Whites should remain white and black should remain black. Africa is our country and that's where we want to go—to the soil of Liberia.

Mrs. Gordon produced a letter from Edwin Barclay, President of Liberia, in which he said that the country "would welcome selected emigrants who were fitted for the pioneering life." "The Government should use the relief money now being spent on blacks here to transport all self-respecting blacks to Liberia," said Mrs. Gordon, herself on the relief rolls.

The 49th State Movement, launched in Chicago in 1933, is also an offspring of the U.N.I.A. Its avowed purpose is:

> To create and operate a National Movement throughout the United States . . . for the ultimate establishment of a new state in the United States wherein at least a portion of the Negroes can have an opportunity to work out their own economic, political and social

destiny unhampered and unrestrained by ruthless artificial barriers; wherein they can have a chance to raise the lot of their poor masses from exploitation, insecurity and wretchedness; wherein they can become respected, industrious and thrifty, self-governing, self-reliant and self-sustaining American citizens, always to be counted upon as an asset and as unfalteringly loyal to their country and a credit to all that is noblest and best in it. . . . [5]

The proponents of the forty-ninth state have made little progress in their efforts to develop enough pressure to persuade the United States to set up an all-Negro state whether within the present territorial limits of the nation or on land to be purchased from Mexico.

Speculation as to the effects of axis propaganda among American Negroes has been common, and a few organizations superficially suggest the presence of such activity. One such is the Iron Defense Legion, some of whose members dress in a uniform similar to that of Italian fascists or Nazi storm troopers. Along with demands for full representation in all branches of the government and the abolishment of "lynching and discriminatory practices," the Legion advocates "the teaching of military science and tactics." So far as is known, it operates only on Chicago's South Side, and there only to an extremely limited extent.

Much more ambitious was the African Pacific Movement of the Eastern World, the first Illinois appearance of which was in Cairo in the fall of 1934, when a Japanese and Negro from St. Louis, Missouri, talked so persuasively to a meeting of 250 Negroes that 150 of them joined on the spot.[6]

Though it was generally supposed that the Pacific Movement was designed to inculcate pro-Japanese sentiment in the minds of American Negroes, an examination of its by-laws and printed creed does not justify this belief. There are the usual generalities employed by fraternal order, and a cautious reference to "learning the people how to reform through constitutional methods." The members are also pledged "to encourage the people who find no opportunity for development in the United States and establish a government of their own in the land of their fathers." A Grand Captain General's duty was "to organize a military unit in every lodge with the drill manual and executions that will in no way conflict with the laws of our United States government."

A dues book and "charity card" issued in 1938 to an Illinois member from the National Office at 11 N. Jefferson St., St. Louis, Missouri, reveals that dues were 25 cents for "charity." D. D. Erwin was designated as National President, and F. P. Townsend as National Secretary.

The Japanese and Negro organizers established lodges in Mounds, East St. Louis, Pulaski and other places before they quarreled and parted ways in the spring of 1935. Meanwhile, National President George Cruz, a Filipino, was jailed in Arkansas on a fraud charge. It was reported that he had been collecting ten dollars from various people and promising them that the sum entitled to them passage to South America, where free land awaited them.

Though it is reported that the Japanese government has entertained a number of American Negroes in Japan, there is no evidence that the Pacific Movement had an official connection with such visits. Indications are that the movement ceased to function in 1938.

Two organizations striving to foster racial pride have attracted numbers of Chicago Negroes from time to time. These are the Moorish American Science Temple and the Nation of Islam, ordinarily referred to as "cults." Essentially they are religious bodies, opposing the Christian faith. Members of the Moorish American Science Temple insist that they are not Negroes, and avoid the use of the word or of "black" when referring to themselves, maintaining that they are really Moors and that their skin is "olive-hued." On the other hand, the Islamites not only call themselves Negroes but are proud of the name, contending that the Negro is "the original man." Neither endorses the "Back to Africa" Movement.

In 1925, a small Negro wearing a flaming red fez similar to those worn by Turks appeared in empty lots and on street corners of Chicago's South Side to proclaim a startling new doctrine. He was Noble Drew Ali, born Timothy Drew in North Carolina. Prophet of Islam, and founder of the Moorish American Science Temple. Little is known of Drew Ali's early history. He is reputed to have been an expressman in Newark, New Jersey, where he is said to have founded the first Moorish American Science Temple as early as 1913. There is also some evidence to indicate that he had established branches of his cult in Pittsburgh and Detroit before he came to Chicago.

Drew's main contention was that the people commonly known in America as Negroes are of Moorish descent and thus Asiatics. Act six of his "Divine Constitution and By-Laws" reads:

> With us all members must declare their nationally and their Divine Creed that they may know that they are a part and partial [sic] of this said government and that they are not Negroes, Colored Folks, Black People or Ethiopians, because these names were given to slaves, by slave holders in 1779 and lasted until 1865 during the time of slavery, but this is a new era of time now, and all men must proclaim their free national name to be recognized by the government in which they live and the nations of the earth, this is the reason why Allah the Great God of the universe ordained Noble Drew Ali, the prophet, to redeem his people from their sinful ways. The Moorish Americans are the descendants of the ancient Moabites who inhabited the North Western and South Western shores of Africa.

Prophet Noble Drew Ali did not immediately rally many disciples to his banner, the Moorish star and crescent on a field of red. But he persisted, and at length was able to set up permanent headquarters. Though semi-literate, he possessed an eloquent tongue, a persuasive manner, and a native shrewdness which enabled him to sway the poor and unlettered people who listened to him. Most of them remembered the race riots of 1919; all of them had experienced discrimination and other wrongs. Drew Ali was offering them pride of race and dignity. In 1927, a successful convention encouraged Drew Ali to expand his proselytizing activities to other cities. It is difficult to ascertain just how many temples resulted, but those in Pittsburgh; Detroit; Charleston, West Virginia; Lansing, Michigan; and Youngstown, Ohio are fairly well authenticated.

Drew Ali had written and published his "Koran," a slim pamphlet consisting of a curious mixture of the Mohammedan holy book of the same name, the Christian Bible, and anecdotes of the life of Jesus—the whole bound together with the Prophet's own pronouncements and interpretations. The Prophet began to do a profitable business in various nostrums and charms he had concocted, among them Old Moorish Healing Oil, Moorish Purifier Bath Compound, and Moorish Herb Tea for Human Ailments.

More and more "Asiatics" flocked to the star and crescent standard. They flaunted their fezzes on the street and treated the white man with undisguised contempt. The Prophet announced that each devout Moorish American must carry a card bearing his credentials and his real (or Asiatic) name, signed by the Prophet with his seal. Often enough "slave" names were transformed into "real" ones by the simple addition of "El" or "Bey," these being titles signifying Moorish dignity. The membership card and button, when displayed to Europeans, would convince them that the bearer was enlightened and a member of an organization to be feared and respected.

To the Prophet this theory of new-found independence had been a more or less purely ethical or theoretical point, and he had not reckoned on its practical effect among his zealous followers. Alarming reports of street brawls, threats, insults, and minor violence centering around Moorish Americans were brought to his notice. Members were accosting the white enemy on the streets, showing their membership cards and buttons, and proclaiming in the name of their Prophet, Noble Drew Ali, that they had been freed of European domination.

Recalling the downfall of the militant Abyssinians and contemplating the current difficulties of the Garvey movement, Drew Ali issued this ukase:

> I hereby warn all Moors that they must cease from all radical or agitating speeches while on their jobs, or in their homes, or on the streets. Stop flashing your cards before Europeans as this only causes confusion. We did not come to cause confusion; our work is to uplift the nation.

Drew Ali's leadership was soon contested. In 1929, he became embroiled in a quarrel with Claude Greene, politician and former butler of Julius Rosenwald, who previously had joined the temple. One day Drew arrived at his office to find that Greene had moved all the furniture outside and declared himself Grand Sheik. A civil war ensued, each faction enlisting support from temples in other cities. Greene was shot and stabbed to death in his offices at the Unity Club on the night of March 15, 1929.

Drew Ali, arrested as he sat with his wife and a group of followers celebrating (authorities charged) the murder of his rival, was defended by attorneys Aaron Payne and William L. Dawson, temple members who later gained political prominence. The Prophet, from prison, issued a message to his flock:

> To the Heads of All Temples, Islam:
> I, your Prophet, do hereby and now write you a letter as a warning and appeal to your good judgment for the present and the future. Though I am now in custody for you and the cause, it is all right and it is well for all who still believe in me and my father, God. I have redeemed all of you and you shall be saved, all of you, even with me. I go to bat Monday, May 20, before the Grand Jury. If you are with me, be there. Hold on and keep faith, and great shall be your reward. Remember my laws and love ye one another. Prefer not a stranger to your brother. Love and truth and my peace I leave all.
>
> Peace from
> Your Prophet
> Noble Drew Ali.

This proved to be Drew Ali's final official proclamation. Released on bond, he died under mysterious circumstances a few weeks later. One theory is that he succumbed to injuries inflicted by the police during his imprisonment, another is that he was set upon by partisans of Green after his release and beaten so severely that he never recovered.

After Drew Ali's death attorney Aaron Payne attempted unsuccessfully to hold the group together. Each among several of the Prophet's disciples announced that he alone was the rightful inheritor of Drew Ali's leadership. Steve Gibbons El (formerly the Prophet's chauffeur) and Ira Johnson Bey (who had been imported from Pittsburgh to assist in quelling the Greene revolt) each maintained that the dead leader's spirit had entered his body. Johnson, a man of action, invaded the office of Mealy El, another aspirant, and demanded recognition as grand sheik. Mealy El demurred and received a terrific mauling. Johnson then dispatched his henchmen to kidnap Kirkman Bey, who claimed possession of Drew Ali's last will and testament.

Kirkman's wife, secretly surmising that her husband was being detained in Johnson's apartment, directed the police thither. A gun battle ensued in which two policemen and one Moor were killed. Sixty-three Moors were arrested, and Johnson was committed to the State Hospital for the Criminally Insane, where he subsequently died. Steve Gibbons was also apprehended after he had forced his way into Attorney Payne's home in search of Drew Ali's papers.

Gibbons, too, was sent to the insane asylum, but was released several years later. In 1941, he was heading a Chicago temple on East 40th Street and still asserting claim to the title of Grand Sheik of all Moorish American Science Temples. Gibbons was one of six contestants, each one a temple leader and each one designating his own as Temple No. 1.

Services in each temple observe with minor deviations, the pattern established by Drew Ali. First, a minor sheik, a sheikess, or the chairman reads and explains Drew Ali's version of the *Koran*. Then follows a more elaborate discourse by the grand sheik (in some temples called the governor), the whole ceremony being punctuated at intervals by Christian hymns with the words Allah, Drew Ali, and Moslem substituted for God, Christ, and Christian. Friday is observed as a holy day of rest, "because on a Friday the first man departed out of the flesh and on a Friday the first man was formed in flesh and on a Friday the first man departed out of the flesh and ascended unto his father God Allah, for that cause Friday is the Holy Day for all Moslems all over the world."

Since Drew Ali considered Marcus Garvey his forerunner (in a relationship analogous to that of John the Baptist and Jesus) and paid tribute to him in his "Koran" and in his sermons, Moorish Americans frequently laud and quote the Jamaican organizer.

January 8, the Prophet's birthday, is a special occasion in all temples. Full Moorish regalia is worn by those members who can afford it, and there is likely to be feasting and distribution of gifts as in Christmas celebrations in Christian churches. A number of unconverted guests are invited; the customary speeches take on a more evangelistic tone. Expositions of the teachings and principles of the Prophet are offered in a simplified form for the benefit of those still under the influence of "The Folly" (Christianity).[7]

The leader of each of the bickering factions has striven in vain to build up an organization as powerful (and as lucrative) as the parent body disrupted by internal warfare and the death of Drew Ali. According to Attorney Aaron Payne, the Prophet in one year amassed a fortune of $36,000 and commanded a membership of 12,000. Politicians respected and courted him, and Congressman Oscar DePriest was reputed to have joined the temple.

The Asiatic black man is the original man, the ruler of the universe, the eight inhabited planets of this planet earth. Islam is the true religion. A religion which can be proved by mathematics in a limit of time.

The Moslems have the wisdom. We're not afraid of the devil, this so-called white man. We talk right up to them. They're afraid of you if you've got the Truth. Just tell 'em, "White man, you're a devil. You were grafted from the original black man." He'll say, "Yes, you're right." He'll admit it 'cause you got the power. Just say, "You're a beast, you've got one-third animal's blood." He won't deny it, 'cause it's true. When they were driven from the Holy City of Mecca, they lived in the Caves of Europe and mingled with the beasts.

Christianity is the religion of the so-called white man. Have you ever noticed that the very things he teaches us that the Devil does it, the very things *he* is doing? *He* is the Devil!

These quotations from a sermon by a minister of a Chicago Temple of Islam outline certain primary beliefs of the sect, founded in Detroit during 1930 by a Negro peddler named W. D. Fard, who presumably hailed from the orient. Fard, shortly after his appearance in Detroit, announced modestly:

I am W. D. Fard and I came from the Holy City of Mecca. More about myself I will not tell you yet, for the time has not yet come. I am your brother. You have not yet seen me in my royal robes.

He proclaimed that his mission was to secure "freedom, justice and equality" for his "uncle" living in "the wilderness of North America, surrounded and robbed completely by the cave man." Islamites soon employed "uncle" as a symbolical term for all Negroes of North America, while the white man was always referred to as "a cave man," a "Satan," or "Caucasian devil."

The Temple of Islam frequently found itself in conflict with the Detroit authorities. One zealot was involved in a ritual murder, and Islam parents refused to send their children to the "white devil's" schools, preferring the University of Islam where "righteous" learning was imparted. At the university, children were taught Moslem knowledge to enable them to cope with the "tricknollogy" of the Caucasians. The Board of Education intervened; the Moslems retaliated with minor riots. Sensational newspaper accounts so far magnified these incidents that the Nation of Islam assumed the proportions of a serious menace to peace and was labeled "the voo-doo cult."

Temple of Islam Number Two was established in Chicago sometime late in 1933 or during the early part of 1934. At about the same time, Fard vanished from Detroit and, if available records are to be credited, has not been seen since. Many of his followers, identifying Fard with Allah, maintained that he had returned to Mecca, the Islam heaven, whence he came. Fard, according to report, helped Elijah Muhammad to organize Temple No. 2 in Chicago, bestowing "righteous" (i.e., "original") names upon eight hundred new Moslems.

Like the Moorish American Science Temple, the Temple of Islam has been torn by internal dissension, a rival group having been established in 1935 by one of the original Temple ministers shortly after the first Chicago prophet, Elijah Muhammad, departed to spread the gospel of Islam in other localities. Since then Elijah's movements, like those of Fard, have been the subject of almost pure conjecture. Elijah Muhammad's son, Emmanuel

Muhammad, assumed charge on the eve of the Temple of Islam's serious encounter with the police. A street car quarrel participated in by a moslem woman led to a battle in the Woman's Court, with Islamites determined to "stand by their sister." Two Moslems were wounded by gunfire, and forty-three persons were placed under arrest. A newspaper account confused the Temple of Islam with the Moorish American Science Temple and W. D. Fard with Noble Drew Ali.

Services of the temple are based upon manuals prepared by Prophet Fard. Only one of these, *Teachings for the Last Found Nation of Islam in a Mathematical Way, Consisting of Thirty-four Problems*, is printed. *Secret Ritual of the Nation of Islam, Part I, in 14 Secs*, and *Secret Ritual of the Nation of Islam, Part II, in 40 Secs*, must be memorized by each member, and no written copies are in evidence.

These manuals, being largely symbolic, are practically unintelligible to outsiders. The first consists of thirty-four "problems," several of which are read to the congregation at each formal service. This is a typical example:

"A lion, in a cage, walks back and forth sixty feet per minute, seeking a way out of the cage. It took him nearly four centuries to find the door. Now, with modern equipment, he is walking three thousand feet per minute and he has three thousand miles by two thousand miles to go yet. How long will it take him to cover this territory of said three thousand miles by two thousand miles? He also has seventeen million keys, which he turns at the rate of sixteen and seventeen one-hundredth per minute. How long will it take him to turn the whole seventeen million? The above figures do not include rusty locks."

A "registered Moslem" has disclosed that the lion in the cage is the "original man," or Asiatic, held in bondage for four centuries within a trap fabricated by the "Caucasian devil." The seventeen million keys represent a like number of "Asiatics" held in bondage in the "wilderness of North America." "Modern equipment" is the teachings of Islam by which the "original man" progresses rapidly toward emancipation. Rusty locks are recalcitrant "originals" who have not yet accepted Islam.

A few rules for the guidance of temple people, chosen from a list including one for each letter of the alphabet, are:

All persons entering the Temple must be searched—products of the Caucasian devil's art, such as weapons, mirrors, fingernail files, cosmetics, cigarettes, medicines etc., must not be taken into the temple.

Moslems must eat only one meal a day, orange juice or cocoa in the morning, and a big meal at 4 o'clock. The eating of pork and the use of alcohol and tobacco is forbidden.

Moslems fast 18 days per year. Ministers and officials fast three or four days a week.

A Moslem must not cross his legs while seated in the Temple, and a ninety day suspension is given for sleeping during a service.

A Moslem's mother's dress must cover her feet, and Moslem women must wear low heel shoes, a hat covering her hair, and must not use hair preparations or cosmetics.

No Caucasian ever may be permitted to enter the Temple. The "righteous" weight for Moslem men is 150 pounds.

A Moslem woman's place is in the home. A girl must be accompanied by her father or brother.

A follower must attend the Islam University three to nine months and master the teachings to become a Moslem.

"Registered Moslems" maintain that the "white devil's spook civilization" actually ended in 1914, and is now existing on borrowed time. Temple ministers sketch on a blackboard a strange device, apparently designed to represent a new planet discovered by Elijah Muhammad, and explains:

This is the Mother's Airplane, the wheel in a wheel, that Elijah saw. This planet is visible at 3 a.m. . . . it moves a little forward, then a little backwards and then goes straight up. There are 15,000 planes coming out of the Mother's Airplane . . . these planes will drop pamphlets to the earth warning the people of the "Holy War." On one of these planes there will be a black brother (Moslem) who will blow a siren . . . it will be blown by steam and some of our eardrums will burst when it sounds, but it won't be no trumpet. When the siren sounds, there will be a brother on every corner who will tell you to run—so run! Don't stop—because it may take you eight days. Don't go back home, if you have a wife and child . . . there will be a brother there to look after them. The planes will drop bombs with steel points that will go a mile into the earth. Each bomb will destroy fifty square miles. The earth will be turned up and will be a lake of fire and Allah will cut a circuit and start a fire in the air. This planet is forty miles in the air and the people that inhabit it are black people. The Caucasian devil can only go six miles up in the air. The black man controls gravity.

Temple members are emphatic in their denunciations of Roosevelt and the New Deal. In their opinion, the WPA and all other alphabetical agencies are subtle efforts on the part of the white man to save what is left of his dying civilization by getting the black man to sign up with him and be given a number. They eschew social security numbers and relief case numbers as manifestations of the "white devil's" aptitude in "Tricknollogy." "Roosevelt," reads a piece of typewritten temple literature, "gave you a social security number just to hold you and now he's getting ready to call these numbers and give you a stamp. . . . He's going to put a stamp on you, the mark of the beast. You signed up with the devil and he gives you the filthy crumbs from his table like the rich man gave Lazarus."

The most recent and most vociferous exponent of "Africa for the Africans" has been *Negro Youth*, a magazine established in New York in April 1941 and purporting to be the mouthpiece of such organizations as the "National Organization of Negro Youth," the "Afro-American Consumers Economic Union, "The Afro-American Institute of Research, Technology and Culture," and the "Black Legions of the Nile." The latter organization pleaded for "500,000 black men who are not afraid to die! To secure the eternal existence of African people and carry freedom, liberty, and independence to African people in all lands." *Negro Youth* specialized in sensational denunciations of mulattoes ("half-breed mongrels"), with emphasis on their sexual behavior and relations with white people, strangely reminiscent of the pornography dispensed by German fascists.

Funds were solicited for scholarships to be awarded to "outstanding youth, sending them to the best universities in the world, including Japan." Samuel W. Daniels, "Co-ordinator of the Pan-African Republics," says: "Hitler evidently calls the black man a 'dressed up ape' because most of them act like apes. They mimic all the things that men of other races do that are destructive to their racial character and honor." Marcus Garvey, who "trusted and was betrayed by mulattoes," was given credit for the only "bold and realistic attempt by a man who really loved black people to give them proper leadership."

Maintaining that "if one drop of black blood makes a person a 'Negro,' one drop of white blood makes a person a Caucasian." *Negro Youth* vehemently condemned Dr. W. E. B. Du Bois of Atlanta University for frustrating the noble and practical efforts of the late honorable Marcus Garvey through the commands of his (Du Bois's) white fathers and masters." A campaign for " . . . ships to facilitate trade between Black America, Haiti, and Liberia" and "to enable those black men and women who so desire to settle in Haiti and Liberia" was announced.

Marcus Garvey died in London in 1940. In 1938 he had advertised in his magazine *The Black Man* for 1,000 students for his "School of African Philosophy" in that city. The Republic of Liberia, original haven of "Back to Africa" converts, some were saying, was owned by an American rubber company. Garvey's actual following had dwindled to a handful, but his influence had been immeasurable. Hundreds of enterprising "organizers" have used the movements springing directly or ideologically from the U.N.I.A. as meal tickets. Some of them would make Garvey's nationalistic fervor seem feeble indeed.

25. And Churches

This chapter is to be distinguished from chapter nine, "Churches," this one differing in that it covers storefront churches and "cults." In the IWP papers, there is a chapter fragment labeled first draft. There is also a longer twenty-one-page draft written by Arna Bontemps at both the Harsh Research Collection and Newberry Library, which is the one that appears below.

The great numbers of southern Negroes whose migration to Illinois began with the last World War, to fill the numerous jobs vacated by homing nationals of belligerent powers, came mainly to Chicago, largest industrial center of the country. They were prompted to the move as much by hope of better social, political and educational opportunities as by promise of good jobs at living wages. Deeply religious, they brought their habits of worship with them, overflowed the assisting churches, and established many others; indeed, in some instances, virtually whole congregations entrained for "The Promised Land" and upon arrival reestablished their churches in the northern metropolis. Among the migrating thousands were many adherents of the old-line, established orders, Methodists and Baptists notably, but there were great numbers also who instituted new denominations, distinctly unorthodox in the opinion of citizens of longer residence in the community. Although the standard faiths gained many new communicants and the number of their members far exceeds that of the less conventional orders, the latter are today an established part of the new picture of the religious scene and a colorful phenomenon of the period.

Preceding the beginning of the mass hegira to Illinois and Chicago, migrants settling in the state had selected one or another among the orthodox faiths and had been absorbed quietly; but the tremendous influx about the middle of the second decade of the present century swamped the existing facilities and resulted in the mushroom growth of scores of "storefront" churches wherein the less educated faithful could feel at home and play a part in the life of the congregation denied them in the properly housed, decorous homes of God—many of whom by the time had forgotten their own storefront beginnings. However, several new standard churches were born during the Great Migration, among them Monumental Baptist Church, Liberty Baptist Church, Allen Temple A.M.E., Pilgrim Baptist, Grant Memorial A.M.E., and Progressive Baptist Church. In addition, during the period from the start of world war one to date, churches of a number of other established faiths were added to the orthodox list; and the independent churches too multiplied in the latter years of the nearly three decades since 1914.

Storefronts had a special appeal for common people, who came from small communities where everyone knew his neighbor and where the church was the political forum, school, social center, and spiritual guide. The 'fronts have become notable for several unusual features that distinguish them from the more familiar standard churches. Two of their characteristics are the unique names they flaunt and the type of music they sing and play. Willing Workers Spiritualist Church, Israel of God Church, St. John A.M.E. Church, Spiritual Love Circle, Blessed St. Martin Church, Peter's Rock Baptist Church, Prophetic Spiritual Church, Purple Rose Mystical Temple, Crossroads to Happiness, Followers of Exodus, and Church of Lost Souls are names of a random list.[1] Their music is known as Gospel music; choirs are composed of loud, untrained voices whose spirited vocalizing does justice to revival songs and spirituals. In standard churches the music and singing is quite different.

An undeclared religious war exists between the two types of churches. Controversy centering around the issue has become so bitter and widespread that the storefront has assumed an importance it would not have had ordinarily. Many citizens of the community have expressed themselves on the matter; the pros contend that they are homier and a good influence, the cons that they are disseminators of superstition and little better than rackets. A recent study of Chicago's Negro churches on the south side shows that most of the storefronts are located in areas north of Forty-Seventh and west of State Street; their segregation in this territory is attributed to cheap rentals in the least lucrative business districts. Storefronts are usually small and intimate as regards membership. There are about thirty-nine members on an average to each church. Latest surveys show that they attract Negroes from the entire colored community and not only from the surrounding neighborhood. In the area known as the Woodlawn territory, the storefront church is almost non-existent; only one is found there.

In all there are about two hundred fifty storefronts within Chicago's Negro neighborhood on the south side, and they are representative of fifty or more unconventional religious groups to which about eight thousand members of the race belong, at least nominally. The number of active participants at any given time is probably much smaller. Because their forms of worship and their beliefs in certain respects differ from the accepted and traditional religious mores, members of these unorthodox sects generally are designated as cultists.

The several "sanctified" Negro sects in Chicago have established more storefronts and enlisted a larger number of members than any of the other unconventional denominations, and have also erected some substantial edifices housing large numbers of followers. Other congregations, some affiliated with more conventional churches (such as the Baptist), likewise occupy store rooms in the blighted districts and share certain beliefs and practices with sanctified and spiritualist worshippers, including "speaking in tongues," shouting and physical manifestations induced by seizure by the "holy spirit," divine healing, magic, and more rarely communication with the dead.

There have been sanctified churches in Chicago since the beginning of the present century, the Church of the Living God and the Church of God in Christ having been organized before 1900. However, in 1919, long after migration from the South had brought large numbers of Negroes to the city, only 20 Holiness (or sanctified) churches had been established. By 1928 this number had grown to 56, and 19 percent of all Negro church members were affiliated with the faith. In 1938 the number had increased to 107 and the percentage to 22.8. There are several denominations, large and small, among the churches sharing a common belief in the "sanctification of man on earth."

Services in the sanctified churches are conducted by a Presiding Elder, the title being similar to that of Father in the Roman Catholic Church and that of Reverend in most Protestant denominations. Very few of the elders have graduated from grade school, and a great many of them can neither read nor write. This educational lack, however, is thought by some elders and communicants to be a blessing in disguise, because illiterate "saints" are held to be endowed with a gift permitting them not only to perceive every word in the *Bible* [but] to interpret it correctly. They contend that the literate [are] ungodly, beguiled and confused by such frivolous reading as is contained in newspapers and man-written books, [and can] never gain a clear understanding of that one essential volume. The basic philosophy of the sanctified churches is nearly identical with that of the orthodox Christian churches, but it places a literal interpretation upon certain passages regarded by the latter as purely historical. The "saints" often burst forth into unintelligible gibberish during the violent emotional displays typifying Holiness services. These utterances are said to emanate from the Holy Spirit through the unwitting lips of the speaker.

Not a few Holiness churches have preaching every night in the week, the services often lasting four hours or more. In addition to the regular Sunday services, prayer or "tarry" meetings for the purpose of accelerating the sanctification of candidates are conducted. "Refilling" services are held to revive the potency of the Holy Ghost in saints who may be wavering a bit. Healing services are rather unusual because they offer the elder his severest test and demand the exercise of his greatest mental agility. When the miracle does not occur, an inevitable explanation is that the afflicted one did not have faith enough or was too full of sin. The mere presence of skeptics in the audience, according to the elders, is sufficient to thwart the healing power of the Holy Ghost.

Perhaps the best known Holiness church in Chicago is that presided over by Reverend Clarence H. Cobbs, the First Church of Deliverance, whose regularly Sunday night radio broadcast—featured by the singing of accomplished soloists and choir, accompanied by a "swing" electric organ—is heard by thousands, white as well as black. Reverend Cobbs, whose appeal is to the "boys and girls in the streets and taverns" as well as to persons more respectably located, conducts annually a candle-lighting service, a unique and striking ceremony always largely attended.[2]

Another denomination that gained many adherents following the Great Migration is the spiritualist churches, practically unknown before 1920 but numbering 17 churches in 1928 (3.8 percent of the total of Negro churchgoers) and 51 in 1938 (10.7 percent). A majority of the Negro spiritualist churches of Chicago are of the storefront variety, although a few have progressed beyond that state and attract large congregations. Because of the comparative decorum ordinarily observed in their meetings—as compared with the vociferousness of Holiness and "shouting" Baptist services—the spiritualists are enabled to meet in settled, more affluent areas. Such gatherings sometimes, however, are likely to be held in private homes and take on the intimate character of neighborhood clubs. Not a few pursue their explorations into the occult as purely commercial ventures.

There are no denominational affiliations between the various spiritualist groups, although in 1938 "Pope" Davis of California made an attempt to unite them, with himself as the Holy See. Each church has its leader who defines its articles of faith, and all subscribe to the basic belief in prophecy and "communication of the spirit." Only a few churches venture to materialize the spirits; the unusual procedure is to relay the message quite prosaically through a medium of whom even the smaller churches customarily have several. The spirits, when contact is established, may divulge valuable information concerning policy tickets, lost articles, marital fidelity, or any other problem vexing the human mind or heart. Mediums often anticipate, even demand, a "gift" or "love offering," pointing out a number of the congregation to inform him a communication for him has been received from the spirit world. This news being accompanied by an offer to interpret the message. "Communications" may be ordered in advance. Divine healing is a major article of the spiritualist faith. The healing is not effected by prayer alone, but by the laying on of hands, rubbing, and the use of magnetized articles such as flowers, candles, oil, marble chips, and anointed handkerchiefs. True believers are admonished to have no faith in doctors, but to rely on these articles instead. If the church is an abandoned store, its windows are likely to be decorated with holy wares, such as miniature alters, necklaces, medallions, and bracelets bearing the crucified figure of Christ, flanked by placards announcing the sale of "blessed candles," "lucky incense," etc.

In the First Community Church, probably the most elaborate Negro spiritualist institution in Chicago, the choir is led by women wearing nuns' black raiment surmounted by cowls, who lead the white-robed singers in a procession down the aisles preceding the minister's entrance. The latter, attired in a purple velvet robe, white surplice, and priest's headgear, carries in his hand a long baton from which depends a small cross as he marches down the aisle to kneel before the altar and cross himself. Officers and worshippers make similar obeisance upon entering the church. Other phases of the service take a more practical turn. At one point, it is the duty of the assistant minister to solicit fees for "reading," and when at times members display indifference toward tidings from the spirit world she offers special inducements in the way of rate reductions or the promise of revelations more significant than common. "You know, dear ones," she announced on one occasion, "our money has been kinda short. I don't want to be scoldful or no ways fretful, but sometimes we gotta wash down kinda hard. Now all those who gave me fifteen cents raise your hands and Sister Cross will come around and read you."

There are in Chicago at least two schools for the training of Negro mediums. One of these is conducted by Father Morris of the Independent Church of God and Power Center, venerated by his followers as divine Messiah and (on special occasions) a reincarnation of the pre-Mosaic Hebrew priest and king of Salem, Melchisedec. Professor Perry Jones, Father Morris's most successful graduate, now heads his own School of Metaphysics in conjunction with the Inspirational Church and Power Center. The elder teacher one Sunday deplored the irregular practice of a majority of his colleagues: "Ninety-eight percent of all spiritualists are making a regular gambling, voodoo, witchcraft, backbiting, policy number game of it. They play the numbers and give them to their customers, claiming that success will come. They are also the greatest agency for breaking up homes and friendships in existence. All of these things are done under the name of spiritualism!"

[Here sections on the Moorish American Science Temple and Nation of Islam were moved to the previous chapter.]

Numerous minor cults have sprung up in Chicago, but most of them have been short lived. There are also branches of international organizations, such as the "I am" movement, which conducts a Negro section in a South Side storeroom. Father Divine's "Angels" have set up half a dozen or more heavens. The Ahmadiyya Movement in Islam maintains a Chicago mosque, but unlike the other two non-Christian cults above noted entertains no enmity toward the white man.

One more major group of churches, considered another form of cult, is the Pentecostal denomination. Perhaps the most famous preacher of the order is Elder Lucy Smith, a huge black woman who boasts of being the only member of her sex in Chicago ever to have built a church from the ground up; unlike most other church edifices of the race in the district, hers was not purchased from whites. Human sympathies of preachers were typified by Elder Smith in 1932 when she sat up a soup kitchen to feed hundreds of unemployed workers. For six months, over ninety persons daily were fed in her kitchen. Both races were seated at the table, the beneficent elder insisting that no difference be made because of color. Described as a simple, ignorant, untrained but deeply sympathetic woman who believes absolutely in her power to help and heal others, her congregation consists largely of new arrivals from the South and those Negroes who have not and probably never will become urbanized. They are persons of little or no formal education, mostly day laborers, domestic servants, WPA workers, and relief clients. Elder Smith's church for a time broadcast on the air an hour of its Sunday night's service.

As has been stated, although the cults attract a good deal of notice because of their striking unconventionality and hectic vicissitudes, the old-line churches and denominations are still dominant in the religious field. But in contrast to both the latter and the sects, or cults, is a third classification, the independent churches, a number of which were established in the period in protest against what the dissenters considered outmoded forms of unprogressive leadership. The movement was crystallized definitely with the revolt of Dr. W. D. Cook from the African Methodist Episcopal Church to find a community church. On the first Sunday of its existence, the new church attracted a hundred persons. Now at 41st Street and South Parkway, Dr. Cook's organization boasts one of the best-known choirs in the world, called the "radio and prize winning choir," under the direction of Wesley Jones. Officers of the church are a group of intelligent, vigorous men; and the Sunday night forum is outstanding.

Today there are about a dozen independent churches in the colored district of Chicago, the leading ones pastured by Dr. J. C. Winters and by Dr. J. Russel Harvey. This independent movement is a terror to established churches, according to Harold M. Kingsley, head of Good Shepherd Church, a notable member of the group. The leading churches of the new movement, states Kingsley, are St. Thomas P.E., St. Edmunds P.E., Grace Presbyterian and Hope Presbyterian, Lincoln Memorial Congregation, and Michigan Avenue Congregational.

The Good Shepherd Church and its pastor are good examples of the modern independent trend.[3] A practical, positive, and aggressive churchman, Kingsley's emphasis is on the virtue and the value of labor and character. "He is not a religious genius," says

Herbert Morrisson Smith. "Instead he strikes one as a social engineer. His sermons do not discuss the golden streets of the New Jerusalem. He is more concerned with the challenge of the slums and dives of Chicago. The fact that men of this type and temper are so few and far apart in the religious history of Black America makes them all the more valuable and significant when they do appear." Kingsley serves mainly a congregation of professional and upper strata people. Good Shepherd Church has been criticized by Negroes who assert the color line is drawn within the organization, because the great majority of the members are fair skinned, as is the pastor, and they control and direct the activities of the church.

An interesting classification of Negro churches has been outlined by Reverend Kingsley; although the groupings are arbitrary, they are clear cut. Each of the types mentioned has played a role in the life of the colored community.

1. The old line churches: the established Methodist and Baptist churches of the traditional type, all of which have permanent church buildings.
2. The storefront and house-front churches, of which there are 178 out of 278 churches in Chicago. These churches are usually transitory and without deep root in the community, a case of the blind leading the blind.
3. Liturgical churches: the Roman Catholic, the Lutheran, and the Protestant Episcopal.
4. The fringe churches: holiness, spiritualist, and various eastern cults such as the Mohammedan Temple, Moorish cult, and others. Most of this group are thinly camouflaged with religion for exploitation purposes.
5. So-called "intellectual" churches: those which have a rationally expressed application of Christianity, of which the Congregational and Presbyterian are types.

The standard churches of the Negro community have engaged in numerous activities besides ministering to the spiritual needs of the race in Chicago. They have played a leading part of forwarding social and political movements. Two of the many projects sponsored by them are the Young Men's and Young Women's Christian Associations, which furnished healthful recreation and residence to thousands of young Negro men and women arriving in Chicago from the South during the Great Migration and later.

Numerous churches interested themselves in politics and candidates especially during the early twenties, when the Negro's political power was increasing rapidly. Certain ministers in return for services rendered received appointments to state and local offices paying handsome salaries, or dictated appointments of loyal followers. Many churches frankly used their pulpits as forums for rival candidates to plead their causes. The minister frequently played one candidate against the other and endorsed the one making the best bargain. Negroes followed the judgment of their pastors in such matters without question. In several notable instances whole blocks of votes were directly controlled by ministers. In certain mayoralty elections these votes determined the victor.

Other activities of the church were noted by the *Chicago Daily News*, July 12, 1929:

Institutional Negro churches are an important factor in aiding the Negro to take his adjustments to Chicago life. There are several such congregations outstanding and equally meritorious.

Possibly the Olivet Baptist Church affords as good an illustration as any of their gradual development not from a theory but from a condition.

This church literally ministers to the material need of its parishioners from the cradle to the grave, nothing less. It maintains prenatal classes for the instruction of expectant mothers. It has established an undertaking service to reduce the high cost of Christian burial.

One form of service has led to another. The pastor, the Reverend L. K. Williams, came to Chicago for studies at the University of Chicago and to write a book. He remained to carry the burden of a parish into which flowed the tide of northward migration. First he set about finding suitable lodging for the newcomers, who were mostly men. That they might pay for their lodging he established an employment bureau, helping them get jobs. That accomplished, the Negro men brought their families, who ultimately required co-operative apartments. Their daughters needed jobs, and that they might fill them well a training school was launched. To establish the new Chicago financially, that they might pay for the homes found for them, thrift was preached and the financing of Anthony Overton's new famous bank. "Don't think that from all this we neglect worship," says the pastor. "We have plenty of 'rousement' and I think at one of services even one who believes as little as our good friend Clarence Darrow would be 'roused.'"

The depression which began in 1929 found great numbers of the race turning to other agencies for aid, however. Reverend Kingsley has asserted, "The state of a man's soul has some relationship to the kind of living standards, the kind of opportunity that he and his children have. The aesthetic, the political, the social, the economic have a very vital and inseparable connection with the religious. The religious expression of a group's life is not going to be much higher than these other expressions." The church, largely unprepared for the unprecedented catastrophe that followed the market crash, stood helplessly by while other organizations lured away a sizable portion of its membership.

Although economic conditions have propelled masses of Negroes toward civic organizations, political groupings, social service agencies, and labor organizations, the colored community yet maintains approximately 500 churches, half of them storefronts. About 75,000 Negroes attend one or another of the vast variety of religious institutions. The Baptists lead the field, with the Methodists second, and Holiness churches embracing the third largest number of communicants. As has been shown, Protestant orders vie with Catholic, independents with cults, and edifices range from white stone fronts to storefronts, while staidly sophisticate congregations contrast with wildly emotional. Both the independent churches and the cults are an expression of the religious seeking of masses of Negroes whose spiritual needs and daily problems are unsatisfied by the standard denominations. As enumerated by Kingsley, the "fringe" movement comprises esoteric theosophical, Cultural Unity and New Thought, elevated Bahaism, yearning Christian Science and Holy Roller, non-descript store-fronters, Primitive Baptists (once in Christ never out); and there may be added to these the many semi-social, semi-economic, semi-political religious organizations, and burial, fraternal, and uplift societies, as well as eastern mystical cults, genuine Mohammedanism and denatured oriental philosophy thinly disguised for exploitation purposes. And in addition there are the jogi and swami.

Recognizing the weakened position of the conventional church in Negro life, the *Chicago Defender*, leading race organ, in an editorial published September 6, 1941, reviewed its history, stated the conditions in which it finds itself currently, and indicated the role it must assure to regain its former influence.

The Negro church has played a memorable role in the cultural development of the Negro race in the United States. Out of meager resources, schools of various categories and grades have been built and maintained with a view to securing better economic opportunities for the masses. Our early church leaders did not limit their activities to spiritual redemption. They were equally concerned with the economic salvation of their people. They fought in and out of church for the observance of the political tenants for which sacrifice in blood was made by the founders of this republic. No one, therefore, who is familiar with this phase of our evolution would cast aspersions on the past leadership of the Negro church.

The present state of muddled world affairs, the titanic conflict of forces with divergent concepts, the attacks upon democracy and the confusion of aims and purposes that grows out of a Fascist challenge, lead us to inquire what the Negro church of today is doing to advance the thinking of its followers and channel their action. Here and there isolated ministers with courage and intelligence have plunged into the stream of social action, often without the support of their congregations. Such individual acts, however laudable, are not enough. The moment calls for collective, unified action by the Negro church as a whole.

With its splendid tradition and moral prestige born of the battles it has won in behalf of the race, our church should be able and willing to grasp the unusual opportunity presented by the crisis of the hour, and produce a dynamic, progressive leadership capable of bringing order out of chaos. The church should not be content to follow. It should lead.

CHAPTER TWENTY-FIVE

26. Literature

There are three drafts of this chapter in the IWP papers at the Harsh Research Collection, including the most recent version which appears here. One labeled "2nd Draft" has Jack Conroy's name on the first page, indicating he was the author of the chapter. There is a fifty-three-page draft with corrections in Conroy's handwriting. This was reduced to a twelve-page final draft, copies of which are also at Syracuse University and Newberry Library. Earlier writings on African American literature in Illinois were drawn upon. One was an essay by Fenton Johnson written for a booklet prepared for the American Negro Exposition in 1940. Also utilized was a lengthy series of writings by Katherine "Kitty" de la Chapelle, including the essay "Development of Negro Culture in Chicago" and several manuscripts under the heading "Colored Culture in Chicago" that were produced between May 1937 and June 1938.

The Cairo (Illinois) *Bulletin* noted in 1875 that

> . . . the colored people of a literary turn of mind, of Charlestown, Missouri, have a flourishing debating society; and now a number of the young colored people of Cairo, not wishing to be outdone in this respect, are organizing an institution of the same kind.

Actually, the Illinois Negro's interest in literature had been recorded almost a decade before the Civil War by the organization of the Chicago Literary Society. It passed resolutions condemning the Fugitive Slave Law, assisted in resistance to colonizers and kidnappers, and sent a number of its members to fight with the Union Army for emancipation. None of the books, pamphlets, and impassioned handbills written and distributed by these pioneers achieved permanent recognition, but one must bear in mind it was not until 1889 that the right of colored children to attend public schools in Illinois was finally affirmed by an act of the legislature. Indeed, equal facilities have not yet been made available. The Negro's cultural development after the Civil War was rapid, but the color problem, perforce, has engaged the Negro writers' attention, not necessarily to the detriment of his art, but inevitably to the limitation of its scope.

Prior to 1861, there had been thirty-five works of Afro-American authorship published and sold in the United States; at the time of the World's Columbian Exposition in 1893 more than one hundred had been issued. A number of these were written by Illinoisans or by men and women who had lived in the state at one time or another.

John Sella Martin, the first Negro writer in Illinois to emerge from anonymity, born a slave, made his way in 1856 from New Orleans to Chicago. He soon figured as a popular lecturer and contributor of prose and poetry to the press. His poem, "The Hero and the Slave," for years enjoyed a favored position on the repertoires of public entertainers. Martin Robinson Delany, an examining surgeon with the United States Army in Chicago during the Civil War, had written for the *Anglo-African* several chapters of an unfinished novel, *Blake, or the Huts of America*, one of the first works of fiction essayed by an American Negro, and several scholarly treatises.

The era marked by the World's Columbian Exposition, which opened in 1893 on Chicago's lake front, ushered in a new trend among Negro writers. Hitherto, they had had little time for training in such literary forms as poetry, fiction, and the essay (other than political tracts). Biographies of slaves, who had escaped from bondage, predominated their writing for many years, while orations which could be comprehended by illiterate listeners and later printed for the more leisurely contemplation of readers were in demand. Frederick Douglass attended the Columbian Exposition as a representative of the Haitian government, to which he formerly had been assigned as United States minister. Foremost race champion and still regarded by many as the greatest of American Negroes, the leonine orator was also a powerful writer. His biographical volumes, *Narrative of Frederick Douglass, My Bondage and My Freedom*, and *The Life and Times of Frederick Douglass*, are believed to have played a definite role in the liberation of his people. Another representative writer-orator, Richard T. Greener, moved to Chicago after 1907. First Negro graduate of Harvard, Greener was an implacable adversary of Douglass on the question of mass migration of Negroes from the South. His best-known oration is *Charles Sumner*, published in Charleston, South Carolina, in 1874.

Three talented Negro poets living in Chicago during the final decade of the last century were leading figures in a departure from the escaped slave and orator schools. These were Paul Lawrence Dunbar, James Edwin Campbell, and James David Corrothers.

Dunbar, who assisted Douglass at the Exposition's Haitian exhibit, had published at his own expense *Oak and Ivy*, the traditional "slender sheaf" of verse, a short time before. Many of the poems therein, including "Ode to Ethiopia" and "Columbia Ode," were reprinted in his third volume, *Lyrics of a Lowly Life* (1896). Dunbar's first paid work was a prose composition in the *Chicago Record*. His stay in the city was short, but the period was a productive one in building a foundation for the poet's subsequent eminence.

James Edwin Campbell, an Ohioan by birth, was a Chicago newspaper man in the late 1880s and early 1890s, and was also associated with the *Four O'Clock Magazine*, a literary publication which survived several years. Most of Campbell's better verse was written in Gullah dialect, though his later work somewhat resembles that of Dunbar, whom he probably knew. Campbell was a rather prolific writer, but only one book, *Echoes from the Cabin and Elsewhere*, published posthumously in 1905, resulted from his activities.

The third of the triumvirate, James David Corrothers, of Cherokee Indian, Scotch-Irish, French and African blood, was born in Michigan in 1869. After a varied career as saw mill and lumber camp worker, sailor, coachman, janitor, bootblack, and Northwestern University student, Corrothers settled down to a sedentary and reflective life as a preacher and writer. His *The Black Cat Club*, a book of sketches originally printed in Chicago newspapers, appeared in 1907, and was followed by two books of poetry, *Selected Poems* (1907) and *The Dream and the Song* (1914), and he had an autobiography, *In Spite of Handicap* (1916). A number of Corrothers's poems appeared in *The Century*—following several of Dunbar's and attracted considerable attention. Corrothers's dialect verse is patterned closely on that of Dunbar, of whom he wrote appreciatively.

Following the three dialect poets of the 1890s to Chicago, William H. A. Moore symbolizes a departure from versifiers of the "mocking bird" school, so-called because they sedulously imitated the ideology and even the subject matter of white masters. Dunbar, though indubitably more versatile and more forthright than any of his predecessors, had derived some of the attitudes of Thomas Nelson Page and Irwin Russell, white apologists for the antebellum culture of the South.

Technically, Moore's verse is in the conventional mold, yet it reflects themes universal in appeal. He stood at the portal of the new world of Negro poetry—a more sophisticated, deeper, broader, stronger world—though he did not enter therein. One small volume, *Dusk Songs*, is Moore's only tangible moment.

Fenton Johnson, born in 1888, a native of Chicago, was the first Negro employing the free verse medium to attain wide recognition.[1] He is also worthy of note for his almost complete break with the past of Negro poetry, although he had published three volumes, *A Little Dreaming* (1912), *Visions of the Dusk* (1915), and *Songs of the Soil* (1916), in the traditional manner and including some dialect pieces, before his acerbic series appeared in Alfred Kreymborg's magazine, *Others*. These poems expressed passionately the bitterness, disillusionment and despair of sensitive members of the race, and their fatalistic hopelessness startled a sedate public conditioned to the soothing melodies of the "mocking birds." Thus far no Negro poet had given voice in vivid concretized verse sketches to such brutal, inescapable facts.

A great many Negro writers, like their brethren the world over, have convinced themselves that commercial publishers seldom recognize talent in its nascent stages or, if they do, are loath to develop it. Consequently, periodicals dedicated to the encouragement of "mute, inglorious Miltons" and Hemingways-in-the-rough frequently appear. Since they ordinarily operate with little or no funds and even less support from the reading public, the average life span is about two issues. Fenton Johnson edited and published two such ventures: *The Favorite Magazine*, which expired in 1917 after a few months' existence, and *The Champion*, launched the next year, which attained the old age (for little magazines) of three years.[2] Two similar undertakings were *Letters* (1927) and *Savoyager* (1929), both sponsored by a group whose verses had appeared in the *Intercollegian Wonder Book*, a somewhat effusive record of the Negro's role in Chicago history, edited in 1927 by F. H. Robb with a second edition in 1929.

Literary strivers also have presented their bids for immortality in more impressive dress. Some of these bids are encompassed in modest pamphlets, others in ornate bound volumes, and most of them are "privately printed," "published by the author," or bear the unfamiliar insignia of presses not infrequently established for the specific occasion. Demonstrating that a churchman may at times stoop to merriment, Bishop Albert Carter of the African Methodist Church published in 1923 his collection of humorous verse, *Canned Laughter*, a direct descendant of Jefferson King's *Darky Philosophy Told in Rhyme* (1906).

Joseph R. Cay brought out in 1913 a compendium of good advice, *Life Lines of Success*. Bettiola Heloise Fortson's *Mental Pearls*, "original poems and essays," was offered in 1915. In 1920, a "romance" with a revealing title, *Black and White Tangled Threads*, introduced its author, Zara Wright. In 1915, William H. Ashby, executive secretary of the Springfield Urban League, published a short novel, *Redder Blood*.

J. L. Nichols & Co. of Naperville, established in 1886, published a number of books for and by Negroes, including *Booker T. Washington's Own Story of His Life and Work; The Life and Works of Paul Lawrence Dunbar*, edited by Lida Keck Wiggins with an introduction by William Dean Howells; and *The Negro Progress of a Race, or Remarkable Advancement of the American Negro*, edited by W. H. Crogman and J. L. Nichols, with an introduction by R. R. Moton. Another title was *The New Floyd's Flowers*, short stories by Prof. Silas X. Floyd, A.M., D.D., supplemented by Mrs. Alice H. Howard's *A.B.C. Book for Negro Boys and Girls*, a collection of verses similar to these:

A stands for African
The race that proved its worth
One more true, more noble
Can not be found on earth.

V stands for victories
America has won
Our race helped to make her
A place in the sun

Another item was the *National Capital Code of Etiquette*, combined with "short stories for colored people, by Edward S. Green and Silas X. Floyd." This book contains "wonderful pictures of Washington's prominent colored Society Leaders on the street; at the Theatre; at Church; in the Home; at Receptions, Balls, Parties, Weddings, Dinners, etc. The illustrations are so perfect and natural that the well bred, correctly clothed men and women almost speak to you." In addition to instructions on "how to dress and conduct yourself on any and all occasions," there is a chapter, "alone . . . worth the price of the book," telling "how to write every imaginable form of letter—on affairs of business, society, invitation, love, proposals of marriage." Alice Dunbar-Nelson edited this for *The Dunbar Speaker and Entertainer*, illustrated by "interpretive poses by Carribel Coles's Pupils of Rhythmatic Expression."

Shortly after the turn of the century, Negro scholars became more and more identified with the University of Chicago. Prominent among these are Carter G. Woodson, Benjamin G. Brawley, Monroe Nathan Work, Abram Lincoln Harris, Charles S. Johnson, E. Franklin Frazier, Horace Mann Bond, Horace R. Cayton, and Allison Davis.

Joel Augustus Rogers, a graduate of Yale, lived in Chicago for several years and published there his *From Superman to Man*, purporting to be a novel, but actually an encyclopedia of little known facts about the Negro from the dawn of history.

Of a less scholarly nature, but interesting as individual experiences, are *Around the World with Hershaw and Collins*, by Flaurience Sengstacke Collins and Far McKeene Hershaw, and *God Wills the Negro*, by Theodore P. Ford. In 1920, Kathryn M. Johnson and Addie W. Hunton wrote *Two Colored Women With the American Expeditionary Forces*, and in 1939 the Pyramid Press of Chicago issued Miss Johnson's *Stealing a Nation*, an account of the methods by which Swaziland was reduced from political self-rule and economic self-rule and economic self-sufficiency to a condition of near slavery under British rule. Robert S. Abbott, publisher of the *Chicago Defender* and *Abbott's Monthly* found time to write two travels books, *My Trip Abroad* and *Travels through South America*. W. Allison Sweeney, editor of the short-lived *Chicago Leader* and also known as a poet, published in 1919 his *History of the American Negro in the Great World War*.

Most assertive of the "new" poets following the trail blazed by Fenton Johnson, Frank Marshall Davis of Chicago describes himself as "a Duskymerican born December 31, 1905, at Arkansas City, Kansas, and exposed to what is termed education in the public schools there, at Friends' University at Wichita, and at Kansas State College."[3] Davis, designated by Benjamin G. Brawley as one of "those two obstreperous poets (the other being J. Harvey L. Baxter of Roanoke, Virginia) having such assurance as could hardly be equaled in this world or in the world to come," has produced three collections of verse: *Black Man's Verse* (1935), *I Am the American Negro* (1937), and *47th Street* (1942).

Langston Hughes, an intermittent resident of Chicago, was the first Negro writer to cope realistically with the problems attending the great migration. In his first full-length work of fiction, *Not Without Laughter* (1930), Hughes records the tribulations of transplanted black peasants in Chicago. Better known as a poet than as a novelist, he depicts the urban Negro's day-by-day concerns and sorrows in his *Weary Blues* and subsequent collections of verse. In 1939, Waters Edward Turpin, whose first novel, *The Low Grounds*, attracted considerable attention, used Chicago as the locale of a second one, *O Canaan!* With the great migration a central theme, segregation, race riots, depression, and the familiar themes of love and family life enter into the book's complex fabric. William Attaway published in 1939 *Let Me Breathe Thunder*, somewhat remarkable because all the leading characters are white. A disciple of the hard-boiled staccato school, Attaway also published in 1941 *Blood on the Forge*, a story with a steel mill background.

Arna Bontemps, poet, novelist, and editor, has lived in Chicago since 1935. His historical novels, *Black Thunder* (1936) and *Drums At Dusk* (1939) are in marked contrast to the genteel southern conception of Negro docility, while his *God Sends Sunday* (1932) details the vicissitudes of a jockey and a sporting man. Editor of *Cavalcade of the American Negro* (1940); W. C. Handy's autobiography, *Father of the Blues* (1941); and *Golden Slippers*, an anthology of Negro verse; Bontemps is also known for his juveniles *Popo and Fifina* (with Langston Hughes) (1932), *You Can't Pet a Possum* (1934), and *Sad-Faced Boy* (1937).

A young refugee from Mississippi who had fled a poverty-blighted home at the age of fifteen, who had supplemented his meager grade school education with knowledge gleaned from library books obtained by subterfuge (because the Memphis public library did not encourage Negro patrons), Richard Wright was destined to startle the reading public as had no other writer of his race. His first book of four long short stories, *Uncle Tom's Children* (1938), grim recitals of lynching, injustice, and prejudice, won the *Story* magazine $500 prize for the best book by a WPA writer, Wright at that time being employed by the Illinois Writers' Project.[4] But it was with his creation of Bigger Thomas, protagonist of *Native Son* (1939), that Wright attained major stature. The frustrated Negro youth of Chicago's South Side slums, impelled by circumstances beyond his control to commit a particularly brutal murder, is transmuted by Richard Wright's art into a sympathetic character and at the same time one of the great figures of fiction. In 1941, Wright published *Twelve Million Black Voices*, commentary with pictures.

The list of white Illinois writers of prose other than fiction who have dealt with material relative to the Negro is a large and impressive one. One of the first was Frederick Starr of the University of Chicago, who—in consideration of his ethnographic studies of African customs—was in 1915 created a Knight Commander of the Order of African Redemption by the government of Liberia. The work of Edwin Rogers Embree, president of the Julius Rosenwald Fund, was a contributing factor in the Georgia school squabble precipitated by Governor Talmadge in 1941, Mr. Embree's book, *Brown America: The Story of a New Race*, then in its ninth edition, being a target of the Governor's wrath. Melville Jean Herskovits, head of the Anthropology Department of Northwestern University, has published numerous volumes and monographs, the most recent being *The Myth of the Negro Past*. Harold F. Gosnell's *Negro Politicians: The Rise of Negro Politicians in Chicago* is the only work on the subject.

Not only white scholars of Illinois, but novelists and poets as well, have considered the Negro. As far back as 1855, Mrs. Elizabeth A. Roe published in Chicago *Aunt Leanna, or Early Scenes in Kentucky*. Upton Sinclair, in his expose of the Chicago stockyards, *The Jungle* (1905), portrayed sympathetically the role of Negro immigrants as unwitting strikebreakers, while Scott Nearing stresses the problem even more pointedly in his *Free-Born* (1932). The novels on related subjects couched in a somewhat romantic vein followed *The Jungle*. The first of these, Gertrude Sanborn's *Veiled Aristocrats* (1923), is an expression of the conflict of class and consciousness accompanying the rise of the Negro petty bourgeoisie, while the second, Vera Caspary's *The White Girl* (1929), "solves" the mixed-blood heroine's dilemma with poison, a device reminiscent of earlier "octoroon" melodramas. James T. Farrell's *Studs Lonigan* at frequent intervals poses the racial problems of Chicago's South Side. In Nelson Algren's *Somebody in Boots* (1935), a Negro burlesque comedian is one of the few characters possessing dignity and integrity. Vachel Lindsay in "The Congo," "Simon Legree," "John Brown," and other poems recognized the Negro as literary material.

27. Music

There were originally plans for an entire book project to be called "History of Negro Music and Musicians in Chicago" that began in late 1939 and continued to July 1940. When Bontemps was first hired on the Illinois Writers' Project, he supervised this study. An outline by Bontemps lists chapters on ragtime, the blues, spirituals, classical music, work songs, and boogie woogie. Several interviews were conducted by IWP worker George L. Lewis for the study. The chapter that appears here came from the more recent of two draft chapters found in Bontemps's papers at Syracuse University. According to an internal memo, both of the drafts were written by Robert Lucas, with many corrections by Bontemps. The editorial changes were incorporated by the editor, although comments suggest entire sections were to be either eliminated or rewritten. The decision was made by the editor to retain all of the material in the draft chapter as it reveals many details about musical history in Chicago that may be of value to scholars today.

Under slavery a familiar command on Southern plantations was, "Make some noise there!" Let me *hear* you!" The Negro hands usually obliged by singing. Knowing only a few songs and snatches, they were forced to improvise. A sullen, silent slave was not to be trusted. A slave working in a thicket or plowing in a distant corn field might fall asleep at his job or make a break for freedom; there was a double reason to require a song of him.

This tradition may or may not have been responsible for the Northern Negro's inclination toward music. At any rate, a "dandy Negro with his violin" was providing music for a dancing room in Chicago as early as 1833. Not long thereafter a Negro musician caused quite a stir among the citizens of Quincy. In 1851, the *Whig* reported an article from the *Louisville Courier* which describes, "Cary, a Negro, or rather a mulatto, who lived in this city some ten or twelve years since. He was an excellent performer on the fife, flute and other musical instruments, and belonged to the band of the old Louisville Guards. . . . He was recently at Indianapolis and he seemed to have taken the 'Railroad City' completely by storm." The Quincy newspaper recalled that Cary had been to Illinois. "Cary visited this city some years ago. . . . He gave several concerts—which were numerously attended."

It was later, however, that the Negro's talent for classical music was manifested, and groups of Jubilee singers were organized in Illinois as well as in other states. Illinois, like the rest of the world, responded to this new music. These American folk songs had a strange, haunting quality which contrasted vividly with the popular minstrel music. Dr. Alain Locke has said:

> [The] universality of the Spirituals looms more and more as they stand the test of time. They have outlived the particular generation and the peculiar conditions which produced them; they have survived in turn the contempt of the slave owners, the conventionalizations of formal religion, the repressions of Puritanism, the corruptions of sentimental balladry, and the neglect and disdain of second generation respectability. They have escaped the lapsing conditions and the fragile vehicle of folk art, and come firmly into the context of formal music. Only classics can survive such things.

Early newspapers record the success enjoyed by Negro groups singing these classics in Illinois. The Hampton Singers included the state of Illinois in their 1874 tour to raise funds for Hampton Institute. The *Chicago Evening Journal* commented at the close of their engagement. "The singers are superior to the Tennesseans, and their songs are of the same characteristic order. Among the most enjoyable as well as harmonious pieces were 'Keep Me From Sinking Down'; 'My Lord Delivered Daniel'; 'The Old Slave's Farewell,' a bass solo; 'The Little Octroon,' a soprano solo; and a plantation melody called 'Oh, Swing Low Sweet Chariot.' The voices are well trained and blend sweetly together."[1]

The Tennesseans, here referred to, were singing in Illinois at the same time. They too received favorable notices.

During the 1870s and 1880s, Blind Tom, "wonderful musical prodigy," made frequent visits to Chicago.[2] On March 18, 1875, the *Inter Ocean* announced that, "the Hallelujah Band of colored singers, formerly slaves in the South, will sing some of their pathetic slave songs at the Oakland Methodist Episcopal Church, corner of Langley Ave., and Thirty-ninth street, this evening."[3] In 1879, the Temperance Colored Jubilee Singers gave a concert in the Academy of Music at Peoria.[4] Concerts sponsored by churches and other organizations were often commonplace. In 1875, Bethel A.M.E. Church sponsored a "grand jubilee concert and tableaux" at Burlington hall in Chicago, and the Louise Cowen Concert Combination, "a troupe of colored singers," was presented at Quinn's Chapel on Fourth Avenue in 1879.[5]

At Springfield, on May 4, 1880, "A good audience greeted the colored Jubilee singers . . . notwithstanding the rain." The Fisk Jubilee Singers appeared at Central Music Hall in Chicago and sang to large audiences in 1886.[6] The Jinglers, a group of jubilee singers, appeared at the M.E. Church in Kewanee, Illinois, in 1891. This company included an original male quartet which had made a national reputation during the presidential campaign of 1888. They had "recently returned from a successful tour of the Pacific Coast, and have established the reputation of being the finest combination of colored singers ever before the public."[7] The Cantata of Queen Esther was given at Central Music Hall in 1896 by a cast which included Eliza Cowan Harris, Della Ridgeway, Blanch Wright, Senora Seldon, and Marion Adams. Fred Burch's orchestra accompanied the singers and a leading role was sung by Richard B. Harrison, at that time "a singer of rare merit."

One of the earliest music societies in Chicago was the Chicago Choral Study Club, organized in the latter part of the 1890s. This group was among the first to feature the work of Coleridge-Taylor, the gifted Negro composer. It had the added distinction of bringing him to Chicago to direct their presentation of "Hiawatha." Among the Choral Study Club's members were Gertrude Jackson, J. Gray Lucas, George W. Duncan, Martha A. Cole, Anita Patti Brown, Arthur A. Brown, Blanch Wright Page, Mabel Burton and Maude Roberts George. The founder and director, Pedro T. Tinsley, a baritone, was a member of the Apollo Musical Club of Chicago when that group sang on the Chicago Day program at the World's Columbian Exposition in 1893.[8]

On December 2, 1906, there appeared in the *Inter Ocean* an article by Glen Dillard Gunn:

> S. Coleridge-Taylor is to visit Chicago this week under circumstances which make his coming particularly significant. His place in the musical world is sufficiently important to make his appearance an interesting event, and Chicago's appreciation of his art was warmly attested at his concert in Music Hall in 1904.
>
> Then he was brought here by a manager in the regular course of business, but on Monday and Tuesday of this week he comes to the New Pekin Theater at the invitation of some of the leaders of the Negroes of Chicago, who believe that the appearance of this distinguished man before an audience of his own race will stimulate the Negroes of America to more serious endeavor in the field of music, for which their natural aptitude has long been admitted.
>
> Mr. Coleridge-Taylor's career might well serve to inspire his people. A Boston paper has called him "one of the greatest of living composers." In England where they fortunately have no race question to consider, and therefore accept the man upon the merit of his work and on his own culture, he occupies a high position. He is director of the famous Handel Society of London, and Professor of harmony in an important school of music. . . .[9]

Following the great migration of 1910–20, organized music schools mushroomed among Chicago Negroes.[10] The Coleridge-Taylor Music School was the first. Several local musicians pooled their interests in 1913 and opened a school at 35th and State streets. With T. Theodore Taylor, Walter Gossette, Martha B. Anderson, Herbert H. Byron, Theodore Bryant, Estella Bond, and Nannie May Strayhorn on the faculty, the school offered instruction in piano, organ, violin, cornet and dancing. Hazel Thompson Davis, a protégé of Aida Overton Walker, conducted classes in stage dancing. In 1925, the school moved to the old Schuman-Heink residence at 37th and Michigan Boulevard, where it remained until 1928.

In 1922, Pauline Lee founded the National Conservatory of Music. Her school, too, began its existence in the Schuman-Heink residence (but later moved elsewhere on Michigan Avenue). Its faculty was equal in size to that of its contemporary and its curriculum was similar. The Normal Vocal Institute, established by Mrs. E. Azalia Hackley, aimed at popularizing music study among the masses.[11]

In 1922, Nora Holt, then music editor of the *Chicago Defender* started a music magazine which briefly influenced the trend of music instruction and appreciation in Chicago.

The music instruction furnished by Negroes is usually of an elementary nature. The highest grade musical schools have always been open to Negroes, and many of them have taken advantage of this opportunity. As early as 1910, for example, there were no less than a dozen Negroes registered at the Northwestern University School of Music.

This period also saw the growth of a number of musical organizations. In 1901, Major N. Clark Smith, a composer and conductor, organized a group of twelve women into the Ladies Mandolin Club. In 1904, he formed the Young Ladies Orchestra with Irene Howard as cornet soloist and Alberta Riggs as violin soloist. The same year Smith was made director of the Eighth Regiment Band and his excellent work with bands continued when he was made band director at Wendell Phillips High School.

In 1911, a young composer was started on the road to fame by a famous opera singer.

Madame Ernestine Schuman-Heink on Thursday discovered a new composer for whom she predicts a brilliant future in the person of James Dekoven Thompson, 3602 Forest Avenue, porter on a Western Railroad while she was going from Chicago to Appleton, Wisconsin.

The young Negro recognized his passenger as the famous contralto and seized the opportunity to show her some of his songs. Mme. Schuman-Heink looked over the songs and when she came to Thompson's latest composition "If I forget," she was struck with the dignity and tunefulness of the piece. She asked Thompson for a copy of the song and said she would sing it in her concerts where English songs were used. "The air reminds me of Tosti or Nevin at his best," said Mme. Schuman-Heink. "It is so long since a really good love lyric has been composed that one welcomes a new one. The theme is entirely new and is handled in the best manner for a sentimental song, that is, the twelve-eight beat. I think the theme must be some old African melody. Some of these themes have an indescribable appeal to them."

The diva's prediction of Thompson's success came true. A story which was printed in the *Chicago Herald* a few years later was headed, "Colored Composer Wins Success."

As a boy singing in the choir of St. Thomas Episcopal Church (colored) Mr. Thompson composed his first work, a sacred song "Dear Lord Remember Me." It attracted the attention of W. L. Tomlins, one of the associates of the late Theodore Thomas, and brought the young musician to the attention of the public. The composer's most recent work is a lullaby, with lyrics in Negro dialect. Mr. Thompson, who is the son of the late Rev. James C. Thompson, founder and rector of St. Thomas Church, is now in vaudeville with his brother Creighton Thompson and Mrs. Opal Cooper. The team is known as Thompson, Cooper and Thompson. They sing and play the Thompson compositions.

The traditional songs of the Negro were sung by choruses of many voices. The Negro's fondness for group singing is manifested in the many choral societies in Illinois.

The Armour Jubilee Singers began as a group of seven or eight packing house employees who sang as they worked and developed their choral singing ability by meeting in their homes at night. Their first public appearance was at the Wabash Y.M.C.A. in 1919. Officials of Armour and Company heard them sing and decided to subsidize the group. They bought music and hired a director and accompanist for them. This chorus of sixteen men, directed by Cornelius W. Pierce and accompanied by Harriet Hammond, has sung work songs of the South, folk songs, spirituals, operatic and concert music on the radio, on the stage, and in churches and schools.[12]

The Federal Glee Club, organized by William E. Myrick and Curtis T. Jackson in 1932, became well known locally. Formerly its membership was restricted to postal employees.[13] The Mundy Choristers were organized in 1929 by James A. Mundy.[14] This group formed the nucleus of a huge chorus of five hundred voices which sang at the Lincoln Dedication services at Springfield in 1931. In 1928, "after Prof. James A. Mundy's wonderful presentation of the Messiah, friends and well-wishers presented him with a $1,000 diamond medal."

Mundy accepted a position to direct and supervise a chorus under the Federal Music Project in 1937. Since then his chorus, the Federal Jubilee Singers, has sung to many thousands of music lovers.

In Springfield, the Lincoln Liberty Chorus, first organized to sing at the re-dedication of the Abraham Lincoln Tomb, is under the direction of Mr. O. Jerome Singleton.[15] The Modern Troubidors were first organized as the Chocolate Soldiers by Mabel Sanford Lewis in 1939.[16]

There are many church choirs which have sung over the radio and in large downtown halls before large audiences, among them are the Ebenezer Baptist Church Choir, directed by Francis S. Hatch; the Tercentenary A.M.E. Church Choir, led by Tennyson T. Butler; the choir of Olivet Baptist Church, whose former director, Dr. William Henry Smith, was appointed the head of the Department of Music at Wiley College, Marshall, Texas; and the Grace Presbyterian Church Choir, directed by Thomas Theodore Taylor, who was once accompanist for Clarence Cameron White, Abbie Mitchell, and Florence Talbert. He also toured the United States and Canada with the Taylor-Johnson Trio. The Cosmopolitan Community Church Choir sang excerpts from Bach's "Jesu, Priceless Treasure" in the Hall of Religion at the Century of Progress Exposition in 1933. The director, Blanche Smith Walton, has been musical director for many musical shows, including Billy King's "Over the Top," Shelton Brooks' "Canary Cottage," and Blanche Calloway's "Plantation Days." The Metropolitan Community Church Choir is directed by J. Wesley Jones. Jones, mentioned in the 1941 edition of *Who's Who in Music*, has directed his group in a Musical Festival the fourth Sunday in every month for twenty-one consecutive years.

Canaan's Travelers, a gospel chorus in Peoria, directed by H. B. Stone, has travelled throughout Illinois and Iowa, and has broadcast over radio station WMBD as a weekly feature. The group was originally organized as the Ward Chapel Gospel Chorus but eventually expanded to include other singers of merit in the community.[17]

In spite of handicaps, the Negro has done well in opera. La Julia Rhea and William Franklin are the only Negroes to appear in major roles in the United States. They appeared in "Aida" in 1938. In 1928, George Garner, noted tenor, appeared in the role of "King Olaf" in London, England. "Their Majesties King George and Queen Mary; the Prince of Wales; Prince Henry; Premier and Mrs. Baldwin; Ramsey McDonald and his daughter, Mary; Members of the Royal Academy of Letters and Science, and distinguished members of the British Parliament turned out and gave Garner a great and tumultuous ovation."

In 1930–31, Dr. Clarence Cameron White received Rosenwald Fellowships to enable him to study abroad. While in Paris, France, he wrote an opera, "Ouanga," based on the life of the Haitian liberator, Dessalines, first ruler of Haiti. The American Opera Society presented "Ouanga" in concert from, at the Three Arts Club, North Shore Art Center in Chicago.[18] John Greene, baritone, and Cleo Wade sang the leading roles, accompanied by Fred Farrel. Dr. White was presented with the David Bispham medal, an award given to American composers who have written operas of outstanding merit and have made a definite contribution to American opera. He is the thirty-fifth in a list which includes Henry Hadley, Frederick S. Converse, Deems Taylor, Walter, Damrosch, and other distinguished composers.

Antoinette Garnes and Anice Hackly were members of the Chicago Opera Chorus for more than twenty years. Madame Mayme Calloway-Byron, for many years a resident of

Chicago, was one of the great Wagnerian opera stars appearing in Europe, principally Germany. She has had the distinction of appearing with the Philharmonic Orchestras of Munich and Dresden. Caterina (Catherine) Yarborough won much acclaim when she appeared in the title role of "Aida" given by the Chicago Opera Company in the Hippodrome, New York City, on July 22, 1933. She is the first woman colored singer to star in a production given by a major company in the United States. She appeared again as "Aida" at the Hippodrome in 1935.

In 1928, James Mundy directed a performance of "Martha" with a cast which included Nellie Bobson, who played the title role and Mrs. Mary E. Jones. Miss Dobson is now in Detroit where she is a member of the Opera Association of that city. The Wendell Phillips High School, under the direction of Miss Mildred Bryant-Jones, successfully presented the "Bohemian Girl." Among the members of the cast, at least three have become outstanding musicians. They are Maurice Cooper, Louise Combs, and Joseph Cole who played leading roles in the production. Joseph Cole is now a resident of Detroit and a member of the Detroit Opera Association. Maurice Cooper appeared in the "Chimes of Normandy" at the Hippodrome in New York in 1939 and with Joseph Cole sang the temple scene from "Aida" when the National Association of Negro Musicians met in Detroit during the summer of 1939.

Abbie Mitchell (former resident of Chicago and now head of the Music Department at Tuskegee Institute, Alabama) has played the role of Santuzza in the opera "Cavelleria Rusticana."

In 1926, the Verdi Opera Company under the direction of Charles Keep presented "The Mikado" at the Eight Street Theater. In the cast were William Edmonson, bass singer with the Southernaires, and Gladys Bouchree and Mabel Roberts Walker, both of whom sang the same roles which, fourteen years later, they sang in the "Swing Mikado."

The year 1932 marked the birth of the Imperial Opera Company. It was organized and directed by Mrs. Gertrude Smith Jackson, who in 1929 organized the Fleur-de-lis, a women's chorus. Some of the members were Mabel Malarcher,[19] who sang the leading roles in "Bohemian Girl" and "The Chimes of Normandy" and in 1935 was soloist with the Federal Glee Club; Alexander M. Bright, composer and director; and Udell A. Taylor, baritone.

The idea of the "Swing Mikado" was conceived by Harry Minturn, director of the now extinct Works Progress Administration Theater Project. The show enjoyed a five-month run in Chicago, each night playing to a crowded house. The "Swing Mikado" left the city with people clamoring for tickets. The company arrived in New York where the show ran for three months, enjoying the same popularity. But for reasons which no one has been able to explain, the show was forced to close. The "Swing Mikado" is said to have received more unsolicited, unpaid-for publicity than any other show in the past thirty-two years. Louis White, one of the principals, was understudy for Porgy in George Gershwin's folk opera, "Porgy and Bess." Others of the cast were Mabel Carter, Frankie Fambro, Edward Fraction, Herman Greene, Maurice Cooper, William Franklin, Mabel Roberts Walker.

After the untimely death of the "Swing Mikado," Maurice Cooper (Nanki-Poo), James Lillard (Pish-Tush), and Alice Harris (Yum-Yum), were selected to play the same roles in Michael Todd's "Hot Mikado," starring Bill Robinson.

The Chicago Negro Light Opera Company (American Negro Light Opera Associations) was organized in 1939 by Raymond B. Girvin from the ranks of the Chicago Negro

Choral Society for the express purpose of presenting light operas. On April 12, 1940, the company presented a modern rhythmical production of Gilbert and Sullivan's "H.M.S. Pinafore"; the new version was called "Tropical Pinafore." The choreography was created by Katherine Dunham. The principals were Thelma Wade Brown, Ernestine Lyle, Don Pierson, George Bizell, Napoleon Reed, and La Julia Rhea.

Some of the better-known musical clubs and associations in Chicago are the Florence B. Price Club, a group of musicians headed by Herman Billingsley, music critic for the *Pittsburgh Courier* (Chicago branch); the Nathaniel Dett Club; the Artists' Progressive Social Club; The Mid–South Side Orchestra, directed by Dr. Edward J. Robinson; the Excelsior Ensemble, an orchestra of young men; the Criterion Orchestra (Miss Grace Tompkins, music editor for the *Chicago Defender*, is president of the Chicago group). The city of Springfield maintains two municipal bands, one of them all-Negro, furnishes uniforms, and pays the members for each performance.

The list of well-known singers, instrumentalists, directors and composers in Chicago is an impressive one. Many have gained national recognition.[20]

Florence B. Price, one of the outstanding composers of the Middle-West, has won two Wanamaker Prizes: one for her Sonata, and the other for her "Symphony in E. Minor," which was played by the Chicago Symphony Orchestra. She has played with the Women's Symphony Orchestra in Chicago.

In 1932, Margaret Bonds won the Wanamaker Prize for the best song composed by a Negro, and in 1933 she was the piano soloist with the Chicago Symphony Orchestra at the Auditorium Theater when Mrs. Price's "Symphony in E. Minor" was played. In the fall of 1934 she appeared as a guest soloist with the Women's Symphony Orchestra at the Century of Progress Exposition.[21]

Anita Patti Brown, now retired, was the first Negro to give a concert in the new city auditorium at Savannah, Georgia, in 1917. Novella McGhee is soloist at the Eighth Christian Science Temple (colored) where she has been given a contract which will run indefinitely, although usually the soloist is selected in open competition every two years. Etta Moten, contralto, appeared in the films "Golddiggers of 1933" and "Flying Down to Rio." She rose to national popularity and was invited to the White House to sing for the President and Mrs. Roosevelt. Her accompanist Clyde Winkfield, brilliant young pianist, was awarded a prize in the 1934 music competition at the Century of Progress Exposition. More recently, he was awarded a Rosenwald Fellowship (1941) for advanced study. Dr. Harrison Ferrell, noted violinist and former director of the Ferrell Symphony Orchestra, is now head of the Art Department at West Virginia State College.

William Clifford King, now a teacher in a Chicago public school, received a diploma for an outstanding performance at the Johann Strauss Theater in Vienna, Austria. He toured Europe with various orchestras and in Budapest, Hungary, Silber Andor, music critic, called him, "The most perfect musician, Mr. King." William A. Tyler had the distinction of playing at the Pekin Theater with Samuel Coleridge-Taylor in 1907.[22] He was musical director with James Reese's European Orchestra, playing with Mr. and Mrs. Vernon Castle on tour in the United States and Canada. Walter E. Gossette, who has been the organist of the Sunday Evening Club at Orchestra hall, in 1926 collaborated with Marian Anderson to give a joint program at the National Cash Register Plant at Dayton, Ohio. Dr. Robert E. Giles, one of Chicago's leading Negro pharmacists, appeared as cornet soloist before the

United States Senate during the Taft administration. From 1921 to 1923, he was president of Musicians Local 208 and is a member of the Business and Professional Men's Orchestra.

Walter Dyett has had a long career directing orchestras. He was the leader of the orchestra of the old Pickford Theater from 1922 to 1927. He was an instructor in the Coleridge-Taylor School of Music. In 1931, he succeeded Major N. Clark Smith as band master of Wendell Phillips High School. He is now at Du Sable High School. Dyett was made a bandmaster of the Eighth Regiment of the Illinois National Guard. He organized and directed the orchestra for the Negro pageant "O Sing a New Song" in 1934. It was with Dyett's arrangement of a song that John Burdette won the Chicago-land Music Festival prize.[23] Hazel Harrison, pianist, studied in Germany. While there, she played the "Chopin E Minor" and the "Grieg A Minor" concertos with the Berlin Philharmonic orchestra. Oland Gaston, a young pianist and composer, was recently appointed to the faculty of [Johnson C. Smith University in Charlotte, North Carolina—Ed.]. Others who have made a reputation are Cleo Mae Dickerson, pianist and organist; Mahalia Jackson, recording artist; John Tompkins,[24] who led the De Saible Singers at the Century of Progress Exposition; Antionette Tompkins, who also directed a chorus at the exposition; Nelmathilde Ritchie, violinist; Charles Theodore Stone; Charles Manney; Jeanne Fletcher, pianist; Charles Mills and Mrs. Naomi Watson of Quincy, Illinois.

In 1895, the Umbrian Glee Club was organized by Arthur A. Brown and Richard C. Kelly. Edward Ferde Morris, who was then music teacher and organist at Bethel A.M.E. Church, was its first director. Climaxing a long and successful existence, the Umbians presented Marian Anderson in her first two Chicago appearances.[25]

Today, education in music is more democratic than ever before. Under the sponsorship of the Works Project Administration, individual and group instruction is available to both children and adults. The National Youth Administration has a chorus as one of its varied activities.[26] Music is returning to the people, and the Negro, as evidenced by the growing number of young and talented musicians, is continuing to contribute to this phase of American culture.

28. The Theater

Copies of the draft that appears here can be found in the IWP papers and in the papers of Arna Bontemps, both of which are identical. It was written by Joseph Bougere. There is an earlier forty-page draft written by Robert Lucas in the microfilm of the IWP papers. Also included among the source material in the IWP papers is an essay by Fenton Johnson dated March 4, 1940 that was written in preparation for the chapter on theater for the *Cavalcade of the American Negro*.

Commenting on the performance in May 1877 of a Negro troupe playing *Out of Bondage*, the *Daily Inter Ocean* described it as "one of the very best representations of slave life as it existed before the war that has ever been presented to the public," and followed the judgment with an editorial stating:

> No one can see the troupe of colored artists now performing at McCormick's Hall without gaining a higher opinion of the race to which they belong and being agreeably surprised at the excellence of the entertainment. . . . To thoughtful people, however, there is more in the performance of this troupe than the mere amusement and enjoyment derived therefrom. The organization represents the rapid strides which a despised race is making in the road to excellence. . . .

This paper's theater critic had already advised admirers of Negro minstrelsy who desired the unadulterated article that they would find it in the Georgia Minstrels, currently pleasing Chicago audiences.[1]

The minstrel show, originated by whites, had by this date become a stereotyped form of set routine; but the fresh comic realism of its early days was recaptured in performances such as those of Haverly's Colored Minstrels, featuring Billy Kersands, comedian, and Wallace King, tenor. Playing Peoria early in 1880, the troupe drew a local writer's praise:

> The first part was decidedly the best presented in Peoria for several seasons, and the balance of the programme was immense. . . . All in all, the minstrels gave an enjoyable entertainment, and deserved the crowded house welcoming them last night. We agree with many other papers in pronouncing the colored minstrels superior to the boasted Mastodons.[2]

The minstrel influence may have been responsible for the use of specialty numbers and other innovations in dramas like *The Octoroon*, *Uncle Tom's Cabin*, and *Magnolia*. Thus an advertisement in a Chicago paper in 1881 announced an *Uncle Tom's Cabin* company with "2 Topsys, 2 Marks, 2 Donkeys, 6 Bloodhounds," the "Largest, Best, and Only Double Co. in the world." "The Funniest Afterpiece over produced on the Minstrel Stage," *The Black Mikado*, "with its Wealth of Pleasing Surprises and Startling Novelties," was advertised at the Grand Opera House, Chicago, in November 1885. The same opus was to be produced by Negroes of the Federal Theater Project over half a century later, not as an afterpiece but as a full-length feature, the most successful of the government-sponsored productions.

Black Patti (Sissieretta Jones) and her company of "talented colored comedians, vocalists and dancers" appeared frequently in Chicago during the late nineties. In 1898 their bill included such well-favored old acts as "Reminiscences of the Camp and the Plantation," "The Cake Walk," and "Cooney Island," together with new songs, dances and "black grotesqueries." After a stand at the Academy, the company played for a full week at Clifford's cozy playhouse on Washington Street."

A new phase of the Negro's evolution in the theater was ushered in when Sam T. Jacks brought his *Creole Show* to Chicago in 1893. The production was "really an enjoyable one," according to one critic, and "more interesting for being given wholly by colored people." As an added attraction, a troupe of Sandwich Islanders danced "the famous 'hulahula.'" Although it followed the general pattern of the minstrel, the *Creole Show*, with its comely sepia maidens, opened the way for later productions of Cole and Johnson, Tutt and Whitney, Williams and Walker, and others featuring Negro girls. Earlier Negro shows were limited to burlesque houses, but in 1896 the production *Oriental America* received presentation in a legitimate theater.

The same year, according to the *Inter Ocean*, the city narrowly missed seeing a performance that might have made theatrical history of a sort. William Jones, arrested as a vagrant, insisted he was an actor. Justice Underwood was thus thrust into the delicate position of deciding the issue.

> Jones was brought before the court yesterday morning charged with being a man of worthless qualities and no job. In a voice evoked with indignation the prisoner declared he was a son of a thespian and that, since the death of Edwin Booth, he was considered the finest interpreter of Hamlet that ever came over the pike.
>
> "I was born in the second act of The Two Orphans" he exclaimed, "and I am now carrying a gun at the Grand Opera House."
>
> When asked if he could prove his allegiance to the stage, Jones manifested a desire to recite Antony's oration over the dead body of Caesar, providing his honor would come off his high still and assume the role of the martyred Roman. Justice Underwood modestly declined to supe for Jones, but gave the fellow a continuance until this morning to bring in witnesses who would testify in his behalf.

Williams and Walker came to Chicago in 1902 with *Sons of Ham* and returned in 1906 with *Abyssinia*. Of the latter a reviewer wrote:

> There are . . . bright spots in "Abyssinia." Ada Overton Walker is one of them. She is as graceful as the much written of gazelle, as bright as the colors she wears, and is a delight

to hear enunciate, so clear and true is her speaking voice and so careful is she in her use of English. Her dancing is a delight. . . .

We have very, very few comedians as entertaining and as gifted as Williams.

The company this season is larger than usual, and the chorus is an ambitious, well trained group of singers. . . . Walker has a good song, called "Rastus Johnson, U.S.A.," and Mrs. Walker another entitled "I'll Keep a Warm Spot in My Heart for You" . . .

A few seasons later

John Borden, club man and Bon Vivant, put a crimp in the common or garden variety of "house warmings" when he pushed a button and directed that the entire Williams & Walker "Bandanna Land" theatrical company come up to his house at 89 Bellevue Place and make merry for his guests.

"Impossible!" said the manager of the Great Northern.

"How much impossible?" asked Mr. Borden, yawning slightly. "Here's a check."

The manager hung out a sign on the main entrance. "No performance tonight. Money returned or seats exchanged."

It was perhaps a slander to imply, as the newspaper reporter did, that most of the musicians and performers were smuggled into the Borden residence via the coal chute, but the fact was established that dressing rooms were set up in the laundry. The Messrs. William and Walker, of course, entered through the front door, and at ten o'clock, the banqueting finished,

the doors which hid musicians in their banks of greenery slid noiselessly back, and with a blare of minstrelsy the big show was on.

Presently Aida Overton Walker socked them with "Kinky," and George Walker bowled them over with "Bon Bon Buddy." To the surprise of the guests, the latter appeared without his familiar diamond studded cane. As usual, however, Bert Williams stopped the shows. His song about being tired of eating at restaurants tickled the bachelor boys into fits. Bert was required to shuffle on and off the stage four or five times to quiet their applause. When this failed, he motioned for the lights to be turned off. Even so,

instead of leaving, society rose and called for Williams & Walker personally. By this time the stars were in the laundry dressing-room. John Borden rushed down the cellar stairs and sought them out among the piles of costumes and accessories.

Back in the drawing room, the Messrs. Williams and Walker met society. Another reporter interviewed Williams in the wings of the Great Northern during the same engagement.

I had expected to find . . . a grimacing, sluggered actor, who would entertain me with the frivolous chatter that I have listened to in many an interview with other footlight idols not his color, and so when Bert Williams told me that he didn't know any funny stories and revealed that the subject nearest his heart is the uplifting of his race through dramatic productions, I was surprised to say the least.

Said Bert,

In the olden days, when the church and the stage were filled, the drama was a potent agency for the instruction of the people. . . . I am hoping and working for the day when

Negroes on the stage will take themselves and be taken more seriously, when the colored performer can be something more than a minstrel man, a song and dance artist, or a slap stick gentleman. . . . Companies of purposeful players will not only uplift the black man, but they will, through the presentation of proper plays, act toward a more perfect understanding between the races.

With the development of the Negro actor will come the development of the Negro playwright. At first, of course, we shall have to look to the dramatists of England and America for our material, but in time Negro writers will spring up, and their plays will be produced. . . . Let us have a Negro drama such as Shakespeare might have written, and let us raise up a Negro Booth to interpret it.

Meanwhile, McVickers Theater announced a "sensational" two week engagement of J. H. Haverly's Minstrels, showing the "Triumph of Minstrelsy" and featuring Billy Rice, the Nichols Sisters ("The greatest of them all"), Master Martin, Billy Lyons—to name just a few of the performers. The Chicago Opera House featured Powers and Hyde in the "Up-to-date Cake Walk," also the Ford Brothers, billed as "Black-face Comics." The Haymarket had three items built on Negro characterization: Johnson and Dean, "the colored King and Queen," the Wilson Family ("The Newest Cake Walk"), and Zoe Matheus, singing *I Want A Real Coon*. The Great Northern presented the famous team of Montgomery and Stone, "Black Face Comedians," and Josephine Cassman and her "Funny Picaninnies." A few blocks away, at the modern and imposing Masonic Temple Roof Garden, Williams and Walker were billed in "Dynamic Song, Monologue and Dances." Which meant that in a single evening of stage performances, and entire company and eight variety acts all based upon Negro life, showed in the outstanding theaters of Chicago. Only a few of the players were Negroes.

Chicago did not see a Negro-produced musical till 1900, when the comedian Ernest Hogan arrived to star in Bob Cole's *A Trip to Coontown*, a fascinating mixture of light opera and variety, at the old Park Theater. The audiences were about three-quarters white, and the play did not prove to be a great box office attraction. Later, similar companies came into the city for short stays, usually at McVickers, the Park, or the Eighth Street Theater. But the Negro still lacked serious vehicles; only his musical ability, his feeling for the dance, and his gifts for mimicry and satire were given opportunity. Resenting such limitations and exasperated at being barred from box and orchestra seats in downtown theaters, Negro leaders in 1901 envisioned a theater "for colored people exclusively, at which only colored talent will appear." Several influential Negroes backed a scheme to open Havlin's Theater; Dr. George C. Hall for one was prepared to spend $20,000 on the project. Records do not reveal the fate of the plan.

However, in 1905 Robert Motts opened the Pekin Theater at 27th and State Streets. Originally operating a café, saloon, and gambling place, Motts suddenly found his activities opposed by the clergy. A threatening political situation did not help matters. He decided to make a change. In Europe he had observed the continental music halls in which patrons, seated about the stage, were entertained by short plays, musical numbers and variety acts while drinking and eating. On June 18, the "Pekin Theater—Temple of Music" opened its doors. Three or four hundred spectators, seated at tables in cabaret style, witnessed the first locally produced all-Negro show in the city's history. The "Temple of Music" presented a long and lavish bill that night. Many of the acts were typical of the nineties—sentimental, saccharine, "tear-jerkers"—but in between these offerings were the new dances, such as the Cake Walk, and the new music, the early ragtime, already beginning to replace the lush waltz-time airs of an era that was ending.[3]

Before long the Pekin began to attract white visitors. Its popularity grew, and Motts was compelled to expand. In April 1906, "The New Pekin Theater," remodeled into a regular theater with conventional stage and seating arrangement, opened its doors. A full time stock company was organized to provide entertainment. Because the plays presented were essentially musical in character the management employed a group of brilliant, if still obscure, musicians. During the Pekin's existence these men turned out hundreds of tunes and wrote the scores for dozens of two and three-act plays. Many of their songs retained popularity with generations unaware that the Pekin ever existed. Like the Moscow Art Theater and Abbey Theater in Dublin, the Pekin did not practice a star system; however, in time, certain figures did attain prominence.

The production staff of the Pekin was experienced. Its head was W. H. Smith, who had booked and scouted Negro acts for the J. D. Hopkins Theaters. Motts was treasurer, Charles S. Sager, stage manager, and W. A. Moran, advertising manager. Oliver Brymn was the musical director, although there was actually a regular staff of musicians whose duties approximated his. They directed the orchestra, wrote scores and specialty numbers, and sometimes acted.

The new theater's first presentation was a musical comedy, *The Man from Bamm*, book and lyrics by Collin Davis and Arthur Gillespie, musical score by Joe Jordan. Among its principals were Ethel James, Elizabeth Wallace, Delores Thomas, L. D. Henderson and Andrew Trimble. This comedy, with some changes, went through constant revivals as long as the Pekin lasted. More important, it introduced Joe Jordan, young composer of the "Peking Rag," a tune which later became a nationwide hit "Sweety Dear."

The Pekin presented the first all-Negro stock company in America. Enlisting talent from all over the country, its music, librettos, and acting improved rapidly. Variety was seldom employed, except when a play was too short for a full afternoon or evening's entertainment. Shows were billed in advance and advertised, sporadically, in the metropolitan press. All seats were reserved and performances generally began on schedule.

The music department included, besides Perry and Jordan, such talented composers as H. Lawrence Freeman, Shelton Brooks, Tim Brymn, Will Marion Cook, Bernie Adler, and Mill Dixon. There was as little individualism among the musicians as among the actors, the majority of music productions being results of collaboration, despite the writers' dissimilar backgrounds. Freeman, known earlier in New York, wrote melodies of a weird, original sort, and cared little about being a "popular" composer. His operatic work, *The Martyrs*, was produced at the Columbia Theater shortly after his arrival in Chicago. Brooks had been an obscure minstrel man and comedian before coming to the Pekin; soon his fame as a composer led to his abandoning stage work, except for an occasional comic role. Cook came to the Pekin already well known for his part in creating the scores of *Clorindy* and *In Dahomey*, the Williams and Walker success. He was a well-trained musician, having studied composition with Dvorak and violin with Joachim, and although he did not produce as many plays as some of his colleagues his influence and prestige were great.[4]

Will Dixon turned out some notable Pekin favorites, including *The Count of No Account*, words by Alf Anderson. Brymn was the busiest of the group, writing and collaborating on more plays than any of the staff save perhaps Jordan.

The librettos of the plays were loose and simple, consisting of a few situations in which the hero or heroine blundered about until finally extricated. In and out of a series of predicaments, "retort dialogue," and roguish whimsicality ran catchy strains that somehow managed to keep things together. There was no scene so bad it could not be rescued by a clever song. The management often used only the name of a song hit in newspaper ads.

To readers of the old script thirty-five years later, the humor sounded faded, but it was tremendous stuff in its time, especially when handled by gifted actors with a flair for mimicry. With so much accent on farce, the Pekin plays were singularly clean. The double *entendre* of the French farce was missing. The love motif was steadily employed but never permitted to offend. Even an involving bit of theatrical confusion such as Miller and Lyles' *The Husband* was kept well in hand. The audience too, with all their infectious laughter, preserved a dignity which prompted one reviewer to observe that

> the audience was a model of propriety and good behavior, as orderly as any that convened at the higher priced theaters and a lot better mannered than many a grand opera opening.

Although the chorus was the company's particular pride, no attempt was made to costume the girls pretentiously; they appeared in long skirts and light waists or in simple street clothes. There were occasions for butler and maid uniforms, but generally the theater made no effort to imitate the lavishness beginning to characterize Broadway musical shows.

The writers who supplied librettos for the Pekin could not be compared with "legitimate" playwrights. Their musical comedies and operettas required a minimum of situation, but plenty of room for dance specialties, songs and strong comedy leads. The Pekin writers attained these objectives. Leading librettists were Miller and Lyles, Victor Smalley, Stanley Woods, and J. Edward Green, the latter contributing such hits as *The Queen of the Jungles*, *My Friend From Georgia*, and (with Alf Anderson) *Captain Rufus*. For a time Green was director, and later production supervisor; while serving in the latter capacity he created some stage effects that have not been forgotten—for example, the "ghost ship" in *My Friend From Georgia*, a realistic representation of a storm at sea. Miller and Lyles's best productions were *The Bachelor* and *The Mayor of Dixie*. They also wrote *Dr. Night*, and Aubrey Lyles (with Charles Gilpin) *Colored Aristocrats*. Their Broadway hit of the twenties, *Shuffle Along*, was based on *The Mayor of Dixie*. Woods authored *Dr. Dope* and *Peanutville*; also—but not for the Pekin—*Ivan the Terrible* and a dramatic version of Tolstoy's *Resurrection*. Smalley was a writer with a flair for satirizing other plays through a medium he called the "burletta." Three of his best things were lampoons of productions then current in Chicago—*The Merry Widower* (*The Merry Widow*), *The Man from Rome* (*The Man from Home*), and *The Follies of 1908*, after a play of the same name. Smalley worked with the musician Bernie Adler.

One-play writers, besides Davis and Gillespie (*The Man from Bamm*), include H. B. Casson, with *In Honolulu*; C. Adelman, *In Zuzuland*; Hen Wise, *Reception Day in Africa*; and Blaine Gray, with *The Grafter*. Lawyer Harper, of Louisville, Kentucky, contributed *Tally Ho*; and L. Tish Hibbard, the only woman who ever wrote for the Pekin, did *Play without a Name*.

The list of star performers who got their start at the Pekin is long. Charles Gilpin, originator of the name role in Eugene O'Neil's *Emperor Jones*, whose specialty was "heavy" monologues, was probably more respected than enjoyed by Pekin patrons. Bill Robinson, then just an unknown youngster, was another successful member of the company. Abbie Mitchell belonged to the group, as did also Lottie Grady, Nettie Lewis, and Elizabeth Hart Scott. Harrison Stewart, a comedian in the manner of Bert Williams, starred in nearly all Pekin productions, but was not heard from after the theater closed. Other members of the company included Jerry Mills, later a fine dancer and an extraordinary "villain"; Leona Marshall, Madaline Cooper, Harry Crosby, Lawrence Chenault, a baritone who often played romantic leads; Louis Pennington, Valla Crawford, Pearl Brown, Mae White, J. F. Morse, Rosa Lee Taylor, Ada Banks, Elvira Johnson, George White, Jenny Ringgold, Marie White, Willie Ingalls, Josephine DeVance, and Matt Marshall.

The first failure of the Pekin was an unsuccessful effort to establish a North Side branch, for the convenience of white patrons. Every other week a second company replaced the regular Pekin unit at the new theater, the Columbia, at Clark and Division Streets. The Columbia failed, and the star of the Pekin commenced to wane. Revivals became frequent; when the theater closed its doors during the summer of 1908—the first time anything like this had happened—the handwriting was on the wall. For the summer season "moving pictures that talk" were advertised. The Pekin was re-opened in the fall, playing musical comedy and vaudeville, with boxes marked down to fifty cents.

A likely explanation of the Pekin's decline is the development of competition from other Negro-controlled houses. The Monogram opened in 1909; the Grand, in 1910. And the Burons, a family of musicians, began weekly musicals at the Temple of Music on State Street near Thirty-second. The LaFayette and Lincoln Theaters of New York, sometimes erroneously considered the birthplaces of Negro drama in the United States, followed the Pekin by approximately a decade.

Chicago's colored population has always reacted militantly to plays and motion pictures that stir up race hatred. *The Daily Inter Ocean* reported early in 1911 that

> A general movement is on foot by the Negroes of Chicago to have Thomas Dixon's play, "The Sins of the Fathers," suppressed. Petitions will be presented to Mayor Busse today, signed by several hundred Negro citizens, asking him to take action. A big protesting mass meeting will be held under the auspices of the Negro Fellowship League next Wednesday night. Among the backers of the move are Mrs. Ida B. Wells Barnett, the Rev. Dr. A. J. Carey, and C. K. Smith, Secretary of the Negro Social Center on the South Side. . . . [5]

The feeling mounted when Dixon proposed to come to Chicago to "make nightly speeches against the Negro race." Outbreaks, such as had occurred in several southern cities, were feared. In 1915 a bill was introduced into the state legislature prohibiting the showing of the films *The Birth of a Nation* and *The Nigger*, the latter running at the Ziegfeld Theater under the title *The New Governor*.[6]

In 1913 Chicago Negroes began to make motion pictures. Will Foster, a newspaper man, organized a company and produced several comedies, using convenient houses for interiors and the neighborhood streets for outdoor sets. His most popular comedy was *The Pullman Porter*. Among his pictures was one based on a scenario by W. H. A. Moore, a local Negro poet. Foster films were received cordially at Negro movie houses. He ended his brief career in the field with a film presenting features of Negro achievement in the Chicago of that day.

Oscar Micheaux also organized a company in Chicago and filmed a novel he had written, the picture playing local movie theaters. Subsequently, Micheaux moved to New York where several former LaFayette Stock Company stars appeared in his pictures. The Micheaux company was the hardiest of several such Negro organizations.

Between the death of the Pekin, and the advent of the Federal Theater, no local Negro theater movement arose comparable to either. A number of vaudeville houses attracted steady customers, moving picture theaters multiplied, but no Negro stage shows of quality originated in the city. However, several notable productions from the East visited Chicago, bringing back players formerly identified with the city.

Among a dozen or more such hits were Miller and Lyles's *Shuffle Along* and *Keep Shuffling*, *Black Birds*, *In Abraham's Bosom*, *Porgy*, *Harlem*, *Green Pastures*, *Run Little Chillun*, *Stevedore*, and *Porgy and Bess*. Two other plays in which Negroes were featured prominently were *Lulu Bells* and Gertrude Stein's *Four Saints in Three Acts*. *Green Pastures* brought back to the city a former resident, Richard B. Harrison, originator of the role of "De Lawd." Abbie Mitchell appeared in *Stevedore* and *In Abraham's Bosom*. *Mulatto* followed in the latter thirties. Then came *As Thousands Cheer*, *The Little Foxes*, with familiar Negroes in the casts, and these were followed by *Cabin in the Sky*, and *Native Son*. The latter, based on Richard Wright's novel, had as its background the South Side Negro community. Featured in *Cabin in the Sky* was Katherine Dunham, earlier prominent in Federal Theater productions in Chicago.

In the early days of the depression a Negro minstrel group, sponsored by the Illinois Emergency Relief Commission, was formed with about thirty experienced players under the direction of "Doc" Simeon M. Wall, with an orchestra of ten musicians conducted by Will Tyler. With a minimum of scenery and costumes, and no admission fee, the group played in parks, hospitals, and schools.

When the Federal Theater was organized the minstrel company was transferred to it, some of the players going to the theater division and others to the vaudeville. The Negroes employed on the project were given the old Igoe Hall, 5538 South Indiana Avenue, in which to rehearse and perform. Here it was a case of every man for himself. The actors acted, the dancers danced, the singers vocalized, the jugglers juggled, and the tumblers tumbled—all within the space of one fairly large hall. Three plays were produced there: *Did Adam Sin?*, *Everyman in His Humor*, and *Romy and July*. The last named was the work of Robert Dunmore. Adapted from *Romeo and Juliet* and set to music, it told the story of a feud between West Indian and Harlem families. The Igor Hall performers made their own costumes and scenery, shifted their sets, swept and dusted the stage and hall, sold tickets, and wrote their own publicity.

When the Federal Theater leased the abandoned Princess Theater, Clark Street near Van Buren, a real theater with a real stage, the actors themselves rehabilitated it. They rehearsed Paul Green's *Hymn to the Rising Sun*, a one-act drama dealing with conditions in a southern chain gang, but were restrained from opening the play. *Mississippi Rainbow*, by Baker Brownell, was produced later. Theodore Ward's *Big White Fog*, the story of a Chicago Negro family defeated by race prejudice, was presented next at the Great Northern. At

CHAPTER TWENTY-EIGHT

about the same time, the *Ballet Fedre* program featured Katherine Dunham and her dance group, along with Kurt and Grace Graff and Berta Ochsner, in *L'Ag'Ya*, a Chicago Federal Theater creation. Set in a Martinique fishing village and dealing with the folklore of the fishermen and their women, *L'Ag'Ya* emphasized native art.

Little Black Sambo, Charlotte Chorpenning's dramatization of the children's classic, was produced in 1938.

Of all Federal Theater productions, the *Swing Mikado* was perhaps the most novel and most widely publicized. Starting out as a moderate success and evoking only lukewarm, even unfavorable reviews, it attracted enthusiastic audiences and drew nationwide attention. Indeed, it stimulated a new interest in Negro musicals, and was emulated by two eastern producers. After a five months' run in Chicago, it opened at the New Yorker Theater in New York, where it played for another two months before it was purchased from the government by a private promoter. The company was brought back to Chicago and plans had been made for a limited engagement at Mandel Hall, University of Chicago, to be followed by resumption of the broken run at the Great Northern, when Congress abolished the Federal Theater. The *Swing Mikado* was produced and staged by Harry Minturn, Blackstone Theater director. Sammy Dyer, assisted by Hazel Davis, directed the dances. Edward Wurtzback conducted the orchestra, and the special swing arrangements were done by Gentry Warden. John Pratt designed the costumes and Clive Rickabaugh, the sets.

Amateur theater groups have been and continue to be active in Chicago. Early in 1938 a number of young clerks, school teachers, W.P.A. workers, and housewives organized the Negro People's Theater, dedicated to the task of presenting plays by and about Negroes. Langston Hughes's *Don't You Want To Be Free?* was its initial production; given on weekends, it enjoyed a long run. Since that time the company has presented at least one major production each year and many skits and one-act plays before trade unions, clubs, and other groups. The Children's Theater Group, composed of women school teachers, social workers and artists, for a time presented plays for children at the Du Sable High School and at South Side grammar schools. The Negro Drama League was another such organization.

The best known amateur theatrical enterprise on the South Side is the annual *Hi-Jinks*, a musical comedy sponsored by the Du Sable High School Band. Begun at the old Wendell Phillips High School in 1932 as a one-night show, at Du Sable its run was extended to a full school week. At the new building, affording standard size stage and theater switchboard, productions have had more elaborate presentation. The *Hi-Jinks* has started many students on professional careers, some of the more noted graduates being Ray Nance, member of "Duke" Ellington's Orchestra; Herman Hill, guitarist, employed in Television at Radio City, New York; Spencer Odum, pianist and arranger for the Southernaires; the Cats and the Fiddle; and Carol Tucker, café singer.

29. Rhythm

There are two drafts of this chapter, both written by Joseph Bougere. One is an early draft in the IWP papers with extensive corrections by Arna Bontemps. There are also two copies of a second draft, one at Syracuse University, which has "office file" written on it with a few additions. The other in the IWP papers has incorporated the changes and is the version that appears below. Much of the source material for this chapter was collected by Onah Spencer, a jazz critic for *Down Beat* magazine.

On a winter night early in 1900, the First Regiment Armory in Chicago

rocked and swayed with ragtime music . . . for the celebration of the greatest entertainment by colored talent in the city. Armant's colored orchestra fairly carried the dancers off their feet with bursts of staccato harmonies. Colored men and women dressed in the height of fashion swayed and swirled and glided over the waxed floor in the maze of the rag-malia cotillion.[1]

A feature of the evening was a "hot" piano duel in which "three muscular young fellows took turns at the piano in a ragtime contest, and the judges awarded the prize to 'Wing' Bass in time to save the instrument from total destruction." A cake walk contest was won by Alfred and Minnie Hallman, and one of the losers grumbled against the decision, complaining that the judges "didn't know the difference between a 'chicken step' and a 'military flat foot.'"

Chicago enjoyed minstrel music. During the Columbian Exposition, it entertained the *Creole Show*. Later it contributed to the ragtime vogue. Finally, it played host to the bar-room musicians who made the so-called "revolution in 4–4 time." Among the latter were Tom Turpin of St. Louis, who published "The Harlem Rag" and "The Bowery Buck" sometime before 1896; Scott Joplin, who wrote "The Maple Leaf Rag" about 1897; Tony Jackson, called by Clarence Williams (himself a noted song writer and pianist) "probably the greatest blues pianist that ever lived"; Louis Chauvin, Ferdinand "Jelly Roll" Morton, Benjamin Harney, Glover Compton, Ed Harding, and Mrs. Richard B. Harrison, wife of "de Lawd" of *Green Pastures*.[2]

Itinerant colored musicians considered Chicago a good town on the circuit; they "hit" it oftener and stayed longer. The district which welcomed them first was located on State Street between the edge of the Loop and 35th Street; its Center was around 22nd. The two biggest places in the district were Pony Moore's (where Charley Elgar and two companions played in 1903) and the Everleigh Club. In the year preceding the arrival of the first New Orleans jazz band, Tony Jackson had a band at the Elite Café, 30th and State.

In 1911, Emanuel Perez's Creole Band came to town, and the *Chicago Defender* asked its readers, "Have you heard that wonderful jazz music that the people of Chicago are wild about?" The South Side was getting its first taste of a whacky horn, played by Freddie Keppard. The scene was the Grand Theater, 31st and State. Keppard's cornet, fresh from New Orleans, gave the blast that announced the "hot" jazz era.[3]

In the years that followed Keppard's arrival, Chicago Negroes wrote many songs that have become a part of America's musical library. Spencer Williams composed "Shim-me-she-wobble," and "adapted" (from the original by "Papa" Warfield) "I Ain't Got Nobody" for the publisher Will Rossiter; also for Rossiter, he "rewrote" Porter Granger's "On the Puppy's Tail." Arthur wrote "Armour Tech Two-Step," "This Lovin' Gag Ain't Goin' to Pay Expenses, Babe," and "Gracie." Maceo Pinkard won wide popularity with "Sweet Georgia Brown" and "Mammy of Mine"; Tom Lemonier wrote "Just One Word of Consolation" and "You're Up Today, Tomorrow You're Down"; Tony Jackson, "Pretty Baby"; Joe Jordan, "Sweetie Dear"; and "Jelly Roll" Morton, "Jelly Roll Blues," "King Porter Stomp," and "Alabama Bound." At the Pekin, America's first Negro theater, Shelton Brooks produced, acted, directed the orchestra, and composed. His first hit, "You Ain't Talking to Me," was introduced on Broadway by Al Jolson. Subsequent successes of Brooks include "Some O' These Days," "Balling the Jack," "Walking the Dog," "Darktown Strutters' Ball." Sometime later ASCAP rated him third among contemporary Negro composers, following W. C. Handy and H. T. Burleigh.

After 1910, the rag-time vogue gradually faded. But Ma Rainey and her tent shows had already come to town to introduce the blues, and shortly thereafter the new Grand was featuring Wilbur Sweatman and a full orchestra. With them the blues era dawned in Chicago.[4]

In 1920, Mamie Smith recorded "Crazy Blues" and the record sold over a million discs. Bessie Smith, most famous of the five unrelated, blues-singing Smiths, was the second to record. At the age of twelve, Bessie had been a protégé of Ma Rainey on the tent show circuit. Her first recordings were made in Chicago. Later on came Ethel Waters, Alberta Hunter, Ida Cox, Priscilla Stewart, Mary Mack, Edith Wilson, Bertha ("Chippie") Hill, Georgia White, Memphis Minnie, Lil Green, and Rosetta Howard.

Four years after Mamie Smith's debut, Floyd Campbell, first male singer to record blues, made "Market Street Blues." A list of later Chicago men who recorded blues includes Big Bill Broonzie, Joe McCoy, Louis Powell, Richard M. Jones, Ollie Shepard, Rhythm Willie, blues harmonica player Peetie Wheatstraw ("the devil's son-in-law" and "the high sheriff of Hell"), LeRoy Carr, Washboard Sam, "Tampa Red," "Pine Top" Smith (whose "Boogie Woogie Blues" are credited with starting the Boogie craze), "Cripple" Clarence Lofton, Lonnie Johnson (who accompanies himself on the guitar), and Kokomo Arnold.[5]

More widely known than these, however, were Louis Armstrong, trumpeter and originator of "scat" singing, and Cab Calloway, a Chicagoan whose style, while not generally recognized as that of the blues, contained minors that put it in a related category. Cab's career began in the Sunset Café on Chicago's South Side; he has since recounted the tale of "Minnie the Moocher" thousands of times and has written *Swingsters' Jive*, a dictionary of blues and "swing" terms that have worked their way into the American speech.[6]

The blues, based originally on affairs of the heart, have expanded to chronicle fires, floods, tornadoes, gambling. "King Joe," a later recording, celebrates the Negro heavyweight champion.

Because Chicago has such a large Negro population, the titles of many blues refer to the city, or places therein: "The Chicago Gouge," "Mecca Flat Blues," "Little Joe from Chicago," "Big Man from the South" (South Chicago), "29th and Dearborn," and "Dusty Bottom Blues," formerly called "Dusty Bottom." There are also blues about the stockyards, steel mills, and other local work areas.

Historians of Chicago jazz like to recall the arrival of "King" Oliver. Representatives from two "spots" were on hand to greet him. The contingent was made up of members of the bands of the Royal Gardens Café and the Dreamland Café. Both wanted Oliver and were determined to get him. Both did. The solution was profoundly simple. It was worked out over a drink at a bar near the railroad station. Joe joined both bands, and left no doubt about who was the king among Chicago trumpeters. Freddie Keppard, curious, dropped in at the Royal Gardens "to see how the new orchestra was getting along." There followed a battle of cornets in which, according to one reporter, "Joe Oliver beat the socks off Keppard."

> Chicagoans who lived by day first saw Joe Oliver when he was playing in a cart under the El pillars of the Loop. The city was keyed high with war-time tension, teeming with parades. Joe and his friends had volunteered to play for a campaign to sell Liberty Bonds. They hired a cart, climbed into it and put on a "New Orleans Jazz Jam" on Wabash Street for the crowds that swarmed through the Loop. The "tail gate" trombone was something new to Chicagoans. . . . For Chicagoans who lived by night, the band was not such a novelty; they had already discovered Joe playing in two South Side night spots.

There were two main reasons for the rise of Chicago as the "hot" music center of the country: the fall of New Orleans's Storyville, a red-light district closed by federal edict, and the mass hegira of Negroes to the North. New Orleans's loss was Chicago's gain. As the *Chicago Defender* put it:

> The Original Creole Band came to Chicago at the Grand Theater. Keppard and Bill Williams made a hit. Creole brothers down South heard of their success and, one by one, came to the land of free and plenty dollars.

Among the jazz instrumentalists preceding Oliver in Chicago were clarinetists Sidney Bechet and Jimmy Noone. When the "King" organized a band for the Dreamland in 1920 (to play there all the time, and give up the work and Royal Gardens), among those he recruited were Honore Dutrey, trombone; and Lil Hardin, piano; Jimmy Noone, leaving to strike out on his own, was replaced by Johnny Dodds, fresh from New Orleans.

"King" Joe and his men had little use for written music; on the stands were a few scribbled-over sheets with the titles torn off to thwart visiting musicians who had come to purloin.

Oliver left Chicago in the spring of 1927, five years after a new "King" had come upon the scene. Shortly before his departure he wrote a song, "Doctor Jazz," which he peddled from a cart occupied by his band, playing the new tune wherever a crowd gathered. This was probably the last time a New Orleans band played in a wagon. He died in a small southern town, 1938.[7]

The new "King," whom Oliver had brought up from New Orleans in 1922, and who played second trumpet behind the leader, was Louis Armstrong. Musicians and public, discovering the superiority of the younger man, clamored for the positions to be reversed. Armstrong left Oliver to go to the Dreamland as first cornet. In September 1924, Armstrong and his wife, Lil Hardin, pianist, went to New York to make recordings. Armstrong remained in New York to play with Fletcher Henderson's popular Roseland band. Lil returned to Chicago and organized her own orchestra for the Dreamland Café.

A dozen years later Lil was still playing the piano and singing her "Brown Gal" number around Chicago. In the middle thirties, she opened a "swing shack" on Chicago's South Side, serving a meal guaranteed to be "a solid sender right in the groove," choice of "Tisket Biscuits and Tasket Hash, Rug Cutter's Roast and Killer Diller Waffles."

Other Negroes promoting the new music in Chicago during the years following the First World War include Erskine Tate, Charley Cook, Clarence Jones, Luis Russell, Billy Ward, Lawrence Harding, Dave Peyton, Carrol Dickerson, Robert ("Bob") Schaffner, Sammy Stewart, and Hartzell ("Tiny") Parham. Later came Les Hite, Willie Bryant, Earl ("Fatha") Hines, Lionel Hampton, Jack Ellis, Walter Barnes, and a host of others.

Three occurrences highlight the story of jazz in Chicago: King Oliver's arrival with the new music, Louis Armstrong's origination of "Scat" singing, and the recording of Clarence ("Pine Top") Smith's Boogie Woogie piano, in March 1928. Boogie Woogie was nothing new. A primitive method of piano playing developed by Negro ear-musicians, it had been played up and down the Mississippi for many decades, but it remained for Smith to put it on wax.[8]

The real vogue for this sort of thing, however, followed the appearance of two of "Pine Top's" Chicago friends, Albert Ammons and Meade Lewis, at Carnegie Hall in New York City. A predecessor of these two, Cleo Brown, had played in many Chicago "spots" before recording her version of the "boogie woogie."

Another early exponent of the style was Jimmy Yancey. Settling in Chicago in 1913 after a long career in vaudeville, Yancey was for years a welcome guest at "house-rent" parties and at taverns. "Cripple" Clarence Lofton is still another Chicago exponent of the "fast blues."

Still another type of music to come out of Chicago and gain popularity in recent years is the so-called "gospel song." In less than twelve years, these "swing spirituals" have pushed all other sacred music into the background in many Negro churches. According to Thomas A. Dorsey, the leading writer and purveyor of the new religious songs, they are "gospel sermons preached in music." Though this type of music made its appearance in 1905, it was in the thirties that it gained wide popularity, its rise being due mainly to Dorsey, formerly a composer of blues. When he started writing these "new spirituals" in 1928, he found no market. For a number of years he and his associates traveled the country over singing them to the people. Many churches closed their doors to him. But despite opposition he established a reputation and before his travels ended, many of the same churches were clamoring for his and other gospel composers' works.[9] The Gospel Choral Union of America, a national organization promoting this music, was formed in 1932 by Dorsey, with headquarters in Chicago and branches throughout the country. Although of Negro origin, "gospel songs" appealed to others as well, as revealed by Dorsey's statement that thirty to forty percent of his customers were white. Most popular of these compositions were two by Dorsey, "How About You?" and "Precious Lord Take My Hand," and one by Roberta Martin, "Didn't It Rain?" Blues and spirituals being closely related, it was not surprising to find a number of prominent Negro women blues singers, among them Sara Martin and Virginia Liston, finishing their careers singing spirituals and "gospel songs" in churches.[10]

Every year a new crop of young hopefuls gather outside night "spots," trying to extract music from home-made instruments: cigar-box guitars, tin-can cymbals, soap-box drums. Eventually some of these toy instruments are exchanged for second-hand clarinets, drums, and trombones, thus a new generation of swing musicians is born. This is the pattern.

As one observer pointed out, places of entertainment in Chicago Negro neighborhoods often close, but the music goes on. When a place "folds," it's "Bring yo' stuff on over to my house an' we'll have a party an' sweat." That's all! It's different in uptown Chicago; there "they glow and may even perspire, but the jazzmen seldom sweat."

In the spring of 1939, Johnny Dodds gave a concert at Mandel Hall, University of Chicago, and proved there was at least one clarinet that could span the years between the New Orleans days of famed Storyville and the present. With Lil Hardin at the piano, according to one reporter, he showed there was still "as much fire, as much of the blues, in his instrument, as there always was." After the concert he was seen wrapping his clarinet in a newspaper; probably he had never had a case to carry it in.

Bibliography

This list of sources was compiled from a 1942 bibliography found in the papers of Arna Bontemps at Syracuse University.

Documents (official records, and federal, state, county, and municipal publications and reports)

Chicago Board of Education. *Annual Reports of Superintendent of Schools*.

Chicago Commission on Race Relations. *The Negro in Chicago: A Study of Race Relations and a Race Riot*. Chicago: University of Chicago Press, 1922.

Chicago Housing Authority. *Report of 1940*.

Illinois State Commission on the Condition of the Urban Colored Population. *Report of 1941*.

Illinois State Historical Library. *Illinois Census Returns, 1820*. Edited by Margaret Cross Norton, 1934.

Illinois State Housing Board. *Report of 1938*.

Illinois State Militia. *Biennial Report of Adjutant-General*. January 1878.

Provident Hospital. *Annual Report*. 1938.

United States Bureau of the Census. *Reports*.

United States Bureau of Labor. *Slums of Baltimore, Chicago, New York and Philadelphia*. 1894.

United States Department of Labor, Division of Negro Economics. *Negro Migration in 1916–17*. Bulletin, 1919.

United States Housing Authority. *The Negro and Low-Rent Housing*. Leaflet by Robert C. Weaver, 1938.

United States President's Conference on Home Building and Home Ownership. *Report of Committee on Negro Housing*. 1932.

United States Public Health Service. *Mortality among Negroes in the United States*. Bulletin No. 174. 1928.

United States Supreme Court. *The Dred Scott Decision*. New York: Van Evrie, Horton, 1863.

Histories (published historical and sociological collections, reports, and books dealing specifically with the Negro or Illinois)

Aldrich, O.W. "Slavery or Involuntary Servitude in Illinois Prior to and after Admission as a State." *Illinois State Historical Society Journal*, 1916: 119–32.

Allen, James S. *The American Negro*. New York: International, 1932.

Alvord, Clarence Walworth, ed. *Centennial History of Illinois*. Springfield and Chicago: Illinois Centennial Commission and A. C. McClurg, 1917–22.

———. *Governor Edward Coles, Second Governor of Illinois, and of the Slavery Struggle of 1823–4*. Springfield: Trustees of the Illinois State Historical Library, 1920.

Alvord, Clarence Walworth and Evarts Boutell Greene Ed. *The Governor's Letter-Books, 1818–1834, 1840–1853*. Edited by C. W. Alvord and E. B. Greene. Springfield: Trustees of the Illinois State Historical Library, 1909–11.

Andreas, A. T. *History of Chicago, from the Earliest Period to the Present Time*. Chicago, 1884–86.

Baird, H. C. *Washington and Jackson on Negro Soldiers*. Philadelphia: Johnson, 1863.

Baker, Ray Stannard. *Following the Color Line: An Account of Negro Citizenship in the American Democracy*. New York: Doubleday, Page, 1908.

Bowen, Louise de Koven. *The Colored People of Chicago: An Investigation Made for the Juvenile Protective Association, by A. P. Drucker, Sophia Boaz, A. L. Harris, Miriam Shaffner*. Chicago: Rogers Hall, 1913.

Brawley, Benjamin G. *Negro Builders and Heroes*. Revised edition. Chapel Hill: University of North Carolina Press, 1937.

———. *The Negro in Literature and Art in the United States*. New York: Duffield, 1921.

Brown, Ina Corrine. *The Story of the American Negro*. London: Student Christian Movement, 1936.

Brown, Sterling A. *The Negro in American Fiction*. Washington, D.C.: Associates in Negro Folk Education, 1937.

———. *Negro Poetry and Drama*. Washington, D.C.: Associates in Negro Folk Education, 1937.

Brown, Sterling, Arthur P. Davis, and Ulysses Lee. *The Negro Caravan: Writings by American Negroes*. New York: Dryden, 1941.

Cayton, Horace, and George Mitchell. *Black Workers and the New Unions*. Chapel Hill: University of North Carolina Press, 1939.

Chandler, Frank. *Che-cau-gou: A History; A Romance in the Evolution of a Great City from the Garden of Eden to the End of the Twentieth Century*. Chicago: Fauthorn, 1924.

Child, Lydia Maria. *The Freedmen's Book*. Boston: Fields, Osgood, 1869.

Culp, D. W., ed. *Twentieth Century Negro Literature*. Naperville, Ill.: Nichols, 1912.

Currey, J. Seymour. *Chicago: Its History and Its Builders*. Chicago: Clarke, 1912.

Davis, Elizabeth. *Lifting as They Climb*. Washington, D.C.: National Association of Colored Women, 1933.

Detweiler, Frederick. *The Negro Press in the United States*. Chicago: University of Chicago Press, 1922.

Dowd, Jerome. *The Negro in American Life*. New York: Century, 1926.

Du Bois, W. E. B. *Black Reconstruction*. New York: Harcourt, Brace, 1938.

Duke, Charles. *The Housing Situation and the Colored People of Chicago*. Chicago, 1919.

Eleazer, Robert B. *Singers in the Dawn*. Atlanta: Conference on Education and Race Relations, 1934.

Embree, Edwin R. *Brown America*. New York: Viking, 1931.

Eppse, Merl R. *The Negro, Too, in American History*. Chicago: National Education, 1938.

Frazier, E. Franklin. *The Negro Family in Chicago*. Chicago: University of Chicago Press, 1932.

———. *Negro Youth at the Crossways*. (Prepared by the American Youth Commission.) Washington, D.C.: American Council on Education, 1940.

Gannett, Henry. *Occupations of the Negroes*. Occasional papers. Baltimore: Trustees of the John F. Slater Fund, 1895.

Goode, W. T. *The Eighth Illinois*. Chicago: Blakely, 1899.

Gosnell, Harold. *Negro Politicians: The Rise of Negro Politics in Chicago*. Chicago: University of Chicago Press, 1935.

Green, Elizabeth. *The Negro Contemporary American Literature*. Chapel Hill: University of North Carolina Press, 1928.

Hare, Maud Cuney. *Negro Musicians and Their Music.* Washington, D.C.: Associated, 1936.

Harris, Abram L. *The Negro as Capitalist: A Study of Baking and Business among American Negroes.* Philadelphia: American Academy of Political and Social Science, 1936.

Harris, I. C. *Directory of Professional and Business Colored Men of Chicago.* Chicago: 1885.

Harris, Norman D. *The History of Negro Servitude in Illinois, and the Slavery Agitation in that State, 1719–1864.* Chicago: McClurg, 1904.

Henderson, Edwin Bancroft. *The Negro in Sports.* Washington, D.C: Associated, 1939.

Herbst, Alma. *The Negro in the Slaughtering and Meat Packing Industry in Chicago.* Boston: Houghton, Mifflin, 1932.

Howe, S. G. *The Refugees from Slavery in Canada West: A Report to the Freedmen's Inquiry Commission.* Boston: Wright and Potter, 1864.

Illinois Writers' Project. *Cavalcade of the American Negro.* Chicago: Diamond Jubilee Exposition Authority, 1940.

———. *Illinois: A Descriptive and Historical Guide.* American Guide Series. Chicago: McClurg, 1939.

Johnson, Charles S., ed. *Ebony and Topaze.* New York: National Urban League, 1927.

———. *The Negro College Graduate.* Chapel Hill: University of North Carolina, 1938.

Johnson, James Weldon. *Book of American Negro Poetry.* New York: Harcourt, Brace, 1931.

Johnson, Kathryn M., and Addie D. Hunton. *Two Colored Women with the American Expeditionary Forces.* Brooklyn: Brooklyn Eagle, 1920.

Jones, John. *The Black Laws of Illinois and a Few Reasons Why They Should Be Repealed.* Chicago: Tribune, 1864.

Julius Rosenwald Fund. *Negro Hospitals: A Compilation of Available Statistics.* 1931.

Kenney, John A. *The Negro in Medicine.* Tuskegee: Tuskegee Institute Press, 1912.

Kerlin, Robert T. *Negro Poets and Their Poems.* Washington, D.C.: Associated, 1923.

Kletzing, H. F., and W. H. Crogman. *Progress of a Race, or The Remarkable Advancement of the Afro-American.* Naperville, Ill: Nichols, 1903.

Locke, Alain. *The Negro in Art.* Washington, D.C.: Associates in Negro Folk Education, 1940.

———. *The New Negro.* New York: Boni, 1925.

Loggins, Vernon. *The Negro Author: His Development in America.* New York: Columbia University Press, 1931.

MacNaul, Willard C. *The Jefferson-Lemen Compact: The Relations of Thomas Jefferson and James Lemen in the Exclusion of Slavery from Illinois and the Northwest Territory, with Related Documents, 1781–1818.* A paper read before the Chicago Historical Society. Chicago: University of Chicago Press, 1915.

Nelson, J. H. *The Negro Character in American Literature.* Bulletin of the University of Kansas. Lawrence: Department of Journalism Press, 1926.

Nichols, J. L., and W. H. Crogman. *The New Progress of a Race.* Naperville, Ill: Nichols, 1920.

Page, Thomas Nelson. *The Negro: The Southerner's Problem.* New York: Scribner's, 1904.

Penn, I. Garland. *The Afro-American Press and Its Editors.* Springfield, Mass: Willey, 1891.

Pierce, Bessie Louise. *A History of Chicago.* New York: Knopf, 1937.

Quaife, Milo. *Checagou: From Indian Wigwam to Modern City.* Chicago: University of Chicago Press, 1933.

Redding, J. Saunders. *To Make a Poet Black.* Chapel Hill: University of North Carolina Press, 1939.

Reid, Ira De Augustine. *Adult Education Among Negroes.* Washington, D.C.: Associates in Negro Folk Education, 1936.

Richardson, Clement, ed. *The National Cyclopedia of the Colored Race.* Montgomery, Ala.: National, 1919.

Robb, Frederick H., ed. *Intercollegian Wonder Book: The Negro in Chicago; A Survey of the Negro's Educational, Athletic, Civic and Commercial Life from 1779 to 1927.* Chicago: Washington Intercollegiate Club, 1927.

Sandburg, Carl. *The Chicago Race Riots, July 1919.* New York: Harcourt, Brace and Howe, 1919.

Scott, Emmett J. *Negro Migration during the War*. New York: Oxford University Press, 1920.

Siebert, Wilber H. *The Underground Railroad from Slavery to Freedom*. New York: Macmillan, 1898.

Sinclair, William A. *The Aftermath of Slavery: A Study of the Condition and Environment of the American Negro*. Boston: Small Maynard, 1898.

Smith, Samuel Denny. *The Negro in Congress, 1870–1901*. Chapel Hill: University of North Carolina Press, 1940.

Spero, Sterling, and Abram L. Harris. *The Black Worker: The Negro and the Labor Movement*. New York: Columbia University Press, 1931.

Sweeney, W. Allison. *History of the American Negro in the Great World War*. Chicago: Cuneo-Hennebery, 1919.

Tilley, John L. *A Brief History of the Negro in Chicago, 1799–1933*. Chicago, 1933.

Trotter, James M. *Music and Some Highly Musical People*. New York: Dillingham, 1878.

Virginia Writers' Project. *The Negro in Virginia*. New York: Hastings, 1940.

Washington, Booker T. *The Negro in Business*. Boston: Hertel, Jenkins, 1907.

———. *The Story of the Negro: The Rise of the Race from Slavery*. New York: Doubleday, Page, 1909.

Wells, Ida B. et al. *The Reason Why the Colored American Is Not in the World's Columbian Exposition*. Chicago, 1893.

Wesley, Charles H. *Negro Labor in the United States, 1850–1925: A Study in American Economic History*. New York: Vanguard, 1927.

Whipple, Leon. *The Story of Civil Liberty in the United States*. New York: Vanguard, American Civil Liberties Union, 1927.

Williams, Charles H. *Sidelights on Negro Soldiers*. Boston: Brimmer, 1923.

Williams, George W. *History of the Negro Race in America from 1619 to 1880*. New York: Putnam's, 1882.

———. *Negro Troops in the Rebellion: A Review of the Military Services of Negroes in Ancient and Modern Times*. New York: Harper, 1888.

Wood, Junius B. *The Negro in Chicago*. Chicago: Chicago Daily News, 1916.

Woods, Norman B. *The White Side of a Black Subject: A Vindication of the Afro-American Race*. Chicago: American, 1897.

Woodson, Carter G. *A Century of Negro Migration*. Washington, D.C.: Association for the Study of Negro Life and History, 1918.

———. *Negro Makers of History*. Washington, D.C.: Associated, 1928.

Work, Monroe Nathan, ed. *Negro Year Book: An Annual Encyclopedia of the Negro*. Nashville: Nashville Sunday School Union, 1912.

Diaries, Memoirs, Autobiographies, Biographies, Travel Books

Brawley, Benjamin. *Paul Laurence Dunbar*. Chapel Hill: University of North Carolina Press, 1936.

Coffin, Levi. *Reminiscences of Levi Coffin*. Cincinnati: Clark, 1880.

Cromwell, John W. *The Negro in American History*. Washington, D.C.: American Negro Academy, 1914.

Douglass, Frederick. *The Life and Times of Frederick Douglass*. Revised ed. New York, Pathway, 1941.

Garvey, Marcus. *Philosophy and Opinions of Marcus Garvey*. New York: Universal, 1923.

Mott, Abigail. *Biographical Sketches and Interesting Anecdotes of Persons of Color*. New York: Mahlon Day, 1826.

Simmons, William J. *Men of Mark*. Cleveland: Rewell, 1887.

Villard, Oswald Garrison. *John Brown: A Biography Fifty Years After*. Boston: Houghton, Mifflin, 1910.

Washburne, Elihu. *Sketch of Edward Coles, Second Governor of Illinois, and the Slavery Struggle of 1823–4*. Chicago: Jansen, McClurg, 1882.

Washington, John E. *They Knew Lincoln*. New York: Dutton, 1942.

Who's Who in Colored America. New York: Who's Who in Colored America Corporation, 1927.

General Sources (broader histories and other sources that address subject)

Asbury, Herbert. *Gem of the Prairie: An Informal History of the Chicago Underworld*. New York: Knopf, 1940.

————. *The French Quarter: An Informal History of the New Orleans Underworld*. New York: Garden City, 1938.

Collins, H. O. *History of the Illinois National Guard, from the Organization of the First Regiment, in September 1874, to the Enactment of the Military Code, in May 1879*. Chicago: Black and Beach, 1884.

Commager, Henry S., and Samuel E. Morison. *The Growth of the American Republic*. London: Oxford University Press, 1930.

Graham, Stephen. *The Soul of John Brown*. New York: Macmillan, 1920.

Hesseltine, William B. *A History of the South, 1607–1936*. New York: Prentice Hall, 1936.

Houghteling, Leila. *The Income and Standard of Living of Unskilled Laborers in Chicago*. Chicago: University of Chicago Press, 1927.

Philbrick, Francis Samuel, ed. *The Laws of Indiana Territory 1801–1809*. Springfield: Trustees of the Illinois State Historical Library, 1930.

Ramsey, Frederic, Jr., and Charles Edward Smith. *Jazzmen*. New York: Harcourt, Brace, 1939.

Stackhouse, Perry James. *Chicago and the Baptists: A Century of Progress*. Chicago: University of Chicago Press, 1933.

Stein, Davis, et al. *Labor Problems in America*. New York: Farrar and Rinehart, 1940.

Turner, L. D. *Anti-Slavery Sentiment in American Literature Prior to 1865*. Washington, D.C.: Association for the Study of Negro Life and History, 1929.

Wooldridge, C. R. *Hands Up in the World of Crime; Or, 12 Years a Detective*. Chicago, Thompson and Thomas, 1901.

Magazines and Periodicals

The American Journal of Sociology
Crisis
The Journal of Negro History
Opportunity: A Journal of Negro Life
Survey
Southern Workman
The Negro World
Negro Youth

Newspapers

Afro-American Press
Alton Observer
Atlanta Constitution
Aurora Beacon
Broad Ax
Belleville Advocate
Birmingham Age-Herald
Bulletin (Louisville, KY)
Cairo Bulletin
Cairo City Times

Cairo Daily Democrat
Cairo Gazette
Cairo Weekly Times
Central Illinois Gazette
Champlain Gazette
Chicago Appeal
Chicago Bee
Chicago Daily Bulletin
Chicago Daily Democrat
Chicago Daily Inter Ocean
Chicago Daily Journal
Chicago Daily Mirror
Chicago Daily News
Chicago Defender
Chicago Enterprise
Chicago Evening American
Chicago Evening Journal
Chicago Leader
Chicago Times
Chicago Tribune
Chicago World
Cleveland Leader
Conservatore
Daily Democrat Press
Daily Drover's Journal
Daily North Western
Dynamite
East St. Louis Gazette
East St. Louis Journal
Edwardsville Spectator
Evanston Right Way
Free West
Gary Tribune
Genius
Genius of Liberty
Genius of Universal Emancipation
Illinois Chronicle
Illinois Daily State Register
Illinois Idea
Illinois Register and People's Advocate
Illinois State Journal
Illinois State Register
Indianapolis Freeman
Journal
Liberator
Liberty Banner
London Times
Macon Sun (Georgia)
Memphis Commercial Appeal
Memphis Confederate Appeal

Memphis Free Speech
Missouri Republican
Morgan Journal
National Era
Negro Youth
New York Age
New York Herald
New York Sun
New York Tribune
Peoria Daily National Democrat
Peoria Daily Transcript
Philanthropist
Pittsburg Courier
Port Gibson Reveille (Mississippi)
Quincy Herald
Quincy Whig
Sangamon Spectator
Shawneetown Local Record
Spectator
Springfield Chronicle
State Capital (Springfield, Ill.)
St. Louis Globe-Democrat
St. Louis Observer
St. Louis Post-Dispatch
St. Louis Times
Telegraph
Western Appeal (St. Paul, Minn.)
Western Citizen
Western Opinion
Whip
Wilmington Star (North Carolina)

Manuscript and Mimeographed Studies, Theses, etc.

Davis, R. N. *The Negro Newspapers in Chicago*. Thesis, University of Chicago, 1939.

Dixon, Herman. *The Near West Side*. Thesis, University of Chicago, n.d.

Drake, St. Clair. *Churches and Voluntary Associations in the Chicago Negro Community*. WPA District 3, Project No. 165–54–6999 Official Report. Chicago, 1939.

Reddick, Lawrence Dunbar. *A Sociological History of the Negro in Chicago*. WPA monograph, n.d.

Rood, Alice Q. *Social Conditions among Negroes on Federal Street Between 45th and 53rd Streets*. Thesis, University of Chicago, 1924.

Scott, Estelle. *Occupational Changes among Negroes in Chicago*. WPA monograph, 1939.

Semper, Joseph. *Business in the Negro Community*. WPA monograph, 1939.

Smith, Herbert Morrison. *Three Negro Preachers in Chicago: A Study in Religious Leadership*. Thesis, University of Chicago, 1935.

Sutherland, Robert I. *An Analysis of Negro Churches in Chicago*. Thesis, University of Chicago, 1930.

Urban League. *Second Annual Report for the Fiscal Year Ending Oct. 31, 1918: On Urban Conditions among Negroes*. 1918.

Work, M. N. *Negro Real Estate Holders of Chicago*. Thesis, University of Chicago, 1903.

Wright, Richard R. *The Industrial Conditions of Negroes in Chicago*. University of Chicago Thesis, 1901.

Poetry, Novels, Essays, Articles, Orations, Plays, and Miscellaneous Works

Blazer, D. N. "History of the Underground Railroad of McDonough County, Illinois." *Illinois State Historical Society Journal* 15, nos. 3–4 (October 1922–January 1923).

Bowen, Louise de Koven. "The Colored People of Chicago, Where Their Opportunity Is Choked, Where Open." *Survey* 1 (November 1913): 117–20.

Cayton, Horace. "Negro Housing in Chicago." *Opportunity*, December 1937–January 1938.

Cooley, Verna. "Illinois and the Underground Railroad to Canada." *Transactions of the Illinois Historical Society* 23 (1917): 76–98.

Du Bois, W. E. B. "The Negro in Literature and Art." *Annals*, American Academy of Political and Social Science. Vol. 49 no. 138 (1913).

Fanning, John W. "Negro Migration." *Bulletin of the University of Georgia* 30, no. 8b (1930).

Mann, Charles W. "The Chicago Common Council and the Fugitive Slave Law of 1850." *Chicago Historical Society Proceedings* 2 (1903–5): 75–86.

Rogers, J. A. *From Superman to Man*. New York: Rogers and Hubner, 1917.

Schmidt, O. L. "An Address on the Illinois Underground Railroad." *Illinois State Historical Society Journal*, October 1925, 703–17.

Schomburg, Arthur. *A Bibliographical Checklist of American Negro Poetry*. New York: Heartman, 1916.

Work, M. N. "Crime among the Negros of Chicago." *American Journal of Sociology*, September 1900, 541–62.

Editor's Afterword

When *The Negro in Illinois* was closed down, the editors Arna Bontemps and Jack Conroy did not leave behind a conclusion to the twenty-nine chapters they had compiled. As a result, the narrative drops off precipitously at the end of the chapter on "Rhythm." The incompleteness of this text may cause us to reflect on what has been characterized as a lack of self-awareness or cohesiveness to Chicago's Black Renaissance. Surely, the failure to publish this work further contributed to the neglect of the movement. Under the supervision of Bontemps and Conroy, this office was arguably the most productive and best staffed of Sterling Brown's seventeen projects. We can only speculate today how publication of *The Negro in Illinois* may have given greater exposure to the number of talented writers that congregated in Chicago during the Depression. The cancellation of the Illinois Writers' Project also contributed to the eventual breakup of this community.

Literary scholar Lawrence Jackson includes writers of the Chicago Renaissance among those he calls the "indignant generation." The success of some black artists during this period, he writes, has "overshadowed history's awareness of their 'positive action' or contribution to a group 'historical destiny.' Individual black writers did so well, especially between 1940 and 1953, that the idea of the artists operating as a cohort has been obscured" (3). With Richard Wright's rapid rise to world-renowned fame, he became removed from the South Side community that had produced him. Returning to his Chicago roots also requires that we reexamine the number of talented young writers whom he worked with and struggled alongside.

There was admittedly no apparent attempt to theorize the Chicago Renaissance or advocate for a unified approach by those who were involved. There was no anthology equivalent to Alain Locke's *New Negro*. The few black literary magazines that were launched in Chicago, such as Fenton Johnson's *Favorite Magazine*, Robert S. Abbott's *Abbott's Monthly*, and Alice Browning's *Negro Story*, were short-lived. The closest thing to a manifesto is Richard Wright's much anthologized "Blueprint for Negro Writing," although the essay is typically attributed solely to Wright, and members of the South Side Writers' Group with whom he wrote the essay have been pushed into the background. The fall 1937 issue of *New Challenge* where the essay first appeared was co-edited by Marian Minus and featured poetry by Frank Marshall Davis, Robert Davis, and Margaret Walker, all founding members of the South Side Writers' Group. In the final section of "Blueprint for Negro Writing," Wright urged black writers to overcome their isolation and work collectively. Members of the South Side Writers' Group had come together to work in a collective environment. Wright had learned the importance of working collectively in the Chicago chapter of the John Reed Clubs. He and others experienced it while working on the Illinois Writers' Project.

Writers of the Chicago Renaissance did not immediately record their experiences as did those who were in Harlem for the New Negro movement. When Wright wrote about his time in Chicago, much of it was viewed through an anti-Communist lens. Scholars have often treated his years in Chicago as a temporary way station between his youth in the South, which he had escaped, and New York, where he achieved his literary fame. It was not until several decades later that Margaret Walker published her account of working with Wright on the Illinois Writers' Project in her biography of the author, *Daemonic Genius* (1988). Autobiographies by Horace Cayton (1965) and Gwendolyn Brooks (1972) appeared more than a decade after the accepted dates of the Chicago Renaissance. Other recollections were written for small publications and not reprinted. It was not until the 1980s that Katherine Dunham sat down to write her autobiography, fragments of which went unpublished until 2005 when the collection *Kaiso!* was released. Many of these writers were simply trying to make a living and did not have the time to document their memories.

When the Illinois Writers' Project closed its doors, it took away an important source of income for writers, and they often found themselves unemployed once again. Not long after the project shut down, some left Chicago to find work elsewhere. Arna Bontemps finished his schooling and moved to Nashville a year later to take a job at Fisk University. Margaret Walker went on to graduate school in Iowa, started a family, and later became a teacher in Jackson, Mississippi. Frank Yerby also went to teach in the South and made a deliberate decision to spend his career churning out commercially successful novels. Other ambitious young writers went to New York or Hollywood to try to make it. Some remained in Chicago and sustained themselves by writing for black publications like the *Chicago Defender*, *Chicago Bee*, or *Negro Digest*. Some wrote scripts for Chicago-based radio stations, which would dedicate an occasional hour to "race" programming. Sadly, others found it too difficult to make a living by their pen and years later died in obscurity.

Despite its short-lived existence, the Illinois Writers' Project played a major role in supporting black writers when there were few opportunities available to them. At this time, the American "free" press remained segregated, with white magazines and newspapers refusing to hire black writers. During World War II, black war correspondents were for the first time sent to Europe to cover the war, but they were all reporting for black newspapers. The publishing industry, after fulfilling a temporary appetite for books about the "race problem" during the war, soon lost interest in publishing black authors.

One of those who is today little known but was able to carve out a living as a writer was Robert Lucas, who worked on the Illinois Writers' Project from 1938 to 1942. In the years immediately after the project, he worked several jobs writing for radio in order to provide for his wife and children. In his application for a 1948 Rosenwald fellowship, he described the difficult conditions he faced in the field of radio. "It is quite apparent," he observed, "that since the end of World War II the number of radio shows dealing with the Negro has dropped sharply." Despite what he called an "uncertain market," he was convinced he could make it as a freelance radio writer. There remained much work to be done by black writers in radio "as far as inter-cultural relations are concerned."[1]

After former IWP worker Robert Davis moved to Hollywood in 1946, he acted in a couple of movies, but he found it increasingly difficult to gain acting jobs as the blacklist settled in. He worked at a Chrysler assembly plant in the mid-1950s. In a 1957 letter to Langston Hughes, he said that there had been no roles in film and television. "The Blacklist still persists," he wrote.[2] Davis continued to teach amateur acting classes and perform in community theater. To get by, he did handyman work for friends. It was not until the 1960s that he began to get more consistent work.

At a time when many were unwilling to hire African American writers, the WPA gave them a job. Before becoming editor of *Ebony* magazine, Era Bell Thompson spent five years working for the WPA typing letters and filing documents. When she created a newspaper for staff members called the *Giggle Sheet*, her supervisor suggested she was better suited for the Writers' Project, but Thompson turned down the offer because she would have to take a pay cut. Without the help of WPA, Thompson would have had to resort to domestic work like most other black women. Even having obtained a college degree, she was repeatedly turned down for jobs. The WPA opened doors for thousands like Thompson and increasingly there were more black faces behind desks. As she observed in her 1946 autobiography, *American Daughter*, the growing numbers of black workers in white-collar jobs "has brought about a healthy change in public attitude" (298). Due to the WPA and its cultural projects, the United States experienced a significant democratization of the workforce.

More than just a job, the Federal Writers' Project gave a generation of African American writers the hope that they could continue to follow their dreams. Although they were "on relief," they still took pride in their work. Many looked back fondly on their time at the Illinois Writers' Project. They developed friendships that would last for several decades after the project ended. The contacts they made helped them to get published in journals and anthologies. A few of them would collaborate on other fruitful ventures. The Writers' Project sustained many who were struggling to survive during the bleak years of the Depression when jobs were scarce for most, but for black writers trying to make their way in the white-dominated media, the road was a weary one.

Would *The Negro in Illinois* have been published in its day, we would surely have a greater appreciation for the special convergence of African American writers in Chicago during the Depression. Publication of, for example, the "Literature" chapter may have provided a much-needed summary of the literary precursors and influences behind the Black Chicago Renaissance. Yet the editors Arna Bontemps and Jack Conroy should not be faulted for failing to see the project through to its end. We should not overlook the importance of government sponsorship of the arts during the 1930s. It was particularly of great benefit to black writers who were otherwise marginalized from the American mainstream. We can only imagine how Chicago's literary legacy might be remembered if the ten-chapter manuscript on the black press, the Dunham-headed study of black cults, the Bontemps-directed project on black music, or Kitty Chapelle's seven-hundred-page manuscript on black culture would have been published. If the "WPA Poems" by Fenton Johnson had finally found a publisher, this early black poet may have received his long overdue recognition. With the final reuniting of the twenty-nine chapters of *The Negro in Illinois*, we now have a document that may begin to bring writers of the Chicago Renaissance their due credit.

Editor's Notes

Editor's Introduction

1. Although *The Negro in Illinois* drew upon some of the WPA studies conducted under the supervision of Horace Cayton, those on the Illinois Writers' Project had a much different purpose, and the manuscript they produced has little resemblance to *Black Metropolis*.

2. See Robert Bone's 1986 essay, "Richard Wright and the Chicago Renaissance," as well as the book *The Muse in Bronzeville: African American Creative Expression in Chicago, 1932–1950* (2011) in which literary scholar Richard A. Courage completes Bone's project on Chicago.

3. See Bill Mullen, *Popular Fronts: Chicago and African-American Cultural Politics, 1935–46* (1999); Adam Green, *Selling the Race: Culture, Community, and Black Chicago, 1940–1955* (2007); Davarian Baldwin, *Chicago's New Negroes: Modernity, the Great Migration, and Black Urban Life* (2007); Christopher Reed, *The Rise of Chicago's Black Metropolis, 1920–1929* (2011); Anne Meis Knupfer, *The Chicago Black Renaissance and Women's Activism* (2006).

4. The notable African American writer Willard Motley worked for the Illinois Writers' Project, but there is no indication that he contributed any writings to *The Negro in Illinois*. Motley was encouraged to apply for the IWP by Jack Conroy and Nelson Algren, who were also working there, and in April 1940 he was hired. As he wrote in his diary, the time on the project gave him "security to write, to think about writing, to go on writing." During these years he was working intensely on his bestselling novel *Knock on Any Door* (1947). Motley was periodically on and off project working for the Chicago Housing Authority, the Pan-American Unit, and a map project. For more see *The Diaries of Willard Motley* (1979), edited by Jerome Klinkowitz.

5. For more about Henry Alsberg and the creation of the American Guide Series, see Monty Noam Penkower, *The Federal Writers' Project: A Study in Government Patronage of the Arts* (1977).

6. For more on John P. Davis, see the chapter on the National Negro Congress in Brian Dolinar, *The Black Cultural Front: Black Writers and Artists of the Depression Generation* (2012).

7. See Kathleen O'Connor McKinzie's dissertation from Indiana University (1970), "Writers on Relief, 1935–1942," 136–37. For more about Brown's time as Editor of Negro Affairs, see John Edgar Tidwell, "Recasting Negro Life History: Sterling A. Brown and the Federal Writers' Project."

8. "New Deal Agencies" microfilm, reel 23, #956.

9. Rollins to Alsberg, December 11, 1936 ("New Deal Agencies" microfilm, roll 23, #573).

10. Brown to Frederick, September 24, 1937 ("New Deal Agencies" microfilm, roll 23, #901). Frederick's WPA-issued notice to appear for work is dated August 20, 1937, and is held in his papers at the University of Iowa (box 45).

11. Despite some claims, I could find no evidence that William Attaway worked for the Illinois Writers' Project. Attaway's novels are discussed in the "Literature" chapter herewith, but there is no mention that Attaway ever worked on the IWP. For more, see the entry on Attaway by Richard Yarborough in *Writers of the Black Chicago Renaissance* (2011), edited by Steven Tracy.

12. Frederick to Brown, September 28, 1937 ("New Deal Agencies" microfilm, reel 23, #771).

13. Cronyn to Rollins, September 28, 1936 (National Archives, Records of the WPA, box 15).

14. The list is dated March 3, 1937 (FWP papers, Abraham Lincoln Presidential Library, box 199).

15. The report is dated April 22, 1937. Copies of it can be found in Springfield, at the Library of Congress, and the National Archives.

16. Brown to Alsberg, June 8, 1937 ("New Deal Agencies" microfilm, reel 23, #989).

17. Jerrold Hirsch, *Portrait of America: A Cultural History of the Federal Writers' Project* (2003).

18. Brown to Gorham Munson, January 9, 1940 ("New Deal Agencies" microfilm, reel 23, #440).

19. Dated November 18, 1939 ("New Deal Agencies" microfilm, reel 23, #466).

20. Brown to Alsberg, June 17 and June 22, 1938 ("New Deal Agencies" microfilm, reel 24, #11; reel 23 #1000–1).

21. Ten of these articles were published with an introduction by Brian Dolinar in *Southern Quarterly*, Winter 2009: "Ethnographical Aspects of Chicago's Black Belt" (December 11, 1935), "The Chicago Urban League" (January 8, 1936), "On the Ethnography of the Negro (Additional)" (January 13, 1936), "White City—Recreational Center," "Hotels" (March 3, 1937), "A Survey of the Amusement Facilities of District #35" (March 3, 1937), "Washington Park" (March 27, 1937?), "Amusements in Districts 38 and 40" (1937), "Agriculture and Farm Life" with Merrell Gregory (undated), "Bibliography on Negro in Chicago" (undated).

22. A copy of the short story is in the IWP papers at the Vivian G. Harsh Research Collection of Afro-American History and Literature (box 53, folder 3).

23. Hazel Rowley, in her biography of Richard Wright, cites two articles, "Outdoor Theatre in Chicago" (January 5, 1936) and "Playwrights in Chicago" (January 28, 1936), documenting his time on the Federal Theatre Project.

24. *Chicago Defender*, October 24, 1936.

25. Barnett to George Davis, June 24, 1936 (Claude Barnett papers, Chicago History Museum, box 289, folder 26). This letter also seems to contradict Wright's claim in "I Tried to Be a Communist" that by May Day 1936 he was back on the Writers' Project.

26. Rollins to Barnett, August 27, 1936 (Claude Barnett papers, Chicago History Museum, box 289, folder 26).

27. A copy of the proposal is in Barnett's papers (box 289, folder 26).

28. Claude Barnett to Sterling Brown, March 2, 1937 ("New Deal Agencies" microfilm, roll 23, #760).

29. Sterling Brown to Barnett, March 9, 1937 (Barnett papers, Chicago History Museum, box 289, folder 26).

30. Wright would eventually be transferred to the New York Writers' Project where he would write the chapter "Portrait of Harlem" for the state guidebook, *New York Panorama* (1938).

31. Undated letter (Louis Wirth papers, University of Chicago, box 2, folder 5).

32. Cayton to Louis Wirth, May 28, 1937 (Louis Wirth papers, University of Chicago, box 2, folder 5).

33. A full report from Cayton under the heading "Memorandum Regarding the General Study of the Negro Community in Chicago" can be found in the Wirth papers (box 2, folder 5).

34. *Chicago Defender*, January 21, 1939.

35. A collection of letters exchanged between Cayton and Myrdal can be found in the Wirth papers.

36. Other works that utilized the Cayton-Warner papers include Richard Wright's *12 Million*

Black Voices (1941) and W. Lloyd Warner's *Color and Human Nature* (1941). Cayton family biographer Richard S. Hobbs compiled a list of ten graduate studies that used the materials (2002, 221n26).

37. Cayton to Wirth, May 28, 1937 (Wirth papers, University of Chicago, box 2, folder 5).

38. Margaret Walker, "Life of Horace Cayton," in Horace Cayton papers at Harsh Research Collection (box 20, folder 1).

39. A copy of the "Outline and Program for a Study of the Negro Press in Chicago," dated November 31, 1938, exists in the IWP papers at the Abraham Lincoln Library. A copy of the "Manual for the Study of the Negro Press in Chicago" is included in IWP papers at the Harsh Research Collection (box 42, folder 1).

40. Questionnaires filled out by Richard Durham are dated from February to May 1939 (FWP papers, Abraham Lincoln Library).

41. For example, Margaret Walker reported on several art exhibits sponsored by the WPA. She also wrote a summary "from personal observation" of the Midwest Federation of Arts and Professions, a conference in June 1936 called by the Chicago Writers' Group (formerly the John Reed Club of Chicago), and attended by, among others, representatives from the South Side Writers' Group, of which she was a member. Documents from Margaret Walker's work on the project are dated from September 1936 to March 1939 (FWP papers, Abraham Lincoln Library).

42. In her account from "How I Wrote *Jubilee*," Margaret Walker writes, "In 1939, Congress passed a law saying all boondogglers were wasting the government's money and must get off the WPA if they had been employed for as many as eighteen months. I discovered I was a boondoggler and must get off the government's payroll, and I vowed not to go back to the Project when the necessary interim period of unemployment expired" (13).

43. The chapter titles in the ten-chapter outline for the book project differ slightly from some of the ones that were written (IWP papers, Harsh, box 41, folder 2).

44. A copy of this essay can be found in the Claude Barnett papers at the Chicago History Museum.

45. For more on Richard Durham, see the forthcoming biography by Sonja Williams, *Destined for Freedom*.

46. Copies of this chapter and the outline for the study of the black press can be found in box 41 of the IWP papers.

47. A nearly complete manuscript can be found at the Abraham Lincoln Library in Springfield. Large portions are also contained in the IWP papers (IWP papers, Harsh, box 47).

48. Pages 62–63.

49. Among the John T. Frederick papers at the University of Iowa are his WPA identification card, dated August 30, 1937, his letter rejecting the offer to replace Alsberg in Washington, D.C., and copies of his letter of resignation sent to IWP workers (box 45).

50. There is evidence that Bowling also worked later on the project. He compiled a bibliography on the Eighth Regiment that is dated June 18, 1940 (IWP papers, Harsh, box 19, folder 2).

51. See Amiri Baraka's review of Marable's biography of Malcolm X dated May 4, 2011 and circulated widely online.

52. For more about Dunham's time on the Federal Theatre Project see Joyce Aschenbrenner, *Katherine Dunham: Dancing a Life* (2002).

53. John T. Frederick also helped to convince Henry Holt to publish *Journey to Accompong* in 1946. According to Dunham, Frederick had courted her "madly" by bringing her large bouquets of flowers (Aschenbrenner 112).

54. Papers of John T. Frederick, memo dated October 5, 1938 (box 45).

55. This is the only known document of Katherine Dunham's time on the Illinois Writers' Project (WPA papers, Library of Congress, container A876).

56. Yerby's writings can be found at the Abraham Lincoln Library in Springfield.

57. *Illinois Writers' Newsletter*, October 4, 1940. Other issues of the *Illinois Writers' Newsletter* can be found at the Abraham Lincoln Library in Springfield.

58. A copy of this essay can be found in the FWP papers at the Abraham Lincoln library (box 186, folder 1).

59. For this account of his hiring, see the introduction Bontemps wrote for the 1968 Beacon Press edition of *Black Thunder*. In a letter of recommendation accompanying a 1942 application for a Rosenwald Fund grant, Frederick said the novel was "the finest single creative work of fiction yet produced by an American Negro" (Julius Rosenwald papers, Fisk University, box 394, folder 15).

60. The outline is dated January and although the year is not provided it was probably 1940 (IWP papers, Harsh, box 48, folder 1). There are completed drafts of chapters for "The Heritage" (dated April 1940 by Robert Lucas), "Spirituals of Today" (by George D. Lewis), "Divas and Divans," and "Boogy Woogy in Chicago" (dated June 1940 by Barefield Gordon).

61. Library of Congress, container A113.

62. Bontemps to Jackman, October 15, 1943 (Bontemps papers, Syracuse University, box 15).

63. Bontemps to Du Bois, February 19, 1941 (Bontemps papers, Syracuse University, box 7).

64. There are other documents with the heading "Negro in Illinois" dated as early as January 1940.

65. The launching of *The Negro in Illinois* was announced in an article by Jack Conroy that appeared in the October 18, 1940 issue of the *Illinois Writers' Newsletter*.

66. While Writers' Projects in southern states were segregated, at offices in northern states, blacks and whites worked alongside one another. Still, the overwhelming number of writers who collected material on African Americans for the Illinois Writers' Project or worked on *The Negro in Illinois* were black.

67. For more about the relationship between Bontemps and Conroy, see Douglas Wixson's, "'Black Writers and White!'": Jack Conroy, Arna Bontemps, and Interracial Collaboration in the 1930s" as well as his biography, *Worker-Writer in America: Jack Conroy and the Tradition of Midwestern Literary Radicalism, 1898–1990* (1994).

68. For Conroy's account of the strike organized by project workers in St. Louis see the article "Writers Disturbing the Peace" in the *New Masses*, November 17, 1936. For a fictionalized account of the St. Louis project see Jack Balch's novel *Lamps at High Noon* (1941).

69. Letters from John T. Frederick are in Conroy's papers, as well as many of the folk tales he wrote while on the project (Conroy papers, Newberry, boxes 10 and 41).

70. For an explanation by Curtis MacDougall of his editorial approach, see "The Problem Was Burocrats." See Conroy's account of his promotion in the essay "Memories of Arna Bontemps."

71. This quotation was used in a letter promoting Conroy's writing class at the Abraham Lincoln School (Conroy papers, Newberry, box 45, folder 1904).

72. This story is told by Annie Oliver in two separate interviews conducted by IWP workers, one in 1938 and the other in 1941 (IWP papers, Harsh, box 38, folder 21; box 2, folder 8).

73. A full copy of the thesis can be found at the Newberry Library in the papers of Jack Conroy. There are fragments of it contained in the IWP papers at the Harsh Research Collection, although it was not conducted under the auspices of the IWP.

74. See Norman R. Yetman, "The Background of the Slave Narrative Collection."

75. *Chicago Defender*, September 18, 1937.

76. The paper was printed in the January 1937 issue of *The Journal of Negro History*.

77. For a more recent study see Glennette Tilley Turner, *The Underground Railroad in Illinois* (2001).

78. For more on Illinois African Americans in the military see Christopher Reed, *Black Chicago's First Century* (2005).

79. For more on the Great Migration see James Grossman, *Land of Hope: Chicago, Black Southern-*

ers, and the Great Migration (1989), Nicholas Lemann, *Promised Land: The Great Black Migration and How it Changed America* (1991), Farah Jasmine Griffin, *Who Set You Flowin'? The African American Migration Narrative* (1995), Isabel Wilkerson, *Warmth of Other Suns: The Epic Story of America's Great Migration* (2010).

80. For more on this period see Randi Storch, *Red Chicago: American Communism and its Grass-roots, 1928–35* (2007).

81. There was growing interest in the conditions of black domestic workers during the 1930s, as evidenced in the investigative essay "The Bronx Slave Market" by Marvel Cooke and Ella Baker published in the November 1935 issue of *Crisis* magazine.

82. In their 1945 book *They Seek a City*, Arna Bontemps and Jack Conroy gave a much more dubi-ous assessment of Garveyism. The chapter "Beloved and Scattered Millions" ends by questioning why Garvey had never visited Africa himself. "Curiously enough," they wrote, "he had never found the time or the opportunity to visit the land of his ancestors." Garvey's wife subsequently wrote a letter to Bontemps complaining about the unflattering image of her husband in the book (Bontemps to Conroy, October 3, 1945, Conroy papers, Newberry, box 3, folder 151).

83. Conspicuously absent from the outline for *The Negro in Illinois* is a chapter dedicated to art. Two drafts of an "Art" chapter were written by Robert Lucas, but they were not included. There were several black artists in Chicago whose works later became highly sought after: Charles White, Archibald Motley, Charles Davis, Charles Sebree, Elizabeth Catlett, Eldzier Cortor, Mar-garet Burroughs, and Marion Perkins.

84. In his memoir *Dreams From My Father: A Story of Race and Inheritance* (1994), Obama recalls the conversations and advice he received from a character named "Frank." Indeed, Davis lived the last years of his life in Honolulu, Hawaii, where Obama grew up. According to biographer John Edgar Tidwell, Davis had joined the Communist Party some time in the mid-1940s. Yet it is doubtful that the Marxist views of Frank Marshall Davis had a longstanding effect on President Obama.

85. Conroy to Bontemps, June 9, 1942 (Bontemps papers, Syracuse, box 5).

86. Edwin Embree to Merle Colby, September 12, 1942 (Conroy papers, Newberry, box 3, folder 151).

87. Conroy to Lieber, undated (Conroy papers, Newberry, box 41b, folder 1863a).

88. Lieber to Conroy, January 6, 1943 (Conroy papers, Newberry, box 17, folder 898).

89. Moon to Lieber, March 2, 1944 (Bontemps papers, Syracuse, box 18).

90. Lieber to Conroy, March 6, 1944 (Conroy papers, Newberry, box 17, folder 898).

91. Julia Waxman to Bontemps, September 9 and September 13, 1943 (Bontemps papers, Syra-cuse, box 24).

92. Bontemps to Conroy, October 12, 1943 (Conroy papers, Newberry, box 3, folder 151).

93. The five chapters in *They Seek a City* that resemble earlier ones are: "Du Sable: Man of the Midlands," "John Brown's Friend," "Leave a Summer Land Behind," "The Exodus Train," and "Beloved and Scattered Millions."

94. There are news clippings of book reviews in Jack Conroy's papers (Conroy papers, New-berry, box 51, folder 2021).

95. Bontemps to Conroy, July 19, 1945 (Conroy papers, Newberry, box 3, folder 151).

96. Bontemps to Conroy, September 25, 1945 (Conroy papers, Newberry, box 3, folder 151).

97. Conroy to Bontemps, September 13, 1945 (Bontemps papers, Syracuse, box 5).

98. Bontemps to Conroy, September 25, 1945 (Conroy papers, Newberry, box 3, folder 151).

99. Bontemps to Robert Davis, October 13, 1943 (Bontemps papers, Syracuse, box 6).

100. Letters that Robert Davis wrote to Langston Hughes, a fellow black radical poet he spoke to in confidence, are revealing. In 1938, Davis told Hughes he had participated in the May Day parade, "It was swell!" Around this same time, he published an article explaining his political journey, "A Christian Becomes a Communist." After the 1939 Nazi-Soviet Pact, Davis considered

resigning from the Communist Party, "I'm just hanging on because I'd have no associates if I got out. I've lost practically all contact with my pre-party friends" (Hughes papers, Yale, box 53, folder 982).

101. On October 24, 1939, Robert Davis wrote to Langston Hughes in a letter, "The 18 month law got me" (Hughes papers, Yale, box 137, folder 2552).

102. Robert Davis to Langston Hughes, January 5, 1940 (Hughes Papers, Yale, box 53, folder 982).

103. Robert Davis to Bontemps, October 7, 1943 (Bontemps papers, Syracuse, box 6).

104. Robert Davis to Langston Hughes, February 19, 1945 (Hughes papers, Yale, box 53, folder 984).

105. Conroy to Bontemps, undated (Bontemps papers, Syracuse, box 6).

106. For more on Robert Davis see the September 1981 article about him in *Ebony* magazine, "The Man Everybody Has Seen but Nobody Knows."

107. *Chicago Defender*, Oct. 12, 1940.

108. George Coleman Moore to Bontemps, February 10, 1946 (Bontemps papers, Syracuse, box 20).

109. Moore to Bontemps, June 19, 1944 (Bontemps papers, Syracuse, box 20).

110. Moore to Bontemps, August 9, 1944 (Bontemps papers, Syracuse, box 20).

111. Robert Lucas to Bontemps, April 23, 1944 (Bontemps papers, Syracuse, box 18).

112. Lucas had also applied for a Rosenwald grant in 1945 and 1947. Biographical details on Lucas are contained in grant applications which can be found in the Julius Rosenwald papers at Fisk University.

113. Lucas to Bontemps, April 21, 1948 (Bontemps papers, Syracuse, box 18).

114. Lucas to Bontemps, July 13, 1949 (Bontemps papers, Syracuse, box 18).

115. Onah Spencer's "Stackolee" was included in Benjamin Botkin's *A Treasury of American Folklore* and before that in the Summer 1941 issue of *Direction* magazine. See also Onah Spencer's article "More about John Henry, The River Giant," *Abbott's Monthly*, July 1933.

116. Conroy to Bontemps, April 24, 1958 (Bontemps papers, Syracuse, box 6).

117. Bontemps to Conroy, May 22, 1958 (Conroy papers, Newberry, box 3, folder 153).

118. Spencer to Conroy, January 16, 1963 (Conroy papers, Newberry, box 29, folder 1476).

119. Spencer to Conroy, January 30, 1968 (Conroy papers, Newberry, box 29, 1476).

120. Conroy to Bontemps, December 15, 1948 (Bontemps papers, Syracuse, box 5).

121. On October 9, 1943, S.I. Hayakawa dedicated one of his weekly columns in the *Defender* to "The Visionaries," who were holding an upcoming poetry reading at the South Side Community Art Center. Among others in the group were Gwendolyn Brooks, Margaret Taylor Goss (later Burroughs), Fern Gayden, Ed Bland, and former IWP worker Robert Davis.

122. Bontemps to Frederick, May 4, 1946 (Frederick papers, Iowa, box 7).

123. Huff to Frederick, July 25, 1944 (Frederick papers, Iowa, box 7).

124. *Chicago Tribune*, December 1, 1981.

125. "The Problem Was Burocrats."

126. *Chicago Tribune*, March 22, 1981.

127. Bontemps to Conroy, October 7, 1949 (Newberry, box 3, folder 153).

128. A small number of selections from the IWP papers were published by Maren Stange in the book *Bronzeville: Black Chicago in Pictures, 1941–43* (2003).

Chapter 1. First, the French

1. This is actually not a direct quote but from a summary of Milo Quaife's *Checagou*, written by IWP worker Ann Williams, who collected it from the book at the residence of Annie Oliver, founder of the Du Sable Memorial Society. The nine-page summary is dated January 30, 1941 (IWP papers, Harsh, box 2, folder 6).

2. Much of this account is based on Milo Quaife's book *Checagou* published in 1933, although there are details that are incorrect. There is, for example, no evidence that Du Sable was ever educated in France. This error is attributable to a pamphlet produced by what was first called the National De Saible Memorial Society for the display of a replica of the settler's cabin at the 1933 World's Fair in Chicago, and among the source material used for this chapter. Although documents indicate that Du Sable was a "free Negro," this does not mean that he had been freed from slavery. The location of Du Sable's birth is unknown.

3. The information on these pictures was taken from Quaife's *Checagou*. This collection of pictures was also significant to Kitty Chapelle, who in her notable essay, "Development of Negro Culture in Chicago" began by analyzing these revealing art objects (IWP papers, Harsh, box 47, folder 1).

Chapter 2. Slavery

1. Sections of this paper were copied by IWP workers L. Pearson and Josephine Copeland at the Harper Library on the University of Chicago campus in 1940 (IWP papers, Harsh, box 3, folder 13).

2. This is taken from an account copied by IWP worker Lillian Harper on October 1, 1941, although the source is not given (IWP papers, Harsh, box 4, folder 11).

3. Some of this material is taken from the manuscript "Slavery or Involuntary Servitude in Illinois Prior to and after Admission as a State" by O. W. Aldrich. It was copied by IWP worker George D. Lewis on December 6, 1940 (IWP papers, Harsh, box 4, folder 29).

4. Material on Edward Coles came primarily from Elihu Washburne's 1882 book, *Sketch of Edward Coles*, copied by Josephine Culpepper. IWP worker Leonard Pearson copied sections of Clarence Walworth Alvord's *Governor Edward Coles, Second Governor of Illinois, and of the Slavery Struggle of 1823–4*. There is also a short biography on Coles written by Edward Condon, an IWP worker in East St. Louis dated March 5, 1936. Also cited was *The Governor's Letter-Books, 1818–1834, 1840–1853*, edited by Clarence Walworth Alvord and Evarts Boutell Greene, as well as the letters of Edward Coles published in the *Journal of Negro History* 3 (1918), copied by IWP worker Julius C. Simms at the George C. Hall Branch of the Chicago Public Library (IWP papers, Harsh, box 3, folders 8, 9, and 12).

Chapter 3. Abolition

1. This quotation was taken from a chapter titled "The Martyrdom of Elijah Lovejoy" in the 1927 publication by the ACLU, *The Story of Civil Liberty in the United States* by Leon Whipple. It was copied by IWP worker W. L. Garner on January 8, 1941 in the Harper Library at the University of Chicago (IWP papers, Harsh, box 5, folder 7).

2. Much of the material on Elijah Lovejoy is taken from a twenty-six-page manuscript titled "And If I Die . . ." written by IWP worker James Phelan, who worked as one of six editors on an Illinois state guidebook published in 1939 (IWP papers, Harsh, box 5, folder 11).

3. This quotation was also taken from an essay titled "The Martyrdom of Elijah Lovejoy" in Leon Whipple's study *Civil Liberty in the United States*, copied by IWP worker M. L. Garner (IWP papers, Harsh, box 5, folder 7).

4. The historian cited here is Norman D. Harris in *The History of Negro Servitude in Illinois, and the Slavery Agitation in that State, 1719–1864*.

5. Information on Owen Lovejoy's indictment was copied from John P. Hand's *Negro Slavery in Illinois* by IWP worker Grace Levy on April 15, 1940.

6. Biographical material on Hooper Warren was taken from the *Historical Encyclopedia of Illinois* by Newton Bateman and Paul Selby (IWP papers, Harsh, box 4, folder 2).

7. There is a nine-page biographical summary of Benjamin Lundy as well as a timeline among

the IWP source materials, the author of which is unknown (IWP papers, Harsh, box 4, folder 1). There is also a newspaper article from the *Inter Ocean* copied by Julius Simms dated April 16, 1941 (IWP papers, Harsh, box 5, folder 10).

8. Biography material on Lyman Trumbull was collected by Emily J. Brennan from the IWP office at 17 E. Erie Street in December 1939 (IWP papers, Harsh, box 5, folder 14).

Chapter 4. The Underground Railroad

1. A copy of this advertisement is contained in the source material for *The Negro in Illinois* (IWP papers, Harsh, box 7, folder 18).

2. This is from the section of L. D. Reddick's unpublished manuscript, "A Sociological History of the Negro in Chicago," which was again utilized for this chapter.

3. The writer was O. L. Schmidt, president of Chicago Historical Society and Illinois State Historical Society, who gave an address on the Underground Railroad that was published in the *Journal of the Illinois State Historical Society*. Copied by IWP worker George D. Lewis on November 25, 1940 (IWP papers, Harsh, box 7, folder 7).

4. D. N. Blazer wrote this notable history of his parents' involvement in the Underground Railroad. It was originally published in the *Journal of the Illinois Historical Society* 15, nos. 3–4 (October 1922–January 1923). Sections of it were copied by IWP workers George D. Lewis on November 22, 1940, and Herman Dixon on March 27, 1941 (IWP papers, Harsh, box 7, folder 8).

5. This material on the Underground Railroad in Jacksonville was collected by IWP worker in Springfield, Jennie Oggs, who took it from the 1884 publication by Charles D. Eames, "Historical Morgan and Classic Jacksonville," which includes interviews with those who had direct involvement with the movement (IWP papers, Harsh, box 7, folder 14).

6. The information on Peoria and Tazewell County was copied from the *Peoria Daily Transcript* by IWP worker Eugene Covington (IWP papers, Harsh, box 7, folder 11).

7. Some of these details were taken from a city guide for Cairo collected by IWP worker John J. Sheard on September 18, 1941 (IWP papers, Harsh, box 7, folder 21).

8. This account was gathered by IWP worker Laura B. Richardson (IWP papers, Harsh, box 7, folder 15).

9. Taken from L. D. Reddick's "A Sociological History of the Negro in Chicago."

10. This story, as well as the following accounts of "Young Tom," and "Charlie," are taken from a manuscript written by W. D. Trowbridge for the *American Guide Series*, but which never reached publication (IWP papers, Harsh, box 7, folder 3).

11. This account was taken from O. L. Schmidt's address, cited in note 3 of this chapter.

Chapter 5. Lincoln and the Negro

1. A quotation from Lincoln appeared in an earlier chapter draft but was deleted by the editor, who was probably Arna Bontemps. The quote was taken from *The Negro in Virginia*, the study which when it was published in 1940 gave Bontemps inspiration for *The Negro in Illinois*. Lincoln's quote reads, "And why should the people of your race be colonized and where? . . . You and we are different races. We have between us a broader difference than exists between almost any other two races. Whether it is right or wrong I need not discuss; but this physical difference is a great disadvantage to us both as I think. Your race suffered very greatly, many of them living among us, while ours suffers from your presence. In a word we suffer side by side. If this be admitted it affords a reason, at least, why we should be separated." See *The Negro in Virginia*, 117.

2. The collection of information on William Fleurville is an example of the state-wide resources that the project drew upon. Arna Bontemps sent a memorandum to Clarence A. Fricke, a foreman at the Springfield office for "a copy of all references to the de Fleurville clan." Fricke located two sources, *Early Settlers of Sangamon County* (1876) by John Carroll Power and *History of Sangamon*

County, Illinois (1881) and copied information, which he then sent to Bontemps on April 2, 1942. Additionally, Fricke interviewed Clara Ware, a granddaughter of Fleurville, who was able to trace the family tree to the present generation. He also sent Bontemps a summary of this interview. Of note is the testimony of Mrs. Ware that Lincoln's barber always signed his name William Florville, but that others who wished to downplay his racial identity had misspelled his name, making it appear more French. In the two historical sources found by Fricke his name is also spelled Florville (IWP papers, Harsh, box 8, folders 8, 9).

3. This story was recorded by IWP worker Eugene Covington on July 31, 1941. The source is not provided (IWP papers, Harsh, box 8, folder 7).

Chapter 6. John Brown's Friend

1. Fenton Johnson wrote a five-page essay titled "Chicago Negro Aristocrats" while he was an IWP worker. Among this crowd of middle-class blacks, he says, Mrs. John Jones was "the first of all of them" (IWP papers, Harsh, box 9, folder 14).

2. A report of the verdict published in the *Chicago Daily Inter Ocean*, October 7, 1874, was recorded by IWP worker Joseph O'Neal on Dec. 31, 1940, at the main branch of the Chicago Public Library (IWP papers, Harsh, box 9, folder 7).

3. The report of the thirtieth anniversary celebration of John Jones's arrival in Chicago, published in the *Chicago Evening Journal*, was copied by Joseph Bougere from records at the Newberry Library on May 1, 1941 (IWP papers, Harsh, box 9, folder 4).

Chapter 7. Leave a Summer Land Behind

1. This quotation and other material came from a fifteen-page essay on "Pap" Singleton by Lillian Harper (Conroy papers, Newberry, box 41b, folder 1863d).

2. This quote was copied from the *Inter Ocean* by M. L. Garner on February 21, 1941, at the Chicago Public Library (IWP papers, Harsh, box 10, folder 15).

3. This quotation was copied and sent in a memo to Arna Bontemps by IWP worker Olive Hill (IWP papers, Harsh, box 10, folder 43).

4. This letter was copied from the *Inter Ocean* by IWP worker Julius C. Simms on March 26, 1941 (IWP papers, Harsh, box 10, folder 12).

5. Some of this story was retold by IWP worker W. R. Wood in a brief essay on African Americans in Springfield and Sangamon County (IWP papers, Harsh, box 11, folder 3).

Chapter 8. Rising

1. The above material on Cairo was taken from a short essay titled "The Beginning 1853–1900," by Lloyd W. Owens, an IWP worker based in Cairo. It was written after interviews with Lydia Amos, Ada Ross, and Wilson Ricks (IWP papers, Harsh, box 14, folder 5).

2. This account from the October 12, 1870, issue of the *Champaign County Gazette* was copied by IWP worker Ethel Chase at the University of Illinois library (IWP papers, Harsh, box 15, folder 13).

3. This quotation came from the March 24, 1874, issue of the *Chicago Evening Journal* and was copied by IWP worker Joseph Bougere at the Chicago Public Library on February 27, 1941 (IWP papers, Harsh, box 13, folder 1).

4. This editorial was copied by IWP worker Joseph O'Neal at the Chicago Public Library on December 30, 1940 (IWP papers, Harsh, box 12, folder 8).

5. An account of the 1882 riot in the September 13, 1882, issue of the *Chicago Tribune* was copied by IWP worker Ann Williams on May 14, 1941 (IWP papers, Harsh, box 14, folder 27).

6. Copied from the April 28, 1880, issue of the *Inter Ocean* by William Page on January 30, 1941 (IWP papers, Harsh, box 14, folder 21).

7. Copied from the November 14, 1902, issue of the *Inter Ocean* by Julius C. Simms on June 5, 1941 (IWP papers, Harsh, box 14, folder 22).

8. This incident at Northwestern in 1902 was described in newspaper articles from the *Inter Ocean* copied by Julius C. Simms in 1941 (IWP papers, Harsh, box 14, folder 15).

9. This quotation was taken from the July 22, 1907, issue of the *Chicago Tribune*. This article and others from the *Inter Ocean* were copied by IWP worker William Page in May and June of 1941 (IWP papers, Harsh, box 14, folder 22).

10. Copied from the July 19, 1876, issue of the *Champaign County Gazette* by Ethel Chase (IWP papers, Harsh, box 15, folder 6).

11. Copied from the June 15, 1877, issue of the *Chicago Tribune* by Lillian Harper (IWP papers, Harsh, box 15, folder 11).

12. Copied from the June 16, 1877, issue of the *Chicago Evening Journal* by Robert Hunter on July 7, 1938 (IWP papers, Harsh, box 15, folder 8).

13. Copied from the July 21, 1894, issue of the *Inter Ocean* by an IWP worker listed only as B. Hall on June 12, 1941 (IWP papers, Harsh, box 14, folder 16).

14. Copied from the June 23, 1895, issue of the *Inter Ocean* by IWP worker B. E. Swindall on February 22, 1941 (IWP papers, Harsh, box 14, folder 16).

15. Copied from the June 20, 1901, issue of the *Inter Ocean* by IWP worker O. Hunter on February 28, 1941 (IWP papers, Harsh, box 14, folder 16).

16. Copied from the May 17, 1904, issue of the *Inter Ocean* by Julius C. Simms on June 14, 1941 (IWP papers, Harsh, box 14, folder 20).

17. The story of this black girl genius was taken from the *Journal of Negro Education*, April 1935. It was copied by Onah Spencer at Crerar Library in Chicago (IWP papers, Harsh, box 14, folder 13).

18. Taken from the February 28 issue of the *St. Louis Daily Journal*. Copied and sent to Arna Bontemps by Olive Hill whose title appears as Research Editor (IWP papers, Harsh, box 15, folder 24).

19. Copied from the September 7, 1902, issue of the *Inter Ocean* by Julius C. Simms on June 2, 1971 (IWP papers, Harsh, box 14, folder 25).

Chapter 9. Churches

1. Information about the Second Baptist Church in Galesburg was gathered by Jennie Elizabeth Oggs, who wrote a short report on July 28, 1941 (IWP papers, Harsh, box 17, folder 20).

2. Information about the Morning Star Free Will Baptist Church in Cairo was collected by John J. Sheard, who interviewed six members of the current congregation and wrote an essay about his findings dated July 26, 1941 (IWP papers, Harsh, box 17, folder 2).

3. Copied by Joseph Bougere on April 3, 1941 (IWP papers, Harsh, box 17, folder 1).

4. Copied by Joseph Hussion on May 8, 1941 (IWP papers, Harsh, box 17, folder 20).

5. Copied by IWP worker George Coleman Moore on April 4, 1941 (IWP papers, Harsh, box 17, folder 18).

6. This article was copied on April 16, 1940, at the Carnegie Library in Marion, Illinois, although the worker responsible for it is not indicated (IWP papers, Harsh, box 17, folder 31).

7. This account came from the March 5, 1915, issue of the *Chicago Daily News* and was copied at the Chicago Public Library by IWP worker Lulu Perle Holstein on April 11, 1941 (IWP papers, Harsh, box 18, folder 3).

8. Fenton Johnson's poem "Aunt Jane Allen" was first published in Alfred Kreymborg's *Others* magazine in February 1919.

9. This quotation was taken from *Early Twentieth Century Churches (Chicago)* and copied by E. Jennings at the Chicago Public Library on June 18, 1941 (IWP papers, Harsh, box 18, folder 16).

10. This quotation was taken from St. Clair Drake's *Churches and Voluntary Associations in the Chicago Negro Community* (IWP papers, Harsh, box 18, folder 18).

Chapter 10. Soldiers

1. Some of the material for this chapter came from a 4,800-word essay titled "The Military Record of the Illinois Negro," written by IWP worker Bernard MacGillian and dated June 17, 1941 (Conroy papers, Newberry, box 42, folder 1868).

2. This article was copied from the July 28, 1875, issue of *Inter Ocean* by IWP worker James Council on January 10, 1941 (IWP papers, Harsh, box 20, folder 8).

3. This news item was copied from the May 20, 1879, issue of the *Inter Ocean* by Julius C. Simms (IWP papers, Harsh, box 20, folder 9).

4. This editorial was copied from the May 12, 1895, issue of *Inter Ocean* by B. E. Swindall on February 12, 1941 (IWP papers, Harsh, box 20, folder 14).

5. This article was copied from the July 17, 1895, issue of the *Chicago Tribune* by Alvin N. Cannon at the Chicago Public Library on July 9, 1940 (IWP papers, Harsh, box 20, folder 14).

6. Copied by William H. Parham on May 3, 1940 (IWP papers, Harsh, box 19, folder 7).

7. Copied by William H. Parham on January 24, 1941 (IWP papers, Harsh, box 23, folder 11).

8. This observation was taken from a speech by Robert R. Jackson, Alderman of the Third Ward, at Marshall's funeral. It was gathered by IWP worker Lillian Harper who wrote about the funeral services (IWP papers, Harsh, box 23, folder 2).

9. Other details about Marshall were found in an article from the *Chicago Daily News* dated July 22, 1898, and copied by O. Hunter at the Newberry Library on October 9, 1940 (IWP papers, Harsh, box 23, folder 2).

10. Some of the information from this paragraph came from a personal reminiscence by Fenton Johnson dated July 25, 1940 (IWP papers, Harsh, box 23, folder 1).

11. Copied from the August 12, 1916, issue of the *Chicago Defender* by Bernice Hall in 1940 (IWP papers, Harsh, box 21, folder 7).

12. Copied from the May 2, 1914, issue of the *Chicago Defender* by Bernice Hall in April 1940 (IWP papers, Harsh, box 21, folder 6).

13. Copied from the May 9, 1914, issue of the *Chicago Defender* by Bernice Hall in April 1940 (IWP papers, Harsh, box 21, folder 6).

14. Copied from the June 24, 1916, issue of the *Chicago Tribune* by Onah Spencer on August 7, 1941 (IWP papers, Harsh, box 21, folder 7).

15. Copied from the November 4, 1916, issue of the *Chicago Defender* by Bernice Hall in April 1940 (IWP papers, Harsh, box 21, folder 7).

16. This article was copied from the April 16, 1917, issue of the *Chicago Tribune* by Onah Spencer on Sept. 4, 1941 (IWP papers, Harsh, box 21, folder 7).

17. This report was copied by William H. Parham (dated May 31, 1940) and Mathilde Louise Bunton (undated) (IWP papers, Harsh, box 23, folder 19).

18. Copied from the October 25, 1917, issue of the *Chicago Tribune* by Louise Henry on April 2, 1941 (IWP papers, Harsh, box 21, folder 8).

19. Copied from the *Chicago Defender* by Bernice Hall in 1940 (IWP papers, Harsh, box 23, folder 10).

20. Copied from the February 11, 1939, issue of the *Chicago Defender* by M. L. Garner on September 20, 1940 (IWP papers, Harsh, box 23, folder 10).

21. Copied from the May 23, 1939, issue of the *Chicago Bee* by Benjamin Jack. To knowledge, no records of the *Bee* from the 1930s remain, except what was copied by IWP workers. Other material from the *Bee* was collected for the newspapers chapter (IWP papers, Harsh, box 22, folder 8).

22. Copied by Mathilde Louise Bunton in June 1939 (IWP papers, Harsh, box 22, folder 5).

23. Copied by Mathilde Louise Bunton in June 1939 (IWP papers, Harsh, box 22, folder 6).

24. Copied by Mathilde Louise Bunton (IWP papers, Harsh, box 22, folder 9).

25. Copied by Mathilde Louise Bunton (IWP papers, Harsh, box 22, folder 11).

Chapter 11. Business

1. This quotation was taken from Booker T. Washington's *The Negro in Business*. It was copied by Andrew G. Paschal on December 9, 1940 (IWP papers, Harsh, box 26, folder 16).

2. Some of this information was found in an article from the Dec. 13, 1903, issue of the *Inter Ocean*, copied by M. L. Garner on July 2, 1941 (IWP papers, Harsh, box 26, folder 40).

3. Copied from the August 25, 1880, issue of the *Inter Ocean* by William Page on February 4, 1941 (IWP papers, Harsh, box 26, folder 8).

4. This material on H. C. Haynes was taken from Booker T. Washington's *The Negro in Business*. It was copied by Mathilde Bunton (IWP papers, Harsh, box 26, folder 39).

5. This material is based on an interview conducted with Mrs. Malone by Lillian Harper (IWP papers, Harsh, box 26, folder 19).

6. According to an earlier draft, this building was located at 4647 Indiana Avenue. In *Native Son*, "Ernie's Kitchen Shack" is listed at 47th and Indiana. Richard Wright lived at 3743 Indiana Avenue, a few blocks north of the restaurant.

7. Information on "jitneying" was taken from a pamphlet titled "We Expose the Taxi-Cab Racket" published by the Midwest Federation for Constitutional Liberties. It was found by Matilde Bunton at the office of Lloyd Warner at the University of Chicago on June 3, 1941 (IWP papers, Harsh, box 26, folder 7).

Chapter 12. Work

1. Articles on the Spring Valley riots were copied from the *Inter Ocean*, *Chicago Tribune*, and *Times-Herald* by E. Diehl, Bernice Hall, Bertha E. Swindall, and Ann Williams (IWP papers, Harsh, box 27, folder 2).

Chapter 14. The Migrants Keep Coming

1. This quotation was taken from a five-page summary of the report by the congressional committee that investigated the East St. Louis riots. The name of the IWP worker who wrote it is not indicated (Conroy papers, Newberry, box 41b, folder 1863e).

2. A fascinating account of the 1919 Chicago riot was written by Fenton Johnson while he was working on the project, a nine-page essay titled "Racial Friction in Chicago" (IWP papers, Harsh, box 31, folder 3).

3. Copied from the August 9, 1919, issue of *The Nation* by Onah Spencer on November 20, 1940 (Conroy papers, Newberry, box 41b, folder 1863e).

Chapter 15. The Exodus Train

1. This and the previous quotation were copied from the February 10, 1917, issue of the *Chicago Defender* by Lillian Harper (IWP papers, Harsh, box 33, folder 2).

2. Copied from the June 2, 1917, issue of the *Chicago Defender* by Lillian Harper (IWP papers, Harsh, box 33, folder 2).

3. Copied from the March 10, 1917 issue of the *Chicago Defender* by Lillian Harper (IWP papers, Harsh, box 33, folder 2).

4. This came from a series of letters by Negro migrants that were collected by Emmett J. Scott which were published in the *Journal of Negro History* 4 (1919), 290–340. They were copied by Lillian Harper. A year later, in 1920, Scott published his book *Negro Migration During the War* (Conroy papers, Newberry, box 41b, folder 1863c).

5. Copied from the May 19, 1917 issue of the *Chicago Defender* by Lillian Harper (IWP papers, Harsh, box 33, folder 2).

Chapter 16. Slave Market

1. This quotation came from an interview with young labor organizer Kathryn Williams that was conducted by IWP worker Robert Davis on August 6, 1937 (IWP papers, Harsh, box 34, folder 3).

Chapter 18. Health

1. This anecdote came from a brief history of Provident written by Eleanor Welch, a reporter for *Time* magazine, in an internal memo to Dave Hulburd, chief of correspondents for *Time*, dated August 21, 1941 (IWP papers, Harsh, box 36, folder 2).

2. In an article from the *Inter Ocean*, May 13, 1896, copied by Josephine Copeland, the following section was circled with a note by Bontemps to use this as the first quote of the chapter (IWP papers, Harsh, box 36, folder 2).

3. The initial story was copied from the July 22, 1893, issue of the *Inter Ocean* by L. Pearson. A second account in Eleanor Welch's history of Provident made mention of the presence of other surgeons during the operation (IWP papers, Harsh, box 36, folder 2).

4. Some of the information on this fundraising campaign came from an article in *Crisis*, Feb. 1930, copied by Onah Spencer on January 3, 1941. Also of note is an article on Provident by Frank Marshall Davis from the rare publication *National Negro Digest*, although it originally appeared in *World Call*, February 1935. The Davis article was catalogued as "Pamphlet 384" at the George Cleveland Hall Library and was copied by Ann Williams on November 14, 1940 (IWP papers, Harsh, box 36, folder 2). For an original copy of the article see the George Cleveland Hall Branch Archives at the Harsh Research Collection (box 14, folders 275, 276).

Chapter 19. Houses

1. Population numbers were taken from a two-part article by Horace Cayton that appeared in the December 1937 and January 1938 issues of *Opportunity* magazine, titled "Negroes Live in Chicago." Cayton's figures were based on U.S. census data. The articles were copied by IWP worker Ann Williams on November 12 and 13, 1940 (IWP papers, Harsh, box 37, folder 10).

2. This material on the bombings during and after WWI came from part one of Cayton's articles for *Opportunity*, December 1937.

3. This account comes from an interview conducted by Joseph Bougere with a man listed only as "Mr. X." Bougere said the informant did not want his identity revealed, but that he was well known to many on the South Side and he had "no doubt of the authenticity of the information given" (IWP papers, Harsh, box 37, folder 18).

4. This quote also comes from the interview with "Mr. X."

5. The Committee on Negro Housing produced a report titled "Housing Conditions and Delinquency in Chicago," sections of which were copied by Mathilde Bunton on December 4, 1940 (IWP papers, Harsh, box 37, folder 16).

6. IWP worker Juanita Henson collected all the research on Colp, Illinois, a small African American community located three miles east of the all-white community of Herrin. On August 18, 1941, Henson conducted an interview with Herrin Mayor Fred A. Henderson (IWP papers, Harsh, box 37, folder 30).

Chapter 20. Social Life and Social Uplift

1. Copied from the July 30, 1874, issue of the *Cairo Bulletin* by Anna Casey on October 16, 1941 (IWP papers, Harsh, box 39, folder 3).

2. Copied from August 3, 1875, issue of the *Inter Ocean* by James Council at the Newberry Library on January 10, 1941 (IWP papers, Harsh, box 39, folder 3).

3. Copied from the August 2, 1876, issue of the *Inter Ocean* by Onah Spencer (IWP papers, Harsh, box 39, folder 3).

4. Copied from the September 23, 1881, issue of the *Inter Ocean* by William Page on February 18, 1941 (IWP papers, Harsh, box 39, folder 2).

5. Copied from the September 24, 1887, issue of the *Cairo Democrat* by Anna Casey on July 28, 1941 (IWP papers, Harsh, box 39, folder 2).

6. Information on the Phyllis Wheatley Home came from an essay by IWP worker Orange Winkfield (IWP papers, Harsh, box 38, folder 12).

7. Taken from *The Story of the Illinois Federation of Colored Women's Clubs, 1900–1922* by Elizabeth Lindsay Davis. Copied by IWP worker Ethel Chase (IWP papers, Harsh, box 38, folder 10).

8. Much of the material on the formation of the YWCA was provided by Josephine Copeland who wrote an essay on the organization dated May 26, 1941 (IWP papers, Harsh, box 38, folder 5).

9. On May 26, 1941, Josephine Copeland also wrote an essay on the history of the YMCA and its branches on Wabash, Maxwell, and in Evanston (IWP papers, Harsh, box 38, folder 4). Information about the initial meeting at the Odd Fellows Hall was provided by an *Inter Ocean* article dated January 5, 1911, that was copied by IWP worker Preston Bowie on April 3, 1941 (IWP papers, Harsh, box 38, folder 9).

10. Copied from the May 19, 1911, issue of the *Inter Ocean* by Onah Spencer on May 5, 1941 (IWP papers, Harsh, box 38, folder 8).

11. Some of the information on the NAACP came from an essay by George Coleman Moore dated May 17, 1941 (IWP papers, Harsh, box 38, folder 1).

Chapter 21. Recreation and Sports

1. Copied from the May 30, 1914, issue of the *Chicago Defender* by Orange Winkfield on April 16, 1940. This and other articles were found on-site at the *Defender* office at 3435 Indiana Ave. (IWP papers, Harsh, box 40, folder 15).

2. Copied from the September 2, 1897, issue of the *Inter Ocean* by Josephine Copeland on April 1942 (IWP papers, Harsh, box 40, folder 4).

3. Copied from the November 6, 1897, issue of the *Inter Ocean* by Julius C. Simms on April 21, 1942 (IWP papers, Harsh, box 40, folder 16).

4. Again, information from this paragraph was collected by Orange Winkfield at the *Defender* office. Material on Farrell Jones came from the December 6, 1913, issue of the *Defender* copied on April 1, 1940 and the October 4, 1913, issue copied on April 3, 1940 (IWP papers, Harsh, box 40, folder 18).

5. Copied from the December 15, 1918 issue of the *Defender* by Orange Winkfield on June 25, 1940 (IWP papers, Harsh, box 40, folder 18).

6. Information about Bernard Jefferson and James Smith was copied from the September 30, 1939, issue of the *Chicago World* by Alonzo Bowling on July 5, 1940 (IWP papers, Harsh, box 40, folder 21).

7. Copied from the July 7, 1917, issue of the *Chicago Defender* by Orange Winkfield on May 17, 1940 (IWP papers, Harsh, box 40, folder 25).

8. Copied from the May 22, 1915, issue of the *Chicago Defender* by Orange Winkfield on May 6, 1940 (IWP papers, Harsh, box 40, folder 24).

9. Copied from the March 31, 1891, issue of the *Chicago Globe* by IWP worker listed only as Sgallio (IWP papers, Harsh, box 40, folder 13).

10. While the editors have the correct address, they have mistaken the name of Jack Johnson's club which was called the Café de Champion. There are many articles on Jack Johnson that were written by IWP workers by Preston Bowie, William Page, Onah Spencer, and Orange Wakefield but never utilized (Conroy papers, Newberry, box 42, folder 1866).

11. An essay on Policy Sam was written by Mathilde Bunton from the files at Lloyd Warner's office (IWP papers, Harsh, box 35, folder 18).

12. Some of this explanation of how the policy game operated came from an essay by Mathilde Bunton titled "The System of Policy," written with consultation at Lloyd Warner's office. This and other information on policy in Chicago was originally collected for the "Professions" chapter but was later moved to "Recreation and Sports" (IWP papers, Harsh, box 35, folder 12).

13. These names and other material on this topic came from an essay by Andrew Paschal titled "Policy: Negroes' Numbers Game" (IWP papers, Harsh, box 35, folder 15).

14. This anecdote came from Andrew Paschal's essay on the numbers.

Chapter 22. Defender

1. This and other material came from a fifteen-page essay by Lillian Harper, "Robert Sengstacke Abbott and the Chicago Defender" (Conroy papers, Newberry, box 41b, folder 1863d).

2. In the 1941 draft of this chapter, a footnote by Arna Bontemps makes mention of the recently published autobiography of W. C. Handy, *Father of the Blues*, a book he helped to write, in which Handy recalls how he "bootlegged" copies of the *Defender* in the South.

3. Material on the *Chicago Whip* and its campaign for jobs was taken from Richard Durham's insightful essay "Don't Spend Your Money Where You Can't Work!" (IWP papers, Harsh, box 41, folder 7).

Chapter 23. Politics

1. Some of the material initially collected for the "Iola" chapter ended up being used in the "Politics" chapter such as this article, which was copied from the November 14, 1870, issue of the *Cairo Bulletin* by IWP worker Flora H. Sedberry on September 8, 1941 (IWP papers, Harsh, box 29, folder 13).

2. Entire sections were copied and notes were taken from Howard Gosnell's influential 1935 book *Negro Politicians: The Rise of Negro Politics in Chicago* by IWP workers Josephine Copeland, Ann Williams, and Andrew Paschal (IWP papers, Harsh, box 43, folders 2–16).

Chapter 24. What Is Africa to Me?

1. Copied by Ethel Chase at the University of Illinois library (IWP papers, Harsh, box 10, folder 7).

2. An interview with William A. Wallace was conducted by Lillian Harper (IWP papers, Harsh, box 44, folder 2).

3. A copy of Garvey's statement on "Why I have Not Spoken in Chicago Since 1920," published in *The Negro World*, was copied by Lillian Harper (IWP papers, Harsh, box 44, folder 1).

4. Much of the material on the Abyssinian Movement was collected by Frank Yerby. See the essay "Abyssinians" (FWP papers, Abraham Lincoln Library, box 188).

5. Copied from the April 1936 issue of the *49th Compass Magazine* by Eunice Jennings (Conroy papers, Newberry, box 41b, folder 1865).

6. A report on the African Pacific Movement was written by John J. Sheard, dated September 12, 1941 (Bontemps papers, Syracuse, box 72).

7. This material comes from the essay "The Prophet's Birthday" written by Frank Yerby dated January 16, 1939 (FWP papers, Abraham Lincoln Library, box 188).

Chapter 25. And Churches

1. A first-hand report on the Purple Rose Mystic Temple was written by Onah Spencer (Bontemps papers, Syracuse, box 72).

2. There were several articles observing the First Church of Deliverance, its practices, sermons, and hymns, written by Frank Yerby, dated October 3 through October 21, 1938 (FWP papers, Abraham Lincoln Library, box 187).

3. A brief history of the Good Shepherd Church was written by Josephine Copeland in a document dated June 18, 1941 (IWP papers, Harsh, box 45, folder 18).

Chapter 26. Literature

1. According to Kitty Chapelle, Fenton Johnson was mentored by William H. A. Moore (IWP papers, Harsh, box 47, folder 5).

2. The editors appear to have got these two publications mixed up. *The Champion* came first and was followed by *The Favorite Magazine*, published 1918–1921. The same mistake was made in the earlier fifty-three-page draft.

3. These lines in the introduction to *Black Man's Verse* were also cited earlier by Kitty Chapelle in her musings about poetry and prose for "Colored Culture in Chicago" (IWP papers, Harsh, box 47, folder 4).

4. A manuscript of "Big Boy Leaves Home," with corrections, was left in the Illinois Writers' Project papers, indicating it was written while he was on the project and submitted it as evidence of his work hours, a privilege afforded to few writers on the Federal Writers' Project.

Chapter 27. Music

1. This article was copied by Joseph Bougere on March 21, 1941 (IWP papers, Harsh, box 49, box 8).

2. The reference to Blind Tom as the "wonderful musical prodigy" was taken from an advertisement of his appearance at Farwell Hall copied from the *Inter Ocean*, June 15, 1875, by James Council on January 9, 1941 (IWP papers, Harsh, box 51, folder 2).

3. Copied by James Council on January 7, 1941 (IWP papers, Harsh, box 49, folder 9).

4. Copied from the *Peoria Transcript*, February 13, 1879, by IWP worker Ray Baum on February 3, 1939, from the Peoria Public Library (IWP papers, Harsh, box 49, folder 19).

5. Copied from the *Inter Ocean*, April 4, 1879, by Julius C. Simms on March 18, 1941 (IWP papers, Harsh, box 49, folder 12).

6. This was according to an article copied from the *Inter Ocean*, April 23, 1886, by George Coleman Moore on March 27, 1941 (IWP papers, Harsh, box 49, folder 6).

7. Copied from the *Kewanee Courier*, April 15, 1891, by IWP worker V. V. Headland at the Kewanee Public Library on March 27, 1939 (IWP papers, Harsh, box 49, folder 10).

8. A history of the Chicago Choral Study Club was compiled by George D. Lewis from interviews he conducted with its members (IWP papers, Harsh, box 49, folder 4).

9. Copied by William Page on May 8, 1941 (IWP papers, Harsh, box 48, folder 6).

10. The following material came directly from an essay by William A. Harrison, who worked extensively on the music study, titled "Music Schools and Teachers" (IWP papers, Harsh, box 48, folder 10).

11. An essay on the Normal Vocal Institute was written by Louise Henry, who was also heavily involved in the study of black music in Chicago. It is dated November 29, 1939 (IWP papers, Harsh, box 48, folder 10).

12. A history of the Armour Jubilee Singers was written by George D. Lewis, including a list of seventy performances by the group between 1936 and 1939 (IWP papers, Harsh, box 49, folder 2).

13. This material was gathered from an interview with Curtis T. Jackson conducted by George D. Lewis (IWP papers, Harsh, box 49, folder 5).

14. George D. Lewis wrote a biography of James A. Mundy for the "History of Negro Music and Musicians in Chicago" (IWP papers, Harsh, box 49, folder 16).

15. A history of the Lincoln Liberty Chorus was written by Jennie Elizabeth Oggs for *The Negro in Illinois* (IWP papers, Harsh, box 49, folder 11).

16. There are two reports filed by George D. Lewis after interviewing Mabel Sanford Lewis. One is a document covering her entire life up to 1939 (IWP papers, Harsh, box 49, folder 29). A summary of the Modern Troubidors was written separately from an interview with both Mabel Sanford Lewis and director James Bar (IWP papers, Harsh, box 49, folder 15).

17. Information about Canaan's Travelers was collected by Eugene Covington (IWP papers, Harsh, box 49, folder 3).

18. This material came from Kitty Chapelle's writings on "Colored Culture in Chicago" (IWP papers, Harsh, box 47, folder 7).

19. A brief biography of Mabel Malarcher was written by George D. Lewis (IWP papers, Harsh, box 49, folder 31).

20. This information comes from a brief report by Jennie Elizabeth Oggs (IWP papers, Harsh, box 49, folder 11).

21. Biographies of Margaret Bonds, Novella McGhee, Napoleon Reed, Charles Theodore Stone, Joseph Cole, and Blanch Smith Walton were written by Robert Lucas for a chapter to be called "Divas and Divans" (later renamed "Concert and Parlor Music" for the "History of Negro Music and Musicians in Chicago" (IWP papers, Harsh, box 48, folder 12).

22. Onah Spencer wrote a brief biography of William A. Tyler dated August 14, 1940 (IWP papers, Harsh, box 48, folder 12).

23. From an interview with Walter Dyett by George D. Lewis (IWP papers, Harsh, box 49, folder 28).

24. A biography of John Tompkins was written by George D. Lewis after he conducted an interview with the singer, dated December 14, 1939 (IWP papers, Harsh, box 49, folder 33).

25. From an interview with Arthur A. Brown by George D. Lewis (IWP papers, Harsh, box 49, folder 20). The Umbrian Glee Club brought Marian Anderson to Chicago for performances on June 5, 1922, and January 29, 1923.

26. A brief report on the N.Y.A. Chorus was written by Louise Henry (IWP papers, Harsh, box 49, folder 17).

Chapter 28. The Theater

1. This comment makes reference to a statement in the *Inter Ocean*, January 13, 1876, praising the Georgia Minstrels that was copied by James Council on January 14, 1941 (IWP papers, Harsh, box 50, folder 5).

2. Copied from the *Peoria Transcript*, January 17, 1880, by IWP worker Ray Baum from the Peoria Public Library on March 7, 1939 (IWP papers, Harsh, Box 49, folder 39).

3. Material on the Pekin Theater was collected by Fenton Johnson who wrote a short summary, and Lillian Harper who wrote a thirty-four-page essay (Bontemps papers, Syracuse, box 71). There was also produced a four-page essay by Barefield Gordon, dated February 1, 1940, and an undated forty-nine-page essay on the Pekin Theater (FWP papers, Abraham Lincoln Library, box 78).

4. A fascinating personal reminiscence of Will Marion Cook was written by Fenton Johnson in May 1940. According to Johnson, he first met Cook in 1914 at the office of the *New York News*. When Cook was informed that Johnson was a poet, he suggested they work together. "Joe Jordan—yore know Joe Jordan, of course—and I are composing music. Why not hook up with us and write the words for us? Ta-ta-ta-de boom, something like that" (IWP papers, Harsh, box 51, folder 4).

5. Copied from the *Inter Ocean*, March 20, 1911, by Preston Bowie on April 16, 1941 (IWP papers, Harsh, box 50, folder 7).

6. Several articles on this incident were collected by IWP workers William Page, Preston Bowie, and Lulu Perle Holstein in April and May of 1941 (IWP papers, Harsh, box 50, folder 7).

Chapter 29. Rhythm

1. This quotation was copied from the *Inter Ocean*, February 20, 1900, by Oscar Hunter (IWP papers, Harsh, box 51, folder 6).

2. Material on ragtime came from two essays by IWP worker Barefield Gordon, "Ragtime in Chicago: Ragging the Keys," dated February 23, 1940, and "Ragtime: Music in Chicago Prior to 1913," dated January 4, 1939 (IWP papers, Harsh, box 51, folder 5).

3. Included in the source material for this chapter is an article from the magazine *Music and Rhythm* by Onah Spencer, "Trumpeter Freddie Keppard Walked Out on Al Capone!" copied by Spencer while he was working on the IWP (IWP papers, Harsh, box 15, folder 13).

4. An essay by Onah Spencer, "The Blues: A Historiette of an American Musical Art" covers the careers of Ma Rainey, Mamie Smith, Bessie Smith, and other pioneer blues singers (IWP papers, Harsh, box 52, folder 1).

5. As part of his job with the IWP, Onah Spencer created discographies for Kokomo Arnold, Lonnie Johnson, Ollie Shepard, and others (IWP papers, Harsh, box 52, folder 7).

6. The 1940 article "How Cabell (Cab) Calloway Got to the Top" by Robert Crandall was copied from the magazine *Music and Rhythm* by Onah Spencer on January 2, 1941 (IWP papers, Harsh, box 51, folder 9).

7. Among the source material for this chapter was an article by Onah Spencer that appeared in the *Down Beat* magazine, May 1938, on the occasion of King Oliver's passing, titled "Death Claims Him" (IWP papers, Harsh, box 41, folder 15).

8. Oscar Hunter wrote an essay titled "Piano Boogie Woogie and the Blues" that includes a discography dated February 1940 (IWP papers, Harsh, box 51, folder 22).

9. A survey of black churches that had incorporated the new gospel songs of Thomas A. Dorsey was conducted by IWP worker George D. Lewis, who wrote a brief report of his findings (IWP papers, Harsh, box 52, folder 15).

10. Much of the material for this section on Thomas A. Dorsey came from an earlier chapter titled "Spirituals of Today" by George D. Lewis, written for the "History of Negro Music and Musicians in Chicago" (IWP papers, Harsh, box 49, folder 24).

Editor's Afterword

1. Julius Rosenwald Papers, Fisk University, box 432, folder 4.

2. Robert Davis to Langston Hughes, April 11, 1957 (Hughes papers, Yale, box 53, folder 985).

Editor's Works Cited

Aschenbrenner, Joyce. *Katherine Dunham: Dancing a Life*. Urbana: University of Illinois Press, 2002.

Balch, Jack. 1941. *Lamps at High Noon*. Urbana: University of Illinois Press, 2000.

Baldwin, Davarian. *Chicago's New Negroes: Modernity, the Great Migration, and Black Urban Life*. Chapel Hill: University of North Carolina Press, 2007.

Bone, Robert. "Richard Wright and the Chicago Renaissance." *Callaloo*, Summer 1986: 446–68.

Bone, Robert, and Richard A. Courage. *The Muse in Bronzeville: African American Creative Expression in Chicago, 1932–1950*. New Brunswick: Rutgers University Press, 2011.

Bontemps, Arna. 1936. *Black Thunder*. "Introduction." New York: Beacon, 1968.

———. "Famous WPA Authors." *Negro Digest*, June 1950, 43–47.

Bontemps, Arna, and Jack Conroy. *They Seek a City*. New York: Doubleday, Doran, 1945.

———. *Anyplace but Here*. New York: Hill and Wang, 1966.

Bontemps, Arna, and Langston Hughes. *Arna Bontemps-Langston Hughes Letters 1925–1967*. Edited by Charles H. Nichols. New York: Paragon, 1980.

Burns, Ben. *A White Editor in Black Journalism*. Jackson: University of Mississippi Press, 1996.

Cayton, Horace. *Long Old Road*. New York: Trident, 1965.

Conroy, "Memories of Arna Bontemps, Friend and Collaborator." *American Libraries*, December 1974, 602–6.

———. "Writers Disturbing the Peace." *New Masses*, November 17, 1936, 13.

Dolinar, Brian. *The Black Cultural Front: Black Writers and Artists of the Depression Generation*. Jackson: University Press of Mississippi, 2012.

———. "Richard Wright on Relief: The Illinois Writers' Project Essays (1935–1937); Introduction." *The Southern Quarterly*, Winter 2009, 84–90.

Drake, St. Clair, and Horace Cayton. *Black Metropolis: A Study of Negro Life in a Northern City*. New York: Harcourt, Brace, 1945.

Dunham, Katherine. *Kaiso! Writings by and about Katherine Dunham*. Edited by Vèvè Clark and Sara E. Johnson. Madison: University of Wisconsin Press, 2005.

Flug, Michael. "Vivian Gordon Harsh (1890–1960)." *Black Women in America: An Historical Encyclopedia*. Edited by Darlene Clark Hine. New York: Carlson, 1993.

———. "Vivian Gordon Harsh." *Women Building Chicago 1790–1990: A Biographical History*. Edited by Rima Lunin Schultz and Adele Hast. Bloomington: Indiana University Press, 2001.

Glasco, Laurence, ed. *The WPA History of the Negro in Pittsburgh*. Pittsburgh: University of Pittsburgh Press, 2004.

Green, Adam. *Selling the Race: Culture, Community, and Black Chicago, 1940–1955*. Chicago: University of Chicago Press, 2007.

Griffin, Farah Jasmine. *Who Set You Flowin'?: The African American Migration Narrative*. New York: Oxford University Press, 1995.

Grossman, James. *Land of Hope: Chicago, Black Southerners, and the Great Migration*. Chicago: University of Chicago Press, 1989.

Handy, W. C. *Father of the Blues: An Autobiography*. Ed. Arna Bontemps. New York: Macmillan, 1941.

Hill, Herbert, Horace Cayton, Saunders Redding, and Arna Bontemps. "Reflections on Richard Wright: A Symposium on an Exiled Native Son." *Anger, and Beyond*. Edited by Herbert Hill, 196–212. New York: Harper & Row, 1966.

Hirsch, Jerrold. *Portrait of America: A Cultural History of the Federal Writers' Project*. Chapel Hill: University of North Carolina Press, 2003.

Hobbs, Richard. *The Cayton Legacy: An African American Family*. Pullman: WSU Press, 2002.

Jackson, Lawrence P. *The Indignant Generation: A Narrative History of African American Writers and Critics, 1934–60*. Princeton: Princeton University Press, 2011.

Jones, Kirkland. *Renaissance Man from Louisiana: A Biography of Arna Wendell Bontemps*. Westport, Conn.: Greenwood, 1992.

Joyce, Donald Franklin. "Vivian G. Harsh Collection of Afro-American History and Literature, Chicago Public Library." *Library Quarterly*, January 1988: 67–74.

Knupfer, Anne Meis. *The Chicago Black Renaissance and Women's Activism*. Urbana: University of Illinois Press, 2006.

Lemann, Nicholas. *Promised Land: The Great Black Migration and How It Changed America*. New York: Knopf, 1991.

MacDougall, Curtis. "The Problem Was Burocrats." *Chicago Tribune*, October 8, 1972.

Mangione, Jerre. *The Dream and the Deal*. Boston: Little, Brown, 1972.

McDonogh, Gary, ed. *The Florida Negro: A Federal Writers' Project Legacy*. Jackson: University Press of Mississippi, 1993.

McKinzie, Kathleen O'Connor. "Writers on Relief, 1935–1942." PhD diss., Indiana University, 1970.

Motley, Willard. *The Diaries of Willard Motley*. Edited by Jerome Klinkowitz. Ames: Iowa State University Press, 1979.

Mullen, Bill. *Popular Fronts: Chicago and African-American Cultural Politics, 1935–1946*. Urbana: University of Illinois Press, 1999.

"New Deal Agencies and Black America in the 1930s," microfilm. Frederick, Md.: University Publications of America, 1983.

Obama, Barack. *Dreams from My Father: A Story of Race and Inheritance*. New York: Times Books, 1995.

Ottley, Roi. "Hall Branch Library Rates as Culture Nugget of City." *Chicago Daily Tribune*, November 8, 1959.

———. "Hall Library Becomes Negro Cultural Center." *Chicago Daily Tribune*, February 21, 1954.

———. *New World A-Coming*. Boston: Houghton Mifflin, 1943.

Ottley, Roi, and Wiliam Weatherby, eds. *The Negro in New York: An Informal Social History*. New York: New York Public Library, 1967.

Penkower, Monty Noam. *The Federal Writers' Project: A Study in Government Patronage of the Arts*. Urbana: University of Illinois Press, 1977.

Reed, Christopher. *Black Chicago's First Century*. Columbia: University of Missouri Press, 2005.

———. *The Rise of Chicago's Black Metropolis, 1920–1929*. Urbana: University of Illinois Press, 2011.

Rowell, Charles H. "'Let Me Be with Ole Jazzbo': An Interview with Sterling A. Brown." *After Winter: The Art and Life of Sterling A. Brown*. Edited by John Edgar Tidwell and Stephen C. Tracy, 287–309. New York: Oxford University Press, 2009.

Rowley, Hazel. *Richard Wright: The Life and Times*. New York: Holt, 2001.

Slaughter, Adolph. "Historian Who Never Wrote." *Chicago Daily Defender*, August 29, 1960.

Stange, Maren. *Bronzeville: Black Chicago in Pictures, 1941–1943*. New York: New Press, 2003.

Storch, Randi. *Red Chicago: American Communism at its Grassroots, 1928–35*. Urbana: University of Illinois Press, 2007.

Tate, Claudia. "Black Women Writers at Work: An Interview with Margaret Walker." *Fields Watered with Blood: Critical Essays on Margaret Walker*. Edited by Maryemma Graham, 28–43. Athens: University of Georgia Press, 2001.

Thompson, Era Bell. *American Daughter*. Chicago: University of Chicago Press, 1946.

Tidwell, John Edgar. *Livin' The Blues: Memoirs of a Black Journalist and Poet*. Madison: University of Wisconsin Press, 1992.

———. "Recasting Negro Life History: Sterling A. Brown and the Federal Writers' Project." *Langston Hughes Review*, Winter/Summer 1995: 77–82.

Tracy, Steven. *The Writers of the Black Chicago Renaissance*. Urbana: University of Illinois Press, 2011.

Travis, Dempsey. *An Autobiography of Black Jazz*. Chicago: Urban Research Institute, 1983.

Turner, Glennette Tilley. *The Underground Railroad in Illinois*. Glen Ellyn, Ill.: Newman Educational, 2001.

Walker, Margaret. "New Poets." *Phylon*, 4th Quarter, 1950: 345–54.

———. *How I Wrote* Jubilee. Chicago: Third World, 1972.

———. *Richard Wright: Daemonic Genius*. New York: Warner, 1988.

Warner, W. Lloyd Warner. *Color and Human Nature: Negro Personality Development in a Northern City*. Washington, D.C.: American Council on Education, 1941.

Wilkerson, Isabel. *Warmth of Other Suns: The Epic Story of America's Great Migration*. New York: Random House, 2010.

Wixson, Douglas. *Worker-Writer in America: Jack Conroy and the Tradition of Midwestern Literary Radicalism 1898–1990*. Urbana: University of Illinois Press, 1994.

———. "'Black Writers and White!': Jack Conroy, Arna Bontemps, and Interracial Collaboration in the 1930s." *Prospects*, 1998, 401–30.

Wright, Richard. 1941. *12 Million Black Voices*. New York: Thunder's Mouth, 1991.

———. "Amusements in Districts 38 and 40" (1937).

———. "Agriculture and Farm Life" with Merrell Gregory (undated).

———. "Bibliography on Negro in Chicago" (undated).

———. 1945. *Black Boy*. New York: Harper, 1991.

———. "The Chicago Urban League" (January 8, 1936).

———. "Ethnographical Aspects of Chicago's Black Belt" (December 11, 1935).

———. "The Illinois Writers' Project Essays." Introduction by Brian Dolinar. *Southern Quarterly*, Winter 2009: 84–128.

———. "Introduction" to *Black Metropolis*. New York: Harcourt, Brace, 1945. i–xxxiv.

———. "I Tried to Be a Communist." *Atlantic Monthly*. August 1944–September 1944.

———. "On the Ethnography of the Negro (Additional)" (January 13, 1936).

———. "A Survey of the Amusement Facilities of District #35" (March 3, 1937).

———. "Washington Park" (March 27, 1937?).

———. "White City—Recreational Center," "Hotels" (March 3, 1937).

Yetman, Norman R. "The Background of the Slave Narrative Collection." *American Quarterly*, Autumn 1967, 534–53.

Archival Collections

Claude Barnett Papers, Chicago History Museum Research Center.

Arna Bontemps Papers, Syracuse University Special Collections Research Center.

Horace R. Cayton Papers, Vivian G. Harsh Research Collection of Afro-American History and Literature.

Jack Conroy Papers, Newberry Library.

John T. Frederick Papers, Iowa University Special Collections.

Langston Hughes Papers, Beineke Rare Book and Manuscript Library, Yale University.

Illinois Writers' Project/"Negro in Illinois" Papers, Vivian G. Harsh Research Collection of Afro-American History and Literature, Chicago Public Library.

Illinois Writers' Project Papers, Abraham Lincoln Presidential Library & Museum, Springfield, Illinois.

Julius Rosenwald Papers, Fisk University Franklin Library Special Collections.

Louis Wirth Papers, University of Chicago Special Collections Research Center.

Richard Wright Papers, Beineke Rare Book and Manuscript Library, Yale University.

Index

MacNeal, Arthur Clement, 187
Madison Anti-Slavery Society, 17
Malone, Annie, xxxi, 99–100
Mangione, Jerre, xi, xl
Marshall, Col. John R., xx, 84–90, 184
Martin, John Sella, 218
Maryland State Colonization Society, 196
Maxwell, John, 99
McClure, G. Wellington, 67
McIntosh, Bernice, 151
McIntosh, Francois, 16
McLean, Dr. Franklin C., 153
mediums, 212
Melendy, Thomas W., 25
Messer, Wilbur, 172
Metcalfe, Ralph, xxxi, 180
Micheaux, Oscar, 238
Michigan Boulevard Garden Apartments, 159
Minnie, Memphis, 241
minstrelsy, xxxiii, 231–35, 238, 240
Mitchell, Abbie, xxxiv, xxxviii, 227, 228, 237, 238
Mitchell, Arthur W., 192
Modern Troubidors, 227, 273n16
Monumental Baptist Church, 209
Moon, Bucklin, xxxv
Moore, George Coleman, xxxvii
Moore, Joseph W., 39
Moore, William H. A. 219, 237, 272n1
Moorish American Science Temple, xxii–xxiii, xxxiii, 201–6, 214
Morning Star Free Will Baptist, 7
Morris, Edward H., 184
Morris, Father, 212
Morton, Ferdinand "Jelly Roll," 240, 241
Mosley, Beauregard F., 121
Moten, Etta, 229
Motley, Willard, xxix, xxxvii, 257n4
Moton, Robert Russa (R. R.), 220
Motts, Robert T., 193
Mound City, Illinois, xxxii, 70, 71, 84, 163, 189
Muhammad, Elijah, 22, 205–7
Mundy, James A., 226, 227, 228
Mundy Choristers, 226
Myrdal, Gunnar, xviii

Nance, Black, 39
National Afro-American Press Convention, 13
National Association for the Advancement of Colored People (NAACP), xxxvii, 117, 170, 175, 192
National Conservatory of Music, 225
National Du Sable Memorial Society, xxix, xxx, 262n1
National Equal Rights League, 113, 117
National Labor Congress, 105
National Labor Union, 105
National Negro Business League, 100
National Negro Congress, xi, xx, 129, 160

National Youth Administration, 172, 230
Nation of Islam, xxii–xxiii, xxxiii, 205–6
Nearing, Scott, 222
Negro Digest, xli, 254
Negro Fellowship League, 117, 237
Negro in Virginia, The, xiv, xxvii, 264n1
Negro Labor Relations League, 188
Negro National Baseball League, xxxi, 179
Negro People's Theater, 239
Negro World, The, 198
Neighbors, Williams A., 186
New Deal, ix, x, xi, xx, xxxiv, 207
New York Age, 113
Nichols, J. L., 220
Ninth Infantry Battalion, 81
Noone, Jimmy, 242
Normal Vocal Institute, 225
Northwestern Railroad Company, 146
Northwestern University, 66, 67, 113, 173, 180, 218, 222, 225
numbers racket, 103, 181–82, 212

Occomy, Marita Bonner, xii
Ogden, Mary Elaine, xviii
Old Folk's Home, 72, 171
"Old Sixteenth" Battalion, 80–81
Oliver, Annie, xxix, xxx, xxxiv, 260n72, 262n1
Oliver, Joe "King," 242–43
Olivet Baptist Church, 74, 113, 214
Original Creole Band, 242
Ottley, Roi, xiv, xxxv–xxxvi, xli
Overton, Anthony, xx, 101, 187, 215

Pace, Harry H., 162
Page, William, xii, xxiii
Page Fence Giants, 178
Palm Tavern, 102
Paschal, Andrew G., xxxix
Payne, Aaron, 203
Peace Movement of Ethiopia, 200
Pekin Theater, xxxiv, 193, 225, 229, 234–38, 241, 273n3
Penn, I. Garland, 111, 113, 117
Peoria, Illinois, xxvii, 2–6, 62, 70, 106, 128, 163, 164, 169, 171, 224, 227, 231
Peters, W. S., 178
Phillips, Wendell, 110
Pickett, Miss Tyde, 180
Pierce, Albert, 177
Pilgrim Baptist Church, 209
Pinchback, Gov. P. B. S., 54, 168
Pittsburgh Courier, 96; Chicago Edition, 188, 229
Platt, Ida, 67
Platt, Jacob F., 98
Pollard, Fritz, 180
Poro College, xxxi, 99–100, 102
Porter, Joanna Snowden, 173
Progressive Baptist Church, 209

Provident Hospital, xvii, xxxi–xxxii, 72, 151, 152–55, 167, 171, 184, 269n4
Pullman Car Cleaners, 145
Purple Rose Mystical Temple, 210

Quaife, Milo M., 3, 262n1
Quincy, Illinois, xxxii, 24–27, 57, 65, 70, 71, 79, 84, 190, 223
Quinn, William Paul, 70
Quinn Chapel, xxxii, 67, 69, 70, 72–73, 179

Railway Men's International Benevolent Industrial Association, 147
Rainey, Ma, 241
Randolph, A. Philip, xxxiii
Ransom, Rev. Reverdy C., xx, 73
Reddick, Lawrence Dunbar (L. D.), xxix–xxx, 23
Redding, Grover Cleveland, 199
Renault, Phillip Francois, 1–2
rent strikes, xxxii, 160, 162
Republican Party, 18, 28, 47, 105, 117, 186, 192
restrictive covenants, xvii, xxxii, 156, 161, 175, 188
Rhea, La Julia, 227, 229
Richardson, George, 59–60
Richardson, Mary, 43–44, 265n1
Robb, Frederick H., 219
Robbins, Illinois, 126
Roberts, Adelbert H., 191
Roberts, Dr. Carl, 154
Roberts, Joseph Jenkins, 195
Robinson, Bill "Bojangles," xxxiv, 102, 228, 237
Robinson, John, 68
Roe, Elizabeth A., 222
Rogers, Joel Augustus (J. A.), 220
Rogers, Leslie L., 185
Rollins, Charlemae, xxxi, 151
Rollins, Dr. Ida Nelson, 151
Rollins, George A., xii, xvi
Roosevelt, Franklin D., ix, x, xi, 89, 96, 207, 229
Rosenwald, Julius, 153, 159, 172–73, 203
Rust, Horatio N., 58

Sanborn, Gertrude, 222
sanctified churches, xxiii, 210–11
Sandburg, Carl, 121
Scott, Dred, 13, 30, 47
Scott, Sparrell, 142
Scott, W. S., 113
Sengstacke, John H., 186
Sharp, Granville, 195
Shedecker, Isaac, 25
Sherman, Esau, 190
Sinclair, Upton, 222
Singleton, Benjamin "Pap," 52–55, 57, 120
Slater, Duke, 180
Smiley, Charles H., 99
Smith, Amanda, 72

Smith, Bessie, 241
Smith, Clarence "Pine Top," 241
Smith, Elder Lucy, 213
Smith, E. P., 106
Smith, "Gypsy," 157
Smith, James, 180
Smith, Major N. Clark, 225, 230
Smith, William Henry, 227
Society for the Recognition of the Brotherhood of Man, 114
South Park M.E. Church, 76
South Side Community Art Center, x
South Side Tenant's League, 162
Spencer, Onah, xxv, xxix, xxxvii, 262n115
Spiritual Love Circle, 210
Spiritualist churches, xxiii, 182, 210, 211–12, 214
Springfield, Illinois, xxxiii, 25, 37–40, 47, 59, 60, 65, 72, 84, 105, 117, 128, 157, 164, 169–70, 175, 192, 198, 224, 226, 227, 229
Springfield Conservator, 187, 188
Springfield Riot (1908), xxxi, 39, 59–60, 157, 175
Stanley, Mrs. Joe, 98
Starr, Frederick, 222
St. Edmunds Episcopal Church, 213
Stern, Alfred K., 153
Stewart, Zephyr Holman, 151
St. John A.M.E. Church, 210
St. Mark M.E. Church, 76
St. Mary's Church, 73
St. Monica's Church, 73
St. Paul Colored Methodist Church, 76
St. Stephen's A.M.E. Church, 73
St. Thomas Episcopal Church, 226
Summers, Lillian, 151
Supreme Liberty Life Insurance Company, 101
Sweeney, W. Allison 134–35, 185, 221
Swing Mikado, 228, 239

Tanner, Gov. John R., 83–87
Tate, George, 177
Taylor, Julius C., 186
Taylor, Thomas Theodore, 225, 227
Tennesseans, 224
Terkel, Studs, xli
Terry, John Welsey, 106
They Seek a City, ix, xxxv–xxxvi, xxxvii, xliii, 261n82, 261n93
Thomas, John W. E., 190
Thompson, Era Bell, 255
Thompson, James Dekoven, 226
Thompson, Mayor William Hale, 127, 191, 193
Thornton, "Mother" Mattie, xxiii
Tinsley, Pedro T., 225
Tipper, Jacob R., 187
Tolton, Father Augustine, 76
Tourgee, Albion W., 194
Tourgee Club, 194
Trinity Mission, 75

BRIAN DOLINAR is a scholar of African American literature and culture from the Depression era. He is author of *The Black Cultural Front: Black Writers and Artists of the Depression Generation*

The New Black Studies Series

Beyond Bondage: Free Women of Color in the Americas   *Edited by David Barry Gaspar and Darlene Clark Hine*

The Early Black History Movement, Carter G. Woodson, and Lorenzo Johnston Greene   *Pero Gaglo Dagbovie*

"Baad Bitches" and Sassy Supermamas: Black Power Action Films   *Stephane Dunn*

Black Maverick: T. R. M. Howard's Fight for Civil Rights and Economic Power   *David T. Beito and Linda Royster Beito*

Beyond the Black Lady: Sexuality and the New African American Middle Class   *Lisa B. Thompson*

Extending the Diaspora: New Histories of Black People   *Dawne Y. Curry, Eric D. Duke, and Marshanda A. Smith*

Activist Sentiments: Reading Black Women in the Nineteenth Century   *P. Gabrielle Foreman*

Black Europe and the African Diaspora   *Edited by Darlene Clark Hine, Trica Danielle Keaton, and Stephen Small*

Freeing Charles: The Struggle to Free a Slave on the Eve of the Civil War   *Scott Christianson*

African American History Reconsidered   *Pero Gaglo Dagbovie*

Freud Upside Down: African American Literature and Psychoanalytic Culture   *Badia Sahar Ahad*

A. Philip Randolph and the Struggle for Civil Rights   *Cornelius L. Bynum*

Queer Pollen: White Seduction, Black Male Homosexuality, and the Cinematic   *David A. Gerstner*

The Rise of Chicago's Black Metropolis, 1920–1929   *Christopher Robert Reed*

Living with Lynching: African American Lynching Plays, Performance, and Citizenship, 1890–1930   *Koritha Mitchell*

Africans to Spanish America: Expanding the Diaspora   *Edited by Sherwin K. Bryant, Rachel Sarah O'Toole, & Ben Vinson III*

Rebels and Runaways: Slave Resistance in Nineteenth-Century Florida   *Larry Eugene Rivers*

The Black Chicago Renaissance   *Edited by Darlene Clark Hine and John McCluskey Jr.*

The Negro in Illinois: The WPA Papers   *Edited by Brian Dolinar*

The University of Illinois Press
is a founding member of the
Association of American University Presses.

Composed in 9.75/13 Palatino
with Avenir display
by Jim Proefrock
at the University of Illinois Press
Manufactured by Thomson-Shore, Inc.

University of Illinois Press
1325 South Oak Street
Champaign, IL 61820-6903
www.press.uillinois.edu